*Oracle Press*™

Oracle Automatic Storage Management: Under-the-Hood & Practical Deployment Guide

Nitin Vengurlekar

Murali Vallath

Rich Long

New York   Chicago   San Francisco
Lisbon   London   Madrid   Mexico City   Milan
New Delhi   San Juan   Seoul   Singapore   Sydney   Toronto

The McGraw·Hill Companies

Cataloging-in-Publication Data is on file with the Library of Congress

McGraw-Hill books are available at special quantity discounts to use as premiums and sales promotions, or for use in corporate training programs. For more information, please write to the Director of Special Sales, Professional Publishing, McGraw-Hill, Two Penn Plaza, New York, NY 10121-2298. Or contact your local bookstore.

Oracle Automatic Storage Management: Under-the-Hood & Practical Deployment Guide

1 2 3 4 5 6 7 8 9 0 FGR FGR 0 1 9 8 7

ISBN: 978-0-07-149607-0
MHID: 0-07-149607-6

Sponsoring Editor Lisa McClain	**Technical Editors** Charles Kim	**Composition** International Typesetting and Composition
Editorial Supervisor Jody McKenzie	Phil Newlan **Copy Editor**	**Illustration** International Typesetting
Project Manager Madhu Bhardwaj, International Typesetting & Composition	Andy Saff **Proofreader** Deepa Pathak	and Composition **Art Director, Cover** Jeff Weeks
Acquisitions Coordinator Mandy Canales	**Indexer** Valerie Haynes Perry	**Cover Designer** Pattie Lee
Contributing Author Richmond Shee	**Production Supervisor** George Anderson	

I would like to dedicate this book to my kids, Ishan and Nisha, my wife, and most importantly, my parents, whose guidance and support have been invaluable.

—Nitin Vengurlekar

For the Earth and all the Nature in her, thank you for your sacrifice for our happiness.

—Murali Vallath

To my parents and sisters Peggy and Ruth for their continued support in all of my endeavors.

—Rich Long

About the Authors

Nitin Vengurlekar has been in the IT industry for 20 years, initially starting out as a Multiple Virtual Storage (MVS) and DB2 systems programmer supporting large mainframe environments. Later he moved into Unix systems and storage administration roles and managed a team of Oracle DBAs. For the past 12 years, Vengurlekar has been working for Oracle Corporation and has been continually involved with performance tuning projects, backup and recovery planning, as well as numerous storage-related projects with Oracle partners. Additionally, he is author of several Oracle white papers and is a popular speaker at Oracle seminars. Currently Vengurlekar works in Oracle's Clustering and Parallel Storage Technology Group, which includes Cluster Ready Services (CRS), Real Application Clusters (RAC), and Automatic Storage Management (ASM) development.

Murali Vallath has more than 21 years of IT experience including over 15 years using Oracle products. Vallath is an Oracle Certified Database Administrator and his expertise is with Oracle RAC and related technologies; Vallath published his second book, *Oracle 10g RAC, Grid, Services & Clustering*, in March 2006. As president of the Oracle RAC Special Interest Group (www.oracleracsig.org) and the All India Oracle Users Group (IOUG) (www.aioug.org) and as a contributing editor to the *IOUG SELECT* journal, Vallath is known for his dedication and leadership.

Vallath is a regular speaker at industry conferences, on Oracle RAC and Oracle relational database management system (RDBMS) performance- and tuning-related topics. He currently provides independent consulting services in the areas of capacity planning, high availability solutions, and performance tuning of Oracle environments through Summersky Enterprises (www.summersky.biz) with operations in the United States and India. He has successfully completed over 75 successful small-, medium-, and terabyte-sized RAC implementations (Oracle 9*i* and Oracle 10*g*) for reputed corporate firms.

Rich Long is Director of Development for Automatic Storage Management at Oracle and has managed ASM development since the project's inception. He joined Oracle after earning a BS in Mathematical and Computational Sciences and an MS in Computer Science from Stanford University. He initially worked as a developer on parallel query, Oracle Parallel Server, and Enterprise Backup Utility for the Oracle on the IBM SP2. He subsequently managed the development for Oracle Parallel Server on the IBM SP2 and later for all AIX-based systems. He managed the Real Applications Clusters UNIX platform development team before starting the ASM development team.

About the Contributor

Richmond Shee is a strategic advisor for Oracle strategic accounts. He has more than 17 years of experience in multiple practices and disciplines in the telecommunication, manufacturing, and software development industries. Shee is an award-winning author of the highly acclaimed book *Oracle Wait Interface: A Practical Guide to Performance Diagnostics and Tuning* (McGraw-Hill, 2005).

About the Technical Editors

Charles Kim is the Sr. Principal Consultant at Database Technology Solutions. Charles is an Oracle Certified DBA, Redhat Certified Technician, and Microsoft Certified Professional. He has over 17 years of IT experience and has worked with Oracle since 1991. Charles is a coauthor of *Oracle Database 11g New Features for DBAs and Developers.* Charles has presented advanced topics for IOUG and Oracle OpenWorld on such topics as RAC/ASM and 7x24 High Availability Considerations using Oracle Advanced Replication, Hot Standby, and Quest Shareplex. Charles also runs the DBAExpert.com website and provides technical solutions to Oracle DBAs and developers.

    Philip Newlan is a member of Oracle's RAC Pack team. He joined Oracle Corporation in the UK nearly 14 years ago and has worked in the IT industry for almost 25 years. Having previously been part of Corporate Pre-Sales for Oracle in the UK and subsequently a product manager for RAC and Oracle Clusterware at Redwood Shores, he is now enjoying being part of the technical RAC Pack team. He has a specific interest in customers who run Oracle Real Application Clusters and ASM on Linux and Microsoft Windows Operating Systems.

Contents

Foreword

History of ASM

by Bill Bridge, an architect at Oracle for over 18 years and the creator of ASM

The idea for Automatic Storage Management (ASM) first occurred to me in early 1996. A computer manufacturer that I was visiting gave me a presentation on a filesystem for video serving. The manufacturer's plan was to put one or two full-length movies on a single physical disk. The company would make a new copy of the movie for every 10 viewers. The next day I was thinking about this and realized that the plan could not work. I came to the conclusion that the only workable solution was to stripe the movies across a large number of disks with a very large stripe. I was not the first person to figure this out. That was the basic strategy behind the Oracle video server, but I did not know that then.

The number of disks would govern how many video streams could be served. The amount of storage would govern how many movies would be available. It would only require one copy of each movie. However, there was a problem. Eventually the system would need to grow incrementally. The only way to add more disks to handle more video streams was to restripe all the data. This required copying every block of data while the server was down. This could take days, so it was not practical. I worried about this problem off and on for several days.

One morning when I woke up, while I was still lying in bed and staring across the room, it hit me. The solution was to spread the data across the disks using a pointer to every extent rather than a hash function. When a new disk was added, individual extents could be moved to the new disk one at a time by changing the pointer. This could be done automatically in the background while the filesystem was online. Only the extent being moved would be locked out, and then only for a short time. It would only be necessary to move the data that go to the new disk, not all the data. Extents from each existing disk could be relocated to the new disk until all disks were evenly filled.

With 1MB extents and an 8-byte pointer to each extent, a terabyte of data (a very large database in 1996) would require only 8MB of pointers.

I kept thinking about this for a few months. On August 15, 1996, I sent the following e-mail to the managers and architects in Oracle's Server Technologies Division. Remember when you read this that the world was different in 1996. There were no clustered filesystems generally available for Unix systems. The only way to share storage was to use a clustered volume manager. Systems were much smaller than they are today. A terabyte database was considered incredibly huge. Many of the limitations described in the e-mail no longer exist. Here is an excerpt from one of the original e-mails proposing a new filesystem manager:

I propose that Oracle build a portable filesystem to support the RDBMS and other server products. I believe this is important for the very large servers of the future. Currently the RDBMS relies on the OS to provide a filesystem to control placement of data on physical devices and to mirror data for reliability. This causes a number of problems that can be solved with our own filesystem.

- Most OS vendors do not provide a shared disk filesystem for archived logs and backups. Only online logs, control files, and datafiles can be shared via a logical volume manager. Unfortunately the kernel has to assume that the same file name can be used to access the same data on all nodes of a cluster. This causes significant administrative problems for recovery operations.

- The filesystem or logical volume manager hides the physical locations of the files from the kernel. This makes it difficult to properly schedule disk I/O and to provide meaningful statistics on disk performance.

- Administration of storage with existing logical volume managers is difficult when dealing with over 100 disks. Users create thousands of logical volumes to locate their data where they want it for performance and reliability. When they see a disk is heavily used they move volumes from it to another drive. They create so many files because they need to have each table, or small group of tables, independently relocatable. This technology will not work for administration of a server with thousands of drives.

- Neither the operating system nor Oracle gracefully supports a database with a thousand files or more. Operating systems frequently do not allow a process to have that many files open, so Oracle must constantly open and close files. The algorithms in the kernel are not geared to handle thousands of files efficiently.

- Since data placement is handled outside Oracle, a person must specify every file name for file creation. Some operations require specifying the name of a previously created file. This makes for many clumsy user interfaces and difficult design problems.

- OS file system functionality varies widely from port to port. Features such as striping and mirroring are not always available. There are frequent bugs in features such as mirroring, particularly with parallel server clusters. There may be limitations such as a file may not be more than 2GB.

- Files used by Oracle can also be manipulated with standard OS utilities. Oracle is not notified when a file is overwritten or deleted, and cannot prevent unreasonable operations. There have been cases where a logical volume was used both for OS swap space and as part of an Oracle database. There is a lot of code in the kernel to verify that a file has the expected contents, but there are still some situations that we cannot protect against.

My proposed filesystem will solve these problems and allow us to add new file system functionality in the future. The existing media server filesystem may be a good base to work from. This would help ensure the filesystem would be suitable for the media server. The filesystem would have the following features:

- The filesystem will work with the parallel server on clustered or massively parallel machines. It will be tightly integrated with the RDBMS and other server products. For example, the kernel will be able to determine stripe size and location for automatic I/O tuning.

- Administration will be at the hardware replaceable unit. This is a drive or group of drives. When more storage is needed, the administrator adds drives to the file system. The new storage is automatically used without any more administration. If a drive has permanently failed or if it needs to be removed from the filesystem, a command will migrate its data to other drives. Statistics will be reported by drive to diagnose drives with problems, and to decide if more storage is needed.

- Thousands of disk drives will be supportable. The design goal is to support a petabyte of storage on over 10,000 drives with individual files from a megabyte to over a terabyte. Traditional filesystems were designed to divide a disk into a number of small pieces of data on a machine with a few drives. This filesystem is intended to divide a group of disks into pieces which may be larger than a single drive.

- Files will not have names and will not be accessible via OS utilities.

There will not be a directory tree. Files will be accessed and maintained by Oracle server code. Files will be created and deleted by operations such as create tablespace and drop tablespace. Administrators will not be asked to supply file names for operations. They will refer to files via the names of their database objects. Unreasonable operations such as removing the file for a system tablespace will not be possible.

■   All files will be spread evenly over all disks. Disk accesses will be evenly distributed over all drives. There will be no need to decide which data is heavily accessed and move it to a drive with low access data. This will eliminate the need for thousands of files per database for tuning.

■   The filesystem will automatically keep redundant data for reliability. Striping and mirroring can be used to improve throughput. Scheduling algorithms will be used to guarantee real time performance. These options will be settable on a per-to see file basis.

■   The first time an administrator uses the system he will be served a piece of apple pie. If the administrator is also a mother she will get two pieces of pie. This will enhance customer loyalty.

I have some ideas on how to implement this filesystem, but a more detailed design is required. If this plan were approved, the next step would be for me to create a high level design document of around 100 pages. This would take me a few months. I would also need some time from various other people to discuss the design and what it would have to do to satisfy their needs. I would anticipate the implementation to take over a year and require 10–100 man years of effort to get to an alpha release.

Bill Bridge

No one ever mentioned the motherhood and apple pie feature (it is still scheduled for a future release). I started calling the feature Parallel Storage Manager (PSM) because it was a filesystem for Oracle Parallel Server (OPS), the predecessor to Real Application Clusters (RAC). "Parallel" was a good buzzword in those days.

There were two basic responses to this e-mail. Some people thought this was a great idea that should be pursued despite the large development cost. The other response was that this functionality belongs in the OS and should not be provided by Oracle.

Putting a filesystem in user space was a pretty radical idea. Oracle worked closely with other vendors to integrate their volume managers with Oracle. There did not seem to be a need to provide an alternative to OS-based volume managers and filesystems. It would be better to help our partners improve their volume managers and filesystems rather than compete with them. We should patent the technology for spreading data over many disks and license it to our volume manager partners. The lack of clustered filesystems was not such an important issue because very few customers ran Oracle Parallel Server. Implementing my proposed filesystem was a huge task that was not as important as providing other smaller features that our customers have requested. No customer had asked us to solve their storage manageability problems. This view prevailed for over two years.

The e-mail did influence a few of the features implemented in Oracle Database 9*i*. Oracle-managed files (OMF) was a direct result of the proposed feature to create and delete files automatically as needed for database operations such as creating or deleting a tablespace. OMF is still an important manageability feature for integrating the database with ASM. The Oracle Data Manager (ODM) interface was implemented. This is a richer filesystem interface for Oracle to create, delete, read, and write files. It is tailored to work with OMF to simplify management. It has a more CPU-efficient I/O interface. Another project to come out of this proposal was the *Stripe and Mirror Everything (SAME)* white paper. This project produced a white paper on how to achieve the same load-balancing results as my proposal using existing volume manager technology. The configurations were tested and shown to perform well without the need to place data carefully. The only problem was that it was difficult to add storage to a system using the SAME methodology. It required downtime for restripping. This problem was an important validation of the underlying assumptions in the ASM design.

While working on the OMF and ODM features for Oracle Database 9*i*, I continued to tell people about this new filesystem idea. I refined the design to flesh out some details and make the claims more believable. People in other areas of the company saw this as an important manageability feature that would help Oracle compete with other database systems. By implementing this design in user mode, it would not be available to other database vendors. If features of automatically load balancing the disks were available in the OS, then our competitors could use them as well. In any case, the volume manager companies were not interested in licensing a feature they did not invent. That was just human nature. RAC was becoming much more important and the lack of a clustered filesystem was becoming an important problem. It was understandable that customers did not ask us to solve their storage management problems since we never had any features in that area.

Describing my proposal to people in other areas of the company eventually succeeded. They brought the proposal to the attention of top management and recommended that it be funded. By 1999, the project was approved and resources allocated to the project. However, my first task was to refine the design further to the point where developers could create detailed design and functional specifications. This task was not my only responsibility at the time, so it took several months.

By 2000, Rich Long (a coauthor of this book) became the development manager for the project. He formed a team of six developers and the project took off. ASM became my full time job. Several months were spent producing a detailed design document before coding began. The resulting design was amazingly close to the proposal in my first e-mail. We did not use any of the existing media server filesystem code, but some of the developers from that project also worked on ASM. We could not eliminate the need for filenames completely. People needed meaningful names for their files, so we developed a traditional directory tree of filenames and automatically created filenames. We never implemented any real-time performance guarantees. The apple pie and motherhood feature would have been nice, but one ever has enough time to implement everything. Otherwise, ASM lives up to all the promises in that first e-mail.

The most difficult design challenge was managing the metadata so that it was redundant and evenly spread across all the disks, even when disks were added or dropped. Some of the metadata related to just one disk so they could be located at fixed locations on that disk, and they did not need to be redundant because they would not be needed if the disk failed. However, most of the metadata had to be relocatable and redundant. An important design feature was the ability to move an entire diskgroup from one set of disks to another. We solved this problem by keeping the metadata in files just like database data. The metadata file extents are mirrored and relocated just like database file extents. This elegant solution works well, but causes many tricky coding issues to deal with the recursive nature of the metadata. For example, file 1 contains one block for each file describing the size of the file and how to find all the extents of the file. Block 1 of file 1 describes file 1 itself.

Just before development began in 2000, the project name was changed to Oracle Storage Manager (OSM). OPS had been renamed Real Application Clusters (RAC), so the buzzword "parallel" has lost its appeal. Occasionally someone would accidentally call it PMS instead of PSM, so a new name was needed. Most of the development was done under the name OSM. Today there are still many references in the code to OSM rather than ASM. A few months before the product announcement at Oracle Open World, the marketing department decided the name should be Automatic Storage Management (ASM) to stress how management of the database is becoming more automated. The first version of ASM was ready for the production release of Oracle Database 10g Release 1. It was announced at Oracle Open World 2003 as part of the Oracle Database 10g grid announcements. ASM implements the storage grid for Oracle databases. The first release of ASM had phenomenal acceptance by customers. Some customer surveys show as many as 70 percent of the 10g RAC databases are using ASM. This level of adoption is unheard of for a first release feature.

In 2007, Oracle Database 11g was announced at Oracle Open World. Several significant ASM enhancements were introduced in Oracle Database 11g Release 1. The most important new feature is the ability to bring disks back online after a temporary failure that does not lose data. This was a significant development effort that had been planned for the first release of ASM, but the feature had to be dropped to make the release date for Oracle Database 10g Release 1.

Now you have this book, written by the people who know ASM better than anyone else. As the ASM development manager, Rich Long knows more about ASM than anyone else on earth, including me. Nitin Vengurlekar has been working with customers using ASM since the first Beta release. Nitin and I have coauthored a number of ASM white papers. Murali Vallath was an early adopter of ASM and actively evangelizes RAC-ASM through his role as a leader in the Oracle community and as an independent consultant.

This book contains a lot of practical information about how to use ASM in specific situations. This "how to" information is very useful, but more importantly, when you are done reading this book you will understand why ASM works. Some statements about ASM are made by people who jump to incorrect conclusions based on misunderstandings. Some of the claims about ASM sound like marketing hype. When you understand what is really going on, you will understand the advantages and limitations of ASM. You will see there is no magic. This book will give you the knowledge you need to succeed in deploying and maintaining a database that uses ASM.

—Bill Bridge

Acknowledgments

o the entire Vengurlekar and Bhide family, Bill Bridge, the entire ASM development team, the Oracle RAC Pack team, Michael Nowak (for getting me involved in cool projects), Charles Kim and Phil Newlan (you guys are awesome reviewers; thanks for the feedback), Bob Ng, Alan Howiston (for his review of Chapter 1), and Richmond Shee (for his contributions to Chapter 12).

—Nitin Vengurlekar

This book has been a real team effort, with each of us sharing several of the responsibilities and providing a helping hand where required, all with the goal of having a wonderful book as this one, on time without any compromise on quality. This is the first time I have coauthored a book and would like to take this opportunity to thank Nitin and Rich for their patience through the slow periods of my writing process and showing me the correct direction in completing my chapters.

I am always without words in expressing my thanks to Jaya and my two children, Grishma and Nabhas, for accepting the unbelievable amount of time that I have been away from home due to my assignments and travel. Although we missed each other every week, we just kept on going with the understanding that these sacrifices are all for the benefit of the family. I love you all so much.

To the technical review team Charles Kim and Phil Newlan, you guys were awesome in providing excellent feedback. I thank Zafar Mahmood and Anthony Fernandez for the great comments. I wish you had the time to contribute to the entire project.

The book would not be published without help from the friendly folks at Oracle Press, especially Lisa McClain and Mandy Canales. Thanks for all your support and patience the several times that I missed my deadlines, while keeping up the pressure and encouragement to get this out on time.

Thanks are also in order for Madhu Bhardwaj and her team for their great patience and for putting it all together.

I would also like to thank the customers of Summersky Enterprises. In addition to providing sustenance to my family, you have made learning and solving issues an everyday challenge and benefit. Thank you all for your business.

I am proud to have been involved in such an incredible project, and I hope that you benefit from the efforts of so many to bring this book into print. Enjoy.

—Murali Vallath

I would like to start by thanking all of the developers on the Automatic Storage Management (ASM) team who made ASM a success. Without their amazing work we would not have a product to write about. Thanks to Bill Bridge, Tom Sepez, Pat Ritto, Jim Williams, Greg Pongracz, Prasad Bagal, Mary Rhodes, Radek Vingralek, Dave Friedman, Harish Nandyala, Shie-rei Huang, Madhura Sharangpani, Hanlin Qian, Rajiv Wickremsinghe, Mukesh Rathor, Krishnan Yegnashankaran, Yaser Suleiman, Song Ye, Hector Yuen, To-Choi Lau, and Shiva Yarlagadda. I'd like to thank Bill especially, for having the idea for such a great product.

Thanks to Angelo Pruscino for obtaining funding for the ASM project and for giving me the opportunity to lead the development team.

Thanks to Nadim Salah, who has been an invaluable mentor and friend.

Thanks to Annie Chen for offering me a development position at Oracle when my original team dissolved immediately after I joined the company.

Thanks to all of my friends who put up with my long work hours.

As my colleagues who have received writing reviews from me know, my high school English teacher Mary Mecom had a major influence on my writing. I hope that this book honors her memory.

Finally, I would like to thank my coauthors Nitin Vengurlekar and Murali Vallath. Nitin has been a long-time advocate of ASM, and has helped many customers successfully deploy ASM. Nitin had the idea to write this book, and asked me to help. Murali has helped us navigate the waters of the publishing industry. He has also managed to transform my scribbles into figures that I hope have helped explain ASM.

—Rich Long

Introduction

ver since Oracle announced the Automatic Storage Management (ASM) feature, database administrators (DBAs) and their supporting system administrators and storage administrators were eager to see what Oracle had developed and where this product was headed. Not surprisingly, the adoption rate for ASM has been outstanding.

Users were fervent about getting information on how ASM works and how they could integrate it into their environment. The motivation for this book is to satisfy the hunger for those anxiously looking for a "real" deployment guide for ASM.

Before we jump into the book, let's review what's in this book, what's not in this book, and who should read it. Then we will quickly review ASM at a high level and its benefits.

About the Book

This book is intended for technical managers, DBAs, system administrators, and storage architects who want to understand ASM concepts or who will be implementing ASM.

We have designed this book to provide the reader with the essentials of ASM and the best practices for implementation. This design includes a chapter-by-chapter process flow for enabling, configuring, and managing ASM in any environment, as well as ensuring that the databases (relational database management system [RDBMS] instances) are configured correctly to leverage ASM. For those eager to delve "under the hood" of ASM, this book also defines critical ASM internal operations and structures. The last chapter, "From Discussion to Deployment," covers a very important aspect of getting ASM into the user infrastructure and navigating all the organization boundaries affected by introducing this new technology.

Finally, a must-read in this book is the Foreword presenting the history of ASM, written by our good friend and ASM inventor, Bill Bridge. Bill walks through the thought process through which he came up with the idea of ASM.

This book has a unique feel, because the authors have either been associated with ASM since its inception or have been implementing ASM in production environments from the day that ASM was released. This book is based on our background in the development of ASM and our experiences testing and configuring ASM and helping customers migrate to the technology.

Now that we defined what is in this book, let's define what is not is this book. The book does not cover things that can be easily found on the Internet or in Oracle documentation, such as ASM SQL command reference and basic database operations and concepts. Rather than replicate the reference material contained in the Oracle documentation, the authors decided to jam-pack this book with information that would be most useful to the user migrating, implementing, or managing ASM. This book also assumes that the reader is familiar with Oracle Database concepts and is familiar with common Oracle terminology.

ASM Overview

ASM is a management tool designed specifically to simplify database storage management by building filesystem and volume manager capabilities into the Oracle database kernel. This design simplifies storage management tasks, such as creating and laying out databases and disk space management. ASM also offers a simple, consistent storage management interface across all server and storage platforms. Additionally, ASM provides the performance of raw input/output (I/O) with the easy management of a filesystem.

In addition to the aforementioned benefits for single-instance databases, ASM provides a clustered filesystem for Real Application Cluster (RAC) databases and a consistent clusterwide namespace for database files. ASM diskgroups provide much simpler management than shared raw devices while providing the same performance. ASM diskgroups can also store archive logs, Recovery Manager (RMAN) backup sets, and other recovery area files that cannot be stored in raw devices.

Because ASM enables the user to manage disks using familiar create, alter, and drop SQL statements, DBAs do not need to learn a new skill set or make crucial decisions on provisioning. An Enterprise Manager (EM) interface and a command-line utility are also available for those ASM administrators who are not familiar with SQL.

The following is a high-level overview of the benefits of ASM:

- Reduces administration complexity:

  - Simplifies or eliminates daily database storage administration tasks

  - Reduces the number of software layers to manage by vertically integrating filesystem and volume manager functionality.

- Integrates tightly with Oracle-managed files (OMF) to reduce further the need to manage database files.

- Simplifies database storage configuration changes, including automatic data copy on disk, add and drop, and online migration to new storage hardware.

- Prevents accidental file deletion by providing automatic file naming and OMF and protecting ASM files from operating system (OS) utilities.

- Reduces costs of storage management and increases utilization:

  - Reduces the cost of managing storage.

  - Provides a mechanism for database storage consolidation.

  - Makes block devices as simple to administer as file servers.

  - Provides a consistent interface for all storage vendors. Works with any type of storage array from modular storage to network attached storage (NAS) devices to storage area network (SAN) disk arrays.

  - Improves performance, scalability, and reliability.

  - Delivers raw disk I/O performance for all files.

  - Stripes files evenly across all storage disks, providing even I/O distribution.

  - Enables higher storage resource utilization.

  - Overcomes filesystem size limitations.

  - Implements mirroring to protect against component failures.

CHAPTER
1

Storage Stack Overview

his chapter reviews the various components that make up the input/ output (I/O) stack. The objective of this chapter is to provide an overview of the stack's key components and to lay the foundation for the database administrator (DBA) or Automatic Storage Management (ASM) administrator to understand the storage nomenclature. Keep in mind that several of these components—such as Fibre Channel (FC) and small computer system interface (SCSI)—cannot be easily compartmentalized into a specific category because they actually belong in several areas.

The chapter starts with disk drive technology and works its way up to disk interfaces, storage architecture, host bus adapters (HBAs), and finally host-side components such as logical volume managers, which is exactly where ASM picks up.

Disk Drive Technology

The terms *hard disk drive*, *spindle*, *disk drive*, and *disk unit* are all used interchangeably. In our discussion, we use the term *disk drive*. From a component level, all disk drives are created essentially the same—that is, they all use the same types of parts. These parts include several thousand of miniaturized components and several movable parts. The focus of this section is on platters, heads, and actuators.

Platters are circular, flat disks typically made from aluminum or a glass substrate material. They are coated on both sides with a magnetically corrosive media that provides a surface area in which discrete data bits can be recorded into a series of tracks.

Platters have holes cut out from the center disk, similar to a small donut hole. With these holes, the platters are mounted and secured onto a spindle.

The platters are driven by a special spindle motor (see Figure 1-1) connected to the spindle, allowing it to rotate at very high speeds. Special electromagnetic read/write devices called *heads* are mounted onto *sliders* and used either to record information onto the disk or read information from it. The sliders are mounted onto *arms*. Heads, sliders, and arms all are connected into a single assembly and positioned over the surface of the disk by a unit called an *actuator*. This entire enclosure is isolated from outside air to ensure that no contaminants get onto the platters, which could cause damage to the read/write heads.

The *surface* of each platter, which can hold billions of bits of data, is organized into larger units to simplify organization and enable faster access to the data recorded on the platter. Each platter has two heads, one on the top of the platter and one on the bottom, so that a hard disk with three platters has six surfaces and six total heads. As illustrated in Figure 1-2, each platter has its information recorded in concentric circles called *tracks*. Each track is further broken down into smaller pieces called *sectors*, each of which holds 512 bytes of information. However, most

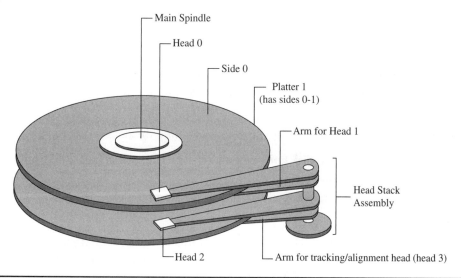

FIGURE 1-1.   *Disk layout*

disk drive manufacturers include 10 bytes for error checking and correction (ECC), making the actual track size 522 bytes.

A *cylinder* is a logical grouping of a single track that all heads can read without perfoming a seek operation, (think of a small slice of pie). Nevertheless, for addressing purposes, a cylinder is equivalent to a track.

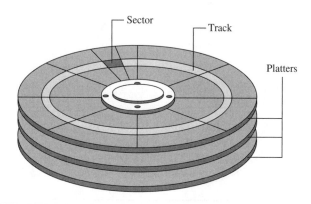

FIGURE 1-2.   *Disk platters*

Disk Drive Performance

The measure of performance for the disk drive shown in Figure 1-3 is dictated by the following factors:

■ **Rotation (spindle) speed** This is the actual speed at which the disk or platters rotate, allowing the read/write heads to retrieve or store the data. This is measured in revolutions per minute (rpm).

■ **Seek time** This is the average time it takes to find the data on the platters.

■ **Speed and size of the disk buffer memory** The effective access time can be illustrated as follows:

Access time = Command overhead time + Seek time + Settle time + Rotational latency

Access time is dominated by the seek time and rotational delay, and thus access time is effectively the sum of the seek time and rotational latency. So for a disk with 5 milliseconds (ms) seek time and 4ms rotational latency, it could take about 9ms between the moment the disk initiates the read request to the moment when it actually starts reading data. The advent of faster disks, which essentially means disks that spin faster (at a higher rpm), translates into a reduced rotational delay, with rotational delays typically around 4ms.

However, by the same measure, the seek time has not decreased significantly over the years. Let's delve a little deeper into this seek time.

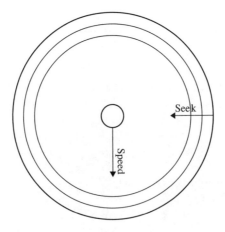

FIGURE 1-3. *Seek time and seek speed*

The *seek time* of a hard disk measures the amount of time required for the read/write heads to move between tracks over the surfaces of the platters. Seek time is one of the most commonly discussed metrics for hard disks, and it is one of the most important positioning performance specifications. Switching between tracks requires the head actuator to move the head arms physically, which, because it is a mechanical process, takes a specific amount of time. The amount of time required to switch between two tracks depends on the distance between the tracks. However, there is a certain amount of overhead involved in track switching, so the relationship is not linear.

Seek time is normally expressed in milliseconds, with average seek times for most drives today in a rather tight range of 5–7ms. However, a millisecond is an enormous amount of time, considering that the speed of the system bus is measured in nanoseconds. That is a difference of about a million. Thus, even small reductions in seek times can improve overall system performance, because I/O waits are typically dominated by the central processing unit (CPU).

There are three different seek time specifications defined by disk drive manufacturers:

- **Average seek time**   The common metric defined by manufacturers, this is the average seek time from one random track (cylinder) to any other.

- **Track-to-track**   This is the amount of time that is required to seek between adjacent tracks. This is similar in concept to the often advertised *track switch time*, and is usually around 0.4ms.

- **Full stroke**   This is the amount of time to seek the entire width of the disk, from the innermost track to the outermost. The range is typically between 10.2ms to 12ms.

Compare the disk drive's track-to-track seek time and then its full stroke seek time. At first glance, it is obvious that it takes a long time for a head to move just to the next track as compared to the head moving across a thousand tracks. However, the difference is only 3 percent, thus it doesn't take a thousand times longer to move the head across a thousand tracks. This is because a significant portion of the seek time is really the settling time and is a predetermined delay programmed in the drive electronics.

The database applications have always favored several disks of smaller capacity, because the limit on I/O operations is determined by the number of disks and not the overall storage capacity of those disks. More disks mean more read/write heads, which in turn mean greater I/O capacity, and this helps in the overall performance of the database. Despite the I/O advantages obtained by basing a system on many disks of small capacity, it is unfortunate that manufacturers these days only make large-capacity disks. To complicate the matters, these days there are choices within and across drive families, such as 73GB 15K rpm, 73GB 10K rpm, 146GB 15K rpm, 300GB 10K rpm, and 750GB 10K rpm.

Considering the preceding observation, it makes sense to have many fewer expensive 10K or even 7,200 rpm disks than to have a few expensive 15K rpm disks.

Moreover, as the drive capacity increases within a particular family of drives, the performance per physical drive does not increase. This is the case, for example, when comparing a 146GB 10K rpm drive with a 300GB drive. Although the *capacity* doubles, the *access density*, or the number of I/Os per gigabyte that the drive can perform, is cut in half. Thus when deploying an appropriate configuration, it is often more important to configure the system for the number of drives required for performance rather than to configure only for the required capacity, striking a balance between performance and capacity.

Disk Interface

The disk drive interface is the language or protocol that a drive uses to communicate with other servers. There are three main types of drive interfaces:

- Integrated Disk Electronics (IDE)/Enhanced Integrated Disk Electronics (EIDE)/Advanced Technology Attachment (ATA)/Parallel Advanced Technology Attachment (PATA)

- SCSI

- Fibre Channel (FC) and Fibre Channel–Arbitrated Loop (FC-AL)

- Serial Advanced Technology Attachment (SATA)

- Serial Attached SCSI (SAS)

IDE/EIDE/ATA/PATA

Parallel ATA, commonly referred to as simply ATA or IDE, is an industry specification that evolved from the original Advanced Technology disk interface. The ATA standard, first developed in 1984, defines a command and register set for the interface between the disk drive and the PC. ATA is currently the standard hard disk drive interconnect in desktop PCs and desktop systems.

Today's ATA-133 interface delivers a maximum data transfer rate of 133MB/sec and supports two parallel ports, with each port supporting two internal hard drives. ATA drives typically are lower-cost devices than SCSI. ATA controller and drive electronics are embedded in the drive itself and thus rely on host CPU cycles for most disk functions. As with most parallel architecture, ATA drives run at half-duplex, meaning that they can send data in one direction at a time.

SCSI (Parallel)

SCSI (pronounced *scuzzy*) is not only a protocol, but a transport as well. SCSI enables host computer systems to perform block data I/O operations to a variety of peripheral devices. Target devices may include devices such as disks, backup tape devices, optical storage devices as well as printers and scanners. The traditional SCSI connection between a host system and the peripheral devices is based on parallel cabling, and hence referred to as parallel SCSI.

The SCSI architecture is based on a client/server model. The client is typically a host system such as file server that issues requests to read or write data. The server is a resource such as a disk array that responds to client requests. In storage parlance, the client is an initiator and plays the active role in issuing commands. The storage array is a target and has a passive role in fulfilling client requests.

NOTE
Keep in mind that the ATA and SCSI interfaces include many subtypes.

Parallel SCSI limitations include the following:

- Allows a maximum of 16 devices on a bus

- Supports of a data transfer rate of up to 320MB/sec (Ultra320)

- Reduces the total length when additional SCSI chains are added

- Runs at half-duplex

The introduction of the SCSI-3 specification provided two dramatic changes to the SCSI infrastructure. First, the SCSI transport specification was separated from the protocol layer. This opened the door for newer interfaces and transport; such as Fibre Channel, Universal Serial Bus (USB), and Firewire (IEEE 1394).

SATA

Serial ATA was borne from the standards of ATA and thus uses the same command set as ATA; however, SATA interface improves that transfer rate to 150MB/sec, although the realistic raw throughput (head read and write data rates) is typically around 60MB/sec.

Serial ATA has thinner cables and hence allows for smaller chassis designs. These cables can extend up to one meter. Serial ATA is not backward-compatible to ATA—that is, it will not work with the same connectors as IDE, SCSI, or any other interface.

SATA supports only one drive per interface. SATA-2 is the current interface available, with transfer rates around 300MB/sec. SATA-3 is on the drawing board and is expected to double the current SATA-2 transfer rates. As with ATA, SATA is half-duplex, and also requires host CPU cycles for most disk functions.

However, unlike ATA, SATA is growing in midrange and certain high-end storage array enclosures. SATA is typically deployed as a low-cost storage solution and has proven to be very effective for applications that rely predominantly on sequential I/O. For example, backups and archived datasets are usually stored as SATA storage. However, SATA drives have higher failures rates than SCSI or FC drives. Nevertheless, SATA consumers can overcome this SATA limitation by double- or triple-mirroring their volumes.

FC and FC-AL

FC serves two purposes: It is both a high-speed switched fabric technology and a disk interface technology. In the context of disk interface, FC-AL is the interface for the FC infrastructure. All devices in an arbitrated loop operate similarly to token ring networking: When one device stops functioning, the entire loop gets interrupted. To overcome this failure, channel hubs are present to connect multiple devices together.

FC-AL is deployed using either copper or fiber-optics (optical). FC over copper is generally the standard for FC drives used inside storage array enclosures.

FC-AL is designed for high-bandwidth, high-end systems and is compatible with mass storage devices and other peripheral devices that require very high bandwidth. Unlike the parallel SCSI interface, FC is a serial interface that employs a full-duplex architecture, thus one path can be used to transmit signals and another to receive signals.

The main features of FC-AL include the following:

- It provides serial data transfer for distances greater than 10Km.

- It offers high data transfer rate.

- It is reliable for data transfer.

- It is compatible with various protocols that already exist.

- An FC-AL loop links as many as 127 devices.

- FC-AL can be connected to two ports to double the data transfer rates. This interface is more expensive than a SCSI interface.

Because FC is the most common environment not only for Oracle ASM–Real Application Clusters (RAC) environments but also for most enterprise systems, this section provides more detail than the other interfaces' sections offer.

FC allows for an active intelligent interconnection scheme, called a *fabric*, to connect heterogeneous computer systems and peripherals with all the benefits. Peripherals can include storage devices such as disk or tape arrays. Today, an FC option is mandatory for high-end mass storage products, such as disk or tape arrays.

FC infrastructure offers the following features:

- Serial data transfer (for greater distances and simplicity).

- Compatibility with various protocols that already exist.

- High data transfer rate.

- Reliable data transfer.

- Packeting (called *frames*).

- Support for a large number of devices.

- Routing information using switches.

- A topology that is the common transport method in a traditional SAN implementation (SAN implementation is discussed later in this chapter).

- Support for a maximum data transfer rate of 400MB/sec (for a full-duplex or half-duplex dual-loop configuration).

- Over 30m of copper cable or 10Km over single-mode fiber-optic links. When implemented in a continuous arbitrated loop (FC-AL), FC can support up to 127 individual storage devices and host systems without a switch.

This interface uses fiber-optic cable to connect the devices to produce a maximum data transfer rate of more than 100MB/sec.

FC was first approved as a standard in 1994 and is primarily implemented in high-end SAN systems. FC has three different types of topologies, as shown in Figure 1-4:

- Point-to-point

- Arbitrated loop

- Fabric topology

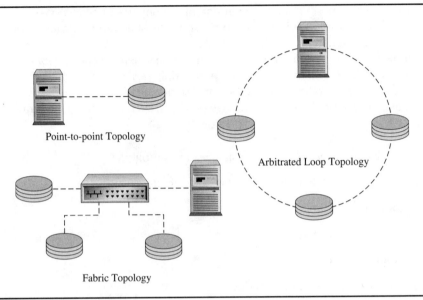

FIGURE 1-4. *FC (not optic) topologies*

Point-to-point is the simplest and least expensive; it is simply two N-ports communicating via a point-to-point connection.

FC-AL (Arbitrated Loop Topology in Figure 1-4) is similar in concept to token ring, in that multiple devices (as many as 126 end nodes) can share a common medium, but must arbitrate for access to it before beginning transmission. FC-AL is not common in the Enterprise Data Center; however, FC-AL is common for the internal loop architecture inside the storage array—that is, the disks in the storage array are part of an FC-AL loop. Due to these limitations of FC-AL, several storage vendors are now moving toward a switched FC back end.

Switched fabric topology, the most common in the Enterprise Data Center, consists of one or more FC (Fabric Topology in Figure 1-4) switches in a single network. Each device has dedicated bandwidth (200 MB/sec full-duplex for 2GB switches), and a device population of as many as 15.5 million devices is supported. This large number is strictly theoretical, because in practice it has been difficult for FC fabrics to support even a few hundred devices.

SAS

SAS, which has evolved from the SCSI standard, is considered the next-generation interface. SAS runs at full-duplex and can therefore achieve transfer rates 300MB/sec in both directions or 600MB/sec aggregate. SAS offers point-to-point serial connection, providing more reliable connection than a traditional shared bandwidth connection, and also allows a much higher level of scalability not attainable by parallel interfaces. SAS is backward-compatible with the SCSI command set and can coexist with SATA on the same interface/controller.

Storage System Architectures

Storage architectures define how servers are connected to the storage array units. This section discusses four popular storage architectures variants:

- DAS

- NAS

- SAN

- iSCSI

Note that Internet Protocol (IP) SANs are a unique breed and thus are covered later in this chapter in the "iSCSI" section.

DAS

Direct attached storage is the term used to describe a storage device that is directly attached to a host system. This storage architecture has been the most common and most mature high-performance storage design for a considerably long period because of its simplicity; however, this model has several drawbacks. The following drawbacks prevent this model from fitting into high-availability, high-performance architectural goals:

- Physical storage cannot be shared with other systems or applications without being served by the host system to which it is attached.

- Storage must be located physically close to the host system because of I/O bus restrictions on distance and performance.

- The scalability of number and capacities of devices are limited, depending on the I/O bus and storage technology being used.

- DAS can be more expensive to manage because unused capacity cannot be redeployed, which results in underutilization.

- DAS inherently creates storage islands distributed throughout the organization, making it difficult to get a consolidated view of the total storage available across the organization.

Nevertheless, DAS still retains its popularity because of its low entry cost and ease of deployment. Because no switches or fabric infrastructure is required for DAS, the learning curve associated with DAS technologies is also a factor that many organizations consider.

DAS is ideal for localized file sharing in environments with a single or a few servers, such as small businesses or departments and workgroups that do not need to share information over long distances or across an enterprise. Small companies traditionally utilize DAS for file serving and e-mail. DAS also offers ease of management and administration in this scenario, since it can be managed using the network operating system of the attached server. However, management complexity can escalate quickly with the addition of new servers, because storage for each server must be administered separately.

From an economic perspective, the initial investment in DAS is cheaper. This is a great benefit for information technology (IT) managers faced with shrinking budgets, who can quickly add storage capacity without the planning, expense, and greater complexity involved with networked storage. DAS can also serve as an interim solution for those planning to migrate to networked storage in the future. For organizations that anticipate rapid data growth, it is important to keep in mind that DAS is limited in its scalability. From both a cost-efficiency and administration perspective, networked storage models are much more suited to high-scalability requirements

NAS

Network attached storage and NAS devices are a specialized file servers optimized for serving storage, using a routable protocol (Transmission Control Protocol/ Internet Protocol [TCP/IP]) over a local area network (LAN). Note that NAS devices provide file I/O access, whereas SAN and DAS architectures provide block I/O storage access. Examples of NAS devices include:

- Hewlett-Packard's StorageWorks NAS 2000s and Hewlett-Packard Proliant Storage Servers (NAS)

- Network Appliance

- EMC Celera

NAS devices (shown in Figure 1-5) contain network interface cards (NICs), which are assigned an IP address and appear on the LAN as a standard network node. Therefore, clients access NAS devices and their storage using standard LAN access. Most environments have standardized on 1GB networks for NAS traffic, placing 10GB on the roadmap for the future.

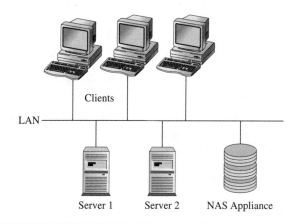

FIGURE 1-5. *NAS configuration*

With NAS, file I/O (file open/close, read/write) is redirected over the network. Thus the block-to-file I/O abstraction layer takes place in the NAS device instead of the host.

Note that NAS devices and NAS I/O traffic run across the LAN, which could impact the enterprise LAN environment. For this reason, it is recommended to configure NAS traffic on a segmented network, isolated from the public network traffic.

The following are the most common NAS-supported protocols:

- **NFS** Network filesystem is typically available on most Unix/Linux servers (as well as Windows).

- **CIFS** Common Internet Filesystem was developed by Microsoft.

- **AFP** AppleTalk Filing Protocol was developed by Macintosh.

- **DAFS** This is the Direct Access Filesystem.

So what is the difference between a NAS device and a standard file server?

- The NAS devices implement a very "slimmed down," customized version of standard operating systems (OSs) such as Windows NT/2000, Unix, and Linux, with a core purpose of serving filesystems to hosts (hence file I/O access). The NAS device acts as a translator between the "served-up" filesystem and clients (hosts) that issue file I/O requests. Therefore, NAS is particularly well suited to network topologies that have a mixture of clients and servers running different operating systems.

- NAS devices employ high-performance, platform-independent data storage technology that uses hardware and software that are optimized to perform a specific task, namely file service. NAS devices are part of a growing category of appliance-like servers that are easy to set up and manage.

- Big advantages of NAS include its expandability. If more storage space is needed, another NAS appliance can be added.

- NAS devices also have built-in utilities and software for backup management and snapshots. Network Data Management Protocol (NDMP)–based tools are an example. NDMP is used to assist in offloading host-based backups, thus reducing host CPU cycles. Snapshots provide the capability to create a point in copy of filesystems or files.

- The NAS OS has enhanced file-level security.

- NAS devices can front end a SAN. When a NAS device is used in this context, it is called NAS Gateway (or NAS Head). The advantage of NAS Gateways is that they provide the accessibility of NAS along with the back-end storage scalability of SAN. With NAS Gateways, logical unit numbers (LUNs) are presented and "percolated" from the SAN to the NAS device; the NAS can either aggregate these LUNs (or present them as is) as a network filesystem.

NAS has the following strengths:

- It is relatively inexpensive.

- It is easy to manage and configure.

- It leverages a standard network infrastructure.

- It is easy to access, as any host with network access can get NAS resources.

Limitations of NAS include the following:

- It can experience high network traffic loads on the LAN and thus is limited by LAN bandwidth.

- The NAS device itself can be a bottleneck.

- I/O performance is still limited by file I/O access—that is, it is not block I/O.

SAN

A storage area network is a specialized network—that is, a communication infrastructure—that provides physical connections and a management layer, as well as access to high performance and highly available storage subsystems using block storage protocols. The SAN is made up of specific devices (or nodes), such as HBAs in the host servers, and front-end adapters that reside in the storage array. SANs use special switches, similar to Ethernet networking switches, as mechanisms to connect these SAN nodes together. Switches help route storage traffic to and from disk storage subsystems.

The main characteristic of a SAN is that the storage subsystems are generally available to multiple hosts at the same time, making SANs scalable and flexible. Unlike DAS or NAS, SANs require careful planning before implementation, because they have more interconnecting components as well as storage security, which is usually done in the fabric network.

SANs differ from NAS in that SANs provide I/O access to hosts, whereas NAS appliances provide file level I/O. SANs also differ from other storage architectures in that they are dedicated storage networks and use their own network protocols (FC) and hardware components.

There are essentially two types of SANs: FC-SANs and IP SANs. However, FC-SANs are the most common and thus SAN has become synonymous with FC. IP SANs are commonly known as iSCSI SANs and will be covered in the "iSCSI" section later in this chapter.

In Figure 1-6, the SAN configuration consists primarily of three tiers: the servers, the switches, and the storage array.

The following are advantages to SAN:

■ Servers and storage can scale independently.

■ Unlike NAS, SAN I/O traffic does not impact IP (LAN) traffic.

■ SANs are the best way to ensure predictable performance and constant data availability and reliability.

The following are disadvantages to SAN:

■ Initial implementation costs are more than that of NAS and DAS.

■ Because SAN has a different network infrastructure than NAS, it can be complex to manage and requires specialized training.

■ Interoperability in heterogeneous environments is usually a constant battle.

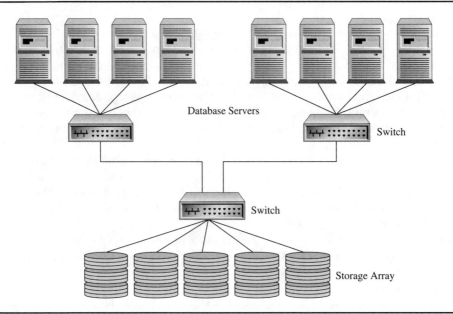

Database Servers

Switch

Switch

Storage Array

FIGURE 1-6. *SAN configuration*

Channel, Networks, and Protocols

In the I/O architecture, the terms *channel*, *network*, and *protocol* are all used interchangeably. This section clarifies these terms and explains how these features fit in a SAN. SAN is specifically discussed here, because it is the most prevalent network infrastructure for Oracle databases.

■ **I/O channel**   An I/O channel is essentially a parallel bus architecture over which I/Os are transmitted—that is, the I/O bus. I/O buses are generally known for transmitting data at high speed for short distances. The I/O channel is a well-structured mechanism designed to transmit data between the caller (host) and the target (I/O device) over a well-known configuration. An example of an I/O channel is the SCSI bus. I/O channels are very static configurations, thus few decisions need to be made. An intelligent hardware HBA or redundant array of independent drives (RAID) controller makes most of the decisions.

■ **Network architecture**   A *network* is defined as an interconnection of three or more communicating entities. However, networks, as opposed to I/O channels, are designed to be dynamic—that is, they adjust to configuration changes, such as the adding or dropping of a network node. An example of a network is Ethernet or FC-SAN networks. Ethernet as well as FC-SAN networks are constantly changing and the associated routing mechanism changes along with it—that is, the decision making is determined in-route and generally in the host. Networks are generally serial architectures and are characterized as spanning long distances but also experiencing higher latencies.

■ **Transport protocols** A protocol is the communication interface into the SAN. Examples include SCSI, IP, and FC. Because Fibre Channel Protocol (FCP) is the most common protocol for SAN (FC-SAN), this chapter focuses on that protocol.

The FC infrastructure serves several functions across the stack, but when it is referred to in the protocol context, FC is generally referred to as FCP. FCP networks are characterized by high speeds, low latency, and longer distances.

More specifically, FCP offers the following:

■ Performance from 266 MB/sec to over 4 GB/sec

■ Support for both optical and electrical media, working from 133 MB/sec up to 1,062 MB/sec with distances up to 10Km

■ High-bandwidth utilization with distance insensitivity

■ Support for multiple cost/performance levels, from small systems to supercomputers

■ Ability to carry multiple existing interface command sets, including IP, SCSI-3, Enterprise Systems Connection (ESCON), High-Performance Parallel Interface–Framing Protocol (HIPPI-FP), Fibre Channel Virtual Interface (FC-VI), and Fibre Channel Audio-Visual (FC-AV).

FC has several layers in its architecture, each of which performs a specific function. FC standards are developed in the National Committee of Industrial Technology Standards (NCITS) T11 standards body, which has defined a multilayer architecture for the transport of block data over a network infrastructure. As shown in Table 1-1, FC layers are numbered from FC-0 to FC-4.

The following describes the layers in greater detail:

■ The upper layer, FC-4, establishes the interface between the FC transport and upper-level applications and operating system. For storage applications, FC-4 is responsible for mapping the SCSI-3 protocol for transactions between host initiators and storage targets.

FC Layer	Layer Title	Comments
FC-4	Upper-layer protocol interface	Encapsulation of other protocols such as SCSI-3, IP, VI, HIPPI, and so on
FC-3	Common services	Services for multiple ports on one node
FC-2	Data delivery	Framing, flow control, sequence management, exchange management, service class, topologies, and segmentation
FC-1	Ordered sets/bytes encoding	8b/10b encoding and link controls
FC-0	Physical interface	Signaling, media specifications, receive/transmitter specifications, optical electrical, and cable plant

TABLE 1-1. *FC Layered Architecture*

- The FC-3 layer is currently under development, and includes facilities for data encryption and compression and for services that require multiple ports.

- The FC-2 layer defines how blocks of data handed down by the upper-level application are segmented into sequences of frames to be handed off to the transport layers. This layer also includes class-of-service implementations and flow-control mechanisms to facilitate transaction integrity.

- The lower two layers, FC-1 and FC-0, focus on the actual transport of data across the network. FC-1 provides facilities for encoding and decoding data for shipment, and defines the command structure for accessing the media. FC-0 establishes standards for different media types, allowable lengths, and signaling.

Collectively, the FC layers fall within the first four layers of the Open Systems Interconnection (OSI) model: physical, data link, network, and transport.

SAN Components

When purchasing hardware components, it is generally a best practice to work from the bottom up—that is, you should first choose the storage array, as this will then help drive the choice of the other components based on the array certification. For example, the storage array may dictate that the fabric switch be a McDATA ED6064 switch, and this subsequently may imply the use of Qlogic 2300F.

This section discusses the following I/O stack components:

- FC (fabric) switches

- HBAs

- Storage arrays

- RAIDs and RAID controllers

FC (Fabric) Switches

FC switches, which are similar to Ethernet switches, contain a switching matrix that allows multiple devices to communicate simultaneously, thus making bandwidth scalable. All of the ports of switches run at full port speed.

A discussion of fabric and FC switches is not complete without discussing switch fabric node security. Fabric node security in this context refers to the security and isolation of ports and resources. This is generally referred to *zoning*.

Zoning allows logical segmentation of fabric devices to servers. These devices typically include components such as servers, storage devices, subsystems, and HBAs. While zoning is performed on a switch, it enforces security by setting up barriers using an access control list (ACL). Zoning can be of two types: hard or soft. As the name indicates, hard zoning is implemented at the hardware level and consists of port- or switch-based zoning and is considered the more secure of the two types of zoning. Soft zoning is implemented at the software level.

Hard Zoning

Hard, or hardware-enforced, zones are the most secure zones. They are created when all members of the zone are specified as switch ports (also called *port zoning*). When a physical fabric port number specifies a zone member, then any and all devices connected to that port are in the zone. If this port is an arbitrated loop, then all devices on the loop are in the zone. Any number of ports in the fabric can be configured as a hard zone. Hard zoning physically blocks access to a zone from any device outside of the zone.

As the name implies, hard zoning occurs within the switch's hardware (specifically, within its circuitry), which reads the destination address of frames entering the switch to determine the output port to which to send them. The switch contains a table of port addresses that are allowed to communicate with each other. If a port tries to communicate with a port in a different zone, the frames from the nonauthorized port are dropped and no communication can occur.

Soft Zoning

Soft, or software-enforced, zones simply influence the list of items returned to by the name server. A host will be given the list of devices available within its zone. Soft zoning uses a filtering method implemented in the FC switches to prevent ports from being seen from outside of their assigned zones. Soft zoning is automatically created whenever any element in the zone is specified by a world wide number (WWN; also called *WWN zoning*). The security vulnerability in soft zoning is that the ports are still accessible if the user in another zone correctly guesses the FC address. A device is included in a zone if either the node WWN or port WWN entries match a defined element in the zone. This enables equipment to be physically relocated to different switches and/or ports and remain within the same zone. However, if the HBA changes for any reason, then zoning must be updated.

NOTE
A WWN is a 64-bit address used to identify each element uniquely in an FC network. It is an identification or addressing mechanism that works similarly to a MAC address being assigned to identify NICs.

Hard zoning is more secure than its software-based counterpart. It also doesn't impose the performance hit that soft zoning does. However, hard zoning is less flexible than soft zoning. Because the zone assignment remains with the port rather than the device, keeping track of configuration changes is more difficult. If a device moves from one port to another, the network manager or administrator must reconfigure the zone assignment, which can result in a significant amount of overhead. This approach can be particularly cumbersome in dynamic environments in which frequent configuration changes are required.

Another intermediate level of zoning is done at the LUN level (called *LUN masking*). Basically, apart from providing protection at the server level, each LUN or set of LUNs can be masked to allow access to only one server or one set of servers. LUN masking is actually performed at a level above zoning—that is, although a zone grants access to only a given port on a storage array, LUN masking grants access to some of the LUNS on a port to one server and the reminder to another server.

HBA

The HBA resides in the host, or more specifically, on the host's system bus. This system bus can be Peripheral Component Interconnect (PCI), Peripheral Component Interconnect Extended (PCI-X), or the latest, PCIe. Having the appropriate system bus can make the difference in system scalability. It is also important to ensure that the bus is not overloaded. This can be achieved by spreading HBAs and NICs across multiple I/O buses. These adapters have the potential to saturate the bus very quickly.

The HBA is essentially a circuit board that provides physical connectivity among a server, a storage device, or any intermediary devices. The HBA's main purpose is to transmit I/O down the SCSI bus. HBAs can be SCSI, FC, or SAS, and have speeds of 1GB, 2GB, or 4GB. Currently, 2GB and 4GB FC are very common HBA types. HBA devices can be either single- or dual-ported, but always run at full-duplex transmission.

The difference between an Ethernet NIC and FC HBA is that the NIC consumes host CPU cycles for flow control, frame sequencing and assembly, and error detection. The FC HBA relieves the host microprocessor of both data storage (flow control) and retrieval tasks (frame assembly and sequencing and so on) onto the application-specific integrated circuit (ASIC) firmware, thus improving the server's performance.

The "iSCSI" section discusses how specialized components can be used to offload the CPU consumption tasks onto a network device.

Storage Arrays

A storage array's internal architecture can vary from vendor to vendor and even model to model. This section describes a typical high-end storage array.

Storage arrays typically have several front-end adapters. These front-end adapters have two sides. One side has one or more ports (port logic) that connect into the FC switch. The host servers also connect into this same fabric switch.

The other side of the front-end adapter connects into the inside of storage array; more specifically, it connects into the cache controller.

The cache controller manages the storage array cache. The storage array cache has a read and write-cache area, with read cache used to store recently accessed data, and the write cache used to buffer writes (write-back cache). The read/write cache can range from 16GB to 256GB for high-end arrays. Note that on some arrays the read/write cache is segmented and separate, whereas others have a common cache area. Moreover, the write cache maybe mirrored in some arrays.

When a read request for a block enters the cache controller via the front-end port, the cache controller checks to see whether that buffer block exists in the cache. If the read request for a data buffer is found in the cache, then this event is called a read-cache hit. This cache hit block is returned through the fabric and eventually to the application, all without requiring physical disk access (which as we discussed earlier is the slowest part of the I/O subsystem).

The cache controller is also responsible for providing prefetch of data blocks for sequentially accessed data. If the cache controller determines that the application is accessing contiguous disk blocks, the prefetch algorithms are triggered (set with thresholds) to prefetch data that are stored in the read cache, providing significant improvement into access time.

If a write request is made to the storage array, it enters the cache controller via the front-end port (just like the read request); however, the write request is written only to the write-cache area and destaged later to the back-end disks. Many people wonder what happens if the storage array crashes before the data are destaged to disks. Most storage arrays have a nonvolatile random access memory (NVRAM) battery system that protects the system from loss of power.

There is some debate about the usefulness of the read cache in databases that are 5TB or larger. Contrast this size with the array cache size of 256GB. To determine whether the cache will be beneficial, you first must know your application and data pattern usage (temporal and spatial locality of reference).

The cache controller also has the back-end adapters (array controllers) connected to it. All the storage array disks are connected to the back-end adapters.

The interface to the hard disks can be dual-ported 4GB/sec FC-AL. The array can contain 15,000 rpm 73GB or 146GB drives or 10,000 rpm 73GB, 146GB, or 300GB drives, as well as the newest 500GB 7,200 rpm drives.

RAID and RAID Controllers

RAID technology expands the capacity of the I/O system while enabling data redundancy. RAID is the use of two or more physical disks to create one logical disk, where the physical disks operate in tandem to provide greater size and more bandwidth. RAID provides scalability and high availability in the context of I/O and system performance.

RAID configurations can be performed in either software or hardware. Software RAID is typically done by host volume managers, such as 1BM, Logical Volume Manager (LVM), Symantec-Veritas Volume Manager (VxVM), and Oracle ASM. This section discusses hardware RAID.

The RAID controller manages the physical storage units in a RAID system and delivers them to the server as logical units (for example, six physical disks may be used to create a one LUN RAID set, but the server sees only one drive).

The controller can be internal to the server, in which case it is a card or a chip, or it can be external, in which case it is an independent enclosure. In either case, although a RAID controller is almost never purchased separately from the RAID itself, the controller is a vital piece of the puzzle. The following are two popular types of RAID controllers:

- **Bus-based or controller card hardware RAID**   This is the more conventional type of hardware RAID, and the type most commonly used, particularly for lower-end systems. A specialized RAID controller is installed into the PC or server, and the array drives are connected to it. It essentially takes the place of the SCSI host adapter or IDE/ATA controller that would normally be used for interfacing between the system and the hard disks; it interfaces to the drives using SCSI or IDE/ATA.

NOTE
Cache incoherency across RAID controllers has proven to be problematic with Oracle Real Application Clusters (RAC) implementations. The cache is not shared across RAID controllers that reside on separate hosts. Due to this limitation, bus-based or controller card hardware RAID is not recommended for Oracle RAC implementations.

■ **Intelligent, external RAID controller**   In this higher-end design, the RAID controller is removed completely from the system to a separate box. Within the box, the RAID controller manages the drives in the array, typically using SCSI, and then presents the logical drives of the array over a standard interface (again, typically a variant of SCSI) to the server using the array. The server sees the array or arrays as just one or more very fast hard disks; the RAID is completely hidden from the machine.

RAID levels ranging from simple striping and/or mirroring have provided benchmarks for the various types of data suited for their respective technology. Several types of RAID configurations are available today; let's briefly discuss some very commonly used types of RAID for Oracle relational database management systems (RDBMS).

RAID 0

RAID 0 provides striping, where a single data partition is physically spread across all the disks in the stripe bank, effectively giving that partition the aggregate performance of all the disks combined. The unit of granularity for distributing the data across the drives is called the *stripe size* or *chunk size*. Typical settings for the stripe size are 32K, 64K, and 128K. In Figure 1-7, there are eight disks all striped across in different stripes or partitions.

RAID 1

In RAID 1, known as *mirroring*, all the writes issued to a given disk are duplicated to another disk. This provides a high-availability solution; if the first disk fails, the second disk or mirror can take over without any data loss. Apart from providing redundancy for data on the disks, mirroring also helps reduce read contention by directing reads to disk volumes that are less busy.

RAID 0+1

RAID 0+1 is a combination of the levels 0 and 1. RAID 0+1 does exactly what its name implies—that is, it both stripes and mirrors disks. For example, it might

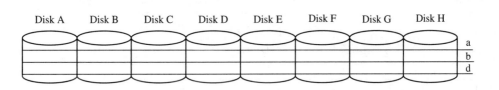

FIGURE 1-7.   *RAID 0*

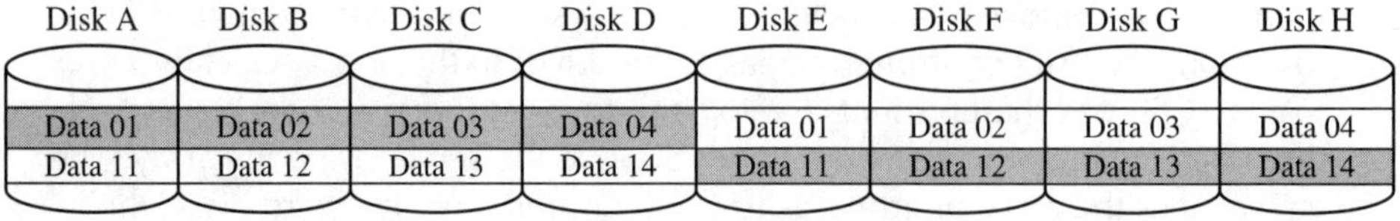

Disk A	Disk B	Disk C	Disk D	Disk E	Disk F	Disk G	Disk H
Data 01	Data 02	Data 03	Data 04	Data 01	Data 02	Data 03	Data 04
Data 11	Data 12	Data 13	Data 14	Data 11	Data 12	Data 13	Data 14

FIGURE 1-8. *RAID 0+1*

stripe first, then mirror what was just striped. This type of RAID incorporates the advantages of both RAID 0 and RAID 1. RAID 0+1 is illustrated in Figure 1-8.

Figure 1-8 illustrates a four-way striped mirrored volume with eight disks (A through H). A given set of data in a file is split/striped across the disks (A through D with the stripe first and then mirrored across disks (E through H). Due to the method in which these disks are grouped and striped, if one of the pieces becomes unavailable due to a disk failure, the entire mirror member becomes unavailable. Thus losing an entire mirror reduces the I/O servicing capacity of the storage device by 50 percent [4].

RAID 1+0

RAID 1+0, or RAID 10, is also a combination of the RAID 0 and RAID 1. In RAID 1+0, the disks are mirrored and then striped—that is, they are mirrored first, and then what was mirrored is striped. All the advantages (mirroring and striping) that apply to the RAID 0+1 configuration apply to this RAID configuration. However, the organization of mirrored sets differs from the previous configuration.

In Figure 1-9, DATA 01 is mirrored on the adjoining disks (DISK A and DISK B), and DATA 02 is mirrored on the subsequent two disks (DISK C and DISK D). This illustration shows eight mirrored and striped disks. Unlike RAID 0+1 (illustrated in Figure 1-8), loss of one disk in a mirrored member set does not disable the entire mirrored volume, thus it does not reduce the I/O servicing capacity of the volume by 50 percent.

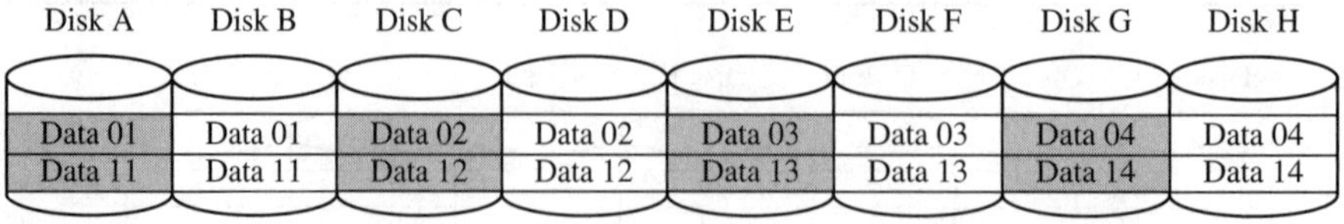

Disk A	Disk B	Disk C	Disk D	Disk E	Disk F	Disk G	Disk H
Data 01	Data 01	Data 02	Data 02	Data 03	Data 03	Data 04	Data 04
Data 11	Data 11	Data 12	Data 12	Data 13	Data 13	Data 14	Data 14

FIGURE 1-9. *RAID 1+0*

NOTE
*RAID 1+0 is the most common type of RAID
solution deployed for Oracle databases.*

RAID 5

Under RAID 5, parity calculations provide data redundancy, and the parity is stored
with the data. This means that the parity (that is, error checking) is distributed across
the number of drives configured in the volume. Parity algorithms contain error
correction code (ECC) capabilities, which calculate parity for a given stripe or
chunk of data within a RAID volume. If a single drive fails, the RAID 5 array can
reconstruct that data from the parity information held on other disks.

Figure 1-10 illustrates the physical placement of stripes (DATA 01 through
DATA 04) with their corresponding parities distributed across the five disks in the
volume. It is a four-way striped RAID 5 illustration where data and parity are
distributed.

RAID 5 is typically not recommended for highly concurrent-random I/O
applications that have a read/write ratio greater than 70:30. This is because the
continuous processes of reading a stripe, calculating the new parity, and writing the
stripe back to the disk (with new parity) make write significantly slower. Several
storage vendors have optimized sequential writes in the array architecture by
calculating the parity in memory and performing the write as a single large I/O.

RAID 5 has proven to be a very good solution where the application is read-
mostly or if the writes are significantly sequential. For this reason, many Oracle
customers have deployed RAID 5 for data warehouse (decision support system
[DSS]) applications and also for Recovery Manager (RMAN) backup areas.

RAID 6

RAID 6 is essentially an extension of RAID level 5, which allows for additional fault
tolerance by using a second independent distributed parity scheme (two-dimensional
parity). It requires the basic number of drives required for storage plus two additional
(N+2) drives to implement because of two-dimensional parity scheme.

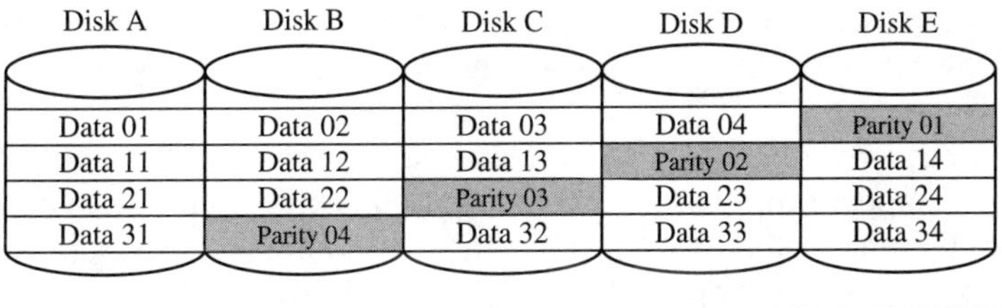

Disk A	Disk B	Disk C	Disk D	Disk E
Data 01	Data 02	Data 03	Data 04	Parity 01
Data 11	Data 12	Data 13	Parity 02	Data 14
Data 21	Data 22	Parity 03	Data 23	Data 24
Data 31	Parity 04	Data 32	Data 33	Data 34

FIGURE 1-10. *RAID 5*

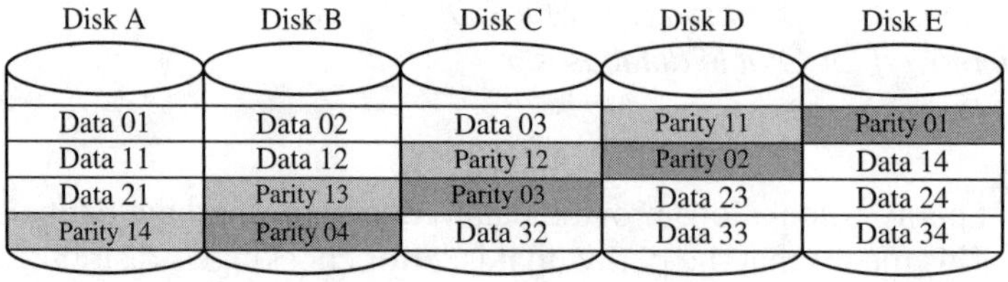

Disk A	Disk B	Disk C	Disk D	Disk E
Data 01	Data 02	Data 03	Parity 11	Parity 01
Data 11	Data 12	Parity 12	Parity 02	Data 14
Data 21	Parity 13	Parity 03	Data 23	Data 24
Parity 14	Parity 04	Data 32	Data 33	Data 34

FIGURE 1-11. *RAID 6*

As with RAID 5, data are striped on a block level across a set of drives, and a second set of parity is calculated and written across all the drives. RAID 6 provides for an extremely high data fault tolerance and can sustain multiple simultaneous drive failures. However, unlike the other RAID levels.

RAID 6 is a good solution for mission-critical applications that require good data protection and disk utilization (better than that offered by RAID 1+0). However, RAID 6 does impose significant controller overhead to compute parity addresses, making it a poor choice for write-intensive applications.

RAID 6 eliminates the risk of data loss if a second hard disk drive fails or an unrecoverable read error occurs while the RAID array is rebuilding. As indicated in Figure 1-11, a second set of parity is calculated, written, and distributed across all the drives. This second parity calculation provides significantly more robust fault tolerance because two drives can fail without losing data.

iSCSI

Internet SCSI (iSCSI), which is a storage protocol based on TCP/IP, encapsulates SCSI-3 commands into the TCP/IP packet and delivers the packet reliably over IP networks. The big advantage of iSCSI is that it enables block I/O data transmission between directly connected IP-enabled storage devices and hosts. This is particularly useful for database applications.

The iSCSI protocol is used on servers (initiators), on storage devices (targets), and in protocol transfer gateways. iSCSI uses standard Ethernet switches and routers to move the data from server to storage. It also enables the IP and Ethernet infrastructure to be used for expanding access to SAN storage and extending SAN connectivity across any distance.

Storage devices are directly plugged into gigabit Ethernet switches and/or IP routers, and then appear simply as any other IP-based device on traditional networks. As with normal IP implementations, direct connection to the IP network pushes responsibility for device discovery and connection establishment to the end devices. Storage devices connected using this protocol also require a list of IP addresses to discover the protocol's intended targets. This list is provided by a lookup table or a domain naming service (DNS)–type service on the network. For the iSCSI interface, such discovery is facilitated by the Internet Storage Name Service (iSNS) protocol and in a storage server implementation; the iSCSI initiator would first query an iSNS server to learn the IP addresses of potential targets resources before establishing TCP/IP connections to them.

System configurations comprise of one or more computers on the front end that do the basic processing of user requests, and on the back end they contain a storage subsystem. The front end is where the request for data is initiated (and thus is called the initiator) and the back end is a target (storage) from where data are retrieved and returned. The iSCSI protocol stack illustrated in Figure 1-5 consists of a stack which is the initiator and another at the target that resides on the gigabit Ethernet interfaces.

As stated previously, the iSCSI layer encapsulates SCSI commands, data, and status-reporting capability. For example, when the application issues a data write operation, the SCSI CDB encapsulates this information and transports it over a serial gigabit link that is then delivered to the target. Similarly, when the initiator makes a read request—for example, using a SQL SELECT statement—the SCSI Command Descriptor Blocks (CDB) encapsulate the request and transport it over the gigabit link to the target; when the data are read, a similar operation is performed to return the data to the initiator.

The iSCSI protocol consists of the following process flow:

1. The application layer initiates and responds to I/O transactions from the OS kernel.

2. The iSCSI layer builds and receives SCSI CDB and relays and receives the CDBs to and from the iSCSI layer.

    Up to this point (above), the process flow is the same as for FC-SCSI, but the following steps are quite different in the iSCSI world:

3. The iSCSI device driver attempts to discover the location of the iSCSI device. This is done using IP address lookup.

4. The iSCSI device driver builds the iSCSI Protocol Data Units (PDUs) with the appropriate CDB and relays to the TCP/IP layer.

5. The TCP/IP layer encapsulates the PDU into TCP segments using one or more TCP connections that form an initiator-target session, and encapsulates TCP segments into IP packets. IPSec is an optional component of this layer.

6. The physical layer transmits and receives IP packets, typically Ethernet packets.

The following are best practices for deploying iSCSI:

■ Use Jumbo frames with 9K maximum transmission units (MTU). Make sure that the overall network infrastructure supports them.

■ Use gigabit Ethernet NICs.

■ Separate the storage SAN from the Oracle Cache Fusion using separate virtual local area networks (VLANs).

■ Use Link Aggregation (NIC teaming) for both the Filer while using single NetApp Virtual Interface (VIF) and the hosts.

■ Use multiple VIFs to different switches to handle switch-level failures.

■ Try to minimize the number of switch/router paths to reduce latency of iSCSI transactions, and use line-rate switches.

■ Maintain separate network paths for management plane access in the event of service network failures.

TCP was designed as a message-passing protocol that provides reliable messaging on unreliable networks. However, TCP was not designed for high-speed, high-throughput, low-latency block data transfers. Because iSCSI uses TCP for sequential delivery and error handling, there is inherent CPU overhead when using the TCP stack. The following subsections review the three types of iSCSI initiators implementations. The correct choice depends on the application I/O rate and the CPU impact that can be tolerated. The iSCSI initiators options are software-iSCSI initiators, TCP offload adapters, and iSCSI HBA.

Software-iSCSI Initiators
TCP implemented in software using a standard NIC requires high CPU utilization (1GB/sec iSCSI requires approximately 60–90 percent utilization from a 1GHz CPU to achieve line-rate performance). This utilization results in potential throughput limitations and/or potentially increased latency.

TCP Offload Engine (TOE) NIC
To mitigate some of this host CPU overhead, the TCP protocol processing functions (the stack) are offloaded onto specialized gigabit Ethernet adapters called TCP Offload Engine (TOE) NICs. TCP processing can be done in firmware or ASICs. However, the host still has to perform SCSI command set processing.

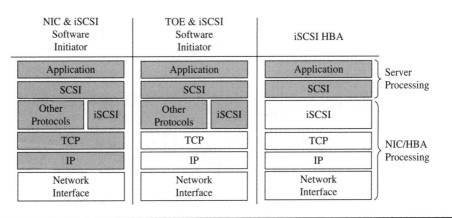

FIGURE 1-12. *iSCSI stack*

iSCSI HBA

To offload the overall overhead of iSCSI further, an incremental solution to TOEs is the iSCSI HBA. The iSCSI HBA not only offloads the TCP stack onto the hardware NIC, but also the SCSI processing; this moves all the I/O processing onto hardware, leaving the server to process the application. When the TCP/IP and iSCSI processing is offloaded to the iSCSI HBA, resulting in less than 10 percent CPU overhead for a 1GHz CPU, which is comparable to that of a FC HBA. iSCSI HBA initiators (shown in Figure 1-12) permit highly scalable iSCSI deployments, iSCSI capabilities such as gigabit-level cryptographic acceleration for end-to-end storage security, diskless server booting, and dynamic failover.

InfiniBand

An InfiniBand fabric uses a switched fabric topology similar to FC and has three key components: a host channel adapter (HCA), a switch, and a target channel adapter (TCA).

An HCA connects a host system to the InfiniBand fabric. An InfiniBand switch connects HCAs to HCAs or TCAs, and a TCA connects noninitiating devices to the InfiniBand fabric.

The demands of the Internet and distributed computing are challenging the scalability, reliability, availability, and performance of servers. InfiniBand architecture represents a new approach to I/O technology and is based on the collective research, knowledge, and experience of the industry's leaders and computer vendors.

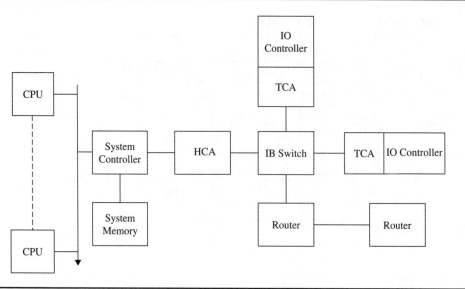

FIGURE 1-13. *InfiniBand architecture*

As shown in Figure 1-13, the InfiniBand architecture specifies channels that are created by attaching HCAs within a server chassis to HCAs in another server's chassis. This is done for high-performance InterProcess Communication (IPC) and to target channel adapters connecting InfiniBand-enabled servers to remote storage and communication networks through InfiniBand switches. InfiniBand links transfer data at 2.5 GB/sec, utilizing both copper wire and fiber optics for transmission. It can carry any combination of I/O, network, and IPC messages.

InfiniBand architecture has the following communication characteristics:

- User-level access to message passing

- Remote direct memory access (RDMA) in read and write mode

- Capability to send a message up to a maximum of 2GB in a single transfer

With RDMA, two or more computers communicate via direct memory access (DMA) from the main memory of one system to the main memory of another. As there is no CPU, cache, or context switching overhead needed to perform the transfer, and transfers can continue in parallel with other system operations, RDMA is particularly useful in applications that require high-throughput, low-latency networking, such as massively parallel Linux clusters. RDMA supports zero-copy networking by enabling the network adapter to transfer data directly to or from application memory, eliminating the need to copy data between application memory and the data buffers in the operating system. Such transfers require no work to be done by CPUs, caches, or context switches, and transfers continue in parallel with other system operations. When an application performs an RDMA read or write request, the application data are delivered directly to the network, reducing latency and enabling fast message transfer. Common RDMA implementations include InfiniBand, Virtual Interface Architecture (VIA), and iWARP.

The memory protection mechanism defined by the InfiniBand architecture allows an InfiniBand HCA to transfer data directly into or out of an application buffer. To protect these buffers from unauthorized access, InfiniBand employs a process called *memory registration.* Memory registration allows data transfers to be initiated directly from user mode, eliminating costly context switches to the kernel. Another benefit of allowing the InfiniBand HCA to transfer data directly into or out of application buffers is that it can make system buffering unnecessary. This eliminates the context switches to the kernel and frees the system from having to copy data to or from system buffers on a send or receive operation, respectively.

Another unique feature of the InfiniBand architecture is the *memory window.* The memory window provides a way for the application to grant another application remote read and/or write access to a specified buffer at a byte-level granularity. Memory windows are used in conjunction with RDMA read or RDMA write to control remote access to the application buffers. Data could be transferred either by the push or pull method—that is, either the sending node would send (push) the data over to the requester or the requester could get to the holder and get (pull) the data.

Oracle and I/O Characteristics

This section discusses the most uppermost part of the I/O stack: the host application I/O layer (specifically Oracle) and the OS handling of the I/O request. This section pulls together all the pieces of the upper layer I/O.

On the host system, applications such as databases, e-mail, or computer-aided design (CAD) systems all issue I/O requests to the underlying I/O infrastructure. However, each application requests I/O in different ways.

The three characteristics of an application are:

- The type of file to access

- The I/O access pattern

- The I/O request call

Types of File to Access

There are two types of files to access: raw files and filesystems.

Raw file access (RAW) (see Figure 1-14) goes through a character device and bypasses the internal page cache. The size of a single I/O is determined by the caller and handed down directly to the SCSI driver. The largest I/O transfer size is dictated by a kernel parameter.

A *filesystem* (FS) goes through a block-oriented device, sometimes called a "cooked" device. Examples of filesystems include Unix File System (UFS), Veritas File System (VxFs), Hierarchical file system (HFS), and Journal File System 2 (JFS2). All I/O requests go through the filesystem through the vfs/vnode structures and generally pass through the internal page cache.

Each page in the internal cache houses at least one filesystem page. The FS is capable of coalescing several I/O requests into a single large I/O call to the device (also known as *clustering I/O*). This reduces the overhead of managing several small I/O requests. Thus sequential reads and writes benefit from filesystem usage. Figure 1-15 shows the filesystem stack to access an Oracle database.

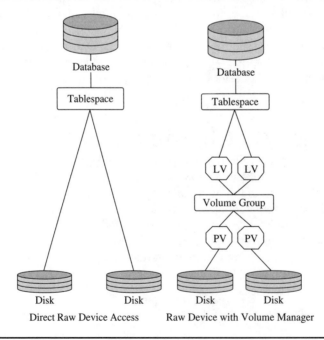

FIGURE 1-14. *RAW device partitions*

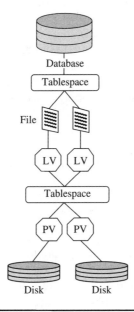

FIGURE 1-15. *Filesystem stack*

I/O Access Patterns

The two primary I/O access patterns are sequential and random.

A *sequential* I/O request is based on physically contiguous file locks—that is, a single I/O request consists of array of buffers. If the underlying OS drivers do not break up the single large request into multiple requests, the whole request is issued as one large I/O. The largest I/O request that Oracle issues is 1MB. Depending on I/O concurrency, sequential access is efficient if it involves all disks in array so that the aggregate bandwidth of all disks is used to satisfy the I/O request.

Random file I/O access varies per access—that is, the previous I/O operation to a block may differ from the subsequent block access. In other words, random file access is not contiguous block access. To optimize random I/O, a single disk is allowed to service the request.

Oracle generates two types of I/O workloads:

■ **Random small I/Os** With type of workload I/Os are the size of the database block, such as 8KB. They consist of random synchronous single reads (which correspond to single block foreground reads) or random asynchronous scatter/gather writes—that is, write requests that are scattered in the buffer and on disk (which correspond to Database Writer [DBWR] writes). Random small I/Os are typical for online transaction processing (OLTP) databases.

■ **Multi-user sequential large I/Os**   With this type of workload I/Os are 1MB on Linux. These workloads are used as multiple streams of sequential I/Os that appear as random I/Os to the storage array, scattered synchronous vector reads (corresponding to multiple block foreground reads, or table scans), sequential asynchronous reads (corresponding to direct path reads), sequential asynchronous writes (corresponding to direct path writes), and synchronous gather writes (corresponding to Log Writer [LGWR] writes). This type of workload is typically used for data warehouses; queries with table or index scans; direct data loads; and backups, restores, and archives.

An application can be characterized as I/O rate or data rate application:

■ **I/O rate**   This is the sum of the read rate and write rate of the application. OLTP applications, which consist of heavy small-block random reads and writes, are typical high I/O rate systems.

■ **Data rate**   This is amount of data that are transferred (requested) per operation. DSS applications, which employ large full-table scans, are examples of high-data-rate systems. DSS applications have low I/O concurrency rates, but the number of data requests per unit of work (I/O request) can be quite high.

I/O Request Calls

Read and write operations usually take the following form:

Read (*fname, open-type, address*)

where *fname* is the filename to open, *open-type* is the file open type flag, and *address* is the file address or offset.

Along with including the I/O request call on the file, you can include certain options to change the behavior of the operation:

■ **Direct I/O**   Although this is implicit in raw interfaces, block devices (on file open) can have the O_DIRECT flag included to provide direct I/O to the FS. Direct I/O is proven to be efficient for sequential accesses that use prefetches.

■ **Synchronous**   This is a standard method of invoking or requesting an I/O operation. The caller blocks, waiting in biowait(), then is interrupted by the device driver indicating that the I/O has completed.

■ **Asynchronous I/O**   Async I/O allows the caller of I/O to queue the I/O request (in the device driver). The return code from the queued request is a confirmed context handle. After the request is queued, the caller can resume activities; that is, unlike synchronous I/O, asynchronous I/O is not blocked. Periodically, the caller polls for the completion of I/O using the context handle as a way to identify this request uniquely. The caller can queue several I/O requests in async mode (there is a system limit). The OS vendor provides async I/O call capability using shared libraries. However, the caller must specifically perform the call (read/write) with the async parameter set.

Basic Variables That Affect I/O Performance

The following are the basic variables that affect I/O performance:

- **I/O size**   This is the unit size of a single I/O operation in bytes.

- **Stripe size**   This is the size of an allocation unit on each disk device in an array unit. Each disk device in the array has the same stripe size.

- **Stripe width**   This is the product of the stripe size and number of disks in that stripe array.

- **Concurrency**   This is the number of distinct concurrent I/O operations against the disk array.

- **Alignment**   This is one of the basic variables affecting I/O.

This section describes how I/O is accomplished, starting from the Oracle user process that issues a system call requesting I/O (via a `SELECT` SQL call), continuing down through the stack with the device transferring the data and finally ending with the driver completing the request. The following subsections describe how a user request results in driver execution.

1. In the User Process

A user process makes an I/O system call and invokes the kernel through the system call interface. The kernel does some processing related to managing the process and resources for the request. This includes the following:

- Checking that the user has permission to access the device

- Obtaining system buffers to use, if necessary

- Using the major number to index into a device switch table

- Calling the driver associated with the device file with the appropriate parameters

2. In the Kernel

Once an Oracle process issues an I/O system call against a disk device, the corresponding driver routine is called based on the device switch table. The device switch table is essentially a table matrix that lists the names of all device drivers and their associated routines. Each device file has a major number and minor number. The kernel uses the major number as an index into the device switch table to locate the device driver for the requested device. Note that each device driver listed has an address for each I/O routine (system call); this address is essentially the entry point into the routine. The minor number is then used to locate the actual device and any device-specific information. There are character and block device switch tables.

The device driver is the software interface to a specific device, such as the SCSI disk, the EIDE disk, tape, printers, and so on. Therefore, each type of device on the system has a device driver.

The kernel uses the major number to index into a device switch table and sets up parameters, if any, to be passed to the device driver.

3. In the Device Driver

The device driver's routine does the necessary setup and begins processing of the I/O request. This involves initializing data structures and setting up a request to process the I/O. After the driver routine sets up a request for I/O, the driver either waits for the I/O to be completed or immediately returns control to the routine that invoked it. Whether the driver returns or waits for the I/O to be completed depends on the characteristics of the device and the needs of the driver. A device driver routine waits by calling `sleep()`, in which case the user process is put to sleep until another routine issues a corresponding call to `wakeup()`.

4. In the Interface Driver

The interface driver processes the request once the device is available. After the hardware completes the I/O request, an interrupt is sent back to the device driver, signaling I/O completion.

The interface driver is the software component that acts as the interfaces between the bus and the physical device. Only the device driver can call the interface driver. There is an interface driver for each interface (hardware adapter) card on the system.

A device driver has two logical components: an upper half and a lower half. A system call from a user program activates the upper half of the driver (the user-mode context). The lower half of the driver, or the interrupt context, processes interrupts from the device. The halves work as follows:

- The upper half initiates activity on the device, then waits.

- The device completes the activity and interrupts, causing the lower half of the driver to tell the upper half that it should/can continue. Interrupts are handled by an interrupt service routine (ISR) and supporting routines in the interface driver.

5. In the Device Driver

If the device driver has called `sleep()` and is waiting for the device to complete the transfer, the interrupt routine calls `wakeup()` to awaken the sleeping process. When the process awakens, it continues to execute from the point at which it put itself to sleep, doing processing appropriate to complete the system call. Then it returns an integer value (indicating the success or failure of the request) to the kernel routine that invoked it, completing the original request.

6. In the Kernel

The kernel interprets the return value from the device driver and sets the return value of the system call accordingly. It then returns control to the user process.

Protecting the Storage Stack from Failures

Unlike direct attached or network attached storage, SANs require careful planning before implementation. SANs differ from NAS in that they store and access data at the block level, whereas NAS appliances store data at the file level. File-level access is preferable for users and applications that need to access a particular file, whereas block-level data access is better for applications that need to access data quickly. SANs also differ from other storage architectures in that they are dedicated storage networks and use their own network protocols and hardware components.

SANs are the best way to ensure predictable performance and constant data availability and reliability. The importance of this is obvious for companies that conduct business on the web and require high-volume transaction processing. It is also obvious for managers who are bound to service-level agreements (SLAs) and must maintain certain performance levels when delivering IT services.

Due to the nature of the vulnerable data that are stored on these servers and the need for today's businesses to keep that data available, the SAN infrastructure should be designed with great care. For a high-availability solution, it is important to consider redundant components of the entire infrastructure stack and not just the storage array. For example, in Figure 1-16, which is a very basic model of SAN configuration, there are several areas of single points of failure:

1. The server's HBA

2. The fibre channel conductor from the server to the first switch

3. The switch (the incoming and outgoing gigabit interface converters [GBICs])

4. The FC conductor between first and second switch

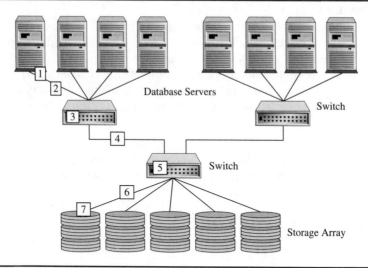

FIGURE 1-16. *SAN failure points*

5. The second switch (the incoming and outgoing GBICs)

6. The FC conductor between second switch and storage array

7. The controller on the storage array

Failure of any of these components will result in unavailability of data to the database server when requests are made or when data is required to be persisted. All these identified components in a SAN configuration (or, for that matter, any storage/infrastructure configuration) should be made redundant in all respects to provide availability and distribution of workload. In Figure 1-17, the preceding SAN configuration has been redone to show how to provide additional redundancy for high availability. The figure shows two data paths of access, A and B, illustrating redundancy and distribution of workload. These components not only provide availability when their counterparts fail, but can also transport data to provide dual connectivity to the database storage arrays.

The architecture illustrated in Figure 1-17 raises another issue. Deep inside the storage array or SAN is the SCSI protocol that basically performs the read/write operation; unfortunately, SCSI was never designed for multipath access. Thus two concurrent operations cannot be made using a SCSI protocol. Several vendors have overcome this limitation using a multipathing software layer:

■ EMC PowerPath

■ SUN Traffic Manager (formerly MP x I/O)

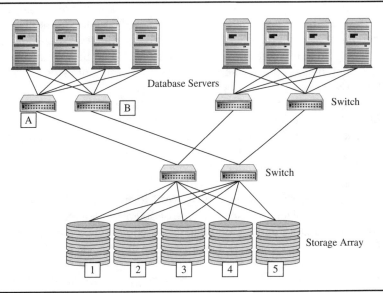

FIGURE 1-17. *SAN with redundant paths*

- Veritas Volume Manager

- Hewlett-Packard SecurePath

- IBM Subsystem Device Driver Path Control Module (SDDPCM)

- Linux DM driver (built on the 2.6 kernel)

- Hitachi Dynamic Link Manager (HDLM)

The primary function of this software that sits between the SAN and the operating system is to present only one path to the operating system at any one time. Apart from this functionality, the multipathing software offers two other functions: failover and load balancing.

One of the very important functions that the multipathing software performs is to automatically tribute I/O to another channel in the case of a fabric failure. Secondly it performs dynamic load balancing by sending streams of data through the least-used path.

Multipathing is the use of redundant storage network components responsible for transfer of data between the server and storage. These components include cabling, adapters, and switches and the software that enables this transfer.

Beyond multipathing, failover, and availability, it is crucial that any one or more sets of servers can access the ports of a SAN. This accessibility is obtained by creating zones. Just as zoning can be applied at the disk level, as you learned earlier in this chapter, zoning can also be applied at the SAN level. In the five storage farms shown in Figure 1-17, farms 1 through 3 may be assigned only to the set of servers on the left, and farms 4 and 5 may be assigned to servers on the right. Zoning can also divide a farm's area; for example, if necessary, farm 3 can be split into two equal zones. Zoning helps protect different servers from seeing or using each other's storage on the SAN.

Another type zoning, called *LUN masking*, is done at the LUN level. Apart from protecting data at the server level, each LUN or set of LUNs can be masked to provide access to only one server or a set of servers. LUN masking is actually performed at a level above zoning—that is, although a zone grants access only to a given port on a storage array, LUN masking grants access to some of the LUNs on the given port to one server and the remainder to another server.

Usually all these LUNs deploy some kind of RAID technology. As discussed earlier, each type of RAID is optimized for a specific type of operation. For example, RAID 5 is good for read-only operations and is found in data warehouse implementations. Each type of RAID has its own pros and cons. Understanding this, Oracle Corporation has developed a methodology based on the RAID 01 technology for best placement of data among all the allocated groups of disks. The methodology is called *SAME (Stripe and Mirror Everything)*.

Summary

The storage stack can get complicated if adequate care is not taken in its configuration. With several choices available today, the right type of configuration should be selected based on careful analysis, in-house expertise, and application data access patterns. In this chapter, we looked at the storage stack overview such as SAN, NAS, iSCSI, and so on as it has existed until now. We covered the basics of the disk technology followed by the various storage protocols and other networking options available.

CHAPTER
2

ASM Instances

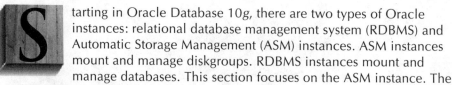tarting in Oracle Database 10*g*, there are two types of Oracle instances: relational database management system (RDBMS) and Automatic Storage Management (ASM) instances. ASM instances mount and manage diskgroups. RDBMS instances mount and manage databases. This section focuses on the ASM instance. The ASM instance is much simpler to manage than an RDBMS instance, because very few parameters are needed to run it. The ASM instance executes only a small portion of the code in the Oracle kernel, thus it is less likely to encounter failures or contention. The ASM instance provides an extent map to the RDBMS instance when a file is opened or created, and subsequently the RDBMS instances read and write directly to the disks based on the extent map. The ASM instance is not in the input/ output (I/O) path. Additionally, the RDBMS instances never directly update ASM metadata. ASM metadata is written only by the ASM instance.

An ASM instance, just like an RDBMS instance, allocates a memory area called the *System Global Area* (SGA) and starts a set of Oracle processes that manage and maintain the instance. This combination of the SGA and the Oracle processes is called an *Oracle instance*.

Starting ASM

The ASM instance is generally named +ASM, and in Real Application Clusters (RAC) configurations, the ASM system identifier (SID) is an +ASM*x* instance, where *x* represents the instance number. The ORACLE_SID environment variable can be as follows:

```
export ORACLE_SID=+ASM1
```

ASM is the volume manager for all databases that employ ASM on a given node. Therefore, only one ASM instance is required per node regardless of the number of database instances on the node. ASM instances can support multiple versions of RDBMS instances. Additionally, ASM seamlessly works with the RAC architecture to support clustered storage environments. In RAC environments, there is one ASM instance per clustered node, and the ASM instances communicate with each other on a peer-to-peer basis using Oracle Cache Fusion and the interconnect.

In a clustered environment, the ASM instance, like the RDBMS instance, leverages the RAC Cache Fusion infrastructure, such as global enqueue serives (GES), global cache services (GCS) and global resource directory (GRD), to communicate with the other instances via the interconnect. ASM instances message other ASM instances to acknowledge or convey changes to diskgroup—for example, disk state changes, diskgroup membership changes, and ASM cluster membership. ASM's distributed lock manager (DLM) traffic typically is minimal and should not impact the RDBMS interconnect throughput.

You can start the ASM instance using SQLPlus, Oracle Enterprise Manager (EM), or the `srvctl` command (if you are using Oracle Clusterware).

The ASM instance is started with the `INSTANCE_TYPE=ASM` set in the init.ora file. Similarly, the RDBMS instance is identified by `INSTANCE_TYPE=RDBMS` (which is the default). Unlike the RDBMS instance, the ASM instance contains no physical files such as logfiles, controlfiles, or datafiles, and requires only a few init.ora parameters for startup.

When the `INSTANCE_TYPE=ASM` parameter is set, it signals the Oracle initialization routine to start an ASM instance and not an RDBMS instance. The startup of an ASM instance is as follows:

```
SQL>STARTUP
```

The following query, when run on the ASM instance, reflects that it is an ASM instance:

```
SQL> SELECT INSTANCE_NAME FROM V$INSTANCE;
INSTANCE_NAME
----------------
+ASM
```

The `STARTUP` clauses for ASM instances are similar to those for RDBMS instances. For example, `NOMOUNT` starts up an ASM instance without mounting any diskgroups. The `MOUNT` option simply mounts all diskgroups defined in the `ASM_DISKGROUPS` init.ora parameter. The `OPEN` startup option performs the same function as the `MOUNT` option. If no diskgroups are listed in the init.ora file, then the message "ORA-15110: no diskgroups mounted" is displayed. If the listed diskgroups cannot be mounted, then the following messages appear: "ORA-15032: not all alterations performed," and, "ORA-15063: ASM discovered an insufficient number of disks for diskgroup <diskgroup name>."

In Oracle Database 11*g*, ASM introduced the `RESTRICTED` startup option for the `MOUNT` command. When an ASM instance is started with the `RESTRICTED` option, the starting ASM instance exclusively mounts all of the diskgroups listed in the `ASM_DISKGROUPS` parameter, and no RDBMS access is permitted in this mode. When the `RESTRICTED` startup option is used on a diskgroup in an ASM clustered (RAC) environment, no other ASM instance in the cluster can access that diskgroup. The `RESTRICTED` option is particularly useful when performing maintenance, such as a rebalance, on a diskgroup or set of diskgroups.

NOTE
The `RESTRICTED` option can be specified during mount at the diskgroup level rather than during startup at an instance level. This option provides a more granular restriction.

The following example illustrates the use of the RESTRICTED option and the STATE reflected in the V$ASM_DISKGROUP view:

```
SQL> ALTER DISKGROUP DATA MOUNT RESTRICTED;
SQL> SELECT NAME, STATE FROM V$ASM_DISKGROUP;
NAME                                 STATE
------------------------------       -----------
DATA                                 RESTRICTED
```

ASM Background Processes

Once the ASM instance is started, all the basic background processes, as well as some that are specific to the operation of ASM, are started. Notice that all the ASM processes begin with *asm,* whereas the RDBMS instance processes begin with *ora.* On Unix, the ASM processes can be listed using the following command:

```
ps -ef|grep asm
oracle     7186    1    0 May30 ?         00:00:13 asm_pmon_+ASM1
oracle     7188    1    0 May30 ?         00:00:01 asm_vktm_+ASM1
oracle     7192    1    0 May30 ?         00:00:02 asm_diag_+ASM1
oracle     7194    1    0 May30 ?         00:00:41 asm_ping_+ASM1
oracle     7196    1    0 May30 ?         00:00:00 asm_psp0_+ASM1
oracle     7200    1    0 May30 ?         00:02:44 asm_dia0_+ASM1
oracle     7202    1    0 May30 ?         00:01:42 asm_lmon_+ASM1
oracle     7204    1    0 May30 ?         00:06:36 asm_lmd0_+ASM1
oracle     7206    1    0 May30 ?         00:04:36 asm_lms0_+ASM1
oracle     7210    1    0 May30 ?         00:00:00 asm_mman_+ASM1
oracle     7212    1    0 May30 ?         00:00:01 asm_dbw0_+ASM1
oracle     7214    1    0 May30 ?         00:00:01 asm_lgwr_+ASM1
oracle     7216    1    0 May30 ?         00:00:02 asm_ckpt_+ASM1
oracle     7218    1    0 May30 ?         00:00:00 asm_smon_+ASM1
oracle     7220    1    0 May30 ?         00:12:46 asm_rbal_+ASM1
oracle     7222    1    0 May30 ?         00:00:43 asm_gmon_+ASM1
oracle     7232    1    0 May30 ?         00:00:04 asm_lck0_+ASM1
oracle     7444    1    0 May30 ?         00:10:04 asm_asmb_+ASM1
```

The following are some of the more important ASM background processes:

- **ARBx** These are the slave processes that do the rebalance activity (where *x* is a number).

- **CKPT** The CKPT process manages cross-instance calls (in RAC).

- **DBWR** This process manages the SGA buffer cache in the ASM instance. DBWR writes out dirty buffers (changed metadata buffers) from the ASM buffer cache to disk.

- **GMON** This process is responsible for managing the disk-level activities (drop/offline) and advancing diskgroup compatibility.

- **KATE** The Konductor or ASM Temporary Errands (KATE) process is used to process disks online. This process runs in the ASM instance and is started only when an offlined disk is onlined.

- **LGWR** The LGWR process maintains the ASM Active Change Directory (ACD) buffers from the ASM instance and flushes ACD change records to disk.

- **MARK** The Mark Allocation Unit (AU) for Resync Koordinator (MARK) process coordinates the updates to the Staleness Registry when the disks go offline. This process runs in the RDBMS instance and is started only when disks go offline in ASM redundancy diskgroups.

- **PING** The PING process measures network latency and has the same functionality in RDBMS instances.

- **PMON** This manages processes and process death in the ASM instance.

- **PSP0** This process spawner process is responsible for creating and managing other Oracle processes.

- **PZ9x** These processes are parallel slave processes (where *x* is a number), used in fetching data on behalf of GV$ queries.

- **RBAL** This opens all device files as part of discovery and coordinates the rebalance activity.

- **SMON** This process is the system monitor and also acts as a liaison to the Cluster Synchronization Services (CSS) process (in Oracle Clusterware) for node monitoring.

- **VKTM** This process is used to maintain the fast timer and has the same functionality in the RDBMS instances.

ASM SGA and Parameter Sizing

This section discusses the parameters typically used in the ASM instance, and explains how to set the appropriate values for these parameters based on best practices.

ASM init.ora Parameters

To enable the ASM instance, you need only configure a few init.ora parameters. The parameter file for ASM can be a Pfile or Spfile. Database Configuration Assistant (DBCA) creates an ASM Spfile by default during database/ASM creation for a single instance. If you initially create a pfile for ASM, the Spfile can be manually configured later if desired. However, if a single Spfile is used in clustered ASM environments, then it must be on a shared access device (that is, a cluster filesystem, shared raw device, or network attached storage [NAS] device). The init.ora parameters specified in the following example are the parameters required to start up ASM:

```
*.instance_type=asm
*.asm_diskgroups=DATA,FLASH
*.processes=100
**** Note that asm_diskstring is site-specific and platform specific
*.asm_diskstring='/dev/rdsk/c3t19d*s4'
*.remote_login_passwordfile='SHARED'

      ******

      **For 11g use only the diagnostics directory.
*.diagnostic_dest='/opt/app/admin/+ASM/diag'

      *******

      **For 10g use the standard dump locations
*.background_dump_dest='/opt/app/admin/+ASM/bdump'
*.core_dump_dest='/opt/app/admin/+ASM/cdump'
*.user_dump_dest='/opt/app/admin/+ASM/udump'

      *******
```

The BACKGROUND_DUMP_DEST, CORE_DUMP_DEST, and USER_DUMP_DEST initialization parameters are deprecated in Oracle Database 11*g* and should not be set in Oracle Database 11*g* ASM. These parameters will be replaced with the Automatic Diagnostic Repository (ADR) DIAGNOSTIC_DEST init.ora parameter. If the DIAGNOSTIC_DEST parameter is not specified, then the default location will be $ORACLE_BASE/diag. For example, the following directory structures will be created:

```
$ORACLE_BASE/diag/<INSTANCE type>/<DB_UNIQUE_NAME>/<ORACLE_SID>
```

Query the V$DIAG_INFO view from the ASM instance as follows to review all the diagnostic information from the ASM instance:

```
SQL> SELECT NAME, VALUE FROM V$DIAG_INFO
NAME            VALUE
---------- ----------------
Diag Enabled    TRUE
ADR Base        /u01/app/oracle
ADR Home        /u01/app/oracle /diag/asm/+asm/+ASM1
Diag Trace      /u01/app/oracle/diag/asm/+asm/+ASM1/trace
Diag Alert      /u01/app/oracle/diag/asm/+asm/+ASM1/alert
Diag Incident   /u01/app/oracle /diag/asm/+asm/+ASM1/incident
Diag Cdump      /u01/app/oracle/diag/asm/+asm/+ASM1/cdump
Health Monitor  /u01/app/oracle/diag/asm/+asm/+ASM1/hm
Default Trace File
```

In Oracle Database 11*g*, all of the ADR can be viewed and tracked using the ADR command-line interface (`adrci`).

Best Practices for ASM init.ora Parameters

In Oracle Database 11*g*, ASM can leverage the Automatic Memory Management (AMM) feature using the init.ora parameters MEMORY_TARGET and MEMORY_MAX_TARGET. Note that these parameters apply not only to ASM but also to the RDBMS instance. Setting these two new parameters automatically manages and tunes all Oracle-related memory for the instance in question (ASM or RDBMS). AMM tunes memory to the target memory size, redistributing and reallocating memory as needed between the instance's SGA and its program global area (PGA).

However, because ASM instances have fairly static memory needs, it is an ASM best practice not to set any Oracle memory parameters, including the MEMORY_TARGET parameter. The result is that the default value for MEMORY_TARGET, 256MB, is used. This value suits most configurations. To modify the memory for ASM, you need only set the MEMORY_TARGET parameter. For example, you can set the MEMORY_TARGET value using the following command:

```
SQL>ALTER SYSTEM SET MEMORY_TARGET=300M;
```

Although it is not recommended, if you want to set the individual memory parameters, disable MEMORY_TARGET by setting it to 0, then set the appropriate SHARED_POOL, LARGE_POOL, or DB_CACHE_SIZE values as needed:

- **DB_CACHE_SIZE** This value determines the size of the buffer cache, which is used to cache ASM metadata blocks. The DB_CACHE_SIZE is based on a metadata block size of 4K. This block size is the buffer page size of the cached metadata and has no bearing or impact on the database block size.

- **SHARED_POOL** This is used for standard memory usage (control structures and so on) to manage the instance. The value is also used to store open file extent maps.

- **LARGE_POOL** The LARGE_POOL value is used for large page allocations.

- **PROCESSES** This ASM init.ora parameter limits the number of processes that can start in ASM instance. You may need to modify this parameter from its default setting for Oracle Database 10*g* ASM instances. The following recommendation pertains to Oracle Database 10.1.0.3 through 10.2.*x* and will work for RAC and non-RAC systems:

```
Processes = 25 + (10 + [max number of concurrent database file
creations, and file extend operations possible])*n
```

where *n* is the number of RDBMS instance (ASM clients) connecting to ASM

The source of concurrent file creations can be any of the following:

- Several concurrent CREATE TABLESPACE commands

- Creation of a partitioned table with several tablespace creations

- RMAN backup channels

- Concurrent archive log file creations

In Oracle Database 10g, ASM does not use the AMM feature, and thus specific SGA parameters must be set. The following guidelines work most configurations:

- SHARED_POOL_SIZE: 128MB

- LARGE_POOL: 12MB

- DB_CACHE_SIZE: 64MB

Once the appropriate SGA values are set for ASM instance, they can be checked using the following SQL*Plus command:

```
SQL> SHOW SGA
Total System Global Area   351682560 bytes
Fixed Size                   1331588 bytes
Variable Size              283242108 bytes
ASM Cache                   67108864 bytes
```

Note that most RDBMS parameters are not allowed or not applicable in the ASM instance. If a nonapplicable parameter is set in the ASM instance, you will receive an ORA-15021 error message. For example, if you try to set the CONTROL_FILES parameter for the ASM instance, you receive the following error message:

```
ORA-15021: parameter "control_files" is not valid in asm instance
```

NOTE
It may seem confusing when you issue a SHOW PARAMETER control_files command on the ASM instance and it shows the following:

```
SQL> SHOW PARAMETER CONTROL
NAME                                  TYPE          VALUE
------------------------------------- ----------- -------------------------------
control_files                         string        /opt/oracle/app/product/10gr2/
                                                       dbs/cntrl+ASM.dbf
```

So what is this cntrl+ASM.dbf file? The control_files parameter points to a dummy (a nonexistent file). This is the internal default value name for the CONTROL_FILES parameter. Nevertheless, it is a meaningless value in the ASM instance.

Two files are stored in the $ORACLE_HOME/dbs directory that are associated with ASM:

- **ab_<ASM SID>.dat**   This file is generated when an ASM instance starts, and is used by the RDBMS instance to determine the appropriate environment information whenever the RDBMS instance connects to the ASM instance. If this file is removed, then RDBMS instances will not be able to connect to ASM. Note that the authentication for the connection is not based on the information in the *.dat file.

- **hc_<SID>.dat**   EM uses this file for instance health-check monitoring. If this file is removed, the health check information for the instance will be inaccurate.

These ASM .dat files should not have any performance effect on ASM. They only have connection details that are needed to talk to the ASM instance.

Note that there will be times when it is necessarily to set some _ (underscore) parameters—for example, when you are debugging issues with Oracle Support. In these cases, in Oracle Database 10*g*, Oracle Support requests that you add a parameter that will allow the ASM instance to process and accept these values. This parameter is called _DISABLE_INSTANCE_PARMS_CHECK (note that this parameter is not required in Oracle Database 11*g*). Set _ parameters only with the assistance of Oracle Support.

ASM and Single Point of Failure

Often users ask whether ASM is a single point of failure and what are the best practices to protect against such failures. Similar to other filesystems or volume managers, ASM instance failure causes the other RDBMS instances on that node to become unavailable. However, when the OS filesystem or volume manager fails, it usually leads to a system crash, whereas the ASM instance can be restarted without restarting the server.

The best-practice approach to mitigating ASM as the single point of failure is to run ASM in a RAC environment and take advantage of high availability through clustering. ASM is able to continue to run on the remaining nodes in a cluster even when one node might restart the RDBMS or ASM instance. An ASM failure is a softer crash and has quicker recovery than traditional filesystems or volume managers.

ASM Installation

In cases where a single ASM instance is managing only one RDBMS instance on a server or node, it may be sufficient to maintain a single ORACLE_HOME for ASM and the RDBMS. However, for systems that have an ASM instance managing the storage for several RDBMS instances and require higher availability, it is recommended that the ASM instance be installed in a separate ORACLE_HOME (ASM_HOME) than the database ORACLE_HOME.

NOTE
In RAC environments, if adding nodes (via `addNode.sh`*) and separate* `ASM_HOMEs` *are deployed, the* `addNode` *procedure needs to be run for the* `ASM_HOME` *as well.*

Starting with Oracle Database 10*g* Release 2, Oracle Universal Installer (OUI-DBCA) and DBCA had been enhanced to allow the user to create and install an ASM instance seamlessly in a separate ORACLE_HOME. OUI-DBCA now has options to install and configure the following:

■ A database that uses ASM for storage management

■ An ASM instance, without creating a database

■ ASM on a system that already has a running database, where subsequently the DBA can use the EM Migration Utility to migrate the database to ASM

Initializing an ASM Instance

This section describes the steps needed to initialize the ASM instance using DBCA. DBCA can be launched using the following command:

```
[oracle11@racnode1~]$  $ORACLE_HOME/bin/dbca
```

This command displays the initial DBCA Welcome page (see Figure 2-1).

Figure 2-2 illustrates Step 1 of the DBCA configuration process. This step provides the option to select the type of operation to be performed. Select the Configure Automatic Storage Management option.

If ASM is not already configured, you receive the message shown in Figure 2-3, indicating that DBCA could not start up ASM. Click Yes to start up and configure ASM.

Next DBCA prompts you to enter a SYS user and password for the ASM instance and make any `init.ora` parameter changes that are necessary. This is shown in Figures 2-4 and 2-5, respectively.

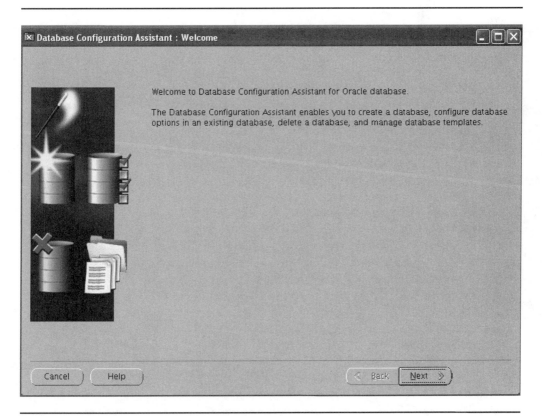

FIGURE 2-1. *The DBCA Welcome screen*

Figure 2-6 shows that the advanced parameters can be listed using the Show Advanced Parameters tab.

Once this is completed , DBCA initiates the startup of the ASM instance, as shown in Figure 2-7. Click on OK to confirm the creation of ASM instances.

Note that for ASM to communicate with the DBCA, the listener should also be started. DBCA verifies whether the listener is running; if it is not, the program prompts the user with a message to click OK to start the listener.

In RAC environments, DBCA creates the ASM instances on all nodes in the cluster.

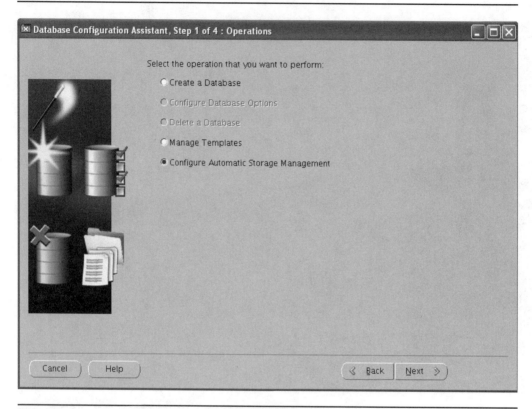

FIGURE 2-2. *Step 1 of the DBCA configuration process*

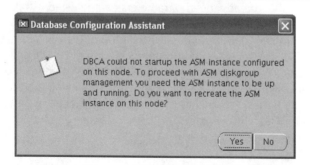

FIGURE 2-3. *The message that you receive when ASM has not yet been configured and DBCA cannot start it up.*

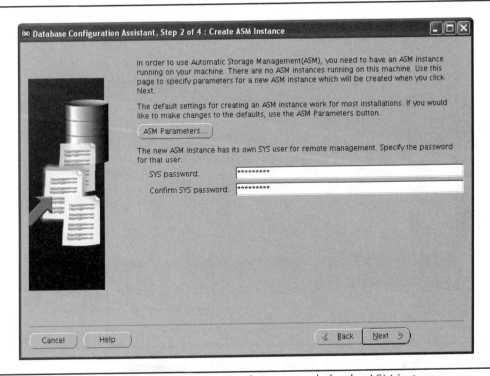

FIGURE 2-4. *Step 2 of DBCA prompts you for passwords for the ASM instance*

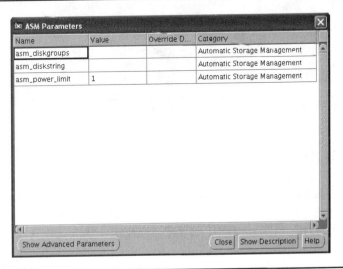

FIGURE 2-5. *The ASM Parameters screen enables you to adjust* `init.ora` *parameters.*

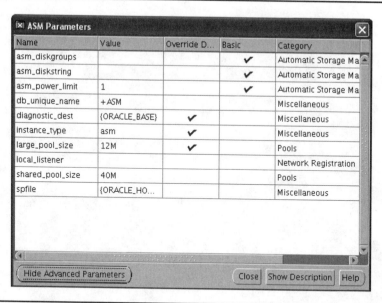

FIGURE 2-6. *Listing advanced parameters*

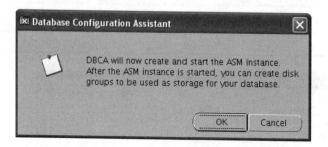

FIGURE 2-7. *DBCA enables you to initiate the startup of ASM instances.*

Upgrading ASM Software

This section discusses the upgrade from Oracle releases 10.1 to 10.2 as well as from Oracle Database 10*g* to Oracle Database 11*g*.

Upgrading the ASM Instance from 10.x to 11.x

There are two methods to use when upgrading ASM to Oracle ASM 11*g*: manually or using the Database Update Assistant (DBUA). With either method, the new Oracle

Database 11*g* software (ORACLE_HOME) should already be installed using OUI. Note that this upgrade is simply a software upgrade; the diskgroup compatibility needs to be advanced as well to take advantage of all the Oracle Database 11*g* features. However, this can be done at a later time. Diskgroup compatibility is explained further in Chapter 4.

Manual Upgrade

With the manual upgrade process, the following needs to be performed:

1. Update the `oratab` entry with the ASM ORACLE_HOME location.

2. Copy over the ASM init.ora and make any appropriate changes, such as the directory locations for the diag and dump directories. In RAC environments, the new ASM home must be modified within the Oracle 11*g* Clusterware OCR disk. This can be done using the `srvctl` command:

   ```
   srvctl modify asm -n racnode1 -i +ASM1 -o \ /opt/oracle/app/
   product/11.1/asm -p init+ASM1.ora
   ```

   This command needs to be performed on all nodes of participating ASM cluster.

3. Once the instance is started, grant `SYSASM` to the `SYSUSER`.

4. For a Windows system, re-create the Windows service using `ORADIM`.

DBUA Upgrade

The ASM upgrade to Oracle Database 11*g* can be performed using DBUA. DBUA performs the following steps:

1. It copies the password file and re-creates init.ora/Spfile in the new home directory.

2. It updates oratab on a Unix/Linux system or re-creates service using `ORADIM` on Windows.

3. It grants the `SYSASM` role to the `SYSUSER`.

To launch DBUA, execute it from the Oracle Database 11*g* ORACLE_HOME directory:

```
[oracle11@racnode1~]$ cd $ORACLE_HOME/bin
[oracle11@racnode1~]$ ./dbua
```

Invoking DBUA from the command prompt displays the DBUA Welcome screen shown in Figure 2-8. Click Next to start the upgrade process.

NOTE
When a separate set of binaries is installed for ASM_ HOME and DBUA must upgrade the ASM instance, DBUA should be invoked from the $ASM_HOME/ bin directory, not from the $ORACLE_HOME/bin directory.

The next screen is the Upgrade Operations screen shown in Figure 2-9. This screen presents two options: to upgrade the RDBMS database to the latest Oracle Database 11*g*, Release 1, or to upgrade the Automatic Storage Management Instance to the latest release of Oracle 11*g*.

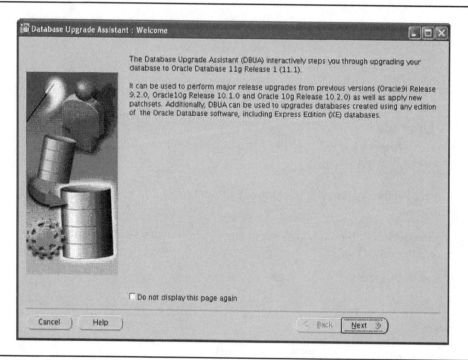

FIGURE 2-8. *DBUA Welcome screen*

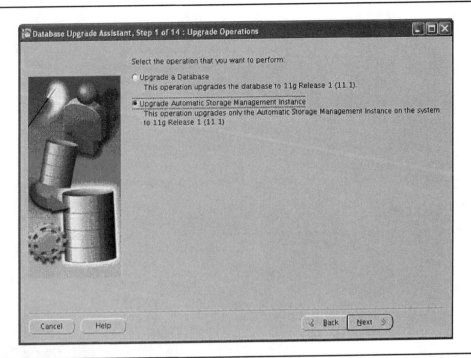

FIGURE 2-9.   *The DBUA Upgrade Operations screen*

From the Upgrade Operations screen, select Upgrade Automatic Storage Management Instance and click Next. This displays the ASM Upgrade Summary screen shown in Figure 2-10. Review the summary, and if everything is correct, click Finish. This starts the upgrade of the ASM instance. At this stage, DBUA displays the Upgrade Results screen (shown in Figure 2-11). When you are finished reviewing the results, click Close.

Figure 2-12 shows the final stage of the upgrade process, where the results of the upgrade are displayed for informational purposes. Click Close to complete the upgrade.

After the upgrade is completed, you can start ASM using the standard methods.

Patching ASM

There is no support for "rolling upgrade" patches in Oracle Database 10*g* ASM. Rolling upgrades patches in Oracle Database 10*g* are supported only with Oracle

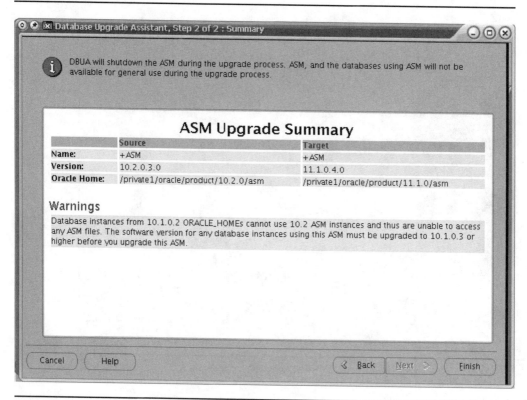

FIGURE 2-10. *The DBUA ASM Upgrade Summary screen*

Clusterware installs and between DataGuard sites. In Oracle Database 10g, if you are installing a patchset or "nonrolling upgrade safe" patches, all the ASM instances in a cluster must be shut down. Additionally, if you are using a separate ASM_HOME, then ASM should be patched accordingly, just like the RDBMS home. This includes applying critical patch updates (CPUs) as well. Starting with Oracle Database 11g, rolling upgrades of ASM are supported. This section covers the ASM Rolling Migration feature of Oracle Database 11g.

With rolling upgrade support for ASM, patchsets and migration to future releases of ASM can be applied in rolling upgrade fashion, providing an even higher level of availability for the underlying applications. Note that the Rolling Migration feature is applicable only if the initial ASM software version is at least version Oracle Database version 11.1. Additionally, Rolling Migration requires that the Oracle Clusterware software be at the highest level.

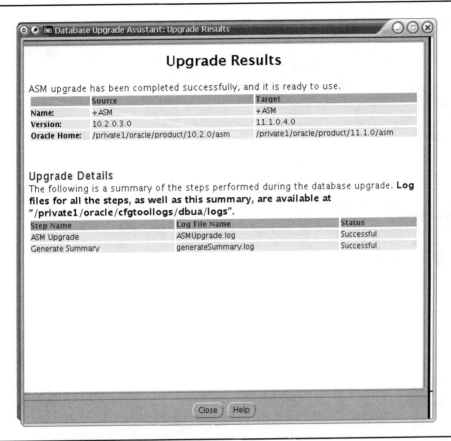

FIGURE 2-11. *The DBUA Upgrade Results screen*

Before initiating a rolling migration, you must first place the ASM instances in the cluster into rolling migration mode by using the following command, for example (for future migrations):

```
ALTER SYSTEM START ROLLING MIGRATION TO 11.2.0.2.
```

Keep in mind that the preceding rolling migration command does not perform the actual migration, it simply prepares the clustered ASM instances for rolling migration. Additionally, the rolling migration is not preserved if all ASM instances fail while in the rolling migration mode.

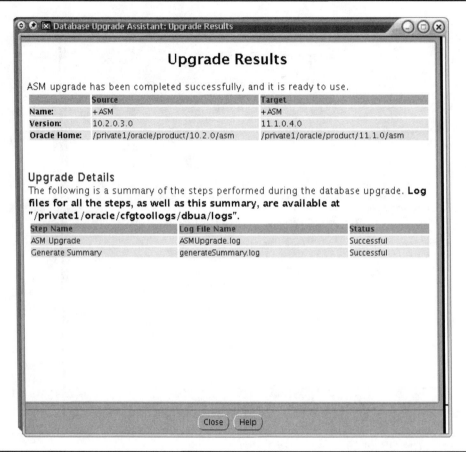

FIGURE 2-12. *The DBUA Upgrade Results screen*

To determine the current state of the cluster, use the following query:

```
SQL> SELECT SYS_CONTEXT('sys_cluster_properties', 'cluster_state') FROM
DUAL;
SYS_CONTEXT('SYS_CLUSTER_PROPERTIES','CLUSTER_STATE')
----------------------------------------------------
Normal
The output above shows that the cluster is in a NORMAL (non-migration) state.
SQL> SELECT SYS_CONTEXT('sys_cluster_properties', 'cluster_state') FROM
DUAL;
SYS_CONTEXT('SYS_CLUSTER_PROPERTIES','CLUSTER_STATE')
----------------------------------------------------
Rolling Migration
```

This output shows that the cluster is in a migration-ready state.

Once the rolling migration mode is enabled, each ASM instance can shut down so that the software upgrade can be started. When the software upgrade for a particular instance is completed, the ASM instance can then be restarted and diskgroups mounted. At this point, the upgraded ASM instance will rejoin the ASM cluster with a higher version than the remaining instances. This configuration is permissible only in rolling migration mode.

The following steps summarize the rolling migration process:

1. Ensure that the software for the new version is installed on all nodes.

2. Ensure that Oracle Clusterware is at the highest version.

3. Ensure that all the ASM instances are on the same Oracle version.

4. Make sure that no rebalance operations are currently in progress. If a rebalance operation is running, then let the operation complete before starting the migration.

5. Place the ASM cluster in rolling migration mode using the following command:

   ```
   ALTER SYSTEM START ROLLING MIGRATION TO 11.2.0.2;
   ```

6. Shut down an ASM running the old software.

7. Start an ASM instance from the ORACLE_HOME with the new software.

8. Repeat steps 4 and 5 until all ASM instances are upgraded.

9. When the software upgrade is complete on all ASM instances, disable the rolling migration mode by using the following command:

   ```
   ALTER SYSTEM STOP ROLLING MIGRATION;
   ```

Only the following operations are permitted in rolling migration mode:

- Diskgroup mount and dismount

- All database file operation, such as file open, close, read, write, resize, and delete

- ASM and RDBMS instance shutdown, startup, and recovery

- Limited access to V$ views

The following operations are not allowed in rolling migration mode:

- Rebalance

- Adding or dropping, online and offline, of disks

After the rolling migration mode is turned off, full functionality for the ASM instance is allowed.

ASM and Security

This section covers various ASM-related security configuration topics, such as configuring userids and/or groupids needed to support ASM; ASM privileges such as SYSOPER, SYSDBA, and the new SYSASM privilege; and finally ASM's the use of Oracle password file, orapwd.

One ASM Instance and Multiple UNIX Userids

If a separate ASM_HOME is created with a different userid than that of the RDBMS instance, then the Oracle user for each of the RDBMS instances must be a member of the dba group for the ASM instance; the ASM Oracle user does not necessarily need to be in the dba group for the RDBMS instances. If you want to have an ASM instance with a different UNIX userid and enable multiple other Unix userids to manage their own database storage, you can do so by making sure that each database has its own dba group that is independent of the dba group for ASM—for example, the databases might be named dba1, dba2, and so on. If you want the RDBMS instances to share the same diskgroups, then all the RDBMS instances need read/write access to the disks in the diskgroup. The ASM instance needs read/write access to all of the disks. For the RDBMS instances, you can restrict which disks they can access.

ASM and Privileges

In Oracle Database 10g, access to the ASM instance via SQLPlus is the same as that of a standard instance, such as SYSDBA and SYSOPER. Note, however, that because there is no data dictionary in the ASM instance, authentication is done from an operating system (OS) level or an Oracle password file. Typically, the SYSDBA privilege is granted through the use of an operating system group. On Unix, this is typically the dba group. By default, members of the dba group have SYSDBA privileges on all instances on the node, including the ASM instance. Users who connect to the ASM instance with the SYSDBA privilege have complete administrative access to all diskgroups in the system.

Note that on Windows systems, Oracle typically runs as under the Local System or Administrator user, and the OSOPER and OSDBA groups are hard-coded groups associated with ORA_OPER and ORA_DBA, respectively.

Starting in Oracle Database 11g, a privilege called SYSASM is the primary means to access the ASM instance, and most administrative commands for ASM instances are deprecated for SYSDBA. SYSDBA is still available for backward compatibility, and if it is used, a warning message is written in the ASM alert log as follows:

```
Warning: Deprecated privilege SYSDBA for command 'STARTUP'
```

The purpose of the SYSASM role is to provide a level of separation between the RDBMS and ASM credentials. The SYSASM role, which has full capability on the ASM instance, is authenticated through the OSASM user group, similar to the SYSDBA role, which is authenticated through OSDBA. For Oracle Database 11*g* ASM, it is a best practice to use the SYSASM privilege instead of SYSDBA.

The following shows how to connect as SYSASM and configure a new user for the SYSASM role:

```
[oracle11@racnode1~]$ sqlplus "/ as sysasm"
```

To create the user ASMUSER, use the following command:

```
SQL> CREATE USER ASMUSER IDENTIFIED BY ASMUSER1;
SQL> GRANT SYSASM, SYSOPER TO ASMUSER;
```

To connect as ASMUSER:

```
[oracle@racnode1 ~]$ sqlplus "ASMUSER/ASMUSER as sysasm"
SQL> select * from v$pwfile_users;
USERNAME                        SYSDBA SYSOPER SYSASM
------------------------------- ------ ------- ------
SYS                             TRUE   TRUE    FALSE
ASMUSER                         FALSE  TRUE    TRUE
```

In Oracle ASM 10*g*, a user connecting as SYSOPER to an ASM instance has most of the same privileges' as one connecting as SYSDBA, except for the ability to query V$ views. To log in as SYSOPER, enter the following command:

```
[oracle11@racnode1~]$ sqlplus " as sysoper"
```

Starting in Oracle Database 11*g*, the ASM SYSOPER privilege has responsibilities similar to those of a database SYSOPER.

The following commands are available to SYSOPER users:

- STARTUP/SHUTDOWN

- ALTER DISKGROUP MOUNT/DISMOUNT

- ALTER DISKGROUP ONLINE/OFFLINE DISK

- ALTER DISKGROUP REBALANCE

- ALTER DISKGROUP CHECK

All other commands—such as CREATE DISKGROUP, ADD/DROP/RESIZE DISK, and so on—require the SYSASM privilege and cannot be used with the SYSOPER privilege.

All administrative SQL commands—including STARTUP, SHUTDOWN, and ALTER/CREATE/DROP DISKGROUP—are logged in the ASM instance. For example, all ALTER DISKGROUP commands are always recorded in the alert log for the instance that issued the command. If required , the operations issued by the SYS USER (from an ASM instance) can be audited in the .aud files. This will require the following initialization parameters to be set:

```
audit_sys_operations = TRUE
_disable_instance_params_check = TRUE
```

Note that, unlike with a RDBMS instance, the audit trail cannot be stored in the AUD$ for the ASM instance, because ASM does not have a database to store these tables. Thus output usually dumps to the .aud file, which is usually located in the default directory, $ORACLE_HOME/rdbms/audit.

The AUDIT_FILE_DEST init.ora parameter controls the location of this audit directory. On Windows systems, it is sent to the Windows System Log.

ASM and orapwd

The ASM instance leverages the Oracle password file (orapwd) for remote ASM access, much like an RDBMS instance does for remote database access.

NOTE
The RDBMS instance is completely independent from ASM instance, and thus ASM has its own password file that is not shared with the RDBMS password file.

To configure EM remote administration of ASM, a password file for the ASM instance must exist. If the ASM instance is configured using DBCA, then the orapwd file is automatically created. If the ASM instance is manually configured, then it must be manually created using the orapwd command:

```
[oracle11@racnode1~]$ orapwd file=$ORACLE_HOME/asm/orapw+ASM1 \
password=oracle
```

The standard orapwd utility is used for password file management for the ASM instance; however, is limited to modifying the sys password only.

NOTE
On RAC systems, each clustered ASM instance must have an orapwd file.

Use the following command to view the contents of the password file from the
ASM instance using the V$PWFILE_USERS view:

```
SQL> SELECT * FROM V$PWFILE_USERS;
USERNAME                         SYSDB SYSOP SYSAS
------------------------------   ----- ----- -----
SYS                              TRUE  TRUE  FALSE
```

In Oracle Database 11*g*, the ASM password file can be updated using the same
commands used in the RDBMS. However, the update only propagates to the local
orapwd file.

ASM Management

With the advent of ASM, the lines of responsibility for volume and storage management
may seem to become blurred. The roles defined around ASM management can have
some variation, depending on the organizational layout. The following are examples of
some typical deployments:

- There is an ASM administrator who specifically manages the ASM instance.
  This ASM administrator can be carved from the Sysadmin department. The
  Oracle software associated with the ASM instance can be installed by a
  distinct user from the RDBMS user. This can help to enforce the ASM
  admin role.

- The standard DBAs or owners of the Oracle software who are responsible
  for managing the enterprise databases also manage the storage for ASM
  instance. The Sysadmin still manages the OS logical unit numbers (LUNs),
  changes the device file ownership, and defines ASM disk isolation from
  other host logical volume manager (LVM) disks.

Regardless of the split of roles and responsibilities, the following activities are
needed to provision storage to ASM:

- Identify storage requirements for ASM.
  - Determine the storage types needed by the application/database, such as
    Serial Advanced Technology Attachment (SATA) or Fibre Channel (FC). This
    is an important question if you are deploying a tiered storage solution. For
    example, the DATA diskgroup may require high-end FC disks, whereas the
    Flash diskgroup may need only SATA disks.

- Determine how much space will be required to house the database(s).

- Determine the potential aggregate database I/O Operations per sec (IOPS). The combination of this and space requirements help dictate the number of back-end spindles (disk units) necessary to accommodate the database requirements. This step must be done with the assistance of the storage and system administrators.

- Prepare disks from the storage array.

  - Create LUNs from the storage array. These LUNs, which can be created from redundant array of independent drives (RAID) group sets (RAID 10 or RAID 5) from the array, are then (in storage array network [SAN] environments) zoned to the appropriate hosts.

  - Prepare the disks on the host.

  - The root user validates that those LUNs presented to the host are seen by the OS. These new LUNs should have their ownerships changed to match the owner of the Oracle software.

- After the ownership/permissions are changed, ASM should discover these disks. These disks can now be added to an existing diskgroup or be used in creating a new diskgroup.

- Create the necessary diskgroups.

  - After ASM has discovered the disks presented from the storage array, determine how many disks will be placed in a diskgroup.

  - Use existing diskgroup or create new diskgroup.

The following V$ ASM views describe the structure and components of ASM:

- **V$ASM_ALIAS**   This view displays all system- and user-defined aliases. There is one row for every alias present in every diskgroup mounted by the ASM instance. The RDBMS instance displays no rows in this view.

- **V$ASM_ATTRIBUTE**   This Oracle Database 11*g* view displays one row for each ASM attribute defined. These attributes are listed when they are defined in CREATE DISKGROUP or ALTER DISKGROUP statements. DISK_REPAIR_TIMER is an example of an attribute.

- **V$ASM_CLIENT**   This view displays one row for each RDBMS instance that has an opened ASM diskgroup.

- **V$ASM_DISK**   This view contains specifics about all disks discovered by the ASM instance, including mount status, disk state, and size. There is one row for every disk discovered by the ASM instance.

- **V$ASM_DISK_IOSTAT**   This displays information about disk I/O statistics for each ASM client. If this view is queried from the database instance, only the rows for that instance are shown.

- **V$ASM_DISK_STAT**   This view contains similar content as the V$ASM_ DISK, except V$ASM_DISK_STAT reads disk information from cache and thus performs no disk discovery. This view is primarily used for quick access to the disk information without the overhead of disk discovery.

- **V$ASM_DISKGROUP**   V$ASM_DISKGROUP displays one row for every ASM diskgroup discovered by the ASM instance on the node.

- **V$ASM_DISKGROUP_STAT**   This view contains all the similar view contents as the V$ASM_DISKGROUP, except that V$ASM_DISK_STAT reads disk information from the cache and thus performs no disk discovery. This view is primarily used for quick access to the diskgroup information without the overhead of disk discovery.

- **V$ASM_FILE**   The V$ASM_FILE view displays information about ASM files. There is one row for every ASM file in every diskgroup mounted by the ASM instance. In a RDBMS instance, V$ASM_FILE displays no rows.

- **V$ASM_OPERATION**   This view describes the progress of an influx ASM rebalance operation. In a RDBMS instance, V$ASM_OPERATION displays no rows.

- **V$ASM_TEMPLATE**   This view contains information on user- and system-defined templates. V$ASM_TEMPLATE displays one row for every template present in every diskgroup mounted by the ASM instance. In a RDBMS instance, V$ASM_TEMPLATE displays one row for every template present in every diskgroup mounted by the ASM instance with which the RDBMS instance communicates.

Table 2-1 summarizes the usage of instance views between the ASM and RDBMS instance.

ASM-Related V$ View	ASM Instance	RDBMS Instance
V$ASM_DISKGROUP	A row per diskgroup discovered	A row per diskgroup available to the local RDBMS instance
V$ASM_CLIENT	A row per client connected	A row for local ASM instance if the RDBMS contains open ASM files
V$ASM_DISK	Row/disk discovered across all diskgroups, as well as disks that are not in diskgroups	A row per disk, across all diskgroups, used by the local RDBMS instance
V$ASM_FILE	Row/file allocated across all client instances and diskgroups	N/A
V$ASM_TEMPLATE	Row/template	Row/template with the associated-attached diskgroup
V$ASM_ALIAS	Row/file alias	N/A
V$ASM_OPERATION	Row per active ASM operation (could be more than one operation per invocation)	N/A
V$ASM_ATTRIBUTE	This Oracle Database 11*g* view displays one row for each ASM attribute defined	N/A
V$ASM_DISK_IOSTAT	Displays information about the disk I/O statistics for each ASM client	N/A

TABLE 2-1. *Views Used in ASM Instances versus RDBMS Instance*

Summary

The ASM metadata is managed by an ASM instance. An ASM instance is similar to any Oracle instance in that it has an SGA and most of the normal background processes. It can use the same executable as the RDBMS instances. ASM instances do not mount databases, but instead mount diskgroups. An ASM instance manages the metadata needed to make ASM files available to RDBMS instances. Both ASM instances and RDBMS instances must have access to all the ASM disks. The ASM instance provides an extent map to the RDBMS instance when a file is opened or created. RDBMS instances read and write the disks directly based on the extent map. The ASM instance is not in the I/O path.

CHAPTER
3

ASM Disks

he first task in building the ASM infrastructure is to discover and place (add) disks under ASM management. This step is best done with the coordination of storage and system administrators. In storage area network (SAN) environments, it is assumed that the disks are identified and configured correctly—that is, they are appropriately zoned or LUN-masked within the SAN fabric and can be seen by the OS.

ASM Storage Provisioning

Before disks can be added to ASM, the storage administrator needs to identify a set of disks or logical devices from a storage array. Note that the term *disk* is used loosely, as a disk can be any of the following:

- An entire disk spindle

- A partition of a physical disk spindle

- An aggregation of several disk partitions across several disks

- A logical device carved from a redundant array of independent drives (RAID) group set

Once the preceding devices are created, they are deemed as logical unit numbers (LUNs). These LUNs are then presented to the operating system (OS) as logical disks. See Appendix B for the specific ASM layout for the storage array.

In this book, we refer generically to LUNs or disks presented to the OS as simply *disks*. The terms *LUN* and disk may be used interchangeably.

DBAs and system administrators are often in doubt as to the maximum LUN size they can use without performance degradation, or as to the LUN size that will give the best performance. For example, will 1TB- or 2TB-sized LUNs perform the same as 100GB- or 200GB-sized LUNs?

Size alone should not affect the performance of an LUN. What is important is the underlying hardware, the number of disks that compose an LUN, and the read-ahead and write-back caching policy defined on the LUN, all of which in turn define the speed of the LUNs. There is no magic number for the LUN size or the number of ASM disks in the diskgroup.

NOTE
The maximum disk size that can be included as ASM disk is 2^{32}MB and the minimum disk size is 4MB.

Seek the advice of the storage vendor for the best storage configuration for performance and availability, because this may vary between vendors. Appendix B presents several sample vendor configurations.

Given the database size and storage hardware available, the best practice is to create larger LUNs (to reduce LUN management) and, if possible, generate LUNs from a separate set of storage array RAID sets so that LUNs do not share drives. If the storage array is a low-end commodity storage unit and storage RAID will not be used, then it is best to employ ASM redundancy and use entire drives as ASM disks. Additionally, the ASM disk size is the minimal increment by which a diskgroup size can change.

ASM Storage Device Configuration

This section details the steps and considerations involved in configuring storage devices presented to the operating system (OS) that were provisioned in the earlier section. This function is typically performed by the System Administrator or an ASM administrator; that is, someone with root privileges.

Typically, disks presented to the OS can be seen in the /dev directory on Unix/Linux systems. Note that each OS has its unique representation of small computer system interface (SCSI) disk naming. For example, on Solaris systems, disks usually have the SCSI name format $cwtxdysz$, where c is the controller number, t is the target, d is the LUN/disk number, and S is the partition. Creating a partition serves three purposes:

- To skip the OS label/volume table of contents (VTOC). Different operating systems have varying requirements for the OS label—that is, some may require an OS label before it is used, whereas others do not. For example, on a Solaris system, it is a best practice to create a partition on the disk, such as partition 4 or 6, that skips the first 1MB into the disk.

- To create a placeholder to identify that the disk is being used, as an unpartitioned disk could be accidentally misused or overwritten.

- To preserve alignment between ASM striping and storage array internal striping.

The goal is to align the ASM file extent boundaries with any striping that may be done in the storage array. The Oracle database does a lot of 1MB input/outputs (I/Os) that are aligned to 1MB offsets in the datafiles. It is slightly less efficient to misalign these I/Os with the stripes in the storage array, as misalignment can cause one extra disk to be involved in the I/O. Although this misalignment may improve the latency of that particular I/O, it reduces the overall throughput of the system by increasing the number of disk seeks. This misalignment is independent of the operating system. However, some operating systems may make it more difficult to control the alignment or may add additional offsets to block zero of the ASM disk.

The disk partition used for an ASM disk is best aligned at 1MB within the LUN as presented to the OS by the storage. ASM uses the first allocation unit of a disk for metadata, and includes the disk header. The ASM disk header itself is in block zero of the file given to ASM as an ASM disk. The disk header block should be aligned to a 1MB boundary in the LUN presented to the OS.

Aligning ASM file extent boundaries to storage array striping only makes sense if the storage array striping is a power of 2; otherwise it is not much of a concern.

The alignment issue would be solved if we could start the ASM disk at block zero of the LUN, but that does not work on some operating systems (Solaris in particular). On Linux you could start the ASM disk at block zero, but then there is a chance that an administrator would run `fdisk` on the LUN and destroy the ASM disk header. Thus we always recommend using a partition rather than starting the ASM disk at block zero of the LUN.

ASM Disk Device Discovery

Once the disks are presented to the OS, ASM needs to discover them. This requires that the disk devices (Unix filenames) have their ownership changed from `root` to `oracle`. The system administrator usually makes this change. In our example, disks c3t19d5s4, c3t19d16s4, c3t19d17s4, and c3t19d18s4 are identified, and their ownership set to the `oracle:dba`. Now ASM must be configured to discover these disks. This is done by defining the ASM `init.ora` parameter `ASM_DISKSTRING`. In our example, we will use the following wildcard setting:

```
*.asm_diskstring='/dev/rdsk/c3t19d*s4'
```

An alternative to using standard SCSI names (such as c*w*t*x*d*y*s*z* or /dev/sdda) is to use special files. This option is useful when establishing standard naming conventions and for easily identifying ASM disks, such as `asmdisk1`. This option requires creating special files using the `mknod` command.

For example, to create a special file called `asmdisk1` for a preexisting device partition called c3t19d7s4, determine the OS major number and minor number using the following:

```
[root@racnode1]# ls -lL c3t19d7s4
crw-r----- 1 root sys 32, 20 Feb 24 07:14 c3t19d7s4
```

NOTE
Major and minor numbers are associated with the
device special files in the /dev directory and are
used by the operating system to determine the actual
driver and device to be accessed by the user-level
request for the special device file.

The preceding example shows that the major and minor device numbers for this
device are 32 and 20, respectively. The *c* at the beginning indicates that this is a
character (raw) file.

After obtaining the major and minor numbers, use the `mknod` command to
create the character and block special files that will be associated with c3t19d7s4.
A special file called /dev/asmdisk can be created under the /dev directory, as
shown:

```
[root@racnode1]# mkdir /dev/asmdisk
[root@racnode1]# cd /dev/asmdisk
[root@racnode1]# mknod asmdisk1 c 32 20
```

Listing the special file shows the following:

```
[root@racnode1]# ls -l
crw-r--r-- 1 root other 32, 20 May 7 07:50 asmdisk1
```

Notice that this device has the same major and minor numbers as the native
device c3t19d7s4.

For this partition (or *slice*) to be accessible to the ASM instance, change the
permissions on this special file to the appropriate `oracle` user permissions:

```
[root@racnode1]# chown oracle:dba disk1
[root@racnode1]# ls -l /dev/disk
crw-r--r-- 1 oracle dba 32, 20 May 7 07:50 disk1
```

Repeat this step for all the required disks that will be discovered by ASM.
Now the slice is accessible by the ASM instance. The `ASM_DISKSTRING` can be
set to /dev/asmdisk/*. Once discovered, the disk can be used as an ASM disk.

ASM discovers all the required disks that make up the diskgroup using "on-disk"
headers and its search criteria (`ASM_DISKSTRING`). ASM scans only for disks that
match that ASM search string. There are two forms of ASM disk discovery: shallow
and deep. For shallow discovery, ASM simply scans the disks that are eligible to be
opened. This is equivalent to executing `ls  -l` on all the disk devices that have the
appropriate permissions. For deep discovery, ASM opens each of those eligible disk
devices. In most cases, ASM discoveries are deep, the exception being when the
*_STAT tables are queried instead of the standard tables. The *_STAT tables are
covered in Chapter 4.

NOTE
*For ASM in clustered environments, it is not
necessary to have the same path name or major
or minor device numbers across all nodes. For
example, node1 could access a disk pointed to
by path /dev/rdsk/c3t1d4s4, whereas node2 could
present /dev/rdsk/c4t1d4s4 for the same device.
Although ASM does not require that the disks have
the same names on every node, it does require that
the same disks be visible to each ASM instance via
that instance's discovery string. In the event that
path names differ between ASM nodes, the only
necessary action is to modify the* ASM_DISKSTRING
*to match the search path. This is a non-issue on
Linux systems that use ASMLIB, because ASMLIB
handles the disk search and scan process.*

Upon successful discovery, the V$ASM_DISK view on the ASM instance reflects which disks were discovered. Note that henceforth all views, unless otherwise stated, are queried from the ASM instance and not from the RDBMS instance.

The following example shows the disks that were discovered using the defined ASM_DISKSTRING. Notice that the NAME column is empty and the GROUP_NUMBER is set to 0. This is because disks that are discovered but are not yet associated with a diskgroup. Thus, they have a null name and a group number of 0.

```
SQL> SELECT NAME,PATH,GROUP_NUMBER FROM V$ASM_DISK
NAME                                PATH              GROUP_NUMBER
----------------------------------- ----------------- ------------
                                    /dev/rdsk/c3t19d5s4          0
                                    /dev/rdsk/c3t19d16s4         0
                                    /dev/rdsk/c3t19d17s4         0
                                    /dev/rdsk/c3t19d18s4         0
```

Disks have various header statuses that reflect their membership state with a diskgroup. Disks can have the following header statuses:

- **Former**   This state declares that the disk was formerly part of a diskgroup.

- **Candidate**   A disk in this state is available to be added to a diskgroup.

- **Member**   This state indicates that a disk is already part of a diskgroup. Note, that the diskgroup may or may not be mounted.

- **Provisioned**   This state is similar to candidate, in that it is available to be added to diskgroups. However, the provisioned state indicates that this disk has been configured or made available using ASMLIB.

The following is a useful query to run to view the status of disks in the ASM system:

```
SQL>SELECT NAME, PATH, HEADER_STATUS, MODE_STATUS FROM V$ASM_DISK;
```

In Oracle ASM 10 Release 1, querying V$ASM_DISK and V$ASM_DISKGROUP was an expensive operation because each execution involved a disk discovery. To minimize overhead, and to allow lightweight access to this dataset, Oracle ASM 10 Release 2 introduced two new views: V$ASM_DISK_STAT and V$ASM_DISKGROUP_STAT. These two views are identical to V$ASM_DISK and V$ASM_DISKGROUP, but $ASM_DISK_STAT and V$ASM_DISKGROUP_STAT views are polled from memory and therefore do not require deep disk discovery. Because these new views provide efficient lightweight access, Enterprise Manager (EM) can periodically query performance statistics at the disk level and aggregate space usage statistics at the diskgroup level without incurring significant overhead.

Third-Party Volume Managers and ASM

Although it is not a recommended practice, host volume managers such as Veritas VxVM or IBM LVM can sit below ASM. For example, an LVM can create raw logical volumes and present these as disks to ASM. However, the third-party LVM should not use any host-based mirroring or striping. ASM algorithms are based on the assumption that I/O to different disks are relatively independent and can proceed in parallel. If any of the volume manager virtualization features are used beneath ASM, then the configuration becomes too complex and confusing and can needlessly incur overhead, such as the maintenance of a dirty region log (DRL). DRL is discussed in greater detail in Chapter 4.

In a cluster environment, such a configuration can be particularly expensive. ASM does a better job of providing this configuration's functionality for database files. Additionally, in RAC environments, if ASM will run over third-party volume managers, then the volume manager must be cluster-aware; that is, it must be a cluster volume manager (CVM).

However, it may make sense in certain cases to have a volume manager under ASM. Such cases include the following:

- The volume manager is providing multipathing. This is the case with the Veritas Volume Manager.

- Easier management and simplified tracking of disk assignments are needed.

ASM and Storage Arrays

ASM is like any other volume manager in that the client (RDBMS instance), not the volume manager, determines the size of the I/O. If the RDBMS makes a request that spans multiple disks, then ASM issues multiple requests, but it cannot do an I/O that is larger than the client's buffer.

It does make sense, however, to let a storage array do the mirroring and striping and present to the OS a virtual LUN, which is then used as an ASM disk in an ASM diskgroup. Most ASM customers create external redundancy diskgroups using LUNs in this way. For example, a 100GB LUN striped over eight disks is typical configuration.

Why is the default size for an ASM coarse stripe 1MB?

- One megabyte is large enough that a sequential scan will spend most of its time transferring data instead of positioning the disk head—that is, the cost of the seek is amortized for the large request.

- One megabyte is small enough that a large I/O operation will not preoccupy a single disk for too long.

- One megabyte is small enough that Oracle's asynchronous read-ahead operations can access multiple disks. Any access hot spot that is smaller than 1MB should fit comfortably in the database buffer cache.

Smaller stripe depths can improve disk throughput for a single process by spreading a single I/O across multiple disks; however, I/Os that are much smaller than 1MB can cause seek time to become a large fraction of the total I/O time and thus reduce the overall efficiency of the storage system. In some cases, it may be worth trading off some efficiency for the increased throughput that smaller stripe depths provide.

Thus the best stripe size (that is, a contiguous space on a single disk) for reading is 1MB. However, few storage arrays support that large a stripe. For efficient writing, it is desirable to have a single ASM extent span all the disks in the RAID 5 set; for example, with four data and one parity, a stripe size of 256K would mean that a full 1MB ASM extent write would hit all disks, and no extra reads would be required for calculating parity. Note that for this to work, the correct alignment is critical.

Interestingly, ASM can create an external redundancy diskgroup consisting of one virtual LUN. The main problem with this is that it is difficult to grow or shrink the diskgroup incrementally. Adding one disk of the same size doubles the diskgroup. Another problem is that the OS may not allow enough I/O to be simultaneously queued to one LUN. The OS assumes it is only one spindle and thus limits the number of simultaneous I/O operations. Thus, best practice is to have multiple LUNs in a diskgroup.

Preparing ASM Disks on OS Platforms

The following section will illustrate the specific tasks need to configure ASM for the specific operating systems and environments

Configuring ASM Disks on Solaris

This section covers some of the nuances of creating disk devices in a Solaris environment. The Solaris format command is used to create OS slices. Note that slices 0 and 2 cannot be used as ASM disks because these slices include the Solaris VTOC. An example of the format command output (partition map) for the device follows:

```
/dev/rdsk/c2t12d29.
```

```
Current partition table (original):
Total disk cylinders available: 18412 + 2 (reserved cylinders)
Part      Tag    Flag     Cylinders         Size            Blocks
  0 unassigned    wm       0                 0          (0/0/0)             0
  1 unassigned    wm       0                 0          (0/0/0)             0
  2     backup    wu       0 - 18411      8.43GB        (18412/0/0) 17675520
  3         -     wu       0 -     2      1.41MB        (3/0/0)          2880
  4         -     wu       4 - 18411      8.43GB        (18408/0/0) 17671680
  5 unassigned    wm       0                 0          (0/0/0)             0
  6 unassigned    wm       0                 0          (0/0/0)             0
  7 unassigned    wm       0                 0          (0/0/0)             0
```

Notice that slice 4 is created and that it skips four cylinders, offsetting past the VTOC.

Use the logical character device as listed in the /dev/rdsk directory. Devices in this directory are symbolic links to the physical device files. For example:

```
[root@racnode1]# ls -l /dev/rdsk/c0t2d0s4
lrwxrwxrwx 1 root root 45 Feb 24 07:14 c0t2d0s4 -> ../../devices/
pci@1f,4000/scsi@3/sd@2,0:e,raw
```

To change the permission on these devices, do the following:

```
[root@racnode1]# chown oracle:dba ../../devices/pci@1f,4000/scsi@3/
sd@2,0:e,raw
```

Now the ASM instance can access the slice. Set the ASM_DISKSTRING to /dev/rdsk/c*s4. Note that the actual diskstring differs in each environment.

Configuring ASM on AIX

This section describes how to configure ASM disks for AIX. It also recommends some precautions that are necessary when using AIX disks.

ASM and PVIDs

In AIX, a disk is assigned a physical volume identifier (PVID) when it is first assigned to a volume group or when it is manually set using the AIX `chdev` command. When the PVID is assigned, it is stored on the physical disk and in the AIX server's system object database, called *Object Data Manager* (ODM). The PVID resides in the first 4K of the disk, and is displayed using the AIX `lspv` command. In the following listing, the first two disks have PVIDs assigned and the others do not:

```
lspv
hdisk11      000f0d8dea7df87c       None
hdisk12      000f0d8dea7a6940       None
hdisk15      none                   None
hdisk16      none                   None
hdisk17      none                   None
```

If a PVID assigned disk is incorporated into an ASM diskgroup, ASM will write an ASM disk header on the first 40 bytes of the disk, which thus overwrites the PVID. Although initially no resultant problems may be evident, on the subsequent reboot, the OS, in coordination with the ODM database, will restore the PVID onto the disk, thus destroying the ASM disk and potentially resulting in data loss.

Therefore, it is a best practice on AIX not to include a PVID on any disk that ASM will use. If a PVID does exist and ASM has not used the disk yet, you can clear the PVID by using the AIX `chdev` command.

NOTE
In RAC environments, the Oracle Clusterware devices, (OCR and Voting devices) need to have PVIDs assigned. See Metalink Note 293819.1 for a discussion on this.

ASM and AIX Disk Attributes

To allow concurrent I/O access to the disk device and prevent the device driver from locking the `hdisks` with a reservation on open, set a no-reservation flag. Use the following `chdev` commands to disable this reservation. For all multipath I/O (MPIO)–capable (ESS, DS8000, and DS6000 devices), use the following command:

```
chdev -l hdisk1 -a reserve_policy=no_reserve
chdev -l hdisk2 -a reserve_policy=no_reserve
```

For EMC (Symmetrix and Clariion), Hitachi Data Systems (HDS), IBM DS4000, and non-MPIO-capable devices, perform the following:

```
chdev -l hdisk1 -a reserve_lock=no
chdev -l hdisk2 -a reserve_lock=no
```

Additionally, change the permissions and ownerships on all required ASM disks.

ASM and Windows

On Windows systems, disks must be defined as basic disks rather than dynamic ones. You can define this by using either the graphical user interface (GUI) Microsoft Management Console (MMC) plug-in Disk Management.(diskmgmt.msc) or the command-line tool `diskpart`.

On Windows systems, disks discovered have the convention of \Device\Harddisk$X$\Partition$Y$, where X is the disk (the name of which starts at 0) and Y is the partition on the disk (the naming of which starts at 1). However, ASM uses a logical name to associate the device name \Device\Harddisk$X$\Partition$Y$.

For each LUN that will be used by ASM, create an extended partition that fills the entire disk. Then, inside this new extended partition, create a logical partition to fill the extended partition. Do not format the partition with any filesystem or assign a drive letter. Additionally, in a RAC cluster environment, you must enable automount for these disks on all nodes. Doing so enables automount for all volumes, as it is a machine global setting.

Enabling automount provides two benefits:

- It allows basic disks. The disks that Oracle will use from an SAN (which must not be dynamic) must allow such basic disks in order to be visible to a Windows application.

- Windows also automatically assigns a drive letter to a volume. Oracle requires that you remove this drive letter.

For these partitions to become visible on other nodes in the cluster, a reboot is required on those nodes. After rebooting, Windows adds drive letters to the unformatted partitions. After the server is rebooted, use the Disk Management plug-in to remove the unneeded drive letters (see Figure 3-1). Then label the partitions using either the GUI tool `asmtoolg` or the command-line version, `asmtool`.

The following examples show the LUNs visible to the Windows OS. Disk Management graphically represents the disks. Note on Windows that the LUNs are numbered starting with 0. Each of the LUNs has an extended partition, represented by the green outer box. Inside the extended partition is a logical partition, represented by the light blue. Logical partitions that completely fill a disk are the best devices to present to ASM.

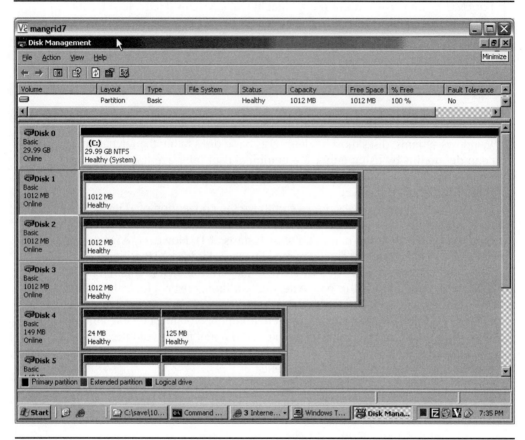

FIGURE 3-1.   *Disk Management on Windows*

You can also view this information by using the Windows command-line utility `diskpart`:

```
C:\windows>diskpart
Microsoft DiskPart version 5.2.3790.1830
Copyright (C) 1999-2001 Microsoft Corporation.
On computer: racnode1
DISKPART> list disk
  Disk ###  Status      Size     Free      Dyn  Gpt
  --------  ----------  -------  -------    ---  ---
    Disk 0  Online        30 GB  8033 KB
    Disk 1  Online      1012 MB     0 B
    Disk 2  Online      1012 MB     0 B
    Disk 3  Online      1012 MB     0 B
```

```
    Disk 4      Online        149 MB      0 B
    Disk 5      Online        149 MB      0 B
    Disk 6      Online         20 MB      0 B
DISKPART> select disk 1
DISKPART> list partition
    Partition ###   Type              Size      Offset
    -------------   ----------------  -------   -------
    Partition 1     Extended          1012 MB   8033 KB
    Partition 2     Logical           1012 MB   8064 KB
```

asmtool

On Windows, Oracle provides the command-line utility `asmtool` and the GUI tool `asmtoolg` to label logical partitions such that they can be discovered by ASM. The following example shows the use of `asmtool`:

```
C:\oracle\product\10.2.0\asm\BIN>asmtool -list
NTFS                         \Device\Harddisk0\Partition1        30710M
                             \Device\Harddisk1\Partition1         1011M
                             \Device\Harddisk2\Partition1         1011M
                             \Device\Harddisk3\Partition1         1011M
Oracle Raw Device file       \Device\Harddisk4\Partition1           23M
Oracle Raw Device file       \Device\Harddisk4\Partition2          125M
Oracle Raw Device file       \Device\Harddisk5\Partition1           23M
Oracle Raw Device file       \Device\Harddisk5\Partition2          125M
Oracle Raw Device file       \Device\Harddisk6\Partition1           20M
```

This example shows seven disks (Harddisk0 – Harddisk6), with three disks, Harddisk1, Harddisk2, and Harddisk3, that will be used for ASM.

Use `asmtool` to label the disks using the `-add` parameter:

```
C:\oracle\product\10.2.0\asm\BIN>asmtool -add \Device\Harddisk1\
Partition1 ORCLDISKDATA0
C:\oracle\product\10.2.0\asm\BIN>asmtool -add \Device\Harddisk2\
Partition1 ORCLDISKDATA1
C:\oracle\product\10.2.0\asm\BIN>asmtool -add \Device\Harddisk3\
Partition1 ORCLDISKDATA2
C:\oracle\product\10.2.0\asm\BIN>asmtool -list
NTFS                         \Device\Harddisk0\Partition1        30710M
ORCLDISKDATA0                \Device\Harddisk1\Partition1         1011M
ORCLDISKDATA1                \Device\Harddisk2\Partition1         1011M
ORCLDISKDATA2                \Device\Harddisk3\Partition1         1011M
Oracle Raw Device file       \Device\Harddisk4\Partition1           23M
Oracle Raw Device file       \Device\Harddisk4\Partition2          125M
Oracle Raw Device file       \Device\Harddisk5\Partition1           23M
Oracle Raw Device file       \Device\Harddisk5\Partition2          125M
Oracle Raw Device file       \Device\Harddisk6\Partition1           20M
```

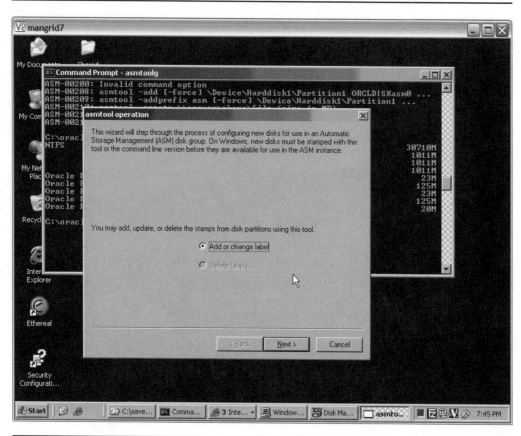

FIGURE 3-2. *asmtoolg operation*

asmtoolg

Alternatively, the GUI version of asmtool, called asmtoolg, can be used to complete the same task. When you start the asmtoolg utility, the first screen displays two options, as shown in Figure 3-2: Add or change label, and delete labels. Select the Add or change label option and click Next.

As shown in Figure 3-3, the three candidate devices are identified and the Generate stamps with this prefix option is selected. This option labels the logical partitions in the same way as asmtool.

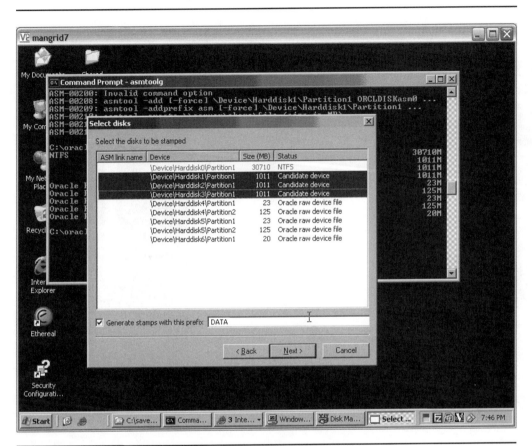

FIGURE 3-3. `asmtoolg` disk selection

Figure 3-4 shows the labels applied to the logical partitions.

In Figure 3-4, the disks are being labeled for ASM. Thus, during the Database Configuration Assistant (DBCA) interview phase, the disks will be automatically visible for diskgroup configuration (see Figure 3-5).

If disks are not automatically visible to DBCA, you can make them visible by assigning the disk discovery string to the ASM_DISK_STRING parameter as shown in Figure 3-6.

ASM and Multipathing

An I/O path generally consists of an initiator port, fabric port, target port, and LUN. Each permutation of this I/O path is considered an independent path. For example, in a high-availability scenario in which each node has two host bus adapter (HBA) ports

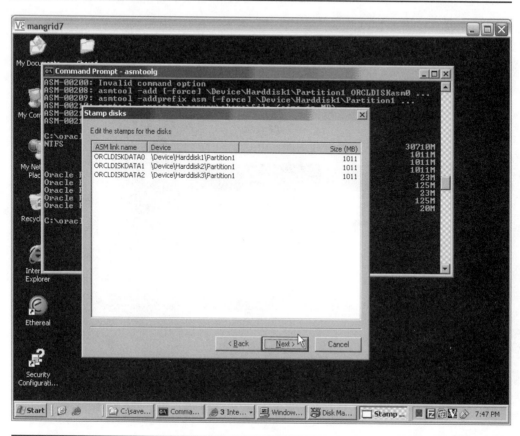

FIGURE 3-4. *asmtoolg stamp disks*

connected to two separate switch ports to two target ports on the back-end storage to a LUN, there are eight paths visible to that LUN from the OS perspective (two HBA ports times two switch ports times two target ports times one LUN equals eight paths).

Path managers discover multiple paths to a device by issuing an SCSI inquiry command (SCSI_INQUIRY) to each operating system device. For example on Linux, the scsi_id call queries an SCSI device via the SCSI_INQUIRY command and leverages the vital product data (VPD) page 0x80 or 0x83. A disk or LUN responds to the SCSI_INQUIRY command with information about itself, including vendor and product identifiers and a unique serial number. The output from this query is used to to generate a value that is unique across all SCSI devices that properly support pages 0x80 or 0x83.

Typically devices that respond to the SCSI_INQUIRY with the same serial number are considered to be accessible from multiple paths.

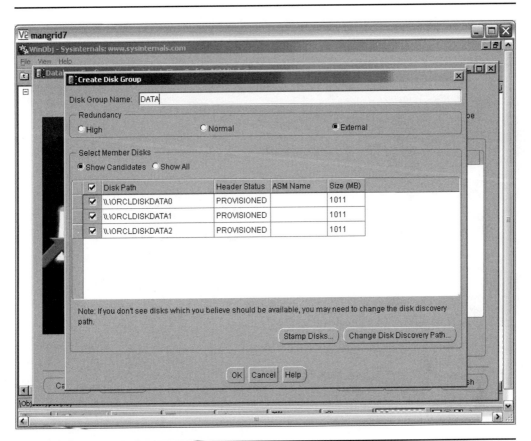

FIGURE 3-5. *The DBCA Create Disk Group dialog box*

Path manager software also provides multipath software drivers. Most multipathing drivers support multi-path services for fibre channel–attached SCSI-3 devices. These drivers receive naming and transport services from one or more physical HBA devices. To support multipathing, a physical HBA driver must comply with the multipathing services provided by this driver. Multi-pathing tools provide the following benefits:

■ They provide a single block device interface for a multipathed LUN.

■ They detect any component failures in the I/O path, including the fabric port, channel adapter, or HBA.

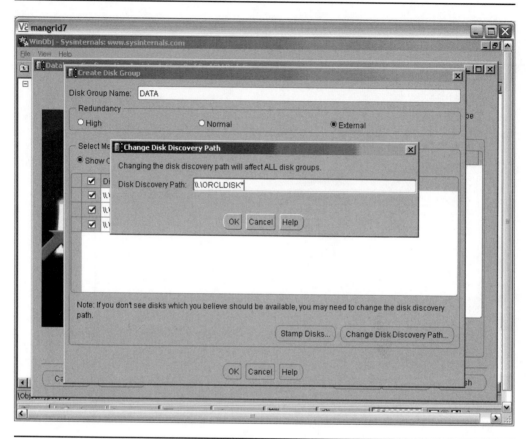

FIGURE 3-6. *ASM's Change Disk Discovery Path dialog box*

- When a loss of path occurs, such tools ensure that I/Os are rerouted to the available paths, with no process disruption.

- They reconfigure the multi-paths automatically when events occur.

- They ensure that failed paths get revalidated as soon as possible and provide auto-failback capabilities.

- They configure the multipaths to maximize performance using various load-balancing methods, such as round robin, least I/Os queued, and least service time.

When a given disk has several paths defined, each one will be presented as a unique path name at the OS level, although they all reference the same physical LUN; for example, the LUNs /dev/rdsk/c3t19d1s4 and /dev/rdsk/c7t22d1s4 could be pointing to same disk device. The multi-path abstraction provides I/O load balancing across the HBAs, as well as nondisruptive failovers on I/O path failures.

ASM, however, can tolerate the discovery of only one unique device path per disk. For example, if the ASM_DISKSTRING is /dev/rdsk/*, then several paths to the same device will be discovered and ASM will produce an error message stating this. A multi-path driver, which generally sits above this SCSI-block layer, usually produces a pseudo device that virtualizes the subpaths. For example, in the case of EMC's PowerPath, you can use the ASM_DISKSTRING setting of /dev/rdsk/emcpower*. When I/O is issued to this disk device, the multi-path driver intercepts it and provides the necessary load balancing to the underlying subpaths.

Examples of multipathing software include EMC PowerPath, Veritas Dynamic Multi-pathing (DMP), Sun Traffic Manager, Hitachi Dynamic Link Manager (HDLM), Windows MPIO, and IBM Subsystem Device Driver Path Control Module (SDDPCM).

Linux 2.6 has a kernel-based multi-pathing driver called *Device Mapper*. Additionally, some HBA vendors also provide multi-pathing solutions, such as Qlogic.

NOTE
Users are advised to verify the vendor certification of ASM/ASMLIB with their multi-pathing drivers, because Oracle does not certify or qualify these multi-pathing tools. Although ASM does not provide multipathing capabilities, it does leverage multipathing tools as long as the path or device that they produce returns a successful return code from an fstat *system call. Metalink Note 294869.1 provides more details on ASM and multi-pathing.*

The use of ASM and pseudo devices is fairly consistent across most products and platforms. The only exception is HP-UX. At the time of this writing, HP-UX does not support pseudo devices; nevertheless, multi-pathing software drivers on HP-UX, such as Hewlett-Packard's SecurePath and EMC's PowerPath, still work as advertised and will route the I/O request to whatever path is available. However, because no pseudo devices exist for the subpaths, ASM must be presented with only a single physical path to each LUN via the ASM_DISKSTRING parameter. Thus, on HP-UX, choose any one given path, change the permissions appropriately, and define it to ASM's discovery string.

NOTE
An alternative to changing the `ASM_DISKSTRING`
parameter is changing the permissions of all the
other physical subpaths or setting the ownership
to Oracle for only one of the set of subpaths. Both
options are workable solutions.

Summary

An ASM disk is the unit of persistent storage given to a diskgroup. A disk can be
added to or dropped from a diskgroup. When a disk is added to a diskgroup, it is
given a disk name either automatically or by the administrator. This is different from
the OS name that is used to access the disk through the operating system. In an RAC
environment, the same disk may be accessed by different OS names on different
nodes. ASM accesses disks through the standard OS interfaces used by Oracle to
access any file (unless an ASMLIB is used). Typically an ASM disk is a partition of an
LUN seen by the OS. An ASM disk can be any device that can be opened through
the OS open system call except for a local filesystem file—that is, the LUN could be
a single physical disk spindle or it could be a virtual LUN managed by a highly
redundant storage array.

CHAPTER
4

Diskgroups and
Failure Groups

he primary component of ASM is the diskgroup, which is the highest-level data structure in ASM (see Figure 4-1). A diskgroup is essentially a container that holds a logical grouping of disks that are managed together as a unit. The diskgroup is comparable to a logical volume manager's (LVM) volume group. Once ASM has discovered the disks, these disks can be used to create a diskgroup.

ASM diskgroups differ from typical LVM volume groups in the following ways:

■ An ASM filesystem layer is implicitly created within a diskgroup.

■ ASM diskgroups have inherent automatic file-level striping and mirroring capabilities. A database file created within an ASM diskgroup is distributed equally across all online disks in the diskgroup, which provides an even input/output (I/O) load.

Diskgroup Management

ASM has three diskgroups types: external redundancy, normal redundancy, and ASM high redundancy. The diskgroup type, which is defined at diskgroup creation, determines the level of mirroring performed by ASM. A diskgroup of external type

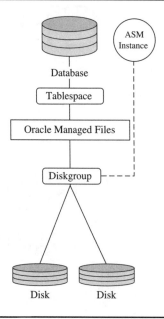

FIGURE 4-1. *ASM layer*

indicates that the mirroring will be handled and managed by the storage array and not by ASM. For example, a user may create an external type diskgroup where the storage array is an EMC DMX or Hitachi USP series. Because the core competency of these high-end arrays is mirroring, external redundancy is well suited for them.

With ASM redundancy, ASM performs and manages the mirroring. ASM redundancy is typically used over low-cost commodity storage, such as the Dell PowerVault MD1000 SAS storage array, or when deploying stretch clusters. For details on ASM redundancy, please see the "ASM Redundancy and Failure Groups" section later in this chapter. The next section focuses on creating diskgroups in an external redundancy environment.

Creating Diskgroups

The creation of a diskgroup involves validation of the disks to be added. The disks must have the following attributes:

- They cannot already be in use by another diskgroup.

- They must not have a preexisting valid ASM header. The FORCE option can be used to override this.

- They cannot have an Oracle file header. for example, from a raw Oracle datafile. The FORCE option can be used to override this for a raw Oracle datafile. Trying to create an ASM disk using a raw device datafile results in the following error:

```
SQL> CREATE DISKGROUP DATA DISK '/dev/sdd3';
create diskgroup data disk '/dev/sdd3'
ERROR at line 1:
ORA-15032: not all alterations performed
ORA-15201: disk /dev/sda3 contains a valid RDBMS file
```

The disk header validation prevents ASM from destroying any data device in use. Only disks with a header status of CANDIDATE, FORMER, or PROVISIONED are allowed to be diskgroup members. To add disks to a diskgroup with a header status of MEMBER or FOREIGN, use the FORCE option. To prevent gratuitous use of the FORCE option, ASM allows it only when using the NOFORCE option would fail. An attempt to use FORCE when it is not required results in an ORA-15034 error ("disk '%s' does not require the FORCE option"). Use the FORCE option with extreme caution, because it overwrites the data on the disk that was previously used as an ASM disk or database file.

A diskgroup can be created using SQL, Enterprise Manager (EM), or Database Configuration Assistant (DBCA) commands. In the following example, a DATA diskgroup is created using four disks that reside in a storage array, with the redundancy being handled externally by the storage array. The following query lists the available that will be used in the diskgroup:

```
SQL> SELECT NAME, PATH, MODE_STATUS, STATE FROM V$ASM_DISK;

NAME         PATH                   MODE_ST STATE
------------ ---------------------- ------- --------
             /dev/rdsk/c3t19d5s4    ONLINE  NORMAL
             /dev/rdsk/c3t19d16s4   ONLINE  NORMAL
             /dev/rdsk/c3t19d17s4   ONLINE  NORMAL
             /dev/rdsk/c3t19d18s4   ONLINE  NORMAL

SQL> CREATE DISKGROUP DATA EXTERNAL REDUNDANCY DISK
'/dev/rdsk/c3t19d5s4',
'/dev/rdsk/c3t19d16s4',
'/dev/rdsk/c3t19d17s4',
'/dev/rdsk/c3t19d18s4';
```

The output, from V$ASM_DISGROUP, shows the newly created diskgroup:

```
SQL> SELECT NAME, STATE, TYPE, TOTAL_MB, FREE_MB FROM V$ASM_DISKGROUP;
NAME                         STATE       TYPE   TOTAL_MB   FREE_MB
---------------------------- ----------- ------ ---------- ----------
DATA                         MOUNTED     EXTERN     34512      34101
```

After the diskgroup is successfully created, metadata information, which includes creation date, diskgroup name, and redundancy type, is stored in the System Global Area (SGA) and on each disk (in the disk header) within the diskgroup. The V$ASM_DISK view reflects this disk header information. Once these disks are under ASM management, all subsequent mounts of the diskgroup reread and validate the ASM disk headers.

The following output shows how the V$ASM_DISK view reflects the disk state change after the disk is incorporated into the diskgroup:

```
SQL> SELECT NAME, PATH, MODE_STATUS, STATE, DISK_NUMBER FROM V$ASM_DISK;

NAME         PATH                   MODE_ST STATE    DISK_NUMBER
------------ ---------------------- ------- -------- -----------
DATA_0000 /dev/rdsk/c3t19d5s4       ONLINE  NORMAL             0
DATA_0001 /dev/rdsk/c3t19d16s4      ONLINE  NORMAL             1
DATA_0002 /dev/rdsk/c3t19d17s4      ONLINE  NORMAL             2
DATA_0003 /dev/rdsk/c3t19d18s4      ONLINE  NORMAL             3
```

The output that follows shows entries from the ASM alert log reflecting the creation of the diskgroup and the assignment of the disk names:

```
SQL> CREATE DISKGROUP DATA EXTERNAL REDUNDANCY DISK
'/dev/rdsk/c3t19d5s4',  '/dev/rdsk/c3t19d16s4',  '/dev/rdsk/c3t19d17s4',
'/dev/rdsk/c3t19d18s4'
NOTE: Assigning number (1,0) to disk (/dev/rdsk/c3t19d5s4)
```

```
NOTE: Assigning number (1,1) to disk (/dev/rdsk/c3t19d16s4)
NOTE: Assigning number (1,2) to disk (/dev/rdsk/c3t19d17s4)
NOTE: Assigning number (1,3) to disk (/dev/rdsk/c3t19d18s4)
NOTE: initializing header on grp 1 disk DATA_0000
NOTE: initializing header on grp 1 disk DATA_0002
NOTE: initializing header on grp 1 disk DATA_0003
NOTE: initializing header on grp 1 disk DATA_0004
NOTE: initiating PST update: grp = 1
Wed Mar 07 15:42:21 2007
NOTE: group DATA: initial PST location: disk 0000 (PST copy 0)
NOTE: group DATA: initial PST location: disk 0001 (PST copy 1)
NOTE: group DATA: initial PST location: disk 0001 (PST copy 3)
NOTE: group DATA: initial PST location: disk 0001 (PST copy 4)
NOTE: PST update grp = 1 completed successfully
NOTE: cache registered group DATA number=1 incarn=0xa311b052
NOTE: cache opening disk 0 of grp 1: DATA_0000 path: /dev/rdsk/c3t19d5s4
NOTE: cache opening disk 1 of grp 1: DATA_0001 path: /dev/rdsk/c3t19d16s4
NOTE: cache opening disk 2 of grp 1: DATA_0002 path: /dev/rdsk/c3t19d17s4
NOTE: cache opening disk 3 of grp 1: DATA_0003 path: /dev/rdsk/c3t19d18s4
```

When mounting diskgroups, either at ASM startup or for subsequent mounts, it is advisable to mount all required diskgroups at once. This minimizes the overhead of multiple ASM disk discovery scans.

ASM Disk Names

ASM disk names are usually assigned by default based on the diskgroup name and disk number, but names can be assigned during ASM diskgroup creation or when disks are added. The following example illustrates how to create a diskgroup where disk names are user-defined:

```
SQL> CREATE DISKGROUP DATA EXTERNAL REDUNDANCY DISK
'/dev/rdsk/c3t19d5s4' name DMX_disk1,
'/dev/rdsk/c3t19d16s4' name DMX_disk2,
'/dev/rdsk/c3t19d17s4' name DMX_disk3,
'/dev/rdsk/c3t19d18s4' name DMX_disk4;
```

If disk names are not provided, then ASM dynamically assigns a disk name with a sequence number to each disk added to the diskgroup:

```
SQL> CREATE DISKGROUP DATA EXTERNAL REDUNDANCY DISK
'/dev/rdsk/c3t19d5s4',
'/dev/rdsk/c3t19d16s4',
'/dev/rdsk/c3t19d17s4',
'/dev/rdsk/c3t19d18s4';
```

The ASM disk name is used when performing any disk management activities, such as DROP DISK or RESIZE DISK.

The ASM disk name is different from the small computer system interface (SCSI) address, and this allows for consistent naming across Real Application Clusters (RAC) nodes. Additionally, ASM disk names persist even if the SCSI address name changes. SCSI address name changes occur due to array reconfigurations and or after reboots.

Diskgroup Numbers

The lowest nonzero available diskgroup number is assigned on the first mount of a diskgroup. However, in an ASM cluster, even if the diskgroups are mounted in a different order between cluster nodes, the diskgroup numbers will still be consistent across the cluster but the diskgroup name never changes. For example, if node 1 has dgA as group number 1 and dgB and group number 2, then if node 2 mounts only dgB, then it will be group number 2, even though 1 is not in use in node 2.

NOTE
Diskgroup numbers are never recorded persistently, thus there is no diskgroup number in a disk header. Only the diskgroup name is recorded in the disk header.

There is a hard-coded limitation of 63 diskgroups in a cluster. There is a six-bit field that holds the diskgroup number and zero is reserved. This is independent of the data in their header. A diskgroup may be mounted on some nodes but not others.

Disk Numbers

Although diskgroup numbers are never recorded persistently, disk numbers are recorded on the disk headers. However, there is no persistent binding of disk numbers to pathnames. When an ASM instance starts up, it discovers all the devices matching the pattern in ASM_DISKSTRING and for which it has read/write access. If it sees an ASM disk header, then it knows the ASM disk number.

Also, disks that are discovered but are not part of any mounted diskgroup are reported in diskgroup 0. A disk that is not part of any diskgroup, mounted or not, will be in diskgroup 0 until it is added to a diskgroup or mounted. When the disk is added to a diskgroup, it will be associated with the correct diskgroup.

ASM Redundancy and Failure Groups

For systems that do not use external redundancy, ASM provides its own internal redundancy mechanism and additional high availability. A diskgroup is divided into failure groups, and each disk is in exactly one failure group. A failure group is a collection of disks that can become unavailable due to failure of one of its associated components. Possible failing components could be any of the following:

- Storage array controllers
- Host bus adapters (HBAs)
- Fibre Channel (FC) switches
- Disks
- Entire arrays

Thus disks in two separate failure groups (for a given diskgroup) must not share a common failure component. If you define failure groups for your diskgroup, ASM can tolerate the simultaneous failure of multiple disks in a single failure group.

ASM uses a unique mirroring algorithm. ASM does not mirror disks; rather, it mirrors extents. When ASM allocates a primary extent of a file to one disk in a failure group, it allocates a mirror copy of that extent to another disk in another failure group. Thus, ASM ensures that a primary extent and its mirror copy never reside in the same failure group.

Unlike other volume managers, ASM has no concept of a primary disk or a mirrored disk. As a result, to provide continued protection in event of failure, your diskgroup requires only spare capacity; a hot spare disk is unnecessary. Redundancy for diskgroups can be either *normal* (the default), where files are two-way mirrored (requiring at least two failure groups), or *high*, which provides a higher degree of protection using three-way mirroring (requiring at least three failure groups). After you create a diskgroup, you cannot change its redundancy level. If you want a different redundancy, then you must create another diskgroup with the desired redundancy, then move the datafiles (using Recovery Manager [RMAN] restore, ASMCMD copy command or `DBMS_FILE_TRANSFER`) from the original diskgroup to the newly created diskgroup.

NOTE
Diskgroup metadata are always triple mirrored with normal or high redundancy

Additionally, after you assign a disk to a failure group, you cannot reassign it to another failure group. If you want to move it to another failure group, then you must first drop it from the current failure group and then add it to the desired failure group. However, because the hardware configuration usually dictates the choice of a failure group, users generally do not need to reassign a disk to another failure group unless it is physically moved.

Creating ASM Redundancy Diskgroups

The following simple example shows how to create a normal redundancy disk group using two failure groups over a NetApp filer:

```
SQL> CREATE DISKGROUP DATA_NRML NORMAL REDUNDANCY
FAILGROUP F1GRP1 DISK '/dev/rdsk/c3t19d3s4','/dev/rdsk/c3t19d4s4',
'/dev/rdsk/c3t19d5s4', '/dev/rdsk/c3t19d6s4','/dev/rdsk/c4t20d3s4',
'/dev/rdsk/c4t20d4s4', '/dev/rdsk/c4t20d5s4', '/dev/rdsk/c4t20d6s4'
FAILGROUP FLGRP2 DISK  '/dev/rdsk/c5t21d3s4','/dev/rdsk/c5t21d4s4',
'/dev/rdsk/c5t21d5s4', '/dev/rdsk/c5t21d6s4','/dev/rdsk/c6t22d3s4',
'/dev/rdsk/c6t22d4s4', '/dev/rdsk/c6t22d5s4', '/dev/rdsk/c6t22d6s4';
```

The same create diskgroup command can be executed using wildcard syntax:

```
SQL> CREATE DISKGROUP DATA_NRML NORMAL REDUNDANCY
FAILGROUP FL1GRP1 DISK  '/dev/rdsk/c[34]*'
FAILGROUP FLGRP2 DISK '/dev/rdsk/c[56]*';
```

In this following example, ASM normal redundancy is being deployed over a low-cost commodity storage array. This storage array has four internal trays, with each tray having four disks. Because the failing component to isolate is the storage tray, the failure group boundary is set for the storage tray—that is, each storage tray is associated with a failure group:

```
SQL> CREATE DISKGROUP DATA_NRML NORMAL REDUNDANCY
FAILGROUP FLGRP1 DISK  '/dev/rdsk/c3t19d3s4','/dev/rdsk/c3t19d4s4',
'/dev/rdsk/c3t19d5s4', '/dev/rdsk/c3t19d6s4'
FAILGROUP FLGRP2 DISK '/dev/rdsk/c4t20d3s4','/dev/rdsk/c4t20d4s4',
'/dev/rdsk/c4t20d5s4', '/dev/rdsk/c4t20d6s4'
FAILGROUP FLGRP3 DISK '/dev/rdsk/c5t21d3s4','/dev/rdsk/c5t21d4s4',
'/dev/rdsk/c5t21d5s4', '/dev/rdsk/c5t21d6s4'
FAILGROUP FLGRP4 DISK  /dev/rdsk/c6t22d3s4','/dev/rdsk/c6t22d4s4',
'/dev/rdsk/c6t22d5s4', '/dev/rdsk/c6t22d6s4';
```

Designing for ASM Redundancy Diskgroups

Note that with ASM redundancy, you are not restricted to having two failure groups for normal redundancy and three for high redundancy. In the preceding example, four failure groups are created to ensure that disk partners are not allocated from the same storage tray.

There may be cases where users want to protect against storage area network (SAN) array failures. This can be accomplished by putting each array in a separate failure group. For example, a configuration may include two NetApp filers and the deployment of ASM normal redundancy such that each filer—that is, all logical unit numbers (LUNs) presented through the filer—are part of an ASM failure group. In this scenario, ASM mirrors extent between the two filers.

If the database administrator (DBA) does not specify a failure group in the CREATE DISKGROUP command, then a failure group is automatically constructed for each disk. This method of placing every disk in its own failure group works well for most customers.

The choice of failure groups depends on the kinds of failures that need to be tolerated without loss of data availability. For small numbers of disks (for example, fewer than 20), it is usually best to put every disk in its own failure group. Nonetheless, this is also beneficial for large numbers of disks when the main concern is spindle failure. To protect against the simultaneous loss of multiple disk drives due to a single component failure, explicit failure group specification should be used. For example, a diskgroup may be constructed from several small modular disk arrays. If the system needs to continue operation when an entire modular array fails, then each failure group should consist of all the disks in one module. If one module fails, all the data on that module are relocated to other modules to restore redundancy. Disks should be placed in the same failure group if they depend on a common piece of hardware whose failure needs to be tolerated with no loss of availability.

It is much better to have several failure groups as long as the data is still protected against the necessary component failures. A small number of failure groups or failure groups of uneven capacity can lead to allocation problems that prevent full utilization of all available storage. Moreover, having failure groups of different sizes can waste disk space. There may be enough room to allocate primary extents, but no space available for secondary extents. For example, in a diskgroup with six disks and three failure groups, if two disks are in their own individual failure groups and the other four are in one common failure group, then there will be very unequal allocation. All the secondary extents from the big failure group can be placed on only two of the six disks. The disks in the individual failure groups fill up with secondary extents and block additional allocation even though plenty of space is left in the large failure group. This also places an uneven write load on the two disks that are full because they contain more secondary extents that are accessed only for writes or if the disk with the primary extent fails.

Allocating ASM Extent Sets

With ASM redundancy, the first file extent allocated is chosen as primary extent, and the mirrored extent is called the secondary extent. In the case of high redundancy, there will two secondary extents. This logical grouping of primary and secondary extents is called an *extent set*. When a block is read from disk, it is always read from the primary extent, unless the primary extent cannot be read. In Oracle Database 11*g*, the preferred read feature allows the database to read the secondary extent first instead of reading the primary extent. This is especially important for RAC Extended Cluster implementations. See the section "ASM and Extended Clusters" later in this chapter for more details on this feature.

Keep in mind that each disk in a diskgroup (and in failure groups) contains nearly the same number of primary and secondary extents. This provides an even distribution of read I/O activity across all the disks.

All the extents in an extent set always contain the exact same data because they are mirrored versions of each other. The only exception is when temporary tablespaces are used. For example, if the relational database management system (RDBMS) instance crashes while writing to a temporary tablespace, there is no need to resilver the mirrors because they will not be read again before they are written.

When a block is to be written to a file, each extent in the extent set is written in parallel. ASM requires that all writes complete before acknowledging the write to the client. Otherwise, the unwritten side could be read before it is written. If one write I/O fails, then that side of the mirror must be made unavailable for reads before the write can be acknowledged.

Disk Partnering

In ASM redundancy diskgroups, ASM protects against a double-disk failure, (which can lead to data loss) by mirroring copies of data on disks that are partners of the disk containing the primary data extent. A *disk partnership* is a symmetric relationship between two disks in a high or normal redundancy diskgroup, and ASM automatically creates and maintains these relationships. ASM selects partners for a disk from failure groups other than the failure group to which the disk belongs. This ensures that a disk with a copy of the lost disk's data will be available following the failure of the shared resource associated with the failure group. ASM limits the number of disk partners to 10 for any single disk.

To illustrate disk partnership, the following example uses the normal redundancy diskgroup DATA_NRML, created previously. The following query shows a disk partnership for a disk (disk 2) that is part of failure group FLGRP1:

```
SQL> SELECT NUMBER_KFDPARTNER, FAILGROUP FROM X$KFDPARTNER A, V$ASM_DISK
A WHERE DISK=2 AND GRP=1 AND A.NUMBER_KFDPARTNER= B.DISK_NUMBER
NUMBER_KFDPARTNER FAILGROUP
----------------- ------------------------------
                7 FLGRP2
                8 FLGRP2
               10 FLGRP2
               12 FLGRP2
               16 FLGRP3
               17 FLGRP3
               19 FLGRP3
               24 FLGRP4
               25 FLGRP4
               26 FLGRP4
```

Notice that ASM did not choose partner disks from its own failure group (FLGRP1); rather, 10 partners were chosen from the other three failure groups. Disk partnership is detailed in Chapter 11, "ASM Operations."

Recovering Failure Groups

Returning to the example in the previous CREATE DISKGROUP DATA_NRML command, in the event of a disk failure in failure group FLGRP1, which will induce a rebalance, the contents (data extents) of the failed disk are reconstructed using the redundant copies of the extents from partner disks. These partner disks are from failure group FLGRP2, FLGRP3, or both. If the database instance needs to access an extent whose primary extent was on the failed disk, then the database will read the mirror copy from the appropriate disk. After the rebalance is complete and the disk contents are fully reconstructed, the database instance returns to reading primary copies only.

ASM and Extended Clusters

The last two years have seen the emergence of extended clusters. An extended cluster, also called a *stretch cluster, geocluster, campus cluster,* or *metro-cluster,* is essentially a RAC environment deployed across two data center locations. Many customers implement extended RAC to marry disaster recovery with the benefits of RAC, all in an effort to provide higher availability.

Within Oracle, the term *extended clusters* is used to refer to all of the stretch cluster implementations.

The distance for extended RAC can be anywhere between several meters to several hundred kilometers. Because Cluster Ready Services (CRS)-RAC cluster group membership is based on the ability to communicate effectively across the interconnect, extended cluster deployment requires a low-latency network infrastructure. For close proximity, users typically use Fibre Channel, whereas for large distances, Dark Fiber is used.

For normal redundancy diskgroups in extended RAC, there should be only one failure group on each site of the extended cluster. High-redundancy diskgroups should not be used in extended cluster configurations unless there are three sites. In this scenario, there should one failure group at each site. Note that it is best to name the failure groups explicitly based on the site name.

NOTE
If a diskgroup contains an asymmetrical configuration, such that there are more failure groups on one site than another, then an extent could get mirrored to the same site and not to the remote failure group. This could cause the loss of access to the entire diskgroup if the site containing more than one failure group fails.

As stated earlier, ASM in Oracle Database 10*g* always reads the primary copy of a mirrored extent set. Thus, a read for a specific block may require a read of the primary extent at the remote site across the interconnect. Accessing a remote disk through a metropolitan area or wide area storage network is substantially slower than accessing a local disk. This can tax the interconnect as well as result in high I/O and network latency.

To assuage this, Oracle Database 11*g* provides a feature called *preferred reads*. This feature enables ASM administrators to specify a failure group for local reads—that is, provide preferred reads. In a normal or high-redundancy diskgroup, when a secondary extent is on a preferred disk and the primary extent is remote, the secondary extent is read rather than the primary one on that node. This feature is especially beneficial for extended cluster configurations.

ASM Preferred Read

The `ASM_PREFERRED_READ_FAILURE_GROUP` initialization parameter is used to specify a list of failure group names that will provide local reads for each node in a cluster. The format of the `ASM_PREFERRED_READ_FAILURE-GROUP` is as follows:

```
ASM_PREFERRED_READ_FAILURE_GROUPS = DISKGROUP_NAME.FAILUREGROUP_NAME,...
```

Each entry is comprised of `DISKGROUP_NAME`, which is the name of the diskgroup, and `FAILUREGROUP_NAME`, which is the name of the failure group within that diskgroup, with a period separating these two variables. Multiple entries can be specified using commas as a separator. This parameter can be dynamically changed.

In an extended cluster, the failure groups that you specify with settings for the `ASM_PREFERRED_READ_FAILURE_GROUPS` parameter should contain only disks that are local to the instance. `V$ASM_DISK` indicates the preferred disks with a *Y* in the `PREFERRED_READ` column.

Note that when adding or dropping a disk, it is a best practice to issue the add or drop command from the site where storage change is occurring. This enables a more efficient rebalance method because the extent relocation is localized within the same failure group—that is, within the same local site.

The following example shows how to deploy the preferred read feature and demonstrates some of its inherent benefits. This example illustrates I/O patterns when the `PREFERRED_READ_FAILURE_GROUPS` parameter is not set, and then demonstrates how changing the parameter affects I/O.

1. First create a diskgroup with two failure groups:

    ```
    CREATE DISKGROUP MYDATA NORMAL REDUNDANCY
    -- these disks are local access from node1/remote from node2
    FAILGROUP FG1 DISK '/dev/sda1','/dev/sdb1', '/dev/sdc1'
    -- these disks are local access from node2/remote from node 1
    FAILGROUP FG2 DISK '/dev/sdf1', '/dev/sdg1','/dev/sdh1';
    ```

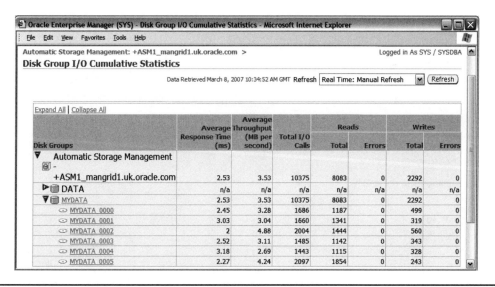

FIGURE 4-2. *The EM Disk Group I/O Cumulative Statistics screen*

2. In this test case, note that under the Reads subheading of the Total table column heading shown in Figure 4-2, and 4-3. The I/Os are evenly distributed across all disks—that is, these are nonlocalized I/Os.

3. Note that you can achieve the same effect by entering the following query:

```
SQL> SELECT INST_ID, FAILGROUP, SUM(READS), SUM(WRITES) FROM GV$ASM_DISK
WHERE FAILGROUP IN ('FG1','FG2') GROUP BY INST_ID, FAILGROUP;

INST_ID FAILGROUP                          SUM(READS) SUM(WRITES)
---------- -------------------------- ---------- -----------
         1 FG1                              3796        2040
         1 FG2                              5538        2040
         2 FG1                              4205        1874
         2 FG2                              5480        1874
```

NOTE
V$ASM_DISK includes I/Os that are performed by the ASM instance for Partnership Status Table (PST) heartbeats, discovery, and so on. The Oracle Database 11g V$ASM_DISK_IOSTAT view was introduced to highlight preferred read. The V$ASM_DISK_IOSTAT tracks I/O on a per-database basis. This view can be used to verify that that an RDBMS instance never does any I/O to a nonpreferred disk.

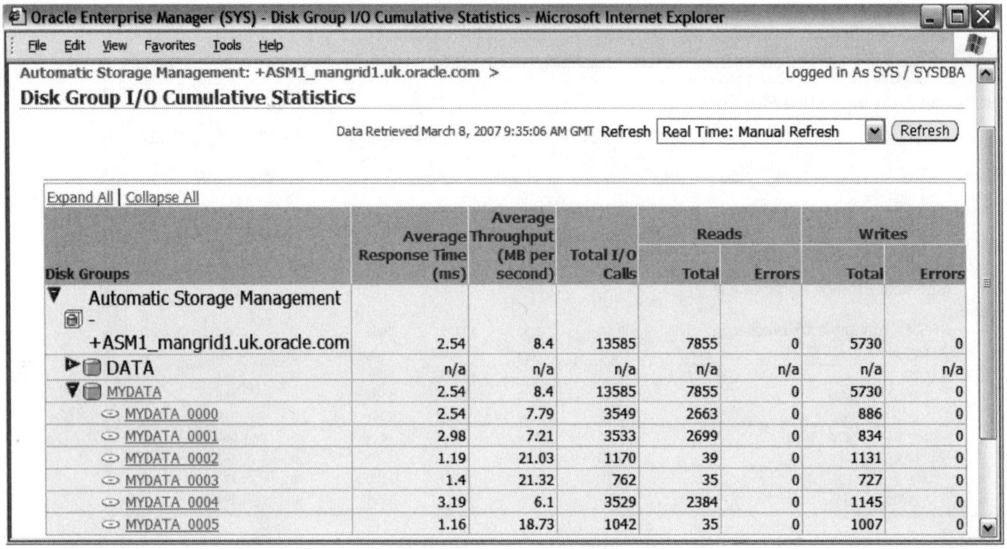
Oracle Enterprise Manager (SYS) - Disk Group I/O Cumulative Statistics - Microsoft Internet Explorer
File Edit View Favorites Tools Help
Automatic Storage Management: +ASM1_mangrid1.uk.oracle.com >
Logged in As SYS / SYSDBA
Disk Group I/O Cumulative Statistics
Data Retrieved March 8, 2007 9:35:06 AM GMT Refresh Real Time: Manual Refresh Refresh
Expand All | Collapse All
Disk Groups | Average Response Time (ms) | Average Throughput (MB per second) | Total I/O Calls | Reads Total | Reads Errors | Writes Total | Writes Errors
Automatic Storage Management - +ASM1_mangrid1.uk.oracle.com | 2.54 | 8.4 | 13585 | 7855 | 0 | 5730 | 0
DATA | n/a | n/a | n/a | n/a | n/a | n/a | n/a
MYDATA | 2.54 | 8.4 | 13585 | 7855 | 0 | 5730 | 0
MYDATA_0000 | 2.54 | 7.79 | 3549 | 2663 | 0 | 886 | 0
MYDATA_0001 | 2.98 | 7.21 | 3533 | 2699 | 0 | 834 | 0
MYDATA_0002 | 1.19 | 21.03 | 1170 | 39 | 0 | 1131 | 0
MYDATA_0003 | 1.4 | 21.32 | 762 | 35 | 0 | 727 | 0
MYDATA_0004 | 3.19 | 6.1 | 3529 | 2384 | 0 | 1145 | 0
MYDATA_0005 | 1.16 | 18.73 | 1042 | 35 | 0 | 1007 | 0

FIGURE 4-3. *The EM Disk Group I/O Cumulative Statistics screen*

4. Now set the appropriate ASM parameters for preferred read. Note that you need not dismount or remount the diskgroup, as this the parameter is dynamic.

   Enter the following for Node1 (site1):

   ```
   +ASM1.asm_preferred_read_failure_groups=MYDATA.FG1
   ```

   Enter this code for Node2 (site2):

   ```
   +ASM2.asm_preferred_read_failure_groups='MYDATA.FG2'
   ```

5. Verify that the parameter took effect by querying `GV$ASM_DISK`. From Node1, observe the following:

   ```
   SELECT INST_ID, FAILGROUP, NAME, PREFERRED_READ FROM G$ASM_DISK
   ORDER BY INST_ID, FAILGROUP;
      INST_ID FAILGROUP    NAME         PREFERRED_READ
   ---------- ------------ ------------ --------------
            1 FG1          MYDATA_0000  Y
            1 FG1          MYDATA_0001  Y
            1 FG1          MYDATA_0004  Y
            1 FG2          MYDATA_0002  N
            1 FG2          MYDATA_0003  N
            1 FG2          MYDATA_0005  N
   ```

```
2 FG1          MYDATA_0000  N
2 FG1          MYDATA_0001  N
2 FG1          MYDATA_0004  N
2 FG2          MYDATA_0002  Y
2 FG2          MYDATA_0003  Y
2 FG2          MYDATA_0005  Y
```

Keep in mind that disks MYDATA_0000, MYDATA_0001, and MYDATA_0004 are part of the FG1 failure group, and disks MYDATA_0002, MYDATA_0003, MYDATA_0005 are in failure group FG2.

6. Put a load on the system and check I/O calls via EM or using V$ASM_DISK_ IOSTAT. Notice in the "Reads-Total" column that reads have a strong affinity to the disks in FG1. This is because FG1 is local to node1 where +ASM1 is running. The remote disks in FG2 have very few reads.

7. Using SQLPlus, the same behavior can be observed. Notice the small number of reads that instance 1 is making to FG2 and the small number of reads that instance 2 is making to FG1:

```
SQL> SELECT INST_ID, FAILGROUP, SUM(READS), SUM(WRITES) FROM GV$ASM_DISK
WHERE FAILGROUP ING ('FG1','FG2') GROUP BY INST_ID, FAILGROUP;

   INST_ID FAILGROUP                        SUM(READS) SUM(WRITES)
---------- ------------------------------ ---------- -----------
         1 FG1                                  8513        3373
         1 FG2                                   118        3373
         2 FG1                                    72        1756
         2 FG2                                  5731        1756
```

Recovering from Transient and Permanent Disk Failures

This section reviews how ASM handles transient and permanent disk failures in normal- and high-redundancy diskgroups. Additionally, this section describes the differences in processing of these failures between Oracle Database 10g and Oracle Database 11g.

Recovering from Disk Failures in Oracle Database 10g

In Oracle Database 10g, as described previously, restoring the redundancy of all extents in the diskgroup following a disk failure is a relatively costly operation. This can be especially expensive in the case of transient errors, which can include cable disconnections, host bus adapter or controller failures, or even disk power interruptions, which cause the entire failure to be dropped. Additionally, a transient failure of the storage interconnect between sites would appear as a failure of an entire failure group. When an ASM disk fails, the ASM disk is taken offline and dropped.

If the ASM diskgroup is created with two failure groups, the loss of one entire failure group is tolerated with no downtime. Messages in the alert log and EM describe the situation. The diskgroup continues to operate normally, allocating space in the one surviving failure group. The failed disks show up in V$ASM_DISK twice (as of 10.1.0.4): once as *missing* and *candidate* statuses for HEADER_STATUS and STATE, respectively, and another as *offline hung*. The reason that you have missing, candidate, and offline hung disks is that you have had a failure group crash, and an insufficient number of surviving failure groups exists to complete a rebalance successfully to restore the contents from the failed disks. The offline hung entries in V$ASM_DISK essentially track the fact that there are extents whose redundancy has not yet been restored.

To restore the disks to a normal status, you need to add back the missing disks. To add the disks back, you must specify the FORCE flag, as in the following example, because they still have their old disk headers:

```
ALTER DISKGROUP DATA_NRML ADD FAILGROUP FLGRP1 DISK
'/dev/rdsk/c3t19d3s4' FORCE,'/dev/rdsk/c3t19d4s4' FORCE,
'/dev/rdsk/c3t19d5s4' FORCE, '/dev/rdsk/c3t19d6s4' FORCE;
```

When adding back the disks, be sure to specify the previously used failure group name. Adding these disks initiates a rebalance. Once the rebalance completes from adding back the disks from the failed failure group, the offline hung entries should go away.

In cases where it is appropriate, you can also use a disk add pattern such as /dev/rdsk/c*'; just make sure that you have the right pattern for the disks you are adding and the appropriate failure group name.

The following are some points to consider when adding back disks into the failgroup:

- Make sure to add the disk back using the same failure group as before the storage failure.

- If upon disk failure the disk to be added back to the failgroup has been physically replaced, then the ASM disk header no longer exists. In this case, the disk cannot be added back to the failgroup using the FORCE option; it must be added using the standard add disk command:

  ```
  ALTER DISKGROUP DATA_NRML ADD FAILGROUP FLGRP1 DISK '/dev/rdsk/c3t13d3s4';
  ```

■ If you are providing a disk name when adding back to the failgroup, ensure that the disk name is different from the previous disk name. Currently, ASM does not support adding a disk back using the same disk name in the diskgroup. It is a best practice to let ASM generate a new disk name for you. If you are using ASMLIB, the default name is provided by the ASMLIB disk name stamped by `oracleasm`. In such cases, with Oracle Database 10*g* the user must explicitly specify a new disk name as part of the add disk.

When disks are added back to reform a second failure group, the rebalance restores redundancy and the hung disks are dropped. Note that adding back an insufficient number of disks can result in the diskgroup running out of space during rebalance. The added storage must be of sufficient capacity to hold a copy of all the data allocated in the surviving failure group. It is also possible to get in a similar state if all but a few disks in a failure group fail. For example, if there are 10 disks in each failure group and 9 of them fail in one failure group, the surviving disk is unlikely to have the capacity to hold a copy of every extent, so the rebalance runs out of space. The easy way to avoid this circumstance is to drop force the one surviving disk.

On some occasions, DBAs need to store data offline in a stretch cluster as part of a planned outage. This essentially drops all the disks in that failure group. However, keep in mind that the rebalance cannot move all of the storage from the dropped disks following a normal drop of all of the disks in a failure group in a two-failure-group diskgroup, because there is nowhere to move the data. Nevertheless, it is part of the design of ASM that any storage reconfiguration—that is, the adding or dropping of disks—always invokes a rebalance. The behavior in Oracle Database 10*g* is as described previously—that is, the disks in the failure group have hung, cached, or member status. Note that the drop disk operation is an asynchronous operation. The "Statement Processed" message indicates only that the drop has been initiated and that no new allocations will occur on that disk if it is in dropping state; the V$ASM_DISK view reveals whether or not a disk is still a member of the diskgroup. Note that a disk is not dropped until all of its contents have been moved to another disk. If such a disk has failed, it will be considered missing. The hung status is documented as a drop disk operation that cannot continue because there is insufficient space to relocate the data from the disk being dropped.

The hung state has been omitted from Oracle Database 11*g*. Disks that are effectively hung continue to be displayed as dropping or forcing.

Recovering from Disk Failures in Oracle Database 11*g*—Fast Disk Resync

The Oracle Database 11*g* feature ASM Fast Disk Resync significantly reduces the time to recover from transient disk failures in failure groups. The feature accomplishes this speedy recovery by quickly resynchronizing the failed disk with its partnered disks.

In Oracle ASM Database 10*g*, disks that go offline because of disk failures are immediately dropped from the diskgroup. To reconstruct a disk's contents, ASM must add the disk back to the diskgroup and perform a full rebalance. This problem can be exacerbated if all disks in a failure group go offline.

With Fast Disk Resync, the repair time is proportional to the number of extents that have been written or modified since the failure. This feature can significantly reduce the time that it takes to repair a failed diskgroup from hours to minutes.

The Fast Disk Resync feature allows the user a grace period to repair the failed disk and return it online. This time allotment is dictated by the ASM diskgroup attribute `DISK_REPAIR_TIME`. This attribute dictates maximum time of the disk outage that ASM can tolerate before dropping the disk. If the disk is repaired before this time is exceeded, then ASM resynchronizes the repaired disk when the user places the disk online. The command `ALTER DISKGROUP DISK ONLINE` is used to place the repaired disk online and initiate disk resynchronization.

Fast Disk Resync requires that the `COMPATIBLE.ASM` and `COMPATIBLE.RDBMS` attributes of the ASM diskgroup be set to at least Oracle 11.1.0.0. In the following example, the current ASM 11*g* diskgroup has a compatibility of 10.1.0.0.0 and is modified to 11.1. To validate the attribute change, the `V$ASM_ATTRIBUTE` view is queried.

```
SQL> SELECT NAME, COMPATIBILITY, DATABASE_COMPATIBILITY FROM
V$ASM_DISKGROUP_STAT;
NAME    COMPATIBILITY    DATABASE_COMPATIBILITY
------  ---------------  ----------------------------------
DATA    10.1.0.0.0       10.1.0.0.0

SQL> ALTER DISKGROUP DATA SET ATTRIBUTE 'COMPATIBLE.ASM' = '11.1';
SQL> ALTER DISKGROUP DATA SET ATTRIBUTE 'COMPATIBLE.RDBMS' ='11.1';

SQL> SELECT NAME, VALUE FROM V$ASM_ATTRIBUTE;
NAME              VALUE
--------------  ------------------------------------
disk_repair_time 12960
compatible.asm    11.1.0.0.0
compatible.rdbms 11.1.0.0.0
```

After you correctly set the compatibility to Oracle Database version 11.1, you can set the `DISK_REPAIR_TIME` attribute accordingly. Notice that the default repair time is 12,960 sec or 3.6 hours. It is a best practice to leave this value at the default, as it should support most disk outages.

If the value of `DISK_REPAIR_TIME` needs to be changed, you can enter the following command:

```
ALTER DISKGROUP DATA SET ATTRIBUTE 'DISK_REPAIR TIME' = '4 H'
```

If the `DISK_REPAIR_TIME` parameter is not 0 and an ASM disk fails, that disk is taken offline but not dropped. During this outage, ASM tracks any modified extents using a bitmap that is stored in diskgroup metadata. (See Chapter 11, "ASM Operations," for more details on the algorithms used for resynchronization.)

ASM's GMON process will periodically (every 3 min) inspect all mounted diskgroups for offline disks. If GMON finds any, it sends a message to a slave process to decrement their timer values (by 3 min) and initiate a drop for the offline disks when the timer expires. This timer display is shown in REPAIR_TIMER column of V$ASM_DISK.

The ALTER DISK GROUP DISK OFFLINE SQL command or the EM ASM Target page can also be used to take the ASM disks offline manually for preventative maintenance. The following describes this scenario using SQLPlus:

```
SQL> ALTER DISKGROUP DATA OFFLINE DISK DATA_0000 DROP AFTER 20 m;

SQL> SELECT NAME, HEADER_STATUS, MOUNT_STATUS, MODE_STATUS, STATE,
REPAIR_TIMER FROM V$ASM_DISK WHERE GROUP_NUMBER=1;

NAME            HEADER_STATU  MOUNT_S MODE_ST STATE     REPAIR_TIMER
--------------- ------------- ------- ------- --------  ------------
DATA_0003       MEMBER        CACHED  ONLINE  NORMAL               0
DATA_0002       MEMBER        CACHED  ONLINE  NORMAL               0
DATA_0001       MEMBER        CACHED  ONLINE  NORMAL               0
DATA_0000       UNKNOWN       MISSING OFFLINE NORMAL             840
```

Notice that the offline disk's MOUNT_STATUS and MODE_STATUS are set to the MISSING and OFFLINE states, and also that the REPAIR_TIMER begins to decrement from the drop timer.

Figure 4-4 shows the EM method for taking disks offline. Figures 4-5 and 4-6 show EM screens confirming the offline operation.

After the maintenance is completed, you can use the ALTER DISK GROUP DISK ONLINE command to bring the disk(s) online:

```
SQL> ALTER DISKGROUP DATA ONLINE DISK DATA_0000
```

Or

```
SQL> ALTER DISKGROUP DATA ONLINE ALL
```

This statement brings all the repaired disks back online to bring the stale contents up to date and to enable new contents. See Chapter 11, "ASM Operations," for more details on how to implement resynchronization.

The following is an excerpt from the ASM alert log showing a disk being brought offline and online:

```
SQL> ALTER DISKGROUP DATA OFFLINE DISK DATA_0000
NOTE: DRTimer CodCreate: of disk group 2 disks  0
WARNING: initiating offline of disk 0.3915947593 (DATA_0000) with mask 0x7e
NOTE: initiating PST update: grp = 2, dsk = 0, mode = 0x15
NOTE: PST update grp = 2 completed successfully
NOTE: initiating PST update: grp = 2, dsk = 0, mode = 0x1
```

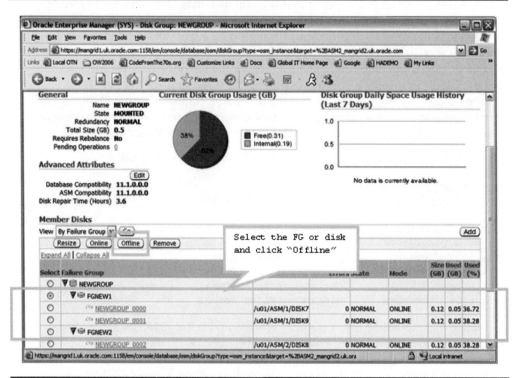

FIGURE 4-4. *EM taking a disk offline for preventive maintenance*

```
NOTE: PST update grp = 2 completed successfully
Tue Mar 20 08:15:37 2007
NOTE: cache closing disk 0 of grp 2: DATA_0000
Tue Mar 20 08:17:50 2007
GMON SlaveB: Deferred DG Ops completed.
Tue Mar 20 08:19:06 2007
......
```

After fixing the disk, you can bring it online using the following command:

```
SQL> ALTER DISKGROUP DATA ONLINE DISK DATA_0000;
SQL> SELECT NAME, HEADER_STATUS, MOUNT_STATUS, MODE_STATUS, STATE,
REPAIR_TIMER FROM V$ASM_DISK WHERE GROUP_NUMBER=1;

NAME          HEADER_STATU MOUNT_S MODE_ST STATE    REPAIR_TIMER
------------- ------------ ------- ------- -------- ------------
DATA_0003     MEMBER       CACHED  ONLINE  NORMAL              0
DATA_0002     MEMBER       CACHED  ONLINE  NORMAL              0
DATA_0001     MEMBER       CACHED  ONLINE  NORMAL              0
DATA_0000     MEMBER       CACHED  ONLINE  NORMAL              0
```

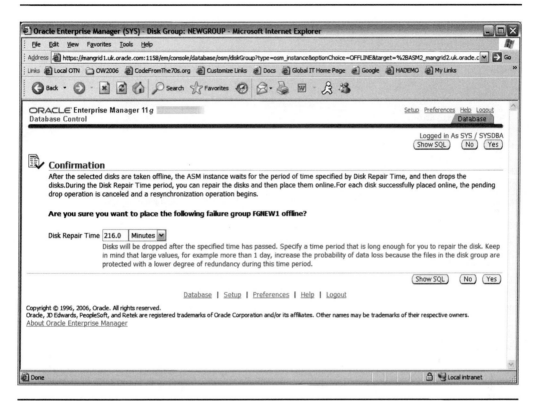

FIGURE 4-5. *EM confirming that it has taken disks offline*

```
SQL> ALTER DISKGROUP DATA ONLINE disk DATA_0000
Tue Mar 20 08:29:06 2007
NOTE: initiating online of disk group 2 disks 0
NOTE: initiating PST update: grp = 2, dsk = 0, mode = 0x19
NOTE: disk validation pending for group 2/0x62087046 (DATA)
NOTE: cache opening disk 0 of grp 2: DATA_0000 path:/u01/ASM/1/DISK7
SUCCESS: validated disks for 2/0x62087046 (DATA)
NOTE: initiating PST update: grp = 2, dsk = 0, mode = 0x1d
NOTE: PST update grp = 2 completed successfully
NOTE: initiating PST update: grp = 2, dsk = 0, mode = 0x5d
NOTE: PST update grp = 2 completed successfully
NOTE: initiating PST update: grp = 2, dsk = 0, mode = 0x7d
NOTE: PST update grp = 2 completed successfully
Tue Mar 20 08:29:17 2007
NOTE: initiating PST update: grp = 2, dsk = 0, mode = 0x7f
NOTE: PST update grp = 2 completed successfully
NOTE: completed online of disk group 2 disks 0
```

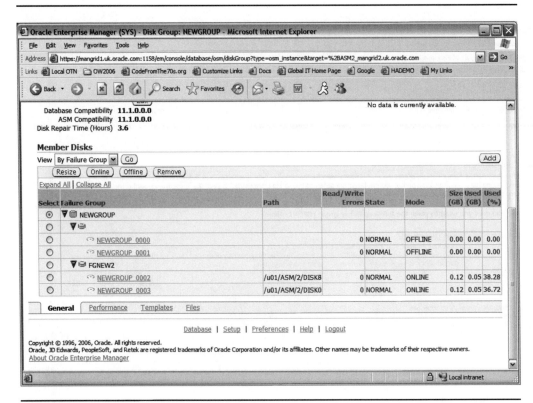

FIGURE 4-6. *The EM Member Disks screen indicates which disks are offline.*

Once the disk is brought back online, the REPAIR_TIMER is reset to 0 and the MODE_STATUS is set to ONLINE.

At first glance, the Fast Disk Resync feature may seem to be a substitute for Dirty Region Logging (DRL), which several logical volume managers such as Veritas VxVM implement. However, Fast Disk Resync and DRL are distinctly different.

DRL is a mechanism to track blocks that have writes in flight. A mirrored write cannot be issued unless a bit in the DRL is set to indicate there may be a write in flight. Because DRL itself is on disk and also mirrored, it may require two DRL writes before issuing the normal mirrored write. This is mitigated by having each DRL bit cover a range of data blocks such that setting one bit will cover multiple mirrored block writes. There is also some overhead for I/O to clear DRL bits for blocks that are no longer being written. You can often clear these bits while setting another bit in DRL.

If a host dies while it has mirrored writes in flight, then it is possible that one side of the mirror is written and the other is not. Most applications require that they get the same data every time if they read a block multiple times without writing it. If one side was written but not the other, then different reads may get different data. DRL mitigates this by constructing a set of blocks that must be copied from one side to the other to ensure that all blocks are the same on both sides of the mirror. Usually this set of blocks is much larger than those that were being written at the time of the crash and it takes a while to create the copies.

During the copy, the storage is unavailable, which increases overall recovery times. Additionally, it is also possible that the failure caused a partial write to one side, resulting in a corrupt logical block. The copying may write the bad data over the good data because the volume manager has no way of knowing which side is good.

Fortunately, when you use ASM, you need not maintain a DRL or blindly copy from one mirror to the other before beginning recovery. The only application that uses ASM is the Oracle database, and Oracle knows how to recover its data so that the mirror sides are the same for the cases that matter. It is not always necessary to make the mirror sides the same. For example, if a file is being initialized before it is part of the database, then it will be reinitialized after a failure, so that file does not matter for the recovery process. For data that does matter, Oracle must always have a means of tolerating a write that was started but which might not have been completed. The redo log is an example of one such mechanism in Oracle. Because Oracle already has to reconstruct such interrupted writes, it is simple to rewrite both sides of the mirror even if it looks like the write completed successfully. The number of extra writes can be small, because Oracle is excellent at determining exactly which blocks need recovery.

Another benefit of not using a DRL is that a corrupt block, which does not report an I/O error on read, can be recovered from the good side of the mirror. When a block corruption is discovered, each side of the mirror is read to determine whether one of them is valid. If the sides are different and one is valid, then the valid copy is used and rewritten to both sides. This can repair a partial write at host death. This mechanism is used all the time, not just for recovery reads. Thus an external corruption that affects only one side of an ASM mirrored block can also be recovered.

I/O Error-Failure Management and ASM

Whereas the previous section covers ASM handling of transient and permanent disk failures in ASM redundancy diskgroups, this section discusses how ASM processes I/O errors, such as read and write errors, and also discusses in general how to handle I/O failures in external redundancy diskgroups.

General Disk Failure Overview

Disk drives are mechanical devices and thus tend to fail. As drives begin to fail or have sporadic I/O errors, database failures become more likely.

The ability to detect and resolve device path failures is a core component of Path Managers as well as HBAs. A disk device can be in the following states or have the following issues:

- **Media sense errors** These include hard read errors and unrecoverable positioning errors. In this situation, the disk device is still functioning and responds to `SCSI_INQUIRY` requests.

- **Device too busy** A disk device can become so overwhelmed with I/O requests that it will not respond to the `SCSI_INQUIRY` within a reasonable amount of time.

- **Failed device** In this case, the disk has actually failed and will not respond to a `SCSI_INQUIRY` request, and when the `SCSI_INQUIRY` timeout occurs, the disk and path will be taken offline.

- **Path failure** The disk device may be intact, but a path component—such as a port or a fiber adapter—has failed.

In general, I/O requests can time out because either the SCSI driver device is unable to respond to a host message within the allotted time or the path on which a message was sent has failed. To detect this path failure, HBAs typically enable a timer each time that a message is received from the SCSI driver. A link failure is thrown if the timer exceeds the link-down timeout without receiving the I/O acknowledgment. After the link-down event occurs, the Path Manager determines that the path is dead and evaluates whether to reroute queued I/O requests to alternate paths.

ASM and I/O Failures

The method that ASM uses to handle I/O failures depends on the context in which the I/O failure occurred. If the I/O failure occurs in the database instance, then it notifies ASM, and ASM decides whether to take the disk offline. ASM takes whatever action is appropriate based on the redundancy of the diskgroup and the number of disks that are already offline.

If the I/O error occurs while ASM is trying to mount a diskgroup, the behavior depends on the release. In Oracle Database 10g Release 1, if the instance mounting the diskgroup is the first instance in the cluster to mount the diskgroup, it attempts to take offline any disks that it cannot discover, such as those that threw I/O errors while trying to read the disk header for mounting. In Oracle Database 10g Release 2, if the instance is not the first to mount the diskgroup in the cluster, it will not attempt to take any disks offline that are online in the diskgroup mounted by other instances. If none of the disks can be found, the mount will fail. The rationale here is that if the disk in question has truly failed, the running instances will very quickly take the disk offline.

If the error is local and you want to mount the diskgroup on the instance that cannot access the disk, you need to drop the disk from a node that the diskgroup mounted. Note that a drop force command will allow the mount immediately. Often in such scenarios, the disk cannot be found on a particular node because of errors in the `ASM_DISKSTRING` or the permissions on the node.

In Oracle Database 11g, these two behaviors are still valid, but rather than choosing one or the other based on whether the instance is first to mount the diskgroup, the behavior is based on the type of mount. The diskgroup MOUNT [NOFORCE], which is the default, requires that all disks in the diskgroup be found at mount time. If any disks are missing (or have I/O errors), the mount will fail. MOUNT FORCE attempts to take disks offline as necessary allow the mount to complete. Note that to discourage the excessive use of FORCE, MOUNT FORCE succeeds only if a disk needs to be taken offline.

ASM, as well as the database, takes proactive measures to handle I/O failures or data corruptions.

When the database reads a data block from disk, it validates the checksum, the block number, and some other fields. If the block fails the consistency checks, then an attempt is made to reread the block to get a valid block read. Oracle can read individual mirror sides to resolve corruption since Oracle Database version 7.3. It was originally implemented with the Veritas volume manager, but now works with a number of volume managers including ASM. For corrupt blocks in datafiles, the database code reads each side of the mirror and looks for a good copy. If it finds a good copy, then the read succeeds and the good copy is written back to disk to repair the corruption, assuming that the database is holding the appropriate locks to perform a write. If the mirroring is done in a storage array (external redundancy), then there is no interface to select mirror sides for reading. In that case, the RDBMS simply rereads the same block and hopes for the best; however, with a storage array, this process will most likely return the same data from the array cache unless the original read was corrupted. If the RDBMS cannot find good data, then an error is signaled. The corrupt block is kept in buffer cache (if it is a cache-managed block) to avoid repeated attempts to reread the block and to avoid excessive error reporting. Note that the handling of corruption is different for each file type and for each piece of code that accesses the file. For example, the handling of datafile corruption during a RMAN backup is different from that described in this section, and the handling of archive logfile corruption.

ASM, like most volume managers, does not do any proactive polling of the hardware looking for faults. Servers usually have enough I/O activity to make such polling unnecessary. Moreover, ASM cannot tell whether an I/O error is due to a cable being pulled or a disk failing. It is up to the operating system (OS) to decide when to return an error or continue waiting for an I/O completion. ASM has no control over how the OS handles I/O completions. The OS signals a permanent I/O error to the caller (the Oracle I/O process) after several retries in the device driver.

NOTE
Starting with Oracle Database 11g, In the event of a disk failure, ASM polls disk partners and the other disks in the failure group of the failed disk. This is done to efficiently detect a pathological problem that may exist in the failure group.

ASM takes disks offline from the diskgroup only on a write operation I/O error, not for read operations. For example, in Oracle Database 10g, if a permanent disk I/O error is incurred during an Oracle write I/O operation, then ASM takes the affected disk offline and immediately drops it from the diskgroup, thus preventing stale data reads. In Oracle Database 11g, if the DISK_REPAIR_TIMER attribute is enabled, then ASM takes the disk offline but does not drop it. However, ASM does drop the disk if the DISK_REPAIR_TIMER expires. This feature is covered in the section "Recovering from Disk Failures in Oracle Database 11g—Fast Disk Resync," earlier in this chapter.

In Oracle Database 11g, ASM attempts to remap bad blocks if a read fails. This remapping can lead to a write, which could lead to ASM taking the disk offline. For read errors, the block is read from the secondary extents (only for normal or high redundancy). If the loss of a disk would result in data loss, as in the case where a disk's partner disk is also offline, ASM automatically dismounts the diskgroup to protect the integrity of the diskgroup data.

NOTE
Read failures from disk header and other unmirrored, physically addressed reads also cause ASM to take the disk offline.

In Oracle Database 11g, if a disk fails, ASM proactively reads all the disk headers of all the partners of the failing disk in an effort to avoid taking disk offline unnecessarily and to ensure partnership availability. After taking a disk offline, ASM checks the disk headers of all disks in that failure group to drop a failure group proactively in the case of failure group. ASM dismounts a diskgroup rather than taking some disks offline and then dismounting the diskgroup in case of apparent failures of disks in multiple failure groups. Also, ASM takes disks in a failure group offline all at once to allow for more efficient repartnering.

If the heartbeat cannot be written to a copy of the PST in a normal- or high-redundancy diskgroup, then ASM takes the disk containing the PST copy offline and moves the PST to another disk in the same diskgroup. In an external redundancy diskgroup, the diskgroup is dismounted if the heartbeat write fails. The heartbeat block is not normally read except at diskgroup mount. At mount time, it is read twice, at least 6 sec apart, to determine whether an instance outside the local cluster mounts the diskgroup. If the two reads show different contents, then the diskgroup has mounted an unseen instance.

In the following example, ASM detects I/O failures as shown from the alert log:

```
Wed May 10 08:13:47 2006
NOTE: cache initiating offline of disk 1  group 1
WARNING: offlining mode 3 of disk 1/0x0 (DATA_1_0001)
NOTE: halting all I/Os to diskgroup DATA_1
NOTE: active pin found: 0x0x546d24cc
Wed May 10 08:13:52 2006
ERROR: PST-initiated MANDATORY DISMOUNT of group DATA_1
```

The following warning indicates that ASM detected an I/O error on a particular disk:

```
WARNING: offlining mode 3 of disk 1/0x0 (DATA_1_0001)
```

This error message alerts the user that trying to take the disk offline would cause data loss, so ASM is dismounting the diskgroup instead:

```
ERROR: PST-initiated MANDATORY DISMOUNT of group DATA_1
```

Messages should also appear in the OS log indicating problems this same disk (DATA_1_0001).

Many users want to simulate corruption in an ASM file in order to test failure and recovery. Two types of failure injection tests that customers induce are block corruption and disk failure. Unfortunately, overwriting an ASM disk simulates corruption, *not* a disk failure. Note further that overwriting the disk will corrupt ASM metadata as well as database files. This may not be the user's intended fault injection testing. You must be cognizant of the redundancy type deployed before deciding on the suite of tests run in fault injection testing. In cases where a block or set of blocks is physically corrupted, ASM, like some other host volume managers, attempts to reread all mirror copies of a corrupt block to find one copy that is not corrupt. So redundancy does matter when recovering a corrupt block. The source of the corruption also matters. If bad data are written to disk through ASM or any other volume manager, they will go to all copies of the mirror. An example of this is a logical corruption, such as bad redo generation. Additionally, normal redundancy would not help if the corruption was systematic so that it affected multiple disks (for example, if a storage administrator changed multiple disks).

Space Management Views for ASM Redundancy

Two V$ ASM views provide more accurate information on free space usage: USABLE_FREE_SPACE and REQUIRED_MB_FREE.

In Oracle Database 10*g* Release 1, the FREE_MB value that is reported in V$ASM_DISKGROUP does not take into account mirrored extents. Oracle Database 10*g* Release 2 introduced a new column in V$ASM_DISKGROUP called USABLE_FILE_MB to indicate the amount of free space that can be "safely" utilized taking mirroring into account. The column provides a more accurate view of usable space in the diskgroup. Note that for external redundancy, the column FREE_MB is equal to USABLE_FREE_SPACE.

Be careful of cases in which USABLE_FILE_MB has negative values in V$ASM_DISKGROUP. USABLE_FILE_MB can go negative due to the relationship among FREE_MB, REQUIRED_MIRROR_FREE_MB, and USABLE_FILE_MB. Although this is not necessarily a critical situation, it does mean that depending on the value of FREE_MB, you may not be able to create new files. The next failure may result in files with reduced redundancy or can result in an out-of-space condition, which can hang the database. If USABLE_FILE_MB becomes negative, it is strongly recommended that you add more space to the diskgroup as soon as possible.

Along with USEABLE_FREE_SPACE, another column, REQUIRED_MB_FREE, has been added to V$ASM_DISKGROUP to indicate more accurately the amount of space that is required to be available in a given diskgroup to restore redundancy after one or more disk failures. The amount of space displayed in this column takes into account mirroring.

Diskgroups and Attributes

Oracle Database 11*g* introduced the concept of ASM attributes. Unlike initialization parameters, which are instance-specific but apply to all diskgroups, ASM attributes are diskgroup-specific and apply to all instances. The ASM diskgroup attributes are shown in the V$ASM_ATTRIBUTES view. However, this view is not populated until the diskgroup compatibility—that is, COMPATIBLE.ASM—is set to 11.1.0.

In Oracle Database 11*g*, the following attributes can be set:

- COMPATIBLE.ASM

- COMPATIBLE.RDBMS

- DISK_REPAIR_TIME

- AU_SIZE

The diskgroup attributes can be set at diskgroup creation or by using the ALTER DISKGROUP command. For example, a diskgroup can be created with 10.1 diskgroup compatibility and then advanced to 11.1 by setting the COMPATIBLE.ASM attribute to 11.1. The discussion on compatibility attributes is covered in the next section.

The following example shows a CREATE DISKGROUP command that results in a diskgroup with 10.1 compatibility (the default):

```
SQL> CREATE DISKGROUP DATA DISK '/dev/rdsk/c3t19d16s4',
'/dev/rdsk/c3t19d17s4' ;
```

This diskgroup can then be advanced to 11.1 using the following command:

```
SQL> ALTER DISKGROUP DATA SET ATTRIBUTE 'compatible.asm' = '11.1.0.0.0';
```

On successful advancing of the diskgroup, the following message appears:

```
SUCCESS: Advancing ASM compatibility to 11.1.0.0.0 for grp 1
```

In another example, the AU_SIZE attribute, which dictates the allocation unit size, and the COMPATIBLE.ASM attributes are specified at diskgroup creation. Note that the AU_SIZE attribute can only be specified at diskgroup creation and cannot be altered using the ALTER DISKGROUP command:

```
SQL> CREATE DISKGROUP FLASH DISK '/dev/raw/raw15', '/dev/raw/raw16',
'/dev/raw/raw17' ATTRIBUTE 'au_size' = '16M', 'compatible.asm' = '11.1';
```

The V$ASM_ATTRIBUTE view can be queried to get the DATA diskgroup attributes:

```
SQL> SELECT NAME, VALUE FROM V$ASM_ATTRIBUTE WHERE GROUP_NUMBER=1;
  NAME                    VALUE
  ------------------ ----------
  disk_repair_time    4 H
  compatible.asm      11.1.0.0.0
  compatible.rdbms    11.1.0.0.0
```

In the previous example, the COMPATIBLE.ASM was advanced, this next example advances the COMPATIBLE.RDBMS attribute. Notice that the version is set to simply 11.1, which is equivalent to 11.1.0.0.0.

```
SQL> ALTER DISKGROUP DATA SET ATTRIBUTE 'COMPATIBLE.RDBMS' = '11.1';
  NAME                    VALUE
  ------------------ ----------
  disk_repair_time    4 H
  compatible.asm      11.1.0.0.0
  compatible.rdbms    11.1
```

The range of values for COMPATIBLE.RDBMS or COMPATIBLE.ASM can be from one version to five versions—for example, from 11.1 to 11.1.0.0.0:

```
SQL> ALTER DISKGROUP ORADATA SET ATTRIBUTE 'DISK_REPAIR_TIME' = '4 H';
```

This is covered in more detail in the next section. For more details on DISK_REPAIR_TIME, see the section "Recovering from Disk Failures in Oracle Database 11*g*—Fast Disk Resync" earlier in this chapter.

ASM and Database Compatibility

When a database instance first connects to an ASM instance, it negotiates the highest Oracle version that can be supported between the instances. There are two types of compatibility settings between ASM and the RDBMS: instance-level software compatibility settings and diskgroup-specific settings.

Instance-level software compatibility is defined using the init.ora parameter COMPATIBLE. This COMPATIBLE parameter, which can be set to 11.1, 10.2, or 10.1 at the ASM or database instance level, defines what software features are available to the instance. Setting the COMPATIBLE parameter in the ASM instance to 10.1 precludes the use of any new features that are introduced in Oracle Database 11*g*, such as disk online/offline and variable extents. Using lower values of the COMPATIBLE parameter for an ASM instance is not useful, because ASM is compatible with multiple database versions. Note that the COMPATIBLE.ASM value must be greater than or equal to that of COMPATIBLE.RDBMS.

The other compatibility settings are specific to a diskgroup and control which attributes are available to the ASM diskgroup and which are available to the database. This is defined by the ASM compatibility (COMPATIBLE.ASM) and RDBMS compatibility (COMPATIBLE.RDBMS) attributes, respectively. These compatibility attributes are persistently stored in the diskgroup metadata.

RDBMS Compatibility

RDBMS diskgroup compatibility is defined by the COMPATIBLE.RDBMS attribute. This attribute, which defaults to 10.1 in Oracle Database 11*g*, is the minimum COMPATIBLE version setting of a database that can mount the diskgroup. RDBMS compatibility also dictates the format of the messages exchanged between ASM and RDBMS instances. After the diskgroup attribute of COMPATIBLE.RDBMS is advanced to 11.1, it cannot be reversed.

ASM Compatibility

ASM diskgroup compatibility, as defined by COMPATIBLE.ASM, controls the persistent format of the on-disk ASM metadata structures. The ASM compatibility defaults to 10.1 and must always be greater than or equal to the RDBMS compatibility level. After the compatibility is advanced to 11.1, it cannot be reset to lower versions. Any value up to the current software version can be set and will be enforced. All five parts of the version number may be specified. For example, valid values for compatibility can be 11.1.0.0, 11.1.0, 10.1.0.0, or 10.1. Oracle Releases 10.1.0.2 through 10.2.0 all use the same ASM and RDBMS compatibility number.

COMPATIBLE.RDBMS and COMPATIBLE.ASM together control the persistent format of the on-disk ASM metadata structures. The combination of the compatibility parameter setting of the database, the software version of the database, and the RDBMS compatibility setting of a diskgroup determines whether a database instance is permitted to mount a given diskgroup. The compatibility setting also determines which ASM features are available for a diskgroup.

The following query shows an ASM instance that was recently software upgraded from Oracle Database 10*g* to Oracle Database 11*g*:

```
SQL> SELECT NAME, BLOCK_SIZE, ALLOCATION_UNIT_SIZE "AU_SIZE", STATE,
COMPATIBILITY "ASM COMP",DATABASE_COMPATIBILITY "DB COMP" FROM V$ASM_DISKGROP;

NAME  BLOCK_SIZE AU_SIZE STATE   ASM_COMP   DB_COMP
----- ---------- ------- ----- --------   ----------

DATA  4096       1048576 MOUNTED 10.1.0.0.0 10.1.0.0.0
```

Notice that the ASM compatibility and RDBMS compatibility are still at the default (for upgraded instances) of 10.1. The 10.1 setting is the lowest attribute supported by ASM.

NOTE
An ASM instance can support different RDBMS clients with different compatibility settings, as long as the database COMPATIBLE init.ora parameter setting of each database instance is greater than or equal to the RDBMS compatibility of all diskgroups.

See the section "Diskgroups and Attributes," earlier in this chapter, for examples on advancing the compatibility.

The ASM compatibility of a diskgroup can be set to 11.0 whereas its RDBMS compatibility could be 10.1, as in the following example:

```
SQL> SELECT DB_NAME, STATUS,SOFTWARE_VERSION,COMPATIBLE_VERSION FROM
V$ASM_CLIENT;
DB_NAME  STATUS        SOFTWARE_V COMPATIBLE
-------- ------------- ---------- ----------

YODA     CONNECTED     11.1.0.6.0 11.1.0.0.0

SQL> SELECT NAME,COMPATIBILITY "COMPATIBLE",DATABASE_COMPATIBILITY
 "DATABASE_COMP" FROM V$ASM_DISKGROUP
NAME                        COMPATIBILE DATABASE_COMP
--------------------------- ----------- -------------

DATA                        10.1.0.0.0 10.1.0.0.0
```

This implies that diskgroup can be managed only by ASM software version 11.0 or higher whereas any database software version must be 10.1 or higher.

Summary

A diskgroup is the fundamental object managed by ASM. It is composed of multiple ASM disks. Each diskgroup is self-describing—that is, all the metadata about the usage of the space in the diskgroup are completely contained within the diskgroup. If ASM can find all the disks in a diskgroup, it can provide access to the diskgroup without any additional metadata.

A given ASM file is completely contained within a single diskgroup. However, a diskgroup may contain files belonging to several databases and a single database may use files from multiple diskgroups. Most installations include only a small number of diskgroups—usually two and rarely more than three.

CHAPTER
5

ASM Space Allocation
and Rebalance

hen a database is created under the constructs of ASM, it will be striped (and can be optionally mirrored) as per the Stripe and Mirror Everything (SAME) methodology. SAME is a concept to make extensive use of striping and mirroring across large sets of disks to achieve high availability and to provide good performance with minimal tuning. ASM incorporates the SAME methodology. Using this method, ASM evenly distributes and balances input/output (I/O) load across all disks within the diskgroup. ASM solves one of the shortcomings of the original SAME methodology, because ASM maintains even data distribution even when storage configurations change.

ASM Space Allocation

This section discusses how ASM allocates space in the diskgroup and how clients such as the relational database management system (RDBMS) initialize and use the allocated space.

ASM Allocation Units

ASM allocates space in chunks called *allocation units* (AUs). An AU is the most granular allocation on a per-disk basis—that is, every ASM disk is divided into AUs of the same size. The ASM 1MB stripe size has proved to be the best stripe depth for Oracle databases and also happens to be the largest I/O request that the RDBMS will issue. This optimal stripe size, coupled with even distribution of extents in the diskgroup and the buffer cache in the RDBMS, prevents hot spots.

Keep in mind that unlike traditional random array of independent drives (RAID) configurations, ASM striping is not done in a round-robin basis. ASM randomly chooses a disk for allocating the initial extent. This is done to optimize the balance of the diskgroup. All subsequent AUs are allocated (as shown in Figure 5.1) in such a way as to distribute each file equally and evenly across all disks and to fill all disks evenly. Thus every disk is maintained at the same percentage full, regardless of the size of the disk.

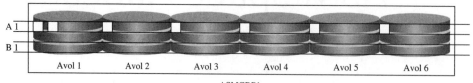

FIGURE 5-1. *ASM extents*

For example, if a disk is twice as big as others, it will contain twice as many extents. This ensures that all disks in a diskgroup have the same I/O load. Because ASM balances load across all the disks in a diskgroup, it is not a good practice to create multiple disk partitions from different areas of the same physical disk and then allocate the partitions as members of the same diskgroup. However, it may make sense for two partitions on a physical disk to be in two different diskgroups.

ASM is abstracted from the underlying characteristic of the storage array (LUN). For example, if the storage array presents several RAID5 LUNs to ASM as disks, ASM will allocate extents transparently across each of those LUNs.

ASM Extents

When a database file is created in an ASM diskgroup, it is composed of a set of ASM extents, and these extents are evenly distributed across all disks in the diskgroup. Each extent consists of an integral number of AUs on an ASM disk.

The following two queries display the extent distribution for a diskgroup (the FLASH diskgroup) that contains four disks. The first query shows the evenness based on megabytes per disk, and the second query lists the total extents for each disk in the FLASH diskgroup (group_number 2) using the `X$KFFXP` base table.

```
SQL> SELECT NAME, TOTAL_MB, FREE_MB FROM V$ASM_DISK WHERE GROUP_NUMBER=2;
NAME                                     TOTAL_MB    FREE_MB
-------------------------------------    ----------  ----------
FLASH_0001                                   8628       4996
FLASH_0000                                   8628       4996
FLASH_0002                                   8583       4970
FLASH_0003                                   8628       4996

SQL> SELECT COUNT(PXN_KFFXP), DISK_KFFXP, GROUP_KFFXP FROM X$KFFXP WHERE
GROUP_KFFXP=2 GROUP BY DISK_KFFXP, GROUP_KFFXP ORDER BY  GROUP_KFFXP,
DISK_KFFXP;
COUNT(PXN_KFFXP) DISK_KFFXP GROUP_KFFXP
---------------- ---------- -----------
            3736          0           2
            3737          1           2
            3716          2           2
            3734          3           2
```

Similarly, the following example illustrates the even distribution of ASM extents for the System Tablespace across all the disks in the DATA diskgroup (group number 3). This tablespace contains a single 100MB datafile called +DATA/yoda/datafile/system.256.589462555.

```
SQL> SELECT F.FILE#, T.NAME TBSNAME, F.NAME FILENAME, BYTES/1024/1024 MB
FROM V$DATAFILE F, V$TABLESPACE T WHERE F.TS# = T.TS#;

FILE#      TBSNAME    FILENAME                                            MB
---------- ---------- --------------------------------------------------- ------
1          SYSTEM     +DATA/yoda/datafile/system.256.589462555           100
```

```
SQL> SELECT DISK_KFFXP, COUNT (DISK_KFFXP) EXTENTS FROM X$KFFXP WHERE
GROUP_KFFXP=3 AND NUMBER_KFFXP=256 AND DISK_KFFXP <> 65534 GROUP BY
NUMBER_KFFXP,DISK_KFFXP

DISK_KFFXP    EXTENTS
----------   ----------
         0          27
         1          25
         2          25
         3          25
```

ASM Striping

There are two types of ASM file striping: coarse and fine-grained. For coarse distribution, each coarse grain file extent is mapped to a single allocation unit.

With fine-grained distribution, each grain is interleaved 128K across groups of eight AUs. Fine-grained striping is intended for latency sensitive files (such as redo and flashback log files). It is also used for very small files (such as controlfile and Spfile) to ensure that they are distributed across disks. Fine-grained striping is generally not good for sequential I/O (such as full table scans) once the sequential I/O exceeds one AU.

As discussed previously, each file stored in ASM requires metadata structures to describe the file extent locations. As the file grows, the metadata associated with that file also grows as well as the memory used to store the file extent locations. Oracle 11*g* introduces a new feature called Variable Sized Extents to minimize the overhead of the metadata. The main objective of this feature is to enable larger file extents to reduce metadata requirements as a file grows, and as a byproduct allows larger file size support [file sizes up to 140PB (petabytes 1,024TB)]. For example, if a datafile is initially as small as 1GB, then the file extent size used will be 1 AU. As the file grows, several size thresholds are crossed and larger extent sizes are employed at each threshold, with maximum extent size capped at 64 AUs. Note that there are two thresholds: 20,000 extents (20GB with 1MB AUs) and 40,000 extents (40GB with 1MB AUs). Valid extent sizes are 1, 8, and 64 AUs (which translate to 1MB, 8MB, and 64MB with 1MB AUs). The database administrator (DBA) or ASM administrator need not manage variable extents; ASM handles this automatically. This feature is very similar in behavior to the Automatic Extent Allocation that the RDBMS uses.

NOTE
The RDBMS layers of the code effectively limit file size to 128TB. The ASM structures can address 140PB.

The following example demonstrates the use of Variable Sized Extents. In this example, the SYSAUX tablespace contains a datafile that is approximately 32GB, which exceeds the first threshold of 20,000 extents (20GB).

```
SQL> SELECT NAME, BYTES/(1024*1024*1024) "SIZE", FILE# FROM V$DATAFILE
  WHERE BYTES/(1024*1024*1024) > 20
NAME                                       SIZE      FILE#
---------------------------------------- ---------- -----
+DATA/yoda/datafile/sysaux.263.62577323 31.9999924    263
```

Now if the X$KFFXP is queried to find the ASM file that has a nondefault extent size, it should indicate that it is file number 263:

```
SQL> SELECT DISTINCT NUMBER_KFFXP, SIZE_KFFXP FROM X$KFFXP WHERE
SIZE_KFFXP = 8 GROUP BY NUMBER_KFFXP, SIZE_KFFXP
NUMBER_KFFXP SIZE_KFFXP
------------ ----------
         263          8
```

The Variable Sized Extents feature is available only for diskgroups with Oracle 11*g* RDBMS and ASM compatibility. For diskgroups created with Oracle database 10*g*, the compatibility attribute must be advanced to 11.1.0. Variable extents take effect for newly created files, but will not be retroactively applied to files that were created with 10*g* software.

Setting Larger AU Sizes for VLDBs

For very large databases (VLDBs)—for example, databases that are 10TB and larger––it may be beneficial to change the default AU size. The following are benefits of changing the default size for VLDBs:

- Reduced SGA size to manage the extent maps in the RDBMS instance

- Increased file size limits

- Reduced database open time, because VLDBs usually have many big datafiles

Increasing the AU size improves the time to open large databases in Oracle 10*g*, also reduces the amount of shared pool consumed by the extent maps. With 1MB AUs and fixed-size extents, the extent maps for a 10TB database are about 90MB, which has to be read at open and then kept in memory. With 16MB AUs, this is reduced to about 5.5MB. In Oracle Database 10*g*, the entire extent map for a file is read from disk at file-open time.

Oracle Database 11*g* significantly minimizes the file-open latency issue by reading extent maps on demand. In Oracle 10*g*, for every file open, the complete extent maps are built and sent to the RDBMS instance from the ASM instance. For large files, this unnecessarily lengthens file-open time. In Oracle 11*g*, only the first 60 extents in the extent map are sent at file-open time. The rest are sent in batches as required by the RDBMS.

Setting Larger AU Sizes in Oracle Database 11*g*

For Oracle Database 11*g* ASM systems, the following `CREATE DISKGROUP` command can be executed to set the appropriate AU size:

```
SQL> CREATE DISKGROUP DATA DISK '/dev/raw/raw15', '/dev/raw/raw16',
'/dev/raw/raw17' ATTRIBUTE 'au_size' = '16M', 'compatible.asm' = '11.1'
'compatible.rdbms' = '11.1';
```

Setting Larger AU Sizes in Oracle 10*g*

In Oracle Database 10*g*, ASM provides two hidden initialization parameters that allow you to create a diskgroup with an AU size of 16MB and fine-grained striping at 1MB (instead of 128K):

```
_asm_ausize
```

```
_asm_stripesize
```

The AU parameter can be used only at diskgroup creation time; furthermore, the AU size of an existing diskgroup cannot be changed after the diskgroup has been created. The following example creates a diskgroup with a 16MB AU and allows for 1MB fine-striping for all database files:

1. Shut down the ASM instance.

2. Edit the ASM init.ora parameter file and add the following:

   ```
   #ASM AU 16MB
   _asm_ausize=16777216
   #ASM fine grain stripesize 1MB
   _asm_stripesize=1048576
   ```

3. Restart the ASM instance. The ASM instance must be restarted for the new parameters to take effect. After you set the underscore parameters and restart the ASM instance, any diskgroup created will have the new AU size and `FINE` stripe size.

4. Create a diskgroup:

   ```
   SQL> CREATE DISKGROUP DATA disk '/dev/sda1', '/dev/sdc1';
   ```

5. Verify that the AU size for the diskgroup is 16MB by querying the `ALLOCATION_UNIT_SIZE` in `V$ASM_DISKGROUP_STAT` or `V$ASM_DISKGROUP`.

   ```
   SQL> SELECT NAME, ALLOCATION_UNIT_SIZE FROM V$ASM_DISKGROUP;
   NAME                          ALLOCATION_UNIT_SIZE
   ----------------------------- --------------------
   XRAID                                     16777216
   ```

6. Query `V$ASM_TEMPLATE` for the diskgroup in question and modify the ASM file templates to set the stripe type to `FINE` for all file types to achieve 1MB striping, as follows:

```
SQL> ALTER DISKGROUP DATA ALTER TEMPLATE <tmpl> ATTRIBUTES (FINE);
```

The purpose of this change is to keep the 1MB extent distribution of files despite the larger AUs. If the files were left with coarse striping, the striping would be done at 16MB. This not necessary in Oracle Database 11*g* when using Variable Sized Extents.

7. Repeat the preceding command for all ASM file types. Query `V$ASM_TEMPLATE` again to ensure that all of the templates are updated correctly.

NOTE
The _asm_ausize and _asm_stripesize parameters are instance parameters. Thus, to create a diskgroup with the normal 1MB AU size and 128K FINE stripe size, you must remove the underscore parameters and restart the ASM instance.

ASM Rebalance

With traditional volume managers, expanding or shrinking striped filesystems has typically been difficult. With ASM, these disk changes are now seamless operations involving redistribution (rebalancing) of the striped data. Additionally, these operations can be performed online.

Any change in the storage configuration— adding, dropping, or resizing a disk— triggers a rebalance. ASM does not dynamically move around "hot areas" or "hot extents." Because ASM distributes extents evenly across all disks and the database buffer cache prevents small chunks of data from being hot areas on disk, it completely obviates the notion of hot disks or extents.

Rebalance Operation

The main objective of the rebalance operation is always to provide an even distribution of file extents and space usage across all disks in the diskgroup. The rebalance is done on a per-file basis to ensure that each file is evenly balanced across all disks. This is critical to ASM's assurance of balanced I/O load. The ASM background process, RBAL, manages this rebalance. The RBAL process examines each file extent map, and the extents are redistributed on the new storage configuration. For example, consider an eight-disk diskgroup, with a datafile with 40 extents (each disk will house five extents).

When two new drives of same size are added, that datafile is rebalanced and distributed across 10 drives, with each drive containing four extents. Only eight extents need to move to complete the rebalance—that is, a complete redistribution of extents is not necessary, as only the minimum number of extents are moved to reach equal distribution.

NOTE
A weighting factor, influenced by disk size and file size, affects rebalancing. A larger drive will consume more extents. This factor is used to achieve even distribution based on overall size

The following is a typical process flow for ASM rebalancing:

1. On the ASM instance, a DBA adds (or drops) a disk to (from) a diskgroup.

2. This invokes the RBAL process to create the rebalance plan and then begin coordination of the redistribution

3. RBAL calculates estimated time and work required to perform the task and then messages the ASM Rebalance (ARBx) processes to handle the request. The number of ARBx processes invoked is directly determined by the init.ora parameter ASM_POWER_LIMIT or the power level specified in an add, drop, or rebalance command.

4. The Continuing Operations Directory (COD) is updated to reflect a rebalance activity. The COD is important when an influx rebalance fails. Recovering instances will see an outstanding COD entry for the rebalance and restart it.

5. RBAL distributes plans to the ARBs. In general, RBAL generates a plan per file; however, larger files can be split among ARBs.

6. ARBx performs rebalance on these extents. Each extent is locked, relocated, and unlocked. Reads can proceed while an extent is being relocated. Writes can still be issued, but may have to be reissued to the new location. This step is shown as Operation REBAL in V$ASM_OPERATION. The rebalance algorithm is detailed in Chapter 11, "ASM Operations".

The following is an excerpt from the ASM alert log during a rebalance operation:

```
SQL> ALTER DISKGROUP GROUPC REBALANCE POWER 5
Mon Feb 12 12:46:16 2007
```

```
NOTE: PST update: grp = 2
NOTE: requesting all-instance PST refresh for group=2
Mon Feb 12 12:46:16 2007
NOTE: PST refresh pending for group 2/0x761086a4 (FLASH)
SUCCESS: refreshed PST for 2/0x761086a4 (FLASH)
Mon Feb 12 12:46:16 2007
NOTE: starting rebalance of group 2/0x761086a4 (FLASH) at power 5
Starting background process ARB0
Starting background process ARB1
ARB0 started with pid=17, OS id=4211
Mon Feb 12 12:46:16 2007
Starting background process ARB2
ARB1 started with pid=20, OS id=4213
Mon Feb 12 12:46:16 2007
Starting background process ARB3
ARB2 started with pid=21, OS id=4215
Mon Feb 12 12:46:16 2007
Starting background process ARB4
ARB3 started with pid=22, OS id=4217
Mon Feb 12 12:46:16 2007
NOTE: assigning ARB0 to group 2/0x761086a4 (FLASH)
NOTE: assigning ARB1 to group 2/0x761086a4 (FLASH)
NOTE: assigning ARB2 to group 2/0x761086a4 (FLASH)
NOTE: assigning ARB3 to group 2/0x761086a4 (FLASH)
ARB4 started with pid=23, OS id=4219
Mon Feb 12 12:46:17 2007
NOTE: assigning ARB4 to group 2/0x761086a4 (FLASH)
...
Mon Feb 12 12:46:17 2007
NOTE: stopping process ARB1
Mon Feb 12 12:46:18 2007
SUCCESS: rebalance completed for group 2/0x761086a4 (FLASH)
```

An ARB trace file is created for each ARB process involved in the rebalance operation. This ARB trace file can be found in the trace subdirectory under the DIAG directory. The following is small excerpt from this trace file:

```
*** 2007-06-21 12:56:39.928
ARB1 relocating file +DATA.257.625774759 (120 entries)
ARB1 relocating file +DATA.257.625774759 (120 entries)
............
ARB1 relocating file +DATA.263.625773231 (120 entries)
ARB1 relocating file +DATA.263.625773231 (120 entries)
ARB1 relocating file +DATA.263.625773231 (120 entries)
```

The preceding entries are repeated for each file assigned to the ARB process.

Resizing a Physical Disk or LUN and the ASM Diskgroup

When increasing the size of a diskgroup, it is a best practice to add disks of similar size. However, there may be cases where it is appropriate to resize disks rather than to add storage of equal size. For these cases, it is a best practice to resize all of the disks in the diskgroup (to the same size) at the same time. This section discusses how to expand or resize the LUN as an ASM disk.

Disks in the storage are usually configured as a LUN and presented to the host. When a LUN runs out of space, you can expand it within the storage array by adding new disks in the back end. However, the operating system (OS) must then recognize the new space. Some operating systems require a reboot to recognize the new LUN size. On Linux systems that use Emulex drivers, for example, the following can be used:

```
echo "- - -" >/sys/class/scsi_host/host{N}/scan
```

where N is the scsi port ordinal assigned to this HBA port (see /proc/scsi/lpfc directory and look for the "port_number" files).

The first step in increasing the size of an ASM disk is to add extra storage capacity to the LUN. To use more space, the partition must be recreated. This operation is at the partition table level, and that table is stored in the first sectors of the disk. Changing the partition table does not affect the data.

In Oracle Database 10g ASM, V$ASM_DISK shows the size of the disk when it was discovered by ASM; this size is reflected in the TOTAL_MB column. However, if the actual size of a disk is 250GB, but ASM uses (or allocates) only 200GB, you cannot determine the true disk size without querying the OS.

Starting in Oracle Database 11g ASM, a new column in V$ASM_DISK called OS_MB gives the actual OS size of the disk. This column can aid in appropriately resizing the disk and prevent attempts to resize disks that cannot be resized.

The general steps to resize an ASM disk are as follows:

1. Resize LUN from storage array. This is usually a noninvasive operation.

2. Query V$ASM_DISK for the OS_MB for the disk to be resized. If the OS or ASM do not see the new size, then review the steps from the host bus adapter (HBA) vendor to probe for new devices. In some cases, this may require a reboot.

3. For 10.2.0.3 and earlier, you need to restart all ASM instances to ensure that they see the new LUN size. Oracle Database 11g ASM can detect new LUN sizes without restarting the instance. Issue ALTER DISKGROUP RESIZE DISK on one ASM instance. Note that a resize invokes an ASM rebalance.

Rebalance Power Management

Rebalancing involves physical movement of file extents. Its impact is usually low because the rebalance is done one extent at a time, so there is only one outstanding I/O at any given time per ARB process. This should not adversely affect online database activity. However, it is generally advisable to schedule the rebalance operation during off-peak hours.

The init.ora parameter ASM_POWER_LIMIT is used to influence the throughput and speed of the rebalance operation. The range of values for ASM_POWER_LIMIT is 0–11, where a value of 11 is full throttle and a value of 1 (the default) is low speed. A value of 0, which turns off automatic rebalance, should be used with caution. In a Real Application Clusters (RAC) environment, the ASM_POWER_LIMIT is specific to each ASM instance. (A common question is why the maximum power limit is 11 rather than 10. Movie lovers might recall the amplifier discussion from *This is Spinal Tap*.)

The power value can also be set for a specific rebalance activity using the ALTER DISKGROUP command. This value is effective only for the specific rebalance task. The following example demonstrates this:

```
"Session1 SQL"> ALTER DISKGROUP DATA ADD DISK '/dev/rdsk/c3t19d39s4'
REBALANCE POWER 11;
```

Here is an example from another session:

```
"Session2 SQL"> SELECT * FROM V$ASM_OPERATION;
OPERA  STAT POWER      ACTUAL     SOFAR    EST_WORK   EST_RATE EST_MINUTES
-----  ---- ---------  ---------- --------- ---------- ---------- ---------
1 REBAL WAIT       11           0         0          0          0         0

(time passes.............)
OPERA STAT   POWER     ACTUAL     SOFAR    EST_WORK   EST_RATE EST_MINUTES
------------ ----- ---- --------- --------- ---------- ---------- ---------
1 REBAL RUN      11       11      115269   217449       6333        16
(time passes.............)
```

Each rebalance step has various associated states. The following are the valid states:

- **WAIT** This indicates that there currently are no operations running for the group.

- **RUN** An operation is running for the group

- **HALT** An administrator is halting an operation.

- **ERRORS** An operation has been halted by errors.

A power value of 0 indicates that no rebalance should occur for this rebalance. This setting is particularly important when adding or removing storage (that has external redundancy) and then deferring the rebalance to a later scheduled time. However, a power level of 0 should be used with caution; this is especially true if the diskgroup is low on available space, which may result in an `ORA-15041` for out-of-balance diskgroups.

The power level is adjusted with the `ALTER DISKGROUP REBALANCE` command, which affects only the current rebalance for the specified diskgroup; future rebalances are not affected. If you increase the power level of the existing rebalance, it will spawn new ARB processes. If you decrease the power level, the running ARB process will finish its extent relocation and then quiesce and die off.

If you are removing or adding several disks, add or remove disks in a single `ALTER DISKGROUP` statement; this reduces the number of rebalance operations that are needed for storage changes. This behavior is more critical where normal- and high-redundancy diskgroups have been configured because of disk repartnering. The following example demonstrates this storage change:

```
SQl> ALTER DISKGROUP DATA ADD DISK '/dev/rdsk/c7t19*' DROP DATA_0012
REBALANCE POWER 8;
```

An ASM diskgroup rebalance is an asynchronous operation in that the control is returned immediately to the DBA after the operation executes in the background. The status of the ongoing operation can be queried from `V$ASM_OPERATION`. However, in some situations the diskgroup operation needs to be synchronous—that is, it must wait until rebalance is completed. In Oracle Database 10g Release 2 and above, the `ASM ALTER DISKGROUP` commands that result in a rebalance have the option of specifying the option to wait. This allows for accurate (sequential) scripting that may rely on the space change from a rebalance completing before any subsequent action is taken. For instance, if you add 100GB of storage to a completely full diskgroup, you will not be able to use all 100GB of storage until the rebalance completes. The `WAIT` option ensures that the space addition is successful and is available for space allocations.

If a new rebalance command is entered while one is already in progress in `WAIT` mode, the command will not return until the diskgroup is in a balanced state or the rebalance operation encounters an error.

The following SQL script demonstrates how the `WAIT` option can be used in SQL scripting. The script adds a new disk, /dev/sdc6, and waits until the add and rebalance operations complete, returning the control back to the script. The subsequent step adds a large tablespace.

```
#An example script to demonstrate WAIT option
#Login to ASM to add the disk
sqlplus  "/ as sysasm" << EOF
```

```
ALTER DISKGROUP data ADD DISK '/dev/sdc6' REBALANCE POWER 2 WAIT;
<< EOF
#login into database & create tablespace for the next month's Order
Entry data
sqlplus  oe_dba/oe1@proddb  << EOF
 CREATE BIGFILE TABLESPACE May_OE  DATAFILE SIZE 800 G
<< EOF
```

Fast Rebalance

When a storage change initiates a diskgroup rebalance, typically all active ASM instances of an ASM cluster and their RDBMS clients are notified and become engaged in the synchronization of the extents that are being rearranged. This messaging between instances can be "chatty" and thus can increase the overall time to complete the rebalance operation.

In certain situations where the user does not need the diskgroup to be user-accessible and needs rebalancing to complete as soon as possible, it is beneficial to perform the rebalance operation without the extra overhead of the ASM-to-ASM and ASM-to-RDBMS messaging. In Oracle Database 11g, the Fast Rebalance feature eliminates this overhead by allowing a single ASM instance to rebalance the diskgroup without the messaging overhead. The primary goal of Fast Rebalance is to improve the overall performance of rebalance operation. Additionally, the rebalance operation can be invoked at maximum power level (power level 11) to provide the highest throttling, making the rebalance operation limited only by the I/O subsystem (to the degree that you can saturate the I/O subsystem with 11 synchronous 1MB I/Os).

To eliminate messaging to other ASM instances, the ASM instance that performs the rebalance operation requires exclusive access to the diskgroup. To provide this exclusive diskgroup access, a new diskgroup mount mode, called RESTRICTED, was introduced in Oracle Database 11g. A diskgroup can be placed in RESTRICTED mode using STARTUP RESTRICT or ALTER DISKGROUP MOUNT RESTRICT.

When a diskgroup is mounted in RESTRICTED mode, RDBMS instances are prevented from accessing that diskgroup and thus databases cannot be opened. Furthermore, only one ASM instance in a cluster can mount a diskgroup in RESTRICTED mode.

At the end of the rebalance operation, the user must explicitly dismount the diskgroup and remount it in normal mode to make the diskgroup available to RDBMS instances.

Effects of Imbalanced Disks

This section illustrates how ASM distributes extents evenly and creates a balanced diskgroup. Additionally, the misconceptions of diskgroup space balance management are covered.

Note the term "balanced" in the ASM world is slightly overloaded. A diskgroup can become imbalanced for several reasons:

■ Dissimilarly sized disks are used in a given diskgroup.

■ A rebalance operation was aborted .

■ A rebalance operation was halted. In this case, this state can be determined by the UNBALANCED column of the V$ASM_DISKGROUP view. Operationally, the DBA can resolve this problem by manually performing a rebalance against the specific diskgroup.

NOTE
The UNBALANCED column in V$ASM_DISKGROUP indicates that a rebalance is in flux—that is, either in progress or stopped. This column is not an indicator for an unbalanced diskgroup.

■ A disk was added to the diskgroup with a ASM_POWER_LIMIT or power level of 0, but the diskgroup was never rebalanced afterward.

This following section focuses on the first reason: a diskgroup being imbalanced due to differently sized disks.

The main goal of ASM is to provide an even distribution of data extents across all disk members of a diskgroup. When an RDBMS instance requests a file creation, ASM allocates extents from all the disks in the specified diskgroup. The first disk allocation is chosen randomly, but all subsequent disks for extent allocation are chosen to evenly spread each file across all disks and to evenly fill all disks. Therefore, if all disks are equally sized, then all disks should have the same number of extents and thus an even I/O load.

But what happens when a diskgroup contains unequally sized disks—for example, a set of 25GB disks mixed with a couple of 50GB disks? When allocating extents, ASM will place twice as many extents on each of the bigger 50GB disks as on the smaller 25GB disks. Thus the 50GB disks will contain more data extents than their 25GB counterparts. This allocation scheme causes dissimilarly sized disks to fill at the same proportion, but will also induce unbalanced I/O across the diskgroup, as the disk with more extents will receive more I/O requests.

The following example illustrates this scenario:

1. The FLASH diskgroup initially contains two disks that are equally sized (8.6GB):

```
SQL> SELECT NAME, TOTAL_MB, FREE_MB FROM V$ASM_DISK WHERE
GROUP_NUMBER =2;
```

```
NAME                            TOTAL_MB   FREE_MB
-----------------------------   --------   --------
FLASH_0001                          8628       1159
FLASH_0000                          8628       1160
```

2. Display the extent distribution on the current diskgroup layout. The even extent distribution is shown by the COUNT(PXN_KFFXP) column.

```
SQL> SELECT COUNT ( PXN_KFFXP), DISK_KFFXP, GROUP_KFFXP FROM
X$KFFXP WHERE GROUP_KFFXP=2 GROUP BY DISK_KFFXP, GROUP_KFFXP
ORDER BY GROUP_KFFXP, DISK_KFFXP;
COUNT(PXN_KFFXP) DISK_KFFXP GROUP_KFFXP
---------------- ---------- -----------
            7461          0           2
            7462          1           2
```

3. Add two more 8.6GB disks to the diskgroup:

```
SQL> ALTER DISKGROUP FLASH ADD DISK '/dev/rdsk/c2t12d13s4',
 '/dev/rdsk/c2t12d14s4' REBALANCE POWER 8 WAIT;
```

4. The following query displays the extent distribution after the two disk were added:

```
SQL> SELECT COUNT(PXN_KFFXP), DISK_KFFXP, GROUP_KFFXP FROM
X$KFFXP WHERE GROUP_KFFXP=2 GROUP BY DISK_KFFXP, GROUP_KFFXP
ORDER BY GROUP_KFFXP, DISK_KFFXP;
COUNT(PXN_KFFXP) DISK_KFFXP GROUP_KFFXP
---------------- ---------- -----------
            3736          0           2
            3737          1           2
            3716          2           2
            3734          3           2
```

5. Then a 1GB disk was accidentally added:

```
sql> ALTER DISKGROUP FLASH ADD DISK '/dev/rdsk/c2t12d29s4'
SIZE 1G;
```

6. Display the space usage from V$ASM_DISK. Notice the size of disk FLASH_0004.

```
SQL> SELECT NAME, TOTAL_MB, FREE_MB FROM V$ASM_DISK WHERE
GROUP_NUMBER=2;
NAME                            TOTAL_MB   FREE_MB
-----------------------------   --------   --------
FLASH_0001                          8628       4996
FLASH_0000                          8628       4996
FLASH_0002                          8583       4970
FLASH_0003                          8628       4996
FLASH_0004                          1024        590
```

7. The extent distribution query is rerun to display the effects of this mistake. Notice the unevenness of the extent distribution.

```
SQL> SELECT COUNT (PXN_KFFXP), DISK_KFFXP, GROUP_KFFXP FROM
X$KFFXP WHERE GROUP_KFFXP =2 GROUP BY DISK_KFFXP, GROUP_KFFXP
ORDER BY GROUP_KFFXP, DISK_KFFXP;
COUNT(PXN_KFFXP) DISK_KFFXP GROUP_KFFXP
---------------- ---------- -----------
            3628          0           2
            3628          1           2
            3609          2           2
            3626          3           2
             432          4           2
```

Myth: Adding and dropping a disk in the same diskgroup requires two separate rebalance activities.

In fact, some disks can be dropped and others added to a diskgroup with a single rebalance command. This is more efficient than separate commands.

NOTE
It is commonly believed that adding and dropping a disk against the same diskgroup requires two separate rebalance activities. In fact, disks can be dropped and then added and a single rebalance command can evenly distribute the I/O.

ASM and Storage Array Migration

One of the core benefits of ASM is the ability to not only rebalance extents within disk enclosure frames (storage arrays) but also across frames. Customers have used this ability extensively when migrating between storage arrays (for example, between an older EMC 8830 to the DMX-3 storage systems) or between storage vendors (for example, from EMC arrays to Hitachi Data Systems [HDS] arrays).

The following example illustrates the simplicity of this migration. In this example, the DATA diskgroup will migrate from an old EMC Symmetrix 8830 storage enclosure to the new EMC DMX-3 enclosure. A requirement for this type of storage migration is that both storage enclosures must be attached to the host during the migration and must be discovered by ASM. Once the rebalance is completed and all the data are moved from the old frame, the old frame can be "unzoned" and "uncabled" from the host(s).

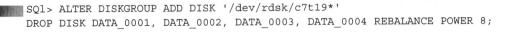

```
SQl> ALTER DISKGROUP ADD DISK '/dev/rdsk/c7t19*'
DROP DISK DATA_0001, DATA_0002, DATA_0003, DATA_0004 REBALANCE POWER 8;
```

This command indicates that the disks `DATA_0001` through `DATA_0004` (from the current EMC 8830 disks) are to be dropped, and that the new DMX-3 disks, specified by `'/dev/rdsk/c7t19*`, are to be added. The `ADD` and `DROP` commands can all be done in one rebalance operation. Additionally, the RDBMS instance can stay online while the rebalance is in progress. Note that migration to new storage is an exception to the general rule against mixing different size or performance disks in the same diskgroup. This mixture of disparate disks is transient; the configuration at the end of the rebalance will have disks of similar size and performance characteristics.

ASM and OS Migration

Customers often ask whether they can move between same endianness systems but different OS, while keeping the storage array the same. For example, suppose that a customer wants to migrate from Solaris to AIX, with the database on ASM over an EMC Clariion storage array network (SAN). The storage will be kept intact and physically reattached to the AIX server. Customers ask whether this migration is viable and/or supported.

Although ASM data structures are compatible with most OSs (except for endianness) and should not have a problem, other factors preclude this from working. In particular, the OS LUN partition has its own OS partition table format. It is unlikely that this partition table can be moved between different OSs.

Additionally, the database files themselves may have other issues, such as platform-specific structures and formats, and thus the database data will need to be converted to the target platform's format. Some viable options include the following:

- Data pump full export/import
- Cross-platform transportable tablespaces (XTTSs)
- Streams

Important Points on ASM Rebalance

The following are some important points on rebalance and extent distribution:

- It is very important that similarly sized disks be used in a single diskgroup, and that failure groups should also be of similar sizes. The use of dissimilar disks will cause uneven extent distribution and I/O load. If one disk lacks free space, it is impossible to do any allocation in a diskgroup because every file must be evenly allocated across all disks. Rebalancing and allocation should make the percentage of allocated space about the same on every disk.

- Rebalance runs automatically only when there is a diskgroup configuration change. Many users have the misconception that ASM periodically wakes up to perform rebalance. This simply is not true.

- If you are using similarly sized disks and you still see diskgroup imbalance, then either a previous rebalance operation failed to complete or was cancelled, or the administrator set the rebalance power to zero via a rebalance command. A manual rebalance should fix these cases.

- If a server goes down while executing a rebalance, the rebalance will be automatically restarted after ASM instance/crash recovery. A persistently stored record indicates the need for a rebalance. The node that does the recovery sees the record indicating that a rebalance is in progress and that the rebalance was running on the instance that died. It will then start a new rebalance. The recovering node may be different from the node that initiated the rebalance.

- Many factors determine the speed of rebalance. Most importantly, it depends on the underlying I/O subsystem. To calculate the lower bound of the time required for the rebalance to complete, determine the following:

  1. Calculate amount of data that has to be moved. ASM relocates data proportional to the amount of space being added. If you are doubling the size of the diskgroup, then 50 percent of the data will be moved; if you are adding 10 percent more storage, then approximately 10 percent of the data will move; and so on.

  2. Determine how long it will take the I/O subsystem to perform that amount of data movement. As described previously, ASM does relocation I/Os as a synchronous 1MB read followed by a synchronous 1MB write. Up to 11 I/Os can operate in parallel depending on the rebalance power. This calculation is a lower bound, because ASM has additional synchronization overhead.

  3. The impact of rebalance should be low, since ASM relocates and locks extents one at a time. ASM relocates multiple extents simultaneously only if rebalance is running with multiple processes—that is, if a higher power level is set. Only the I/Os against the extents being relocated are blocked; ASM does not block I/Os for all files in the ASM diskgroup. I/Os are not actually blocked per se; reads can proceed from the old location during relocation, whereas some writes need to be temporarily stalled or may need to be reissued if they were in process during the relocation I/O. The writes to these extents can be completed after the extent is moved to its new location. All this activity is transparent to the application. Note that the chance of an I/O being issued during the time that an extent is locked is very small. In the case of the Flash diskgroup, which contains archive logs or backups, many of the files being relocated will not even be open at the time, so the impact is very minimal.

■ When a rebalance is started for newly added disks, ASM immediately begins using the free space on them; however, ASM continues to allocate files evenly across all disks. If a diskgroup is almost full, and a large disk (or set of disks) was then added, the RDBMS could get out-of-space (ORA-15041) errors even though there is seemingly sufficient space in the diskgroup. With the `WAIT` option to the `ADD DISK` command, control does not return to the user until rebalance is complete. This may provide more intuitive behavior to customers who run near capacity.

■ If disks are added very frequently, the same data are relocated many times, causing excessive data movement. It is a best practice to add and drop multiple disks at a time so that ASM can reorganize partnership information within ASM metadata more efficiently. For normal- and high-redundancy diskgroups, it is very important to batch the add and drop disks rather than doing them in rapid succession. The latter option generates much more overhead as mirroring and failure groups place greater constraints on where data can be placed. In extreme cases, nesting many adds and drops without allowing the intervening rebalance to run to completion can lead to the error ORA-15074.

Summary

Every ASM disk is divided into fixed size allocation units. The AU is the fundamental unit of allocation within a diskgroup, and the usable space in an ASM disk is a multiple of this size. The AU size is a diskgroup attribute specified at diskgroup creation and defaults to 1MB, but may be set as high as 64MB. An AU should be large enough that accessing it in one I/O operation provides very good throughput—that is, the time to access an entire AU in one I/O should be dominated by the transfer rate of the disk rather than the time to seek to the beginning of the AU.

ASM spreads the extents of a file evenly across all disks in a diskgroup. Each extent comprises an integral number of AUs. Most files use coarse striping. With coarse striping, in each set of extents, the file is striped across the set at one AU granularity. Thus each stripe of data in a file is on a different disk than the previous stripe of the file. A file may have fine-grained striping rather than coarse. The difference is that the fine-grained striping granularity is 128K rather than one AU.

Rebalancing a diskgroup moves file extents between disks in the diskgroup to ensure that every file is evenly distributed across all the disks in the diskgroup. When all files are evenly distributed, then all disks are evenly filled to the same percentage. This ensures load balancing. Rebalancing does not relocate data based on I/O statistics nor is it started as a result of statistics. ASM automatically invokes rebalance only when a storage configuration change is made to an ASM diskgroup.

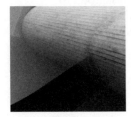

CHAPTER

6

ASMLIB Concepts and Overview

arly in the design of ASM, Oracle decided that an alternative to the standard operating system interface for device management, disk discovery, and provisioning was considered necessary and that this mechanism needed to be easily integrated into ASM. The core concept was to produce a storage management interface API, called ASMLIB. This API enables storage and operating system (OS) vendors to supply a plug-in library to extend the vendors' storage-related features and exploit their storage array strengths and capabilities. ASMLIB is not required to run ASM; it is simply an add-on module that simplifies the management and discovery of ASM disks.

This chapter covers the generic API components and their corresponding benefits. The first few sections cover the basics of the API. Note that these sections do not discuss an implementation of the API, but rather provide an overview of the potential capabilities of the API. The last section covers the implementation and configuration of Oracle ASMLIB, which is Oracle's own implementation of the ASMLIB API on Linux.

Benefits of ASMLIB

The objective of ASMLIB is to provide a more efficient mechanism for managing disks and input/output (I/O) processing of ASM storage. The ASMLIB API provides a set of interdependent functions that need to be implemented in a layered fashion. These functions are dependent on the back-end storage implementing the associated functions. From an implementation perspective, these functions are grouped into three collections of functions:

- Device discovery

- I/O processing

- Performance and reliability

As illustrated in Figure 6-1, each function group is dependent on the existence of the lower-level group. For example, device discovery functions are the lowest-layer functions and must be implemented in any ASMLIB library.

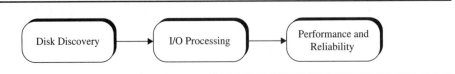

FIGURE 6-1. *ASMLIB Functional Dependencies*

Device Discovery

Device discovery identifies and names the storage devices that are operated on by higher-level functions. This function does not require any operating system code and can be implemented as a standalone library invoked and dynamically loaded by the Oracle database. The discovery function makes the characteristics of the disk available to ASM. Disks discovered through ASMLIB do not need to be available through normal operating system interfaces. For example, storage vendors may provide a more efficient method of discovering and locating disks that their own interface driver manages.

The device discovery function takes a discovery string as input from the user and then performs a disk discovery. The output from this procedure is a set of all qualified disks. In a Real Application Clusters (RAC) environment, the discover procedure executes the discovery function in the node in which the procedure was issued.

The implementer of ASMLIB generally dictates the syntax of the discovery string. The syntax could be something similar to glob on Unix or it could be more customized to the ASMLIB implementation. When implementing the discovery function, a storage or OS vendor enables the ASM administrator to specify storage devices used by ASM with attributes specific to their particular storage architecture. For example, an Oracle storage partner, such as EMC or Hewlett-Packard, could provide an ASMLIB with a discovery function enabling the ASM administrator to specify disks for database use that reside in a particular storage cabinet. The ASM administrator specifies the vendor cabinet and disks using the vendor's nomenclature rather than generic operating system names. The benefit is a tighter integration between the database and the storage hardware.

Disk Management and Discovery

ASMLIB automatically takes the ASM disk name from the name that the ASMLIB administrative tool provides. This simplifies adding disks and correlating OS names with ASM names; also, because disks are prenamed, it eliminates erroneous disk management activities. The user can manually change the name by using the NAME clause while issuing a CREATE DISKGROUP or ADD DISK statement. The default discovery string for ASM is NULL, so with ASMLIB in place, all disks are automatically discovered if NULL is kept as the discovery string. Because the user does not even need to modify the ASM_DISKSTRING, this makes disk discovery much more straightforward.

The ASMLIB permissions are persistent across reboot and in the event of major/ minor number changes, ASMLIB will continue to find its labeled disks. In RAC environments, the disk identification and discovery process is similar to that of a single-instance environment. Once the disks are labeled on one node, the other clustered nodes simply use the default disk discovery string, and discovery is seamless.

I/O Processing

The current standard I/O model imposes OS central processing unit (CPU) overhead partly because of mode and context switches. The deployment of ASMLIB reduces the number of state transitions from kernel-to-user mode by employing a more efficient I/O scheduling and call processing mechanism. A single call to ASMLIB can submit and reap multiple I/Os. This dramatically reduces the number of calls to the operating system when performing I/O. Additionally, all the processes in an instance can use one I/O handle to access the same disk. This eliminates multiple open calls and multiple file descriptors.

I/O processing functions provide an optimized asynchronous interface for scheduling I/O operations and managing I/O operation completion events. These functions, in effect, extend the operating system interface. Consequently, the I/O processing functions must be implemented as a device driver within the operating system kernel.

Future developments by Oracle storage partners, in storage array firmware may allow the transport of database-related metadata to back-end storage devices, which will then be capable of new database-related intelligence.

Reduced Overhead

ASMLIB provides the capability for a process (RBAL) to perform a global open/close on the disks that are being dropped or closed. Every file and device currently open on the system has an open file descriptor, and the system has a finite number (defined at the system level) of these file descriptors. ASMLIB reduces the number of open file descriptors on the system, thus making it less likely that the system will run out of global file descriptors. Also, the open and close operations are reduced, ensuring orderly cleanup of file descriptors when storage configurations change. A side benefit of this capability is that the database starts up faster. Without ASMLIB, file descriptors often cannot be cleaned up for dropped disks until ASM instances are shut down. This is because idle database foreground processes, which have open file descriptors, never get around to closing file descriptors.

Performance and Reliability

The highest-layer functions are the performance and reliability functions, which depend on the existence of the I/O processing functions. The performance and reliability functions use the I/O processing control structures for passing metadata between the Oracle database and the back-end storage devices. They enable additional intelligence on the part of back-end storage. This additional intelligence is achieved when metadata transfer is passed through the ASMLIB API.

Oracle's ASMLIB Implementation

After the ASMLIB API announcement, Oracle produced its own ASMLIB library, called (oddly enough) the Oracle ASMLIB. This implementation of ASMLIB, which is specifically for the Linux platform, makes it easier to manage a clustered pool of storage.

ASMLIB performance benefits are evident when the CPU usage on the server is very high (85 to 90 percent); this is when ASMLIB's reduced context switches and efficient reaping of I/Os really help to minimize CPU overhead. Also, for very big databases with a large number of open data files, ASMLIB efficiently handles file descriptors and thus reduces the number of open file descriptors on the system, making it less likely to run out of global file descriptors. Also, the open and close operations are reduced, ensuring orderly cleanup of file descriptors when the storage configuration changes.

Although it helps reduce CPU overhead, ASMLIB is foremost a device management tool used to simplify ASM disk administration.

Oracle ASMLIB Installation

Oracle's ASMLIB software is available from the Oracle Technology Network (OTN) at http://otn.oracle.com. Users are encouraged to go to the ASMLIB site to download the appropriate Linux rpm files for their platform.

The Oracle ASMLIB implements three key components of the generic ASMLIB API:

- Device discovery

- Performance management

- I/O management

NOTE
Oracle's ASMLIB does not use the kernel asynchronous (async) I/O calls, such as the standard `io_submit(2)` *or* `io_getevents(2)` *system calls. In fact, it does not use* `kioctx` *types at all. ASMLIB uses the interface provided by the ASMLIB kernel driver. Async I/O is automatically used with ASMLIB.*

Three ASMLIB packages are available for each Linux platform. For example, the following three packages are for the Intel IA32 (x86) architecture:

- oracleasm-support-2.0.3-1.i386.rpm

- oracleASMLIB-2.0.2-1.i386.rpm

- oracleasm-2.6.9-42.0.3.ELsmp-2.0.3-1.i686.rpm

The core ASM library is in the oracleASMLIB package. The command-line utilities are part of the oracleasm-support package. The last rpm listed is the kernel driver and is kernel-dependent. Choose the correct kernel driver rpm based on the Linux uname -a command on the system to be installed. For example, if the OS is Red Hat Enterprise Linux 4 AS and the kernel is 2.6.9-5.0.5.ELsmp, then accordingly choose the oracleasm-2.6.9-5.0.5-ELsmp package. Note that the version number listed in the ASMLIB kernel package is the Linux kernel version that was used to compile the driver.

Install the required rpm files using the rpm -Uvh command. For example, if the platform is the Intel IA32 (x86) architecture and the kernel is 2.6.9-42.0.3.EL, then the following would need to be installed:

```
[root@racnode1]# rpm -Uvh oracleasm-support-2.0.3-1.i386.rpm \
oracleasmlib-2.0.2-1.i386.rpm \
oracleasm-2.6.9-42.0.3.ELsmp-2.0.3-1.i686.rpm
```

Installing ASMLIB for Unbreakable Linux Network

For systems registered with Oracle's Unbreakable Linux Network (ULN), all the ASMLIB software can be downloaded directly from ULN. This greatly simplifies ASMLIB installation and upgrades.

The oracleASMLIB rpm is part of the Oracle Software for Enterprise Linux channel. A system must be added to this channel to install the library package. This requires that users log in at the ULN website, https://linux.oracle.com, and select the Systems tag. This brings up a list of systems registered with ULN. Select the system that will install the ASMLIB package, then select the Subscribe button under the Oracle Software for Enterprise Linux link. The system is now able to download the ASMLIB rpm.

Once the system is registered with ULN, it can install the software. Log in as root and run the following:

```
# up2date -i oracleasm-support oracleasmlib oracleasm-`uname -r`
```

This command installs the following packages:

- ASMLIB support tools

- The ASMLIB library

- The ASMLIB kernel driver for the currently running kernel

Registration automatically downloads (and optionally installs) the new upgrade versions of all the ASMLIB packages via the up2date -u command. To upgrade the kernel, make sure to install the matching ASMLIB kernel driver as well, using the following:

```
# up2date -i kernel-smp-2.6.9-100.EL oracleasm-2.6.9-100.ELsmp
```

Setting Up and Configuring ASMLIB

Once the appropriate Linux rpm files are installed, the ASMLIB installation installs a utility in the /etc/init.d directory called oracleasm. This utility is the front-end tool used to perform all device management activities.

The next step is to set up and configure ASMLIB. Typically a system administrator with root access performs this step.

Execute the /etc/init.d/oracleasm script with the configure option. This sets up and configures ASMLIB for the system. You must execute this command on each node of RAC cluster. In our example, the database is running as the oracle user and the oinstall group:

```
[root@racnode1]#/etc/init.d/oracleasm configure
Configuring the Oracle ASM library driver.
This will configure the on-boot properties of the Oracle ASM library
driver. The following questions will determine whether the driver is
loaded on boot and what permissions it will have. The current values
will be shown in brackets ('[]'). Hitting without typing an answer will
keep that current value. Ctrl-C will abort.
Default user to own the driver interface: oracle
Default group to own the driver interface []: oinstall
Start Oracle ASM library driver on boot (y/n) [n]: y
Fix permissions of Oracle ASM disks on boot (y/n) [y]: y
Writing Oracle ASM library driver configuration [ OK ]: OK
Creating /dev/oracleasm
mount point [ OK ]
 Loading module "oracleasm" [ OK ]
 Mounting ASMLIB driver filesystem [ OK ]
 Scanning system for ASM disks [ OK ]
```

At the end of this configuration a virtual filesystem (specific to ASMLIB) called /dev/oraclesasm is created and mounted. This filesystem has two subdirectories called disks and iid. The disks subdirectory lists the ASMLIB scanned and present on the system. The configuration should load the oracleasm.o driver module and mount the ASM driver filesystem, since the on-boot load of the module was selected during the configuration.

Now that ASMLIB is installed, the automatic startup of ASMLIB can be enabled or disabled manually with the enable and disable options. Using the /etc/init.d/ oracleasm utility, the process runs as follows:

```
[root@racnode1]#/etc/init.d/oracleasm enable
 Writing Oracle ASM library driver configuration [ OK ]
 Loading module "oracleasm" [ OK ]
 Mounting ASMLIB driver filesystem [ OK ]
 Scanning system for ASM disks [ OK ]
```

Managing Disks in ASMLIB

After the storage administrator provides disk devices to the server, it becomes available to the server and can be seen in /proc/partitions virtual file on Linux. The system administrator then partitions this disk device using the Linux fdisk utility. The disk device is now ready to be configured as an ASMLIB disk—that is, the system administrator creates an ASMLIB disk. The administrator does this using the `oracleasm createdisk` command. The `createdisk` command takes two input parameters, the user-defined disk name followed by the device name, as follows:

```
[root@racnode1]#/etc/init.d/oracleasm createdisk VOL1 /dev/sdg1
Creating Oracle ASM disk "VOL1" [ OK ]
```

Disk names are limited to 30 characters. They must start with a letter but may otherwise consist of any ASCII characters, including capital letters, numbers, and underscores.

Each disk successfully created is considered a *marked* ASMLIB disk and is listed in the oracleasm filesystem, /dev/oracleasm/disks. This filesystem is a special one that should not be manipulated in any way.

The user can query disk devices to determine whether they are valid ASMLIB disks. To do so, use the following `oracleasm querydisk` commands. The `querydisk` command is applicable to both the raw device and the ASMLIB disk.

```
[root@racnode1]#/etc/init.d/oracleasm querydisk /dev/sdg1
  Checking if device "/dev/sdg" is an Oracle ASM disk [ OK ]

[root@racnode1]#/etc/init.d/oracleasm querydisk VOL1
  Checking for ASM disk "VOL1" [ OK ]
```

Alternatively, all the disks marked and created using ASMLIB can be listed using the following `oracleasm listdisks` command:

```
[root@racnode1]#/etc/init.d/oracleasm listdisks
  VOL1
  VOL2
  VOL3
```

If a disk device is not an ASMLIB, the following is displayed:

```
[root@racnode1]#/etc/init.d/oracleasm querydisk /dev/sdh1
  Checking if device "/dev/sdh1" is an Oracle ASM disk [FAILED]
```

Disks that are no longer needed by ASM can be unmarked and deleted using the `oracleasm deletedisk` command:

```
[root@racnode1]#/etc/init.d/oracleasm deletedisk VOL1
  Deleting Oracle ASM disk "VOL1" [ OK ]
```

When ASMLIB is deployed in an RAC environment, the shared disk architecture of RAC allows the `createdisk` command to be run on only one node; all other nodes of the RAC cluster simply need to pick up the disk list via an ASMLIB scan. For example, in a two-node RAC cluster, node 1 can mark an ASMLIB disk, whereas node 2 can then execute a scan of the ASMLIB disks to discover the marked ASMLIB disks. This process mitigates the need to discover and set up the disks manually on each node and provides each disk with a unique clusterwide name.

```
[root@racnode1]#/etc/init.d/oracleasm createdisk VOL1 /dev/sdg1
Creating Oracle ASM disk "VOL1" [ OK ]
[root@racnode2]#/etc/init.d/oracleasm scandisks
 Scanning system for ASM disks [ OK ]
```

After the appropriate ASMLIB disks are created, the ASM `init.ora` parameter `ASM_DISKSTRING` can either be left with the default (NULL) or it can be set to `'ORCL:*'`. Once this is set, ASM will discover the disks as follows:

```
SQL> SELECT NAME, LIBRARY, PATH FROM V$ASM_DISK;
 NAME            LIBRARY                         PATH
 ----------- -------------------------- ------------------------
 VOL1            ASM Library Generic Linux     ORCL:VOL1
 VOL2            ASM Library Generic Linux     ORCL:VOL2
 VOL3            ASM Library Generic Linux     ORCL:VOL3
```

Note that if ASMLIB is not being used, then the preceding query returns "System" under the LIBRARY column. See the "Troubleshooting" section of this chapter for more details.

Renaming Disks

The `renamedisk` command is used for changing the label of an existing member without losing data. Note that the modification of the disk must be done while ASM is not accessing the disk. Therefore, the diskgroup must be dismounted, and in an RAC environment, all ASM nodes in the cluster must have dismounted the diskgroup as well. Corruption may result if a `renamedisk` operation is done while any ASM instance is accessing the disk to be relabeled. Because this `renamedisk` command is dangerous, ASM indicates this by printing out a gentle message after the command is executed:

```
[root@racnode1]#/etc/init.d/oracleasm renamedisk /dev/sdb3   VOL1

Warning: Changing the label of a disk marked for ASM is a very
dangerous operation. If this is really what you mean to do, you
must ensure that all Oracle and ASM instances have ceased using
this disk. Otherwise, you may LOSE DATA. If you really wish to
change the label, rerun with the force-renamedisk command.

[root@racnode1]#/etc/init.d/oracleasm force-renamedisk /dev/sdb3 VOL1
Renaming disk "/dev/sdb3" to "VOL1" [ OK ]
```

The `force-renamedisk` command takes two parameters: the raw device name followed by the ASM disk name.

Discovering Disks

The command `/sbin/oracleasm-discover` is a simple utility that determines which devices Oracle's Linux ASMLIB sees during discovery. This command is more of debugging tool to validate that the discovery is listing all the required disks. This command also lists the maximum I/O size *(maxio)* per disk—that is, the maximum I/O, in sectors, that ASMLIB can send to the device as one command.

```
[root@racnode1]#/usr/sbin/oracleasm-discover 'ORCL:*'
Using ASMLib from /opt/oracle/extapi/32/asm/orcl/1/libasm.so
[ASM Library - Generic Linux, version 2.0.0 (KABI_V1)]
Discovered disk: ORCL:VOL1 [819200 blocks (419430400 bytes), maxio 512]
Discovered disk: ORCL:VOL2 [1955808 blocks (1001373696 bytes), maxio 512]
```

The maximum I/O size comes from the small computer system interface (SCSI) host bus adapter (HBA) driver and anything else in the disk device chain. In the preceding case, maxio equals 512—that is, 512 byte sectors, or 256K. If maxio shows low values, such as 128, then it is possible that intermediary components, such as multipathing drivers or HBA drivers, may be the limiting factor.

Upgrading ASMLIB

To upgrade ASMLIB, the system administrator can take the following steps. Note that this is strictly a software upgrade and no disk labels are manipulated. Also, this is a node local upgrade, so, as in an RAC/environment, each individual node should be upgraded.

1. Shut down ASM.

2. Execute `/etc/init.d/oracleasm stop`.

3. Execute `rpm -Uvh oracleasm-*.rpm`.

4. Execute `/etc/init.d/oracleasm start`.

5. Start up ASM.

Troubleshooting ASMLIB

The following checklist is intended to be a top-down list of items to review and validate that ASMLIB is installed and working correctly.

1. Use the current release of Oracle ASMLIB. Verify the software versions. ASMLIB requires a driver exactly matching the running kernel, thus matching the oracleasm kernel package with the output of the `uname -a` command:

```
[root@racnode1]# rpm -qa |grep oracleasm
oracleasm-support-2.0.3-1.i386.rpm
oracleasmlib-2.0.2-1.i386.rpm
oracleasm-2.6.9-42.0.3.ELsmp-2.0.3-1.i686.rpm
[root@racnode1]# uname -a
Linux racnode1.us.oracle.com 2.6.9-42.0.3.ELsmp #1Thu May 15
17:03:45 EST 2006 i686 i686 i386 GNU/Linux
```

2. Verify the ASMLIB installation as indicated in the installation documentation.

3. Make sure that the `oracleasm configure` command ran properly. Confirm this configuration with the following:

   a. Execute the `lsmod` command (as root) to show the loaded oracleasm module. The oracleasm module should be listed with a "Used by" column setting of 1.

```
[root@racnode1]# lsmod
Module              Size    Used by     Not tainted
ide-cd              35296   0              (autoclean)
cdrom               35520   0           (autoclean) [ide-cd]
soundcore            7940   0           (autoclean)
oracleasm           16384   1
cpqfc               53376   1
autofs              13796   0           (autoclean)  (unused)
eepro100            21968   2
ext3                70944   6
jbd                 55444   6              [ext3]
cpqarray            26080   10
sd_mod              13920   1
scsi_mod           126812   2              [cpqfc sd_mod]
```

   b. Execute the command `cat /proc/filesystems`, and make sure that an entry named oracleasmfs exists in this filesystem listing.

```
[oracle@racnode1]$ cat /proc/filesystems
nodev   rootfs
nodev   proc
nodev   sockfs
nodev   tmpfs
nodev   shm
nodev   pipefs
        ext2
        iso9660
nodev   devpts
nodev   pcihpfs
        ext3
        ocfs
nodev   oracleasmfs
nodev   autofs
```

   c. Execute the command `df -ha`. This should show you that oracleasmfs
   is mounted on /dev/oracleasm:

```
[oracle@racnode1]$ df -ha
Filesystem       Size  Used   Avail Use%  Mounted on
/dev/ida/c0d0p1  5.0G  1.6G   3.2G  32%   /
none             0     0      0     -     /proc
none             0     0      0     -     /dev/pts
oracleasmfs      0     0      0     -     /dev/oracleasm
```

   Make sure that `oracleasm createdisk` was properly run for the
   candidate disks. To be used for ASM, a disk must be marked by the
   `createdisk` command. When a disk is "marked," a signature is written
   to the header of the disk—that is, the disk is stamped for ASM use. You
   can validate this by using the following commands:

   - Execute the `oracleasm listdisks` command. This command
     displays marked ASMLIB disks. This command will list all marked disks.

   - Execute the `oracleasm querydisk` command for each disk marked
     to ensure that each is marked.

4. Execute `ls -l /dev/oracleasm/disks` to ensure the ownership and
   permissions are `oracle:oinstall` (or whatever was used in the `configure`
   command) for each disk name that was created using the `oracleasm`
   `createdisk` command:

```
[oracle@racnode1]$ ls -l /dev/oracleasm/disks
total 0
brw-rw----   1 oracle   oinstall   8,   32 Apr  9 16:09 VOL1
brw-rw----   1 oracle   oinstall   8,   48 Apr  9 16:09 VOL2
brw-rw----   1 oracle   oinstall   8,   64 Apr  9 16:09 VOL3
brw-rw----   1 oracle   oinstall   8,   80 Apr  9 16:10 VOL4
```

5. Verify that the ASMLIB discovery string (either at the Database Configuration
   Assistant [DBCA] prompt or in the ASM `init.ora` `ASM_DISKSTRING`
   parameter) is set to ORCL:* or to NULL. Also, if the ASM instance is active,
   then check the ASM alert log to see whether the correct string is being used.

6. Use the Unix `grep` command against the ASM alert log to see whether
   ASM is displaying any messages regarding discovery. A successfully loaded
   ASMLIB will display the following general message (depending on the
   version):

```
Loaded ASM Library - Generic Linux, version 2.0.1 library for
ASMLIB interface
```

The following query shows disks that ASMLIB properly discovered:

```
SQL> SELECT LIBRARY, PATH FROM V$ASM_DISK;

LIBRARY                                       PATH
----------------------------------------- ----------------
ASM Library - Generic Linux, version 2.0.0.1  ORCL:VOL1
ASM Library - Generic Linux, version 2.0.0.1  ORCL:VOL2
ASM Library - Generic Linux, version 2.0.0.1  ORCL:VOL3
```

NOTE
If the query shows SYSTEM under the Library column, then the ASM_DISKSTRING is not set correctly—that is, ASMLIB is not used to access the disks. ASMLIB needs to access the disks through the diskstring ORCL:. Check ASM_DISKSTRING and verify that it is set to ORCL:* or to NULL:*

```
SQL> SELECT LIBRARY, PATH FROM V$ASM_DISK;

LIBRARY          PATH
--------------   --------------------------------------------------
System           /dev/oracleasm/disks/DATA1D1
System           /dev/oracleasm/disks/DATA1D2
System           /dev/oracleasm/disks/DATA1D3
```

7. Watch for the following error message in the ASM alert log:

```
ORA-15186: ASMLIB error function = [asm_open],  error = [1],
mesg = [Operation not permitted]
```

This message usually means that the ASMLIB configuration permissions were incorrectly specified during the /etc/init.d/oracleasm configure stage.

Migrating to ASMLIB

There may be cases where you need to convert a "member" ASM raw disk to an ASMLIB disk; for example, you may need to do so when installing ASMLIB after ASM is in place. Conversely, if you're deinstalling ASMLIB, you can convert an ASMLIB disk to a standard ASM disk. All this can be done without destroying the data on the disk. However, the diskgroup must be dismounted before the conversion, as ASM cannot be actively using the disk.

This conversion works without destroying data because of the structures on the disk and what ASM reads on disk open. ASM reads the header off of the disk and recognizes the diskgroup to which it belongs. When a disk is added to a diskgroup,

ASM writes several things on disk. Two of the most important items are the disk marker (or tag) and the ASMLIB label. All ASM disks have the tag ORCLDISK stamped on them. If the tag already exists, then the disk is either currently or was formerly in use by ASM. This tag can be created by ASM or ASMLIB. For example, when ASM initially uses a disk as a raw device via diskgroup creation, ASM automatically adds the tag. Conversely, ASMLIB adds this tag when a disk is configured by the ASMLIB command /etc/init.d/oracleasm createdisk. Regardless of which tool creates the tag, once this tag is added, the disk is considered "marked."

The second part of the disk header that is relevant to ASMLIB is the ASMLIB label. This string of 24 characters allotted for ASMLIB is used to identify the disk. When the disk is configured by ASMLIB using the /etc/init.d/oracleasm createdisk command, the associated label is written to the device. Note that ASM preserves the disk's contents, but it does write to this section reserved for ASMLIB.

The following is a sample dump of an ASM disk (without ASMLIB) that was incorporated into a diskgroup. Notice the ASM disk name in the header, DATA_0002:

```
[root@racnode1]# dd if=/dev/asmdisk17 bs=128 count=1 |od -a
0000000 soh stx soh soh nul nul nul nul stx nul nul nul   : stx   " dc4
0000020 nul nul nul nul nul nul nul nul nul nul nul nul nul nul nul nul
0000040   O   R   C   L   D   I   S   K nul nul nul nul nul nul nul nul
0000060 nul nul nul nul nul nul nul nul nul nul nul nul nul nul nul nul
0000100 nul nul dle  nl stx nul soh etx   D   A   T   A   _   0   0   0
0000120   2 nul nul nul nul nul nul nul nul nul nul nul nul nul nul nul
0000140 nul nul nul nul nul nul nul nul   D   A   T   A nul nul nul nul
```

The following is a sample dump of an ASMLIB disk created using the following /etc/init.d/oracleasm createdisk command. Notice that VOL1 is appended to the ORCLDISK label:

```
[root@racnode1]# /etc/init.d/oracleasm createdisk VOL1 /dev/sdc3
Dump of disk header after ASMLIB, via oracleasm createdisk VOL1 /dev/asmdisk26.
[usupport@jfrac2 bin]$ dd if=/dev/asmdisk26 bs=128 count=1 |od -a
0000000 nul nul nul nul nul nul nul nul nul nul nul nul   V   O   N   5
0000020 nul nul nul nul nul nul nul nul nul nul nul nul nul nul nul nul
0000040   O   R   C   L   D   I   S   K   V   O   L   1 nul nul nul nul
0000060 nul nul nul nul nul nul nul nul nul nul nul nul nul nul nul nul
0000100 nul nul dle  nl stx nul soh etx   D   A   T   A   _   0   0   0
0000120   2 nul nul nul nul nul nul nul nul nul nul nul nul nul nul nul
0000140 nul nul nul nul nul nul nul nul   D   A   T   A nul nul nul nul
```

In this example, the tag ORCLDISK and the label VOL1 are stamped to the disk. The next time that ASMLIB scans for disks, it will see the tag ORCLDISK and the label VOL1 and create an ASMLIB disk-to-device mapping using the name VOL1. Subsequently, ASM will discover this disk via ASMLIB driver. If the disk were not initially managed by ASMLIB—that is, if it were instead managed by ASM's raw device (non-ASMLIB) access—then when ASM discovers the disk, it detects that no ASMLIB label exists, it then bypasses this section of the header and opens the device as native (non-ASMLIB) ASM disk. This is why a disk can move from ASMLIB access to raw device access with no problems.

Using ASMLIB and Multipathing Utilities

As was stated in the chapters on ASM Disks and ASM concepts, multipathing drivers generally virtualize subpaths using pseudo devices. During disk discovery, ASMLIB uses the pseudo file /proc/partitions. This is a Linux file that records all the devices and partitions presented to the machine. To function correctly with multipathing, ASMLIB must operate only on the pseudo devices. Thus behavior of the ASMLIB discovery must be altered to leverage the pseudo devices. You can configure this behavior in file /etc/sysconfig/oracleasm by changing two parameters:

- ORACLEASM_SCANORDER dictates the ASMLIB scan order of the devices, using the generic prefix.

- ORACLEASM_SCANEXCLUDE indicates which devices should not be discovered by ASMLIB.

For example, if you are configuring ASMLIB with EMC's PowerPath, you can use the following setup:

```
ORACLEASM_SCANEXCLUDE=sd
ORACLEASM_SCANORDER=emcpower
```

In this example, ASMLIB scans disks identified under /dev/emcpower* and excludes all the devices /dev/sd*. Please consult your multipathing vendor for details and support matrix.

The following is an example of an /etc/sysconfig/oracleasm file:

```
# This is a configuration file for automatic loading of the Oracle
# Automatic Storage Management library kernel driver.  It is generated
# By running /etc/init.d/oracleasm configure.  Please use that method
#to modify this file
# ORACLEASM_ENABELED: 'true' means to load the driver on boot.
ORACLEASM_ENABLED=true
#
# ORACLEASM_UID: Default user owning the /dev/oracleasm mount point.
ORACLEASM_UID=oracle
#
# ORACLEASM_GID: Default group owning the /dev/oracleasm mount point.
ORACLEASM_GID=dba
#
```

```
# ORACLEASM_SCANBOOT: 'true' means fix disk perms on boot
ORACLEASM_SCANBOOT=true
#
# ORACLEASM_CLEARBOOT: 'true' means clean old disk perms on boot
ORACLEASM_CLEARBOOT=true
#
# ORACLEASM_SCANORDER: Matching patterns to order disk scanning
ORACLEASM_SCANORDER=
```

Summary

ASMLIB is the support library for the ASM feature of Oracle Database 10*g* and Oracle Database 11*g*. ASMLIB allows an Oracle database using ASM more efficient and capable access to diskgroups. The purpose of ASMLIB, which is an add-on to ASM, is to provide an alternative interface to identify and access block devices. Additionally, the ASMLIB API enables storage and operating system vendors to supply extended storage-related features. These features could provide benefits such as improved performance and greater integrity.

CHAPTER
7

ASM Files, Aliases,
and Templates

hen an ASM diskgroup is created, a hierarchical filesystem structure is created. This hierarchical layout is very similar to the Unix or Windows filesystem hierarchy. ASM files, stored within this filesystem structure, are the objects that RDBMS instances access. They come in the form of datafiles, controlfiles, Spfiles, and redo log files, and several other file types. The RDBMS treats ASM-based database files just like standard filesystem files.

ASM Filenames

When you create a database file using the `create tablespace`, `add datafile`, or `add logfile` commands, or even an archive logfile creation, ASM explicitly creates the ASM file in the diskgroup specified, as in the following example:

```
SQL> CREATE TABLESPACE ISHAN DATAFILE '+DATA' SIZE 10GB;
```

This command creates a datafile in the DATA diskgroup. ASM filenames are derived and generated upon the successful creation of a datafile. Once the file is created, the file becomes visible to the user via the standard RDBMS views, such as the V$DATAFILE view. Note that the ASM filename syntax is different from that of the typical naming standards; ASM filenames are in the following format:

+diskgroup_name/database_name/database file type/tag_name.file_number.incarnation

For example, the ASM filename of *+DATA/yoda/datafile/ishan.259 .616618501* for the tablespace named ISHAN can be dissected as follows:

- **+DATA**   This is the name of the diskgroup name where this file was created.

- **yoda**   This specifies the name of the database that contains this file.

- **datafile**   This is the database file type—in this case, *datafile*. There are over 20 file types in Oracle 11*g*. The table at the end of this chapter lists the various tag names and file types.

- **ISHAN.259.616618501**   This portion of the filename is the suffix of the full filename, and is composed of the tag name, file number and incarnation number. The tag name in the datafile name corresponds to the tablespace name. In this example the tag is the tablespace named ISHAN. For redo logfiles, the tag name is the group number; e.g., *group_3.264.54632413*. The ASM file number for the ISHAN tablespace is 259. The file number in the ASM instance can be used to correlate filenames in database instance. The incarnation number is 616618501. The incarnation number, which has been derived from a timestamp, is used to provide uniqueness. Note, that once the file has been created the incarnation number does not change. The incarnation number distinguishes between a new file that has been created using the same file number and another file that has been deleted.

For best practice, every database should implement the Oracle Managed File (OMF) feature. The objective of OMF, which was introduced in Oracle Database 9*i*, is to simplify Oracle database file administration.

Some of the key benefits OMF are:

- **Simplified Oracle file management** All files are automatically created in a default location with system-generated names, thus a consistent file standard is inherently in place.

- **Space usage optimization** Files are deleted automatically when the tablespaces are dropped.

- **Reduction of Oracle file management errors** OMF minimizes errant file creation and deletion, and also mitigates file corruption due to inadvertent file reuse.

- **Enforcement of Optimal Flexible Architecture (OFA) standards** OMF complies with the OFA standards for filename and file locations.

You can enable OMF by setting the DB_CREATE_FILE_DEST and DB_RECOVERY_FILE_DEST parameters. There are other *_DEST variables that can be used for other file types. When the DB_CREATE_FILE_DEST parameter is set to +DATA, the default file location for tablespace datafiles becomes +DATA. Moreover, you need not even specify the diskgroup location in the tablespace creation statement. In fact, when the DB_CREATE_FILE_DEST and DB_RECOVERY_FILE_DEST parameters are set, the create database command can be simplified to the following statement:

```
SQL> CREATE DATABASE;
```

You can use the following command to create a tablespace:

```
SQL> CREATE TABLESPACE ISHAN;
```

This command simply creates a datafile in the ISHAN tablespace under the +DATA diskgroup using the default datafile size of 100MB. However, this file size can be overridden and still leverage the OMF name, as in the following example:

```
SQL> CREATE TABLESPACE ISHAN DATAFILE '+DATA' SIZE 10GB;
```

> **NOTE**
> *OMF is not enabled for a file when the filename is explicitly specified in* create/alter tablespace add datafile *commands. For example, the following is not considered an OMF file because it specifies an explicit filename and path:*
> *SQL> CREATE TABLESPACE ISHAN DATAFILE '+DATA/YODA/ISHAN_01.DBF';*
> *However, the following is considered an OMF file:*
> *SQL> CREATE TABLESPACE ISHAN DATAFILE '+DATA';*

The following listing shows the relationship between the RDBMS files and the ASM file. Note that the file number from V$ASM_FILE is embedded in the filename.

The first query is executed from the ASM instance and the second query is executed from the RDBMS instance.

```
ASM_SQL> SELECT FILE_NUMBER, SUM(BYTES)/1024*1024) FROM V$ASM_FILE
GROUP BY FILE_NUMBER;

FILE_NUMBER SUM(BYTES)/(1024*1024)
----------- ----------------------
        256            360.007813
        257             35.0078125
        259             35.0078125
        261             .002441406
        262            450.007813
        263             23.0078125
        264             10.0004883
        265              5.0078125
        266             10.0004883
        267             10.0004883
        268              2.2109375
        269             23.0078125
        270             28.0078125


RDBMS_SQL> SELECT NAME FROM V$DATAFILE;
NAME
-----------------------------------------
+DATA/yoda/datafile/system.256.589462555
+DATA/yoda/datafile/sysaux.257.621507965
+DATA/yoda/datafile/undotbs1.258.621507965
+DATA/yoda/datafile/ishan.259.616618501
+DATA/yoda/datafile/undotbs2.262.621508063
+DATA/yoda/datafile/nitin.263.621507963
+DATA/yoda/datafile/kiran.269.689507964
+DATA/yoda/datafile/anya.270.689804549
/u01/oradata/yoda/nisha01.dbf
```

```
SQL> SELECT MEMBER FROM V$LOGFILE;
MEMBER
------------------------------------
+DATA/yoda/onlinelog/group_3.264.3
+DATA/yoda/onlinelog/group_2.266.3
+DATA/yoda/onlinelog/group_1.267.3
```

Observe that this database contains ASM files and a non-ASM file named NISHA01.dbf. The NISHA tablespace is stored in a Unix filesystem called /u01/oradata—that is, it is not an ASM-managed file. Because the NISHA01.dbf file is a Unix filesystem file rather than an ASM file, the ASM file list from the SQL output does not include it. This illustrates an important point: an Oracle Database 11*g* (and 10*g*) can have files that reside on filesystems, raw devices and ASM, simultaneously. However, in RAC environments they must all be on shared storage and accessible by all nodes in the cluster.

ASM Directories

ASM provides the capability to create user-defined directories using the ADD DIRECTORY clause of the ALTER DISKGROUP statement. User-defined directories can be created to support user-defined ASM aliases (discussed later). ASM directories must start with a plus sign (+) and valid diskgroup name, followed by any user-specified subdirectory names. The only restriction is that the parent directory must exist before you attempt to create a subdirectory or alias in that directory. For example, both of the following are valid ASM directories:

```
SQL> ALTER DISKGROUP DATA ADD DIRECTORY '+DATA/yoda/oradata';

ASMCMD> mkdir +DATA/yoda/oradata
```

However, the following ASM directory cannot be created because the parent directory of datafiles, *oradata,* does not exist:

```
SQL> ALTER DISKGROUP DATA ADD DIRECTORY '+DATA/oradata/datafiles';
```

Although system directories such as +DATA/yoda cannot be manipulated, user-defined directories, such as the one successfully created in the previous example, can be renamed or dropped. The following examples illustrate this:

```
SQL> ALTER DISKGROUP DATA RENAME DIRECTORY '+DATA/yoda/oradata' to
'+DATA/yoda/oradata_old';

ASMCMD> mv +DATA/yoda/oradata  +DATA/yoda/oradata_old
SQL> ALTER DISKGROUP DATA DROP DIRECTORY '+DATA/yoda/oradata;

ASMCMD> rm +DATA/yoda/oradata_old
```

ASM Aliases

The filename notation described thus far, +*diskgroup_name*/*database_name*/ *database file type*/*tag_name.file_number.incarnation*, is called the fully qualified filename notation (FQFN). ASM alias can be used to make filenaming conventions easier to remember.

Note that whenever a file is created, a system alias is also automatically created for that file. The system aliases are created in a hierarchical directory structure that takes the following syntax:

```
<db_unique_name>/<file_type>/<alias name>
```

When the files are removed, the <alias name> is deleted, but the hierarchical directory structure remains.

ASM aliases are essentially in hierarchical directory format, similar to the filesystem hierarchy (*/u01/oradata/dbname/datafile_name*), and are used to reference a system-generated filename such as +DATA/yoda/datafile/system.256.589462555.

Alias names specify a diskgroup name, but instead of using a file and incarnation number, they take a user-defined string name. Alias ASM filenames are distinguished from fully qualified or numeric names because they do not end in a dotted pair of numbers. Note that there is a limit of one alias per ASM file. The following examples show how to create an ASM alias:

```
SQL> CREATE TABLESPACE ISHAN DATAFILE '+DATA/YODA/ORADATA/ISHAN_01.DBF';
```

Note, as stated above, OMF is not enabled when file alias are explicitly specified in create/alter tablespace add datafile commands (as in the example above).

Aliases are particularly useful when dealing with controlfiles and Spfiles—that is, an ASM alias filename is normally used in the CONTROL_FILES and SPFILE initialization parameter. In following example, the SPFILE and CONTROL_FILES parameters are set to the alias, and the DB_CREATE_FILE_DEST and DB_ RECOVERY_FILE_DEST parameters are set to the appropriate OMF destinations:

```
SPFILE                  = +DATA/yoda/spfileorcl.ora
CONTROL_FILES           = +DATA/yoda/controlfile/control_01.ctl
DB_CREATE_FILE_DEST     = +DATA
DB_RECOVERY_FILE_DEST   = +FLASH
```

To show the hierarchical tree of files stored in the diskgroup, use the following connect by clause SQL to generate the full path. However, a more efficient way to browse the hierarchy is to use the ASMCMD *ls* command or Enterprise Manager. See Chapter 8 for details on the use of *ls* command.

```
SELECT CONNECT ('+'||GNAME,SYS_CONNECT_BY_PATH(ANAME, '/'))
FULL_ALIAS_PATH FROM (SELECT G.NAME GNAME, A.PARENT_INDEX PINDEX,
A.NAME ANAME, A.REFERENCE_INDEX RINDEX FROM V$ASM_ALIAS A,
V$ASM_DISKGROUP G WHERE A.GROUP_NUMBER=G.GROUP_NUMBER) START WITH
(MOD(PINDEX, POWER(2,24))) = 0 CONNECT BY PRIOR RINDEX = PINDEX;
```

```
FULL_ALIAS_PATH

---------------------------------------------------------------------

+DATA/YODA

+DATA/YODA/spfilered.ora

+DATA/YODA/CONTROLFILE

+DATA/YODA/CONTROLFILE/Current.260.629979753

+DATA/YODA/ONLINELOG

+DATA/YODA/ONLINELOG/group_1.261.629979755

+DATA/YODA/ONLINELOG/group_2.262.629979775

+DATA/YODA/ONLINELOG/group_3.265.629979903

+DATA/YODA/ONLINELOG/group_4.266.629979921

+DATA/YODA/TEMPFILE

+DATA/YODA/TEMPFILE/TEMP.263.629979811

+DATA/YODA/PARAMETERFILE

+DATA/YODA/PARAMETERFILE/spfile.267.629979939

+DATA/YODA/DATAFILE

+DATA/YODA/DATAFILE/SYSTEM.256.629979635

+DATA/YODA/DATAFILE/SYSAUX.257.629979639

+DATA/YODA/DATAFILE/UNDOTBS1.258.629979641

+DATA/YODA/DATAFILE/USERS.259.629979643

+DATA/YODA/DATAFILE/UNDOTBS2.264.629979829
```

Templates

ASM file templates are named collections of attributes applied to files during file creation. Templates are used to set file-level redundancy (mirror, high, or unprotected) and striping attributes (fine or coarse) of files created in an ASM diskgroup.

Templates simplify file creation by housing complex file attribute specifications. When a diskgroup is created, ASM establishes a set of initial system default templates associated with that disk group. These templates contain the default attributes for the various Oracle database file types. When a file is created, the redundancy and striping attributes are set for that file, where the attributes are based on the system template that is the default template for the file type or an explicitly named template.

The following query lists the ASM files, redundancy and striping size for a example database.

```
SQL> SELECT NAME, REDUNDANCY, STRIPED FROM V$ASM_ALIAS A, V$ASM_FILE B
     WHERE A.FILE_NUMBER=B.FILE_NUMBER AND A.GROUP_NUMBER=B.GROUP_NUMBER
     ORDER BY NAME;


NAME                                  REDUNDANCY STRIPE
-----------------------------------   ---------- -------
Current.260.616618829                 HIGH       FINE
EXAMPLE.264.616618877                 MIRROR     COARSE
ISHAN.259.616618501                   UNPROTECTED COARSE
NITIN.269.617736951                   MIRROR     COARSE
SYSAUX.257.616618501                  MIRROR     COARSE
SYSTEM.256.589462555                  MIRROR     COARSE
TEMP.263.616618871                    MIRROR     COARSE
KIRAN.269.689507964                   MIRROR     CORASE
ANYA.270.689804549                    MIRROR     CORASE
UNDOTBS1.258.616618501                MIRROR     COARSE
UNDOTBS2.265.616619119                MIRROR     COARSE
GROUP_1.261.616618835                 MIRROR     FINE
GROUP_2.262.616618849                 MIRROR     FINE
GROUP_3.266.616619217                 MIRROR     FINE
GROUP_4.267.616619231                 MIRROR     FINE
spfile.268.616619243                  MIRROR     COARSE
spfileorcl.ora                        MIRROR     COARSE
```

The administrator can change attributes of the default templates if required. However, system default templates cannot be deleted. Additionally, administrators can add their own unique templates, as needed. The SQL command below illustrates how to create user templates (performed on the ASM instance) and then applying this to a new tablespace datafile (performed on the RDBMS).

```
ASM_SQL> ALTER DISKGROUP DATA ADD TEMPLATE NONCRITCAL_FILES ATTRIBUTES
(UNPROTECTED);
```

Once the template is created, it can be applied when creating the new tablespace.

```
RDBMS_SQL> create tablespace ISHAN datafile
'+DATA/ishan(noncritcal_files)' size 200M;
```

Using the ALTER DISKGROUP command, you can modify a template or drop the template using the DROP TEMPLATE clause. The following commands illustrate this:

```
ASM_SQL> ALTER DISKGROUP DATA ALTER TEMPLATE NONCRITICAL_FILES ATTRIBUTES (COARSE);
ASM_SQL> ALTER DISKGROUP DATA DROP TEMPLATE NONCRITICAL_FILES;
```

If you need to change an ASM file attribute after the file has been created, the file must be copied, into a new file with the new attributes. This is the only method of changing a file's attributes. Table 7-1 lists the default templates and their characteristics.

Database File Type	ASM Default Template	ASM File Type	ASM Tag Assigned	ASM Default Striping
Archived Redo Logs	ARCHIVELOG	archive_log	thread_thread#_ seq_sequence#	coarse
Control Files	CONTROLFILE	controlfile	Current	fine
Control File Autobackups	AUTOBACKUP	autobackup	Backup	coarse
Data Files	DATAFILE	datafile	tablespace_name	coarse
Data File Backup Pieces	BACKUPSET	backupset	hasspfile_ timestamp	coarse
DataGuard Broker Configurations	DATAGUARDCONFIG	drc	Drc	coarse
DataPump DUMPSet	DUMPSET	dumpset	Dump	coarse
Flashback Logs	FLASHBACK	rlog	log_log#	fine
Online Redo Logs	ONLINELOG	online_log	log_<thread>	fine
Server Initialization Parameters	PARAMETERFILE	init	Spfile	coarse
TEMPFILEs	TEMPFILE	temp	tablespace_name	coarse

TABLE 7-1.   *ASM Template Characteristics*

Summary

Like most filesystems, an ASM diskgroup contains a directory tree. The root directory for the diskgroup is always the diskgroup name. Every ASM file has a system-generated filename; the name is generated based on the instance that created it, the Oracle file type, the usage of the file, and the file numbers. The system-generated filename is of the form +*disk_group/db_name/file_type/usage_tag .file_number.time_stamp*. Directories are created automatically as needed to construct system-generated filenames.

A file can have one user alias and can be placed in any existing directory within the same diskgroup. The user alias can be used to refer to the file in any file operation where the system-generated filename could be used. When a full path name is used to create the file, the path name becomes the user alias. If a file is created by just using the diskgroup name, then no user alias is created. A user alias may be added to or removed from any file without disturbing the file.

The system-generated name is an OMF name, whereas a user alias is not an OMF name. If the system-generated name is used for a file, then the system will automatically create and delete the file as needed. If the file is referred to by its user alias, then the user is responsible for creating and deleting the file and any required directories.

File templates are used to specify striping (coarse or fine) and, in a normal redundancy diskgroup, the redundancy (unprotected, normal, or high) for a file when it is created. A default template is provided for every Oracle file type. These defaults may be edited or custom templates can be created. Changing a template only affects new file creations, not existing files. When creating a file, you can specify a template by placing the template name in parentheses after the diskgroup name in the file-creation name.

CHAPTER
8

ASM Command-Line

here are many ways to manage and access ASM and its components. Two typical methods are using SQLPlus and using Enterprise Manager (EM) Database Control or Grid Control. A third method leverages the ASMCMD command-line utility, which provides short commands that have the same functionality as their SQL equivalents. This method obviates the need to build complex SQL statements to query ASM information. The ASMCMD syntax is very similar to Unix/Linux shell commands, thus simplifying ASM management for those administrators not accustomed to the SQLPlus interface or SQL coding.

NOTE
Because ASMCMD does not encompass all the functionality of the SQLPlus or EM interface, it is still highly recommended that the EM interface (using either Grid or Database Control) be used as a primary means to manage ASM and utilize ASMCMD for quick, short commands or for batch command processing.

This chapter discusses and illustrates the various ASMCMD commands. Note that the Oracle Database 11g ASMCMD can be used with Oracle Database 10g ASM instances as well; however, certain 11g specific commands will not be operational.

Interactive and Noninteractive Modes

The ASMCMD interface provides both interactive and noninteractive modes. This chapter primarily focuses on the interactive mode of ASMCMD. The interactive mode provides a shell-like environment where the user is prompted to issue the commands listed in this section. The noninteractive mode executes a single command and then exits the utility. Noninteractive mode is made available for scripting and batch processing purposes.

Note that for most ASMCMD commands, the ASM instance must be started and the diskgroups to be managed are mounted—for example, ASMCMD cannot mount or drop diskgroups.

Before invoking ASMCMD, the user must set the ORACLE_SID to the ASM instance name and the ORACLE_HOME to the location where ASM is installed.

The following are examples of using ASMCMD in a noninteractive mode:

```
Noninteractive Mode command line:
[oracle@racnode1]$ asmcmd ls -L +DATA/RAC/DATAFILE
EXAMPLE.267.553536489
```

```
SYSAUX.257.553536323
SYSTEM.256.553536323
UNDOTBS1.258.553536325
UNDOTBS2.268.553536665
USERS.259.553536325

[oracle@racnode1]$ asmcmd find -t DATAFILE +DG1%

+DG1/ORA102/DATAFILE/TEST.256.560274299
```

You must use the percent sign (%) as the wildcard for noninteractive mode queries.

Database administrators (DBAs) can utilize ASMCMD in a noninteractive manner to write shell scripts to query the amount of diskspace available for a given diskgroup and send alerts accordingly. For example, the following ASMCMD command can be piped to awk to determine the percentage free for ASM diskgroups and alert the DBAs accordingly:

```
#!/bin/ksh
export ALERT_THRESHOLD=$1
export ASM_DG_LOGFILE=/tmp/asm_dg.log
[ -f "$ASM_DG_LOGFILE" ] && rm $ASM_DG_LOGFILE

asmcmd lsdg -H |awk '{printf "%.2f\t%.2f\t%.2f\t%s\n",
$8,$9,($9/$8*100),$13}' |while read TOTAL_MB FREE_MB PCT_FREE DG
do
if [ "$PCT_FREE" -lt $ALERT_THRESHOLD ]; then
  echo "$DG - $FREE_MB $PCT_FREE % " >>$ASM_DG_LOGFILE
fi
done
[ -s $ASM_DG_LOGFILE ] && mailx -s "CRITICAL - ASM Diskgroup
exceeded allowable threshold:  $ALERT_THRESHOLD" oracleuser@companya
.com < $ASM_DG_LOGFILE
```

Connected and Nonconnected Modes

In Oracle Database 11g, if a user invokes ASMCMD in interactive mode, it starts in nonconnected mode. A connection to the ASM instance is made when the user issues a command that requires a connection; the session then remains persistently connected until the user exits or the session is disconnected. The lsdsk command is an example of a command that makes use of this facility. Table 8-1 describes several other such commands.

```
The ASMCMD help command provides the most efficient method of finding
the syntax and usage of a given command.
```

Command	Description
`help [command]`	Lists help topics
`pwd`	Shows the current directory
`cd <dir>`	Changes the directory
`find [-t <type>] <dir> <alias>`	Searches the directory
`ls [-lsdrtLaH] [alias]`	Lists the directory
`mkdir <dir1 dir2 . . .>`	Creates a directory
`rm <file1, file2 . . .>`	Removes a file or directory
`mkalias <system_alias> <user_alias>`	Creates a user alias
`rmalias [-r] <user_alias1 user_alias2 .>`	Removes a user alias
`du [-H] [dir]`	Displays the disk usage
`lsdg [-H] [group]`	Lists diskgroup information
`lsdsk`	Lists disk information
`lsct [-H] [group]`	Lists ASM client information
`exit`	Exits

TABLE 8-1. *Commands That Make Use of Connected/Nonconnected Modes*

The following commands were introduced in Oracle Database 11g:

```
md_backup [-o <location_of_backup> ] [-g dgname [-g dgname …]]
md_restore [ -t full|nodg|newdg]-fi <backup_file> -g dgname [-g dgname]
[-o <override>] [-of <override_file>][-i] [-l< log_file>]
remap <disk group name> <disk name> <block range>
```

These commands will be described in greater detail later in the chapter.

The following sets of examples illustrate the use of each of ASMCMD commands previously listed.

```
[oracle@racnode1]$ asmcmd -p
```

When the `-p` option is used to launch ASMCMD, the current path is shown in the prompt. Administrators are encouraged to set up a Unix alias for the `asmcmd` command: `alias asmcmd='asmcmd -p'`

```
ASMCMD [+] > cd DATA
```

Keep in mind the following when using the ASMCMD cd command:

■ cd + is equivalent to cd / in Unix.

■ cd allows wildcard substitutions (such as cd +DG1/ORA102/DATAF*)

■ cd is also case-insensitive.

The example below shows how change directories using the 'cd' command:

```
ASMCMD [+DATA] > cd V102
ASMCMD [+DATA/V102] > ls
CONTROLFILE/
DATAFILE/
ONLINELOG/
PARAMETERFILE/
TEMPFILE/
spfileV102.ora
ASMCMD [+DATA/V102] > cd DATAFILE
```

Table 8-2 lists the flag options for the ls command.

Option	Description
(none)	Displays only filenames and directory names.
-l	Displays extended file information.
-s	Displays file space information.
-d	Displays information about the directory; typically used with -l.
-r	Reverses the sort order of the listing.
-t	Sorts the listing by timestamp (with the latest first) instead of by name.
-L	Lists alias file references; typically used with -l.
-a	Displays the absolute path of the alias that the file references.
-c	Selects from the V$ASM_DISKGROUP view or from the GV$ASM_DISKGROUP view if the -g flag is also specified.
-g	Queries from the GV$ views.
-H	Suppresses column headings.

TABLE 8-2. *ls Command Options*

The example below shows the ASM file listing using the 'ls –l' command:

```
ASMCMD [+DATA/V102/DATAFILE] > ls -l
Type      Redund  Striped  Time             Sys   Name
DATAFILE  UNPROT  COARSE   DEC 08 12:00:00  Y     APPS_TS_TX_DATA.269.608645203
DATAFILE  UNPROT  COARSE   DEC 08 12:00:00  Y     APPS_TS_TX_IDX.268.608645149
DATAFILE  UNPROT  COARSE   DEC 04 12:00:00  Y     SYSAUX.257.605208869
DATAFILE  UNPROT  COARSE   DEC 04 12:00:00  Y     SYSTEM.256.605208869
DATAFILE  UNPROT  COARSE   DEC 04 12:00:00  Y     UNDOTBS1.258.605208869
DATAFILE  UNPROT  COARSE   DEC 12 22:00:00  Y     UNDOTBS2.264.605209043
DATAFILE  UNPROT  COARSE   DEC 04 12:00:00  Y     USERS.259.605208869
```

NOTE
The –l option is similar to the Unix `ls -l`
*command in that it provides a long list output. This
output provides redundancy information, striping
information (coarse or fine), the modification date,
and the file type.*

The example below illustrates the use of the make alias command using the
'mkalias'. In this example, the mkalias command creates an alias for the USERS
tablespace datafile, and then the alias is displayed using the 'ls –l' command:

```
ASMCMD [+DATA/V102/datafile] > mkalias
+DATA/V102/datafile/USERS.259.605208869  USERS_tbs01.dbf
ASMCMD [+DATA/V102/datafile] > ls -l
Type      Redund  Striped  Time             Sys   Name
DATAFILE  UNPROT  COARSE   DEC 08 12:00:00  Y
APPS_TS_TX_DATA.269.608645203
DATAFILE  UNPROT  COARSE   DEC 08 12:00:00  Y
APPS_TS_TX_IDX.268.608645149
DATAFILE  UNPROT  COARSE   DEC 04 12:00:00  Y     SYSAUX.257.605208869
DATAFILE  UNPROT  COARSE   DEC 04 12:00:00  Y     SYSTEM.256.605208869
DATAFILE  UNPROT  COARSE   DEC 04 12:00:00  Y     UNDOTBS1.258.605208869
DATAFILE  UNPROT  COARSE   DEC 12 22:00:00  Y     UNDOTBS2.264.605209043
DATAFILE  UNPROT  COARSE   DEC 04 12:00:00  Y     USERS.259.605208869
                                           N     USERS_tbs01.dbf
=>  +DATA/V102/DATAFILE/USERS.259.605208869
```

The du command is similar to du (disk usage) command in Unix. The following
shows an example of du command on an external redundancy diskgroup:

```
ASMCMD [+DATA/V102/datafile] > du
Used_MB      Mirror_used_MB
   1963              1963
```

The following example shows the output from an Oracle Database 10*g* lsdg
command:

```
ASMCMD [+DATA/V102/DATAFILE] > lsdg
State     Type    Rebal  Unbal  Sector  Block      AU  Total_MB
Free_MB  Req_mir_free_MB  Usable_file_MB  Offline_disks  Name
MOUNTED  NORMAL  N    N    512   4096  1048576   66790   63445   13358
25043    0   DATA/   lsdg [-gCH] [group]
```

Option	10*g*R1	10*g*R2 and Later
No flag	V$ASM_DISKGROUP	V$ASM_DISKGROUP_STAT
-c	V$ASM_DISKGROUP	V$ASM_DISKGROUP
-g	GV$ASM_DISKGROUP	GV$ASM_DISKGROUP_STAT
-cg	GV$ASM_DISKGROUP	GV$ASM_DISKGROUP

TABLE 8-3. *V$ Views Comparison between Oracle Database 10g and 11g*

In Oracle Database 11*g*, the two new flags are added: -g and -c.

The -g flag selects from GV$ASM_DISKGROUP, and presents the INST_ID in the output. If the –g flag is used with the –c flag (as –gc), the GV$ASM_DISKGROUP_STAT will be queried. GV$ASM_OPERATION will also be used for the REBAL column of the output. Note that the *_STAT views did not exist in Oracle ASM version 10 release 1, thus this command will not work if the Oracle ASM instance is version 10 release 1. Table 8-3 lists the views used by the –c and –g options across ASM versions.

The example below uses the lsct command to list the ASM clients (RDBMS instances) connected to the ASM instance.

```
ASMCMD [+DATA/V102/DATAFILE] > lsct

DB_Name   Status      Software_Version   Compatible_version   Instance_Name
V102      CONNECTED   11.1.0.6.0         11.1.0.0.0           RAC1
```

The new –g flag added in Oracle Database 11*g* selects from GV$ASM_CLIENT, and the INST_ID is included in the output.

The following examples illustrate creating and removing directories, as well as removing files:

```
ASMCMD [+DATA/V102] > mkdir dumpsets
ASMCMD [+DATA/V102] > rm dumpsets
ASMCMD [+DATA/V102] > rm +DATA/V102/DATAFILE/USERS.259.605208869
```

The rm command works only if the file is closed. This prevents erroneous deletion of files.

The following example shows the usage of the find command:

```
ASMCMD> find +DATA undo*
+DATA/V102/DATAFILE/UNDOTBS1.258.605208869
+DATA/V102/DATAFILE/UNDOTBS2.264.605209043
```

A new command in Oracle Database 11*g* called lsdsk can be used to list the disks that are discovered—that is, those that are visible to ASM. This command is especially important if the user is currently using another logical volume manager (LVM), such as Symantec-Veritas VxVM, to manage other disk storage. The Sysadmin can use `lsdsk` command with the host LVM (if one exists).

```
lsdsk [-ksptagcHI] [-d <disk group name> [pattern]
```

Table 8-4 lists the parameters for V$ASM_DISK.

The pattern option restricts the output to only disks that match the pattern. In the following example, the pattern option, DATA*, can be used to filter only disk names that start with DATA:

```
lsdsk -k -d DATA DATA*
```

Wildcard characters and slashes (/ or \) can be part of the pattern. This command can run in two modes: connected and nonconnected. In connected mode, ASMCMD uses the V$ and GV$ tables to retrieve disk information. In nonconnected mode, ASMCMD scans disk headers to retrieve disk information, using an ASM diskstring to restrict the discovery set. The connected mode is always attempted, first (unless –I is specified).

Option	Description
None	Displays the PATH column of the V$ASM_DISK view
-k	Displays the basic disk information such as TOTAL_MB, FREE_MB, NAME, REDUNDANCY and PATH
-s	Displays the input/output (IO) statistics
-p	Displays basic diskgroup information
-t	Displays the CREATE_DATE, MOUNT_DATE, and REPAIR_TIMER
-g	Selects from GV$ASM_DISK_STAT, or from GV$ASM_DISK if the -c flag is also specified
-c	Selects from V$ASM_DISK, or from GV$ASM_DISK if the -g flag is also specified
-H	Suppresses column headings
-I	Scans disk headers for information rather than extracting the information from an ASM instance
-d	Restricts results to only those disks that belong to the group specified by diskgroup name

TABLE 8-4. *V$ASM_DISK Parameters*

The -k option provides size and free space information at the disk level. It also provides failure group, disk label, and redundancy information.

```
ASMCMD> lsdsk -k -d DATA

Total_MB Free_MB OS_MB Name         Failgroup  Library  Label    UDID   Product
Redund    Path
13358    12688   13358 DATA_0000    DATA_0000  System   UNKNOWN         /dev/raw/raw10
13358    12691   13358 DATA_0001    DATA_0001  System   UNKNOWN         /dev/raw/raw11
13358    12684   13358 DATA_0002    DATA_0002  System   UNKNOWN         /dev/raw/raw12
13358    12695   13358 DATA_0003    DATA_0003  System   UNKNOWN         /dev/raw/raw8
13358    12687   13358 DATA_0004    DATA_0004  System   UNKNOWN         /dev/raw/raw9
```

The -s option provides information about disk performance metrics in terms of reads to writes and errors encountered at the disk level.

```
ASMCMD> lsdsk -s -d DATA
 Reads   Write  Read_Errs  Write_Errs  Read_time  Write_Time  Bytes_Read  Bytes_Written  Path
  3408   81390          0           0       49.4     3435.18    45616128                  /dev/raw/raw10
164892   81572          0           0     609.24     3459.22  2686983168                  /dev/raw/raw11
 62135   82729          0           0      19.83     3258.27  1009091072                  /dev/raw/raw12
  3161   18497          0           0     226.03     3329.31    39063552                  /dev/raw/raw8
  3628   15028          0           0     206.37     3403.24    49618432                  /dev/raw/raw9
```

The following example uses the lsdsk −t −d command to list the diskgroup disks' creation date, mount date, repair timer and the operating system (OS) path.

```
ASMCMD> lsdsk -t -d DATA
Create_Date   Mount_Date   Repair_Timer   Path
20-DEC-06     20-DEC-06    0              /dev/raw/raw10
20-DEC-06     20-DEC-06    0              /dev/raw/raw11
20-DEC-06     20-DEC-06    0              /dev/raw/raw12
20-DEC-06     20-DEC-06    0              /dev/raw/raw8
20-DEC-06     20-DEC-06    0              /dev/raw/raw9
```

ASM Metadata Backup and Restore in ASMCMD

Backing up your diskgroup is usually unnecessary, as you can easily re-create it and restore its contents. In cases where users create or define numerous user templates, aliases, and directories within ASM and the diskgroup needs to be re-created, you need to re-create these ASM user objects manually as well. To overcome this, Oracle Database 11g introduces a new utility to back up the metadata for the ASM objects. This new utility, ASM Metadata Backup and Restore (AMBR), is a subcomponent of ASMCMD. AMBR provides the ability to re-create a preexisting ASM diskgroup with exactly the same templates, attributes, and alias directory structures, thus preserving the diskgroup structures. AMBR has two modes: backup and restore.

Backup Mode

With the backup mode, information is gathered about ASM disks, diskgroup and failure group configurations, templates, attributes, and alias directory structures. This information is converted into SQL commands and stored in a user-defined metadata backup (MDB) file, which can be used by the `md_restore` command during a diskgroup restore. This file contains enough metadata information that a restore operation can re-create and restore the entire diskgroup as it previously existed. The following is the syntax of the backup metadata:

```
asmcmd md_backup [-b <location_of_backup> ] [-g dgname [-g dgname …]]
```

The `md_backup` command creates one backup file for each execution of the command. The user can control where the script is created and the list of diskgroups that need to be backed up. By default, the MDB file is saved in the current working directory and is called *ambr_backup_intermediate_file*.

The MDB file, by default, builds metadata information of all the mounted diskgroups. Because the MDB file is a text file, users can manually edit the stored information, if they need to restore only certain ASM objects rather than the entire diskgroup. However, care must be taken when editing this file; always create a backup of the MDB file before editing. Mistakes made during editing result in errors in the restore process. Note that the `md_restore` command does not perform any syntax or semantic checks on the input file before it attempts to process it.

The following list reviews each segment of the MDB file. Each section is identified by a unique tag/section ID in the form of an SQL comment. Restore mode uses this tag to locate the section in the backup file. If an exact match for the expected tag is not found, the md_backup command continues searching for the next valid tag and ignores items in between. Errors caused by editing mistakes can cause sections to be skipped. In backup mode, the `md_backup` command connects to an ASM instance to gather the following information:

- Diskgroup information (for each diskgroup being backed up). This is the first section of the file and contains SQL commands to create diskgroup(s).

  - Diskgroup name

  - Redundancy type

  - Both ASM and database (DB) compatibility

  - Allocation unit size

- Disk information (for each disk that belongs to a diskgroup being backed up).

  - Diskgroup name

  - Disk label (name), if user-specified

- Disk path

- Operating system (OS) size and the ASM size of the disk

- Failure group name, if user-specified

- Alias directory information (for each user-created directory).

  - Diskgroup name

  - Full path of the alias entry without the diskgroup name

- Attribute directory.

- Template directory information. There is an entry for each diskgroup template. Users can use the commands in this section to manipulate the templates for restore mode.

  - Edit default/system templates based on the changes to system templates made by user

  - Create user-created templates

    For each template, the following information is built:

    - Diskgroup name

    - Template name

    - Redundancy

    - Stripe

    - System

Restore Mode

The essential task of the AMBR restore mode is to restore the metadata into the diskgroup; this is done using the `md_restore` subcommand of ASMCMD. It is assumed that the user has a good backup of the diskgroup's database files. This database backup will need to be restored via RMAN after the successful restore of the diskgroup.

The restore mode can re-create the diskgroup (based on the specifications listed in the MDB file) or restore the diskgroup into an existing (precreated) diskgroup with any required modifications, such as a change to the diskgroup name.

The `md_restore` command re-creates all user-defined templates and incorporates changes if any are made to system templates, applies appropriate

Option	Description
-b	Specifies which MDB file to read.
-t	Specifies the type of restore.
full	Re-creates the diskgroup with the exact configuration as the backed-up diskgroup, using same diskgroup name, the same set of disks and failure group configurations, and the same attribute values. It then re-creates template and alias directories with the exact same structure as the backed-up diskgroup.
nodg	Restores metadata in an existing diskgroup provided as an input parameter.
newdg	Enables the user to change the disk specification, failure group specification, diskgroup name, and so on.
-f	Specifies the script output file created by the backup command.
-g	Specifies the diskgroup name that needs to be restored.
-o	Provides the capability to rename the diskgroup on restore.
-i	Instructs restore to ignore specific change specifications and display a warning to the user if a particular change line is syntactically incorrect or invalid. Without this option specified, restore would simply terminate with an error in such instances.

TABLE 8-5. *md_restore Command Options*

attribute values, and restores ASM alias directories by re-creating user-created directories as specified by the backup file. The syntax is as follows:

```
asmcmd md_restore [ -t full|nodg|newdg] -f <backup_file> -g dgname
[-g dgname] [-o <override>] -i
```

Table 8-5 describes the md_restore command's options.

The following are examples of the md_restore command. This first example is to restore the diskgroup DATA from the MDB backup file.

```
md_restore -t full -g DATA -f backupfile_out
```

This command restores metadata into an existing diskgroup DATA:

```
md_restore -t nodg -g DATA -i backupfile_out
```

The following example completely restores diskgroup DATA but renames the diskgroup to DATA_NEW:

```
md_restore -t newdg  -o 'DATA:DATA_NEW'  -i backupfile_out
```

Backup and Recovery Example

The following example illustrates the use of md_backup and md_restore:

1. Create some user-defined ASM directories, aliases, and templates.

2. Execute the md_backup command to create the MDB file.

3. Use RMAN to back up the database stored within that diskgroup.

4. To simulate a complete diskgroup failure, drop the diskgroup.

5. Recover the diskgroup using md_restore.

6. Restore and recover the database using RMAN.

Let's look at these steps in more detail:

1. Create user-defined ASM objects:

```
SQL> alter diskgroup data add  template temp_unprot attributes (fine  unprotected)
SQL> alter diskgroup data add  template important_data attributes (fine mirror);
SQL> alter diskgroup data add  alias '+DATA/RAC/USERS_01.DBF'  for '+DATA/RAC/
DATAFILE/USERS.259.609660473';
SQL> alter diskgroup data add directory '+DATA/RAC/oradata';
SQL> alter diskgroup data add alias '+DATA/RAC/oradata/sysaux_01.dbf' for
'+DATA/RAC/DATAFILE/SYSAUX.257.609660473';
SQL> alter diskgroup data add directory '+DATA/RAC/oradata/temp_files';
SQL> alter diskgroup data add alias '+DATA/RAC/oradata/temp_files/temp_01.dbf' for
'+DATA/RAC/tempfile/TEMP.263.609660687'
SQL> select name,REDUNDANCY,STRIPE from v$asm_template where system='N';
NAME                            REDUND STRIPE
----------------------------    ------ ------
TEMP_UNPROT                     UNPROT FINE
IMPORTANT_DATA                  MIRROR FINE
SQL> SELECT NAME,FILE_NUMBER,ALIAS_DIRECTORY FROM V$ASM_ALIAS WHERE
 SYSTEM_CREATED='N' AND ALIAS_DIRECTORY='Y'
NAME                                            FILE_NUMBER A
--------------------------------------------    ----------- -
oradata                                          4294967295 Y
temp_files                                       4294967295 Y
```

2. Invoke the diskgroup backup using the md_backup command:

```
[oracle@racnode1]$ asmcmd md_backup -b datadg_backup -g data
```

This command outputs a message indicating that the backup is generated:

```
###User defined intermediate backup file is :       datadg_backup

Disk group to be backed up: DATA#
```

The `datadg_backup` file contents are displayed as follows (for brevity, the system-generated templates, such as DATAFILE and CONTROLFILE, are omitted):

```
@diskgroup_set = (
        {
        'DISKSINFO' => {
                'DATA_0003' => {
                        'DATA_0003' => {
                          'TOTAL_MB' => '13358',
                          'FAILGROUP' => 'DATA_0003',
                          'NAME' => 'DATA_0003',
                          'DGNAME' => 'DATA',
                          'PATH' => '/dev/raw/raw8'
                                                 }
                                       },
                'DATA_0001' => {
                        'DATA_0001' => {
                          'TOTAL_MB' => '13358',
                          'FAILGROUP' => 'DATA_0001',
                          'NAME' => 'DATA_0001',
                          'DGNAME' => 'DATA',
                          'PATH' => '/dev/raw/raw11'
                                       }
                               },
                'DATA_0000' => {
                        'DATA_0000' => {
                          'TOTAL_MB' => '13358',
                          'FAILGROUP' => 'DATA_0000',
                          'NAME' => 'DATA_0000',
                          'DGNAME' => 'DATA',
                          'PATH' => '/dev/raw/raw10'
                                       }
                               },
                'DATA_0002' => {
                        'DATA_0002' => {
                          'TOTAL_MB' => '13358',
                          'FAILGROUP' => 'DATA_0002',
                          'NAME' => 'DATA_0002',
                          'DGNAME' => 'DATA',
                          'PATH' => '/dev/raw/raw12'
                                       }
                               },
                'DATA_0004' => {
                        'DATA_0004' => {
                          'TOTAL_MB' => '13358',
                          'FAILGROUP' => 'DATA_0004',
```

```
                                      'NAME' => 'DATA_0004',
                                      'DGNAME' => 'DATA',
                                      'PATH' => '/dev/raw/raw9'
                                                     }
                                        }
                      },
      'DGINFO' => {
                  'DGTORESTORE' => 0,
                  'DGCOMPAT' => '10.1.0.0.0',
                  'DGNAME' => 'DATA',
                  'DGDBCOMPAT' => '10.1.0.0.0',
                  'DGTYPE' => 'NORMAL',
                  'DGAUSZ' => '1048576'
                },
      'ALIASINFO' => {
                '1' => {
                  'DGNAME' => 'DATA',
                  'LEVEL' => 2,
                  'ALIASNAME' => 'RAC/oradata/temp_files',
                  'REFERENCE_INDEX' => '16777640'
                          },
                  '0' => {
                    'DGNAME' => 'DATA',
                    'LEVEL' => 1,
                    'ALIASNAME' => 'RAC/oradata',
                    'REFERENCE_INDEX' => '16777587'
                            }
                  },
      'TEMPLATEINFO' => {
                  11' => {
                      'DGNAME' => 'DATA',
                      'STRIPE' => 'FINE',
                      'TEMPNAME' => 'FLASHBACK',
                      'REDUNDANCY' => 'MIRROR',
                      'SYSTEM' => 'Y'
                            },
                    '5' => {
                      'DGNAME' => 'DATA',
                      'STRIPE' => 'COARSE',
                      'TEMPNAME' => 'DATAFILE',
                      'REDUNDANCY' => 'MIRROR',
                      'SYSTEM' => 'Y'
                        }
                    }
      }
  );
```

3. Back up the database contents of the diskgroup using RMAN:

```
[oracle@racnode1]$ rman > BACKUP DATABASE;
```

4. To simulate a diskgroup loss, drop the diskgroup:

```
SQL>ALTER DISKGROUP DATA DISMOUNT;
```

This must be done on all nodes of the cluster that have that ASM diskgroup mounted, except for the instance that will issue the `DROP DISKGROUP` command:

```
SQL> DROP DISKGROUP DATA INCLUDING CONTENTS;
```

5. Restore the diskgroup using `md_restore`.

Now let's restore the diskgroup using the pre-created backup file from the `md_backup` command:

```
[oracle@racnode1]$ asmcmd md_restore -t full -g DATA -b datadg_backup
Disk group to be restored: DATA#
Current Diskgroup being restored: DATA
Diskgroup DATA created!
Template IMPORTANT_DATA created/altered!
Template TEMP_UNPROT created/altered!
```

NOTE
The restore operation mounts the diskgroup only on the node where the md_restore *command was run. Thus, in a Real Application Clusters (RAC) environment, the remaining nodes of the cluster will need to mount the recently restored diskgroup manually.*

6. Now restore and recover the database.

```
[oracle@racnode1]$rman> restore database;
[oracle@racnode1]$rman> recover database;
```

Bad Block Remapping in ASMCMD

Due to the mechanical nature of disk drives, over time bad areas or bad spots develop on disk. The reasons for bad spots can range from moisture or dust accumulation on the drive unit to vibration instability or continuous head misalignment. These bad spots result in bad blocks that the application discovers via a failed read command. If these blocks are being mirrored, then the host volume manager can handle the recovery of these blocks through routine scanning or scrubbing of the disks. However, scrubbing is typically very ineffective if done by the host. Typically, scrubbing is performed by the storage array itself.

Starting in Oracle Database 11g, when ASM redundancy (normal or high) is used, these bad spots can be recovered by restoring the data from their mirror copy from the other failure groups. This new Oracle Database 11g feature is called `remap` and is a subcommand of ASMCMD similar to `md_backup` and `md_restore`. This feature improves the availability characteristics of the diskgroup by moving data out of bad spots on the disks.

Note that the remap functionality does not fix logical errors or corruptions detected by the RDBMS.

Bad block remapping comes into play in two scenarios:

■ When the relational database management system (RDBMS) instance encounters a bad block (input/output [I/O] errors) during a read operation, it attempts to read from the secondary extent. However, ASM initiates a background `remap` operation to find the secondary extent(s) for the bad block. If the secondary extent is valid, then the extent with the bad block is moved to another location on the same disk as the primary extent, and the allocation unit used for the old primary extent is marked as a bad extent.

■ As mentioned earlier, most storage arrays provide some level of scrubbing. Scrubbing is defined as a method by which drives are periodically accessed to detect drive failure or sector read failures. When the scrubbing routine finds blocks that have become unreadable (that is, media errors occur), these errors are logged in the OS logs indicating the small computer system interface (SCSI) disk name and the block affected. Best practice is to mine the system logs routinely to identify the list of blocks with media errors. ASMCMD's `remap` command can then be used to repair these blocks using the following syntax:

```
remap <disk group name> <disk name> <block range>
```

The diskgroup name is the name of the diskgroup in which a disk needs to be repaired, whereas the disk name is the name in `V$ASM_DISK.NAME` of the disk that needs to be repaired. The block range is a range of physical blocks to repair.

Here is an example of an `remap` command:

```
asmcmd> remap DATA DATA_0001 24-48
```

For bad block remapping, ASM currently remaps one file extent range at a time. Therefore, if blocks from different extents need remapping, ASMCMD must separate them into different calls to ASM.

To leverage the `remap` command, the diskgroup needs to be mounted in normal mode.

This `remap` feature can be used by the `SYSASM` privileges in the ASM instance. The user connecting to `SYSASM` needs to be part of the `OSASM` group to be able to use ASMCMD.

ASMCMD Copy

Starting with Oracle Database 11g, ASMCMD includes a mechanism to copy eligible database files into and out of ASM, as well as to other ASM diskgroups. The diskgroup can either be a local diskgroup (existing on same host) or remote (residing on a different server that does not share the storage). The big advantage of this feature is that the ASMCMD copy can be used to transfer files without requiring an active database instance.

This command is particularly useful for archived logfiles or offlined database files.

The ASMCMD copy command is a user interface that resembles standard copy file utilities such as `scp` and `rcp`:

```
cp <ifr> <connection_string:>src_fname <connection_string:>tgt_fname

cp <ifr> <connection_string:>src_fname… <connection_string:>tgt_directory
```

The options are as follows:

`-i` Prompt before copying or overwriting the file.

`-f` If you are copying an existing destination file, remove it and try again without user interaction.

`-r` Copy forwarding subdirectories recursively.

Copy command parameters include the following:

- **src_fname(s)** This identifies the source filename from which to copy. It is either the fully qualified filename (system-generated name) or an ASM alias.

- **tgt_fname** This is a user alias for the created target filename or alias directory name.

- **tgt_directory** This specifies a target alias directory within an ASM disk group. The directory must preexist; otherwise, the file copy returns an error.

- **connection_string** This is the ASMCMD connection string for the case of remote instance copy.

NOTE
The `connection_string` *parameter is not required when the command is used for local instance copy, which is the default. For remote copying, the ASMCMD users need to specify the* `connection_string` *and are prompted to specify a password in a nonechoing prompt. The connect identifier is in the form of* `<host>:<port>`, *with the defaults being* `localhost` *for* `<host>` *and* `1521` *for* `<port>`.

Note that when copying database datafiles, files should either be offlined or be placed in hotbackup mode.

The syntax is as follows:

```
cp [src]... login@<<SID>|<hostname>.<SID>|<hostname>.<port>.<SID>>:<path>
```

The following is an example of a copy of a file from an ASM diskgroup to a filesystem:

```
ASMCMD [+DATA/YODA/datafile] > cp USERS.259.623342167 \ /u01/oradata/
yoda/users.dbf

source +DATA/YODA/datafile/USERS.259.623342167

target /u01/oradata/yoda/users.dbf

copying file(s)...

file, /u01/oradata/yoda/users.dbf, copy committed.
```

Now let's validate the file using the dbverify command:

```
DBVERIFY - Verification starting : FILE = /u01/oradata/yoda/users.dbf

DBVERIFY - Verification complete

Total Pages Examined          : 640

Total Pages Processed (Data) : 37

Total Pages Failing   (Data) : 0

Total Pages Processed (Index): 20

Total Pages Failing   (Index): 0

Total Pages Processed (Other): 569

Total Pages Processed (Seg)  : 0

Total Pages Failing   (Seg)  : 0

Total Pages Empty            : 14

Total Pages Marked Corrupt   : 0

Total Pages Influx           : 0

Total Pages Encrypted        : 0

Highest block SCN            : 274868171 (0.274868171)
```

In the case of a remote ASM file copy, ASMCMD does not allow the user to initiate the file copy among remote instances. The local ASM instance must present either the source or the target sides of the operation.

The following steps are used to configure remote ASMCMD copy:

1. In the remote ASM instance, ensure that the SYSASM privilege is enabled. Chapter 2, "ASM Instances," covers the steps to perform this.

2. Verify that the listener is running and then check that ASM is registered properly.

3. At the source ASM instance, you can type the following, for example:

```
[oracle@racnode1]$ asmcmd -p

ASMCMD [+] > cp +DATA/yoda/tempfile/TEMP.268.627503627
sys@host.+ASM:+DATA_DG/obiwan/tempfile
```

The following are some key points for ASMCMD copy command:

■ The format of copied files can be converted between little-endian and big-endian systems. However, this is possible only if the source files exist in an ASM diskgroup (ASM files), because the underlying ASM API automatically converts the format when allocating and initializing the files. If a source file is not in an ASM diskgroup, the user can copy the file to a different endian platform and use one of the commonly used utilities to convert the file.

■ If the source is a single file, then the destination can be the target directory or a filename; otherwise, it must be a directory.

■ The destination is of the form target/<connect_identifier>, where <connect_identifier> is of the form:

<HOSTNAME>, <HOSTNAME>.SID

or

<HOSTNAME>.[PORT.]SID

where the port is optional.

The following defines the ASMCMD copy support in Oracle Database 10g:

■ To copy a single-source ASM file to a target ASM file, the created filename must be a user alias in an ASM diskgroup.

■ Copying source files fails if the specified user alias already exists in the target ASM diskgroup.

■ Remote copying is not supported.

Summary

The ASMCMD is a Unix-like command-line interface that simplifies the management of an ASM environment. This tool can be especially beneficial for ASM administrators who are not typically exposed to complex SQL querying or for the ASM administrator who needs quick access to ASM. Additionally, ASMCMD can be used for scripting ASM operations.

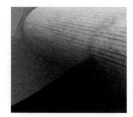

CHAPTER
9

Managing Databases
in ASM

n the chapters so far, we have discussed the various components of ASM and how they all work together to provide a solid storage management solution, taking advantage of Oracle metadata and providing performance benefits by storing data the way that Oracle Databases need them. But how do the relational database management system (RDBMS) and the new storage manager work together? At this point, every reader must be wondering about the answer to this important question. In this chapter, let's discuss the interaction between ASM and the RDBMS. We will also discuss the various interfaces to the ASM instance and how to migrate data into and from ASM storage.

ASM supports both a single-instance version of the Oracle Database and a clustered version. Although from a strategic point of view ASM best fits a clustered configuration such as Real Application Clusters (RAC), but it is not short of any features when it comes to implementing ASM in a single-instance database. So in this chapter, unless otherwise mentioned, all discussions apply to both types of configurations.

Database Interaction with ASM

After the ASM diskgroup is created, the Database Configuration Assistant (DBCA) can now be used to create the database. Starting with Oracle Database 11*g* DBCA provides two options for database file structures: filesystem, or ASM.

NOTE
Oracle Database 10g provided three options filesystem, raw or ASM as options for creating database files.

Database creation can be done in one of two ways: either by using the DBCA, which is a graphical user interface (GUI) provided with the product (this is the recommended method); or manually by using a script. Creation of a Real Application Clusters (RAC) database is different from the regular standalone configuration because a RAC configuration consists of one database and two or more instances.

An advantage of using the GUI over using the script method is that there are fewer steps to remember. This is because when you use DBCA, the steps are predefined and based on the selected template, and the type of database is automatically created, sized, and configured. However, the script approach has an advantage over the GUI approach in the sense that the user can see what is happening during the creation process and physically monitor the process. Another advantage of this option is that you can create the script based on the needs of the enterprise.

DBCA helps in the creation of the database. It follows the standard naming and placement convention defined in the Optimal Flexible Architecture (OFA) standards.

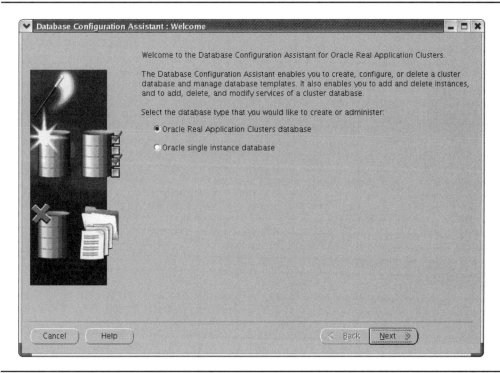

FIGURE 9-1. *The DBCA's Welcome screen enables you to select the database type.*

DBCA can be launched automatically as part of the Oracle installation process or manually by directly executing the DBCA command from the $ORACLE_HOME/bin directory. Figure 9-1 shows the DBCA Welcome screen. From this screen, the type of database to be created is selected. The screen provides two choices: Oracle Real Application Clusters database or Oracle single instance database. Configuration of the database irrespective of using either option should be similar. For the purposes of our discussions, we will select the RAC option. Select the Oracle Real Application Clusters database option, then click Next.

NOTE
The Oracle Real Application Clusters database option is visible only if the Clusterware is configured. If this option is not visible in this screen, the database administrator (DBA) should cancel the configuration process and verify that the Clusterware is running before proceeding.

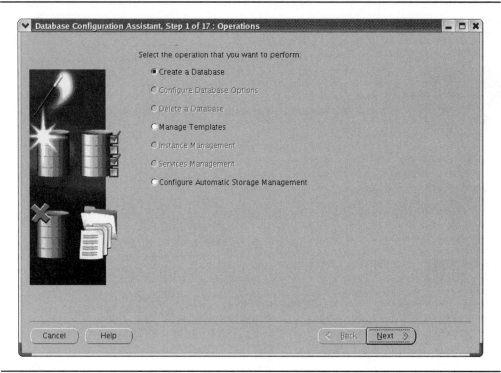

FIGURE 9-2. *The DBCA's Operations window*

The next screen is the Operations window (see Figure 9-2). If this is the first database being configured, DBCA provides three options: create a new database, manage database creation templates provided by Oracle, and configure ASM. From this screen, select the Create a Database option, then click Next.

The next screen (not shown here) is the node selection window. On this screen, the appropriate node where RAC needs to be configured is selected. Because the Oracle Universal Installer (OUI) copies the required files to all nodes participating in the cluster, it is advisable to select all nodes listed, then click Next.

Following the node selection screen is the Database Template screen. Figure 9-3 shows the Oracle templates that can be selected according to the functionality that the database will support.

After the appropriate database template has been selected, the next screen (not shown) is the database identification screen. In this screen, the proposed database name should be provided (for example, SSKYDB) and the Oracle system identifier (SID) (SSKY). The DBCA automatically generates an instance number that will be suffixed to the SID. When the DBCA subsequently creates the database and starts

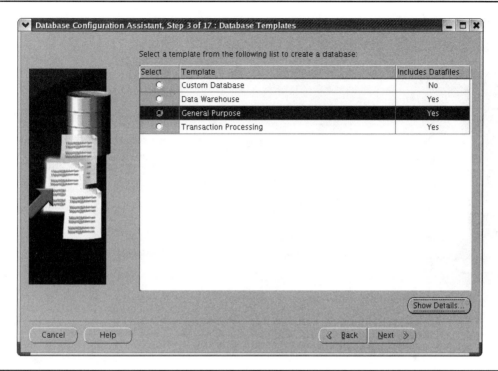

FIGURE 9-3.   *Selecting the template from the DBCA Database Template screen*

the instances, depending on the number of instances being created, the instances will have the following naming convention: SID1, SID2, and so on (for example, SSKY1, SSKY2, SSKY3, and so forth).

Once the database and the instances' names have been identified, click Next. The next screen, shown in Figure 9-4, is the Management Options screen. In this screen, the DBA defines the various monitoring and notification methods that will be used.

The screen presents two options:

- The default option, where the Oracle Enterprise Manager (OEM) console is installed by the DBCA process. Under this option, no repository or data collection process is involved. Only the basic console monitoring and administration functions are available.

- An advanced option that requires the OEM grid control functionality. Under this option, the OEM repository is created and the management agents installed on all nodes that require monitoring.

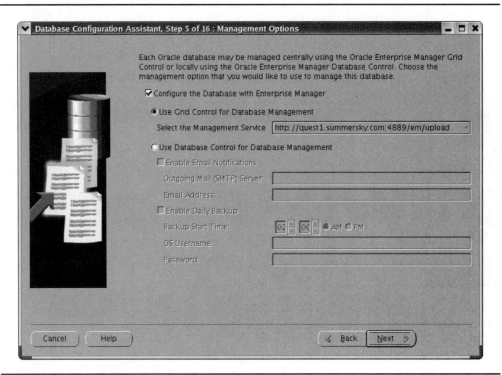

FIGURE 9-4. *The DBCA's Management Options screen*

As Figure 9-4 shows, the management agent has already been installed on the node, and hence the DBCA automatically detects and fills in the appropriate management agent information. Note that under this option, because the OEM will control the e-mail and other administrative functions, only one of the following two options can be selected: Use Grid Control for Database Management or Use Database Control for Database Management.

Once the monitoring control options have been selected, the next step is to assign a name to the database you are creating. Following that, the next step is to define the passwords for the SYS and SYSTEM user accounts. The screen (not shown) illustrates the password definition process. Oracle provides two options on this screen:

■ Assign a default password for all accounts created by Oracle. In this case one single password assigned is applied to all accounts.

■ Define individual passwords specific to each account (for example, SYS, SYSTEM, and DBSNMP).

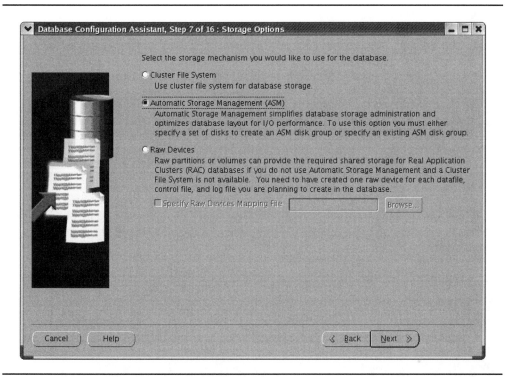

FIGURE 9-5. *The DBCA's Storage Options screen enables you to select the storage mechanism.*

Based on the user requirements and the security policies of the organization, either option could be used. After assigning and verifying the password, click Next.

The next screen (see Figure 9-5) is the Storage Options screen. Oracle Database 10*g* provides three mechanism selection options:

■ Clustered File System

■ Automatic Storage Management (ASM)

■ Raw Devices

NOTE
Starting with Oracle Database 11g, raw devices is not an available option for database files.

Based on the desired storage mechanism for the database files, the required subcomponents will be installed. As illustrated in Figure 9-5, select the ASM option.

Note the following:

- If ASM is the storage management method, the DBCA will verify if ASM is configured on the nodes in the cluster, and if ASM instances are not found, the DBCA will start ASM instances on all nodes participating in the cluster.

- While RAC supports a mixture of storage options (not available from this screen); that is, some datafiles could be created on a Cluster File System such as OCFS, and the others on ASM. As a best practice all datafiles including archive redo log files and RMAN backups should be stored on ASM.

The next screen (see Figure 9-6) in the configuration process enables you to create the ASM instances. In this screen, the DBA provides the password for the ASM instance and type of parameter file to be used for the ASM instances. After completing these choices, click Next.

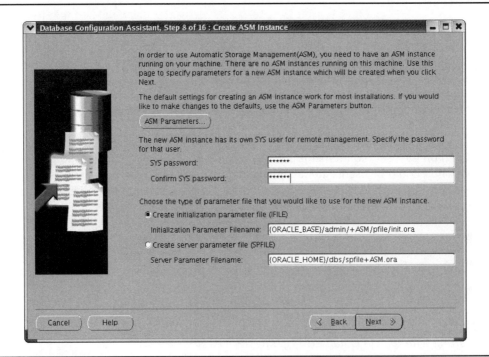

FIGURE 9-6. *The DBCA's Create ASM Instance screen*

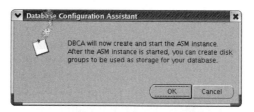

FIGURE 9-7. *The DBCA is ready to create an ASM instance.*

At this point, OUI has all the information required to create the ASM instances on the respective nodes in the cluster. When the new window pops up asking for confirmation (as shown in Figure 9-7), and you are ready, click OK.

The next screen (not shown) is related to the ASM diskgroup definition process. Diskgroups are used by ASM to store database files.

Available diskgroups, if already created for that ASM instance, are listed. Selecting ASM and a diskgroup specifies the DBCA to create a database within ASM. If no diskgroups exist or a new diskgroup is desired, then the DBCA offers the opportunity to create a new diskgroup. Note that an ASM diskgroup can house all the Oracle Database files, ranging from controlfiles, datafiles, redo logs, archive logs, Spfiles, and Recovery Manager (RMAN) backup files. However, Oracle executables, CRS files (OCR and voting disks), and nondatabase files cannot be housed in ASM diskgroups.

An active RDBMS instance that uses ASM storage can operate just like a typical database instance. All file access is directly performed with minimal ASM intervention. When a file is opened or created, the ASM instance sends the file layout to the RDBMS instance and all subsequent inputs/outputs (I/Os) are done using the extent map stored in the RDBMS instance.

All ASM file access can only be done via the RDBMS instance and its utilities. For example, database backups of ASM files can be performed only with RMAN. Note that utilities such as the Unix dd command are not recommended for backing up or restoring ASM diskgroups.

Database instances usually interact with the ASM instance when files are created, resized, deleted, or opened. ASM and RDBMS instances also interact if the storage configuration changes, such as when disks are added, are dropped, or fail.

The database file–level access (read/write) of ASM files is similar to pre–Oracle Database 10g, except that any database filename that begins with a plus sign (+) will automatically be handled and managed using the ASM code path. However, with ASM files, the database file access inherently has the characteristics of raw devices— that is, unbuffered (direct I/O) with kernelized asynchronous I/O (KAIO). Because the RDBMS instance issues I/Os against raw devices, there is no need to set the database parameter FILESYSTEMIO_OPTION unless network file system (NFS) volumes are used as ASM disks. Additionally, because ASYNCIO is enabled by default, no additional parameters are needed to leverage ASM.

In the next screen in the configuration process (see Figure 9-8), the DBA selects the location for the various database files. In the Database File Locations screen, the DBA has the choice to select between user-managed and Oracle-managed files. Note that if the storage mechanism is ASM, then to take advantage of the ASM architecture, select Oracle-managed files (OMF). With OMF, the DBA has further options to multiplex redo logs and control files. After you finish making your selections, click Next.

The next screen (see Figure 9-9) is the Recovery Configuration screen. In this screen, the DBA has the option to create a flashback recovery area (FRA) and enable archiving. For easy sharing of recovery data among the various nodes participating in the cluster, it is a requirement that these areas are located on shared storage. OUI has options to select the appropriate location by browsing through a list.

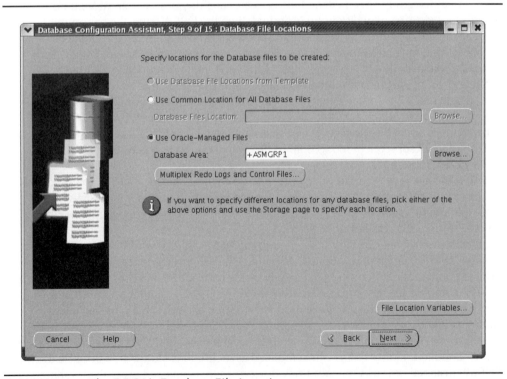

FIGURE 9-8. *The DBCA's Database File Locations screen*

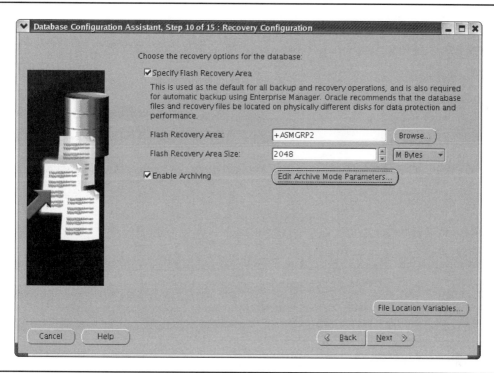

FIGURE 9-9. *The DBCA's Recovery Configuration screen*

Both the archive log files and FRA are to be configured on the same type of storage, (illustrated in Figure 9-9). Following two diskgroups for a database, both the FRA area will contain the archive log files, the backups, and the FRA.

The next screen (step 11 in the DBCA process and not shown here) presents the option to create sample schemas when the database is configured. After making the appropriate selections, click Next.

Next is the Database Services screen (see Figure 9-10). Services play a strategic role and are used in implementing distributed workload management. The next set of screens relates to the service and workload distribution setup process.

Note that as a part of the service definition, the transparent application failover (TAF) policies for the respective services could also be defined using this screen.

After the DBA has selected the storage mechanism and identified the appropriate services (if any), the next few screens are related to the instance definition process. In these screens, the DBA selects various instance-specific information such as memory

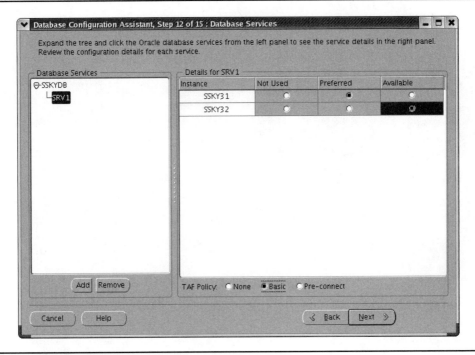

FIGURE 9-10. *The DBCA's Database Services screen*

allocation (for example, shared pool and buffer cache), sizing (such as processes), character modes (for example, UTF8), and the connection methods (dedicated, for instance). The DBA defines these parameters by selecting the respective tabs on the screen shown in Figure 9-11.

For example, when the DBA selects the Connection Mode tab, the DBCA displays options for client connections (see Figure 9-12). From this screen, the DBA can select the type of connection that is intended, such as shared server or dedicated server. After selecting the connection mode, click Next.

The DBCA now displays the database storage window (not shown here). In this screen, the DBA can enter a filename for each type of file, such as the storage definition for the control file, the various tablespaces, the rollback segments, and so on. After defining all the storage for the various files, click Next.

The next screen (see Figure 9-13) shows the database creation options. In this screen, the DBCA provides the option to generate the database creation scripts. The DBA can select both the options, in which case OUI generates the scripts and subsequently creates the database automatically or users can allow DBCA to

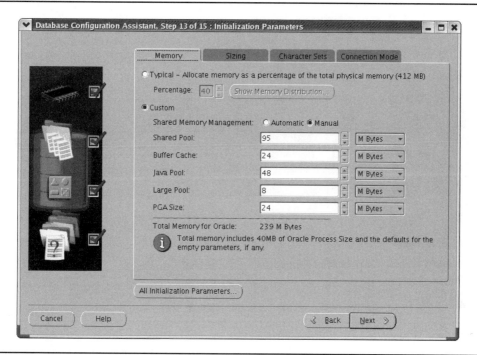

FIGURE 9-11. *The DBCA Initialization Parameters screen*

generate the scripts and execute them manually. Ensure that the Create Database
checkbox is selected, then click Finish.

Figure 9-13 is the final screen where the actual Create Database option is selected.
When the DBA selects the Finish option, the DBCA begins creating the database.
When the process has finished, a new database and the required database instances
are created.

Based on the database configuration specified, the next screen shows the various
stages of the installation process (see Figure 9-14).

After all the stages of the installation are complete, the DBCA starts the instances
on the respective nodes.

Several steps, which were once performed manually in the previous versions of
Oracle, are now automated in Oracle Database 10*g* and Oracle Database 11*g*. For
example, the registry is automatically created, formatted, and initialized during the
installation of Oracle Clusterware. The Oracle Cluster Registry (OCR) is stored in a
system parameter file ocr.loc located in the /etc/oracle directory in a Linux/Unix
environment, whereas the registry is located in a Windows environment.

The initial contents of the OCR file are visible, after Cluster Ready Services (CRS)
configuration, using the `crs_stat` utility.

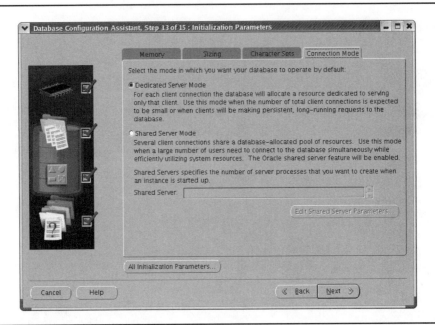

FIGURE 9-12. *The DBCA's Connection Mode tab*

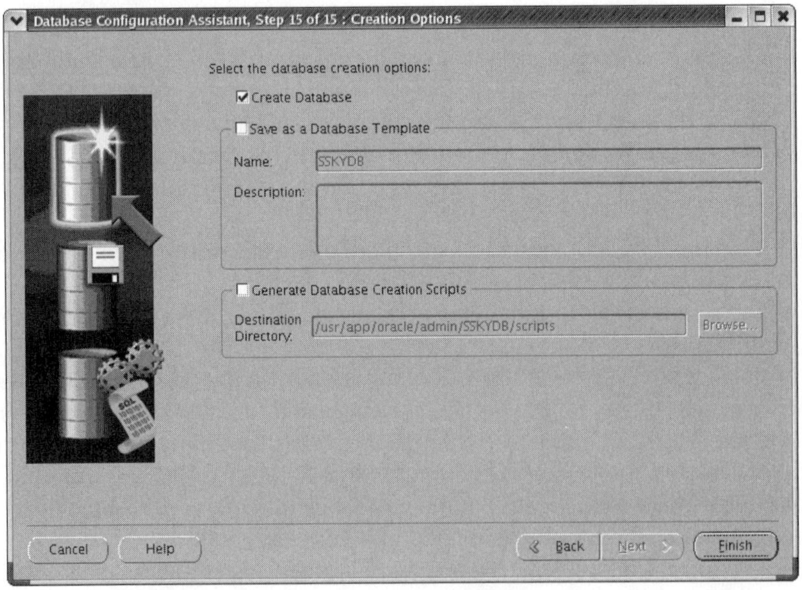

FIGURE 9-13. *The DBCA's Creation Options screen*

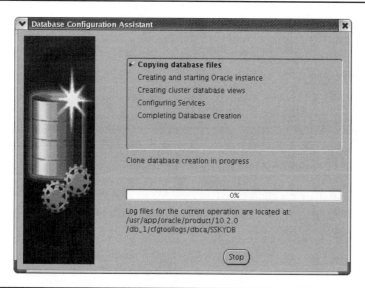

FIGURE 9-14. *The DBCA's database configuration progress screen*

Due to its shared location, one of the primary administrative features of the OCR is that from a single location all the components running on all nodes and instances of Oracle can be administrated, irrespective of the node from where the registry was created.

With the verification if all resources are ONLINE (from output above), it completes the database creation process.

Diskgroups and Databases

A diskgroup can contain files from many different Oracle Database 10*g* or higher databases, and these databases can be either from the same server or can reside on different servers. However, a disk and a database file can be part of only one diskgroup. Furthermore, one Oracle Database may also store its files in multiple diskgroups managed by the same ASM instance. Allowing multiple databases to share a diskgroup provides greater potential for improved disk utilization and greater overall throughput.

To reduce the complexity of managing ASM and its diskgroups, it is recommended to maintain and manage two ASM diskgroups per RAC cluster or single ASM instance. Additional diskgroups may be added to support tiered storage classes in information lifecycle management (ILM) or hierarchical storage management (HSM) deployments. Another variation of this model deployed by customers is where a third diskgroup is created and used to house the temporary tablespaces. In these cases, the temporary tablespace diskgroup is usually on less-expensive storage.

The two primary diskgroups map to the following areas:

- **Database area** This area stores active database files such as datafiles, controlfiles, online redo logs, and change tracking files used in incremental backups.

- **Flash recovery area** This is where recovery-related files are created, such as multiplexed copies of the current control file and online redo logs, archived redo logs, backup sets, and flashback log files.

If chosen at database creation time (via DBCA), an FRA stores an active copy of the controlfile and one member set of the redo log group to provide higher availability for the database. Note that additional copies of the controlfile or extra logfiles can be created and placed in either diskgroup.

NOTE
Refer to the following documentation for a detailed discussion on the usage and best practices of the FRA: http://otn.oracle.com/otn.

What about cases where there are several databases on the server, each one with differing recovery point objectives (RPOs) and recovery time objectives (RTOs)? One solution is to create a single large diskgroup for all the database areas and (possibly) a separate FRA for each database. This caters to environments where the database growth can be contained and where disk utilization is of great importance. There are many other alternatives, such as grouping databases together into a single DATA diskgroup and a single FRA diskgroup. The main point here is not to create too many diskgroups or to mimic a filesystem environment. This just ends up producing "islands of storage pools" and becomes highly unmanageable.

There is also another scenario illustrated later in Figure 9-17, where multiple single-instance databases share diskgroups managed by ASM in a clustered environment. In such situations, the primary objective is database consolidation.

Interaction between ASM and Database

Cluster Synchronization Services (CSS) is part of the Oracle Clusterware in a RAC configuration. Although CSS is automatically installed when Oracle Clusterware is installed in a RAC environment, CSS is also required on a single-instance configuration when the node has an ASM instance (Figure 9-15).

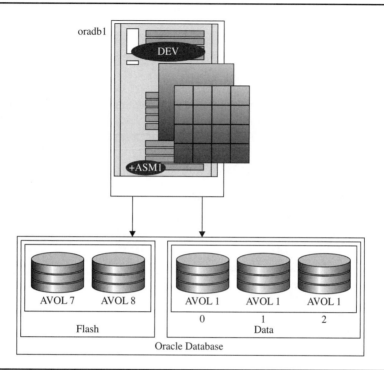

FIGURE 9-15. *ASM in single-instance configuration*

CSS provides cluster group services and node monitoring. It monitors RDBMS and ASM instances. When the ASM instance is started, it updates the CSS with status information regarding the diskgroups along with any connection information. CSS also helps ASM and RDBMS instances in the cluster know when to perform recovery.

An RDBMS instance is the standard Oracle instance and is the client of the ASM instance. The RDBMS to ASM communication is always intranode—that is, the RDBMS will not contact the remote ASM instance (in case of RAC) for servicing diskgroup requests.

It is important to note that RDBMS instances do not pass an I/O request to the ASM instance—that is, RDBMS instances do not proxy the I/O request through ASM. When an RDBMS instance opens an ASM file such as the system tablespace datafile, ASM ships the file's extent map to RDBMS instance, which stores the extents map in its System Global Area (SGA). Given that the RDBMS instance has the extent map for the ASM file cached in the SGA, the RDBMS instance can process reads/writes directly from the disk without further intervention from the ASM instance. As in the case with raw devices, the I/O request size is dictated by the RDBMS instance, not by ASM. Therefore, if the RDBMS needs to read or flush an 8K database block, it will issue an 8K I/O, not a 1MB I/O.

Users often ask whether there is any dependency between Automatic Segment Space Management (ASSM)-based datafiles and ASM. There is no dependency between ASM and ASSM (although their acronyms only differ by one extra letter). ASM manages how datafiles are laid out across disks (among other things) without looking at the data stored in those datafiles. ASSM deals with empty blocks that exist within a single segment (it replaces freelists and freelist groups). ASM does not care if the datafiles contain segments that are freelist-managed or autospace segment–managed via Bitmap Managed Block (BMB), so no conversion of internal structures takes place.

ASM Implementations

ASM can be implemented in following three configurations:

- On a single node

- On multiple nodes

- Consolidating and Clustering databases

Using ASM on a Single Node

ASM supports both a single-node, multiple-database configuration or a clustered configuration such as on RAC. One instance of ASM is required on a node regardless of the number of databases that are contained on the node. Besides configuring ASM, as discussed earlier, you must also configure CSS.

In a single node that supports multiple databases, diskgroups can be shared between multiple databases.

As illustrated in Figure 9-15, `oradb1` supports the DEV database and stores data in two diskgroups: `ASMGRP1` and `ASMGRP2`. If subsequently another database DEV1 is added to the same node, DEV1 can share the diskgroups with the DEV database.

NOTE
ASM instances are identified with the plus sign (+) prefixed to the name of the instance, as in +ASM1, +ASM2, and so on.

Using ASM on Multiple Nodes

Multiple nodes can contain ASM instances supporting their respective databases having diskgroups located on the same disk farm. For example, in Figure 9-16, instance +ASM1 on node `oradb1` and +ASM2 on `oradb2` can support their

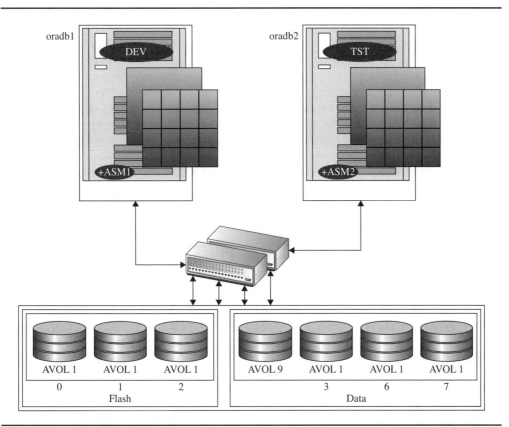

FIGURE 9-16. *ASM on multiple nodes sharing the same diskgroup*

respective databases DEV and TST mapping to their own diskgroups: ASMGRP1, ASMGRP2, and ASMGRP3; +ASM1 manages ASMGRP1 and ASMGRP2, whereas +ASM2 manages ASMGRP3.

Although no specific rules or conditions exist for single-instance databases, the situation changes when ASM instances share diskgroups. For example, if the database needs additional disk space, the DBA has two choices:

■ Add an additional disk to the storage array and either assign the disk to the existing diskgroup ASMGRP3 or create a new diskgroup and a new datafile for the same tablespace in this group.

■ Assign disk space from an existing diskgroup currently owned by instance +ASM1 located on `oradb1`. However, this would not be possible in this case due to configuration limitations. Both +ASM1 and +ASM2 (illustrated in figure 9.17) on `oradb1` and `oradb2`, respectively, are single-instance versions of ASM. If multiple instances of ASM located on different nodes require access to the same set of diskgroups, the nodes should be clustered together using Oracle Clusterware in Oracle Database 10*g* Release 2 or later. This is because ASM has to synchronize the metadata updates between the various instances.

Figure 9-16 shows multiple nodes having different ASM instances and sharing diskgroups on the same storage array. One of the primary benefits of this configuration is storage consolidation, where multiple databases residing on different nodes can share one diskgroup.

Consolidating and Clustering Databases

In Oracle Database 10*g* Release 1, the same ASM instance could not have both RAC and single-instance RDBMS clients. This limitation created challenges in implementing storage grid architectures and consolidated database solutions. Oracle Database 10*g* Release 2 enhances the ASM functionality in a clustered environment, allowing one ASM instance per node to manage all RDBMS instances in the cluster. Therefore, an ASM instance on a given node can now manage storage for single instances or RAC RDBMS instances. This feature relieves the customer from having to maintain more than one ASM instance to serve the different database types that might exist in the cluster, and thus obviates the need for DBAs to manage separate storage pools.

This feature leverages Oracle Clusterware to consolidate multiple islands of databases economically into a single clustered pool of storage managed by ASM. This essentially allows customers to optimize their storage utilization by eliminating overprovisioned storage and save money by reducing their overall footprint of database storage.

After the database is created and the instance is active, the RDBMS instance becomes a client of ASM. This is reflected in the V$ASM_CLIENT view. (This view of RDBMS instances contains rows if the database has open files in ASM [CONNECTED state] or can access any diskgroup [MOUNTED state].) V$ASM_CLIENT contains one row for every ASM diskgroup that is opened by a database instance. In the following output, V$ASM_CLIENT displays two RDBMS instances connected to ASM, with each instance using two diskgroups. Note that instance `cubs1` is a Oracle Database 10*g* Release 2 RAC-enabled database and that instance `brew` is a 10.1.0.5 single instance.

```
SQL> SELECT INSTANCE, NAME, STATUS, SOFTWARE_VERSION, COMPATIBLE_VERSION
FROM V$ASM_CLIENT;
INSTANCE STATUS        SOFTWARE_VRSN COMPATIBLE_VRSN
-------- ------------- ------------- -------------
```

```
cubs1   CONNECTED      10.2.0.3.0    10.2.0.1.0
cubs1   CONNECTED      10.2.0.3.0    10.2.0.1.0
brew    CONNECTED      10.1.0.5.0    10.1.0.2.0
brew    CONNECTED      10.1.0.5.0    10.1.0.2.0
```

If queried from the RDBMS instance, V$ASM_DISKGROUP has a row for every diskgroup that is discovered by the ASM instance on the node. If there are no rows, there are no ASM diskgroups on the node (or the ASM instance is not running). For each diskgroup listed, the view lists the state of the diskgroup. If the state is connected, that means that the RDBMS instance already has the diskgroup open. If the state is mounted, then the diskgroup is mounted by the ASM instance, but not in use at that time by the RDBMS instance. Other states of the diskgroup would indicate that the diskgroup is not available to the RDBMS instance without further action on the ASM instance.

Clustering ASM

A clustered configuration is an environment that consists of one or more servers connected together through an additional layer of software called a clusterware or cluster manager. The clusterware treats all the components of the various servers to behave in a coherent fashion. The basic functioning of ASM in a clustered environment is no different than that of a single-instance configuration. However, in a clustered configuration the various ASM instances share information among themselves. We will look at these details in the following subsection.

Using ASM in a RAC Environment

Every node in a RAC environment will contain one instance of ASM irrespective of the number of databases that exist on that node. As illustrated in Figure 9-17, in a four-node RAC configuration, there will be four instances of ASM. The various instances of ASM communicate with each other through the cluster interconnect using the CACHE FUSION technology available with RAC.

Figure 9-17 is a RAC configuration where multiple RDBMS instances on multiple nodes each of which has an ASM instance that manages the same set of diskgroups. In this configuration, all the instances can write to or read from any of the available diskgroups in the storage array.

Background Processes

In a RDBMS instance, there are three sets of processes added to support the ASM diskgroups and infrastructure:

- **RBAL** This process performs global opens of all the disks in the diskgroups. The primary function of this background process is to open all disks listed under each diskgroup and to make them available for the various clients.

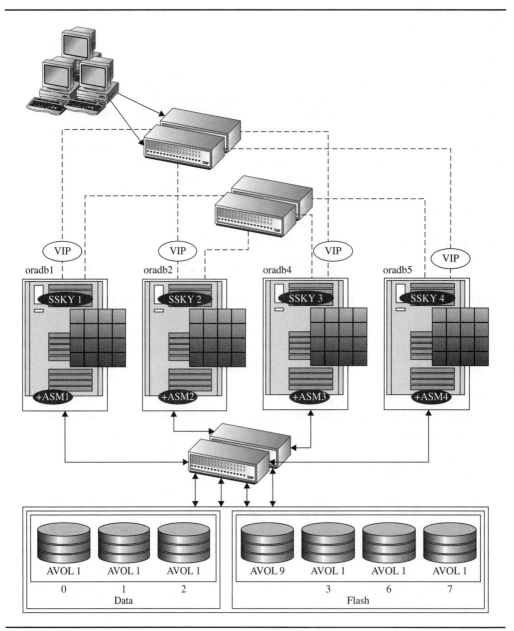

FIGURE 9-17. *ASM configuration in a RAC implementation*

- **ASMB** This process contacts CSS using the diskgroup name and acquires the associated ASM connect string. This connect string is then used to connect into the ASM instance using a bequeath connection. Using this persistent connection, periodic messages are exchanged to update statistics and provide a heartbeat mechanism. During operations that require ASM intervention, such as a file creation by an Oracle 10g RDBMS database foreground, the RDBMS foreground connects directly to the ASM instance to perform the operation. Upon successful completion of file creation, database file extent maps are sent by ASM to ASMB. Additionally, ASMB also sends database I/O statistics to the ASM instance.

- **O0nn** This group of slave processes establishes connections to the ASM instance, where nn is a number from 01 to 10. Through this connection pool, RDBMS processes can send messages to the ASM instance. For example, opening a file sends the open request to the ASM instance via a slave. However, in Oracle Database 10g slaves are not used for long-running operations such as creating a file. Slaves are used for file creation in Oracle Database 11g. The slave (pool) connections eliminate the overhead of logging into the ASM instance for short requests. These slaves are shut down when not in use.

Database init.ora Parameters to Support ASM

The SGA parameters for an RDBMS instance need slight modification to support ASM extent maps and other ASM information. Note if the Oracle Database Automatic Memory Management feature is being used on the RDBMS instance, then the following sizing data can be treated as informational only or as supplemental data in gauging appropriate values for the SGA. Oracle highly recommends using the Automatic Memory Management feature. The following are guidelines for SGA sizing on the database instance:

- **PROCESSES** Add 16.

- **LARGE_POOL** Add an additional 600K.

- **SHARED_POOL** Additional memory is required to store extent maps.

The values from the following queries are aggregated to obtain current database storage size that is either already on ASM or will be stored in ASM. This value is then used in conjunction with the diskgroup redundancy type that is used (or will be used) to calculate the size of the SHARED_POOL.

```
SELECT SUM (BYTES)/(1024*1024*1024) FROM V$DATAFILE;
SELECT SUM (BYTES)/(1024*1024*1024) FROM V$LOGFILE A, V$LOG B WHERE
```

```
A.GROUP#=B.GROUP#;
SELECT SUM (BYTES)/(1024*1024*1024) FROM V$TEMPFILE WHERE
STATUS='ONLINE';
```

For example:

1. For diskgroups using external redundancy = (every 100GB of file space needs 1MB of extra shared pool) + 2MB

2. For diskgroups using normal redundancy: (every 50GB of file space needs 1MB of extra shared pool) + 4MB

3. For diskgroups using high redundancy: (every 33GB of file space needs 1MB of extra shared pool) + 6MB

Migration to ASM

Databases that were already created using raw devices or filesystems or databases that have migrated from Oracle Database 9*i* to Oracle Database 10*g* or to Oracle Database 11*g* may not be using ASM for storage. In these situations, it may be desirable to convert the datafiles to use ASM. Conversion could be performed in one of two available methods: Either the complete database can be converted, or specific tablespaces could be converted to use ASM. Converting the entire database to ASM storage is performed using RMAN. However, there are several methods to convert individual datafiles to ASM.

Converting Non-ASM Databases to ASM Using RMAN

The following are the steps to be followed when migrating an existing database to ASM:

1. Perform a SHUTDOWN IMMEDIATE command on all instances participating in the cluster.

2. Modify the following initialization parameters of the target database:

   DB_CREATE_FILE_DEST

   DB_CREATE_ONLINE_LOG_DEST[1,2,3,4]

   CONTROL_FILES

3. Using RMAN connect to the target database and start up the target database in NOMOUNT mode.

4. Restore control file from its original location to the new location specified in step 2.

5. After the controlfile is restored to the new location and the database is ready to be mounted, mount the database.

6. Using the RMAN copy operation, copy the database into the new location assigned in the ASM diskgroup.

7. Once the copy operation has completed, the database is ready for recovery. Using RMAN, perform database recovery operation.

8. Open the database.

9. During the migration process, the temporary tablespace was not migrated; this has to be created manually.

10. Next step is to create the online redo logs into ASM. This step can be accomplished using Oracle-provided PL/SQL scripts found in Oracle Database documentation.

11. The old datafiles can be deleted from the operating system (OS).

12. If the database had enabled block change tracking, you can re-enable this feature at this stage.

Converting Non-ASM Datafiles to ASM Using RMAN

The following are the steps for migrating a single non-ASM datafile into an ASM-based volume manager:

1. Using RMAN, connect to the target database as follows:

```
[oracle@oradb1 oracle]$ rman
Recovery Manager: Release 10.2.0.3 - Production
Copyright (c) 1995, 2004, Oracle.  All rights reserved.
RMAN> connect target
connected to target database: SSKYDB (DBID=2290365532)
```

2. Using SQL, take the tablespace offline that will be the migration candidate:

```
RMAN> SQL "ALTER TABLESPACE EXAMPLE OFFLINE";
```

3. Using the `BACKUP AS COPY` operation, perform the following operation:

```
RMAN> BACKUP AS COPY TABLESPACE EXAMPLE FORMAT '+ASMGRP1';
Starting backup at 01-OCT-04
allocated channel: ORA_DISK_1
channel ORA_DISK_1: sid=252 devtype=DISK
channel ORA_DISK_1: starting datafile copy
input datafile fno=00005 name=/u14/oradata/SSKYDB/example01.dbf
output filename=+ASMGRP1/sskydb/datafile/example.264.571954419
tag=TAG20041001T221236 recid=2 stamp=538438446
channel ORA_DISK_1: datafile copy complete, elapsed time: 00:01:36
Finished backup at 01-OCT-04
RMAN>
```

4. After receiving the "copy complete" message, indicating a successful copy, switch the tablespace to use the copied datafile:

```
RMAN> SWITCH TABLESPACE EXAMPLE TO COPY;
datafile 5 switched to datafile copy
"+ASMGRP1/sskydb/datafile/example.264.571954419"
RMAN>
```

5. Final step is to put the tablespace online using SQL:

```
RMAN> SQL "ALTER TABLESPACE EXAMPLE ONLINE";
```

6. Verify the operation by connecting to the target database and checking the V$ views.

Moving Datafiles from One Diskgroup to Another

To move files from one diskgroup to another or even from a filesystem into ASM diskgroup, follow these steps:

1. Identify the *datafile#* and the *tablespace_name* for the file that you want to move.

2. Connect using RMAN and enter the following commands:

```
CONNECT TARGET
BACKUP DEVICE TYPE DISK AS COPY DATAFILE datafile# FORMAT '+DG2';
SQL "ALTER TABLESPACE tablespace_name OFFLINE";
SWITCH DATAFILE datafile# TO COPY;
RECOVER DATAFILE datafile#;
SQL "ALTER TABLESPACE tablespace_name ONLINE";
```

Converting ASM Files Using
`DBMS_FILE_TRANSFER`

`DBMS_FILE_TRANSFER` is a stored procedure that was introduced in Oracle Database 9*i*. This package provides a means to copy files between two locations (on the same host or between database servers). Starting in Oracle Database 10*g* Release 1, ASM leverages this utility to copy files between ASM diskgroups and is the primary utility used to instantiate an ASM DataGuard database. In Oracle Database 10*g* Release 2, `DBMS_FILE_TRANSFER` was enhanced to support all combinations of ASM and non-ASM file transfers.

The `DBMS_FILE_TRANSFER` package enables DBAs to copy files between two locations. This procedure is used to move or copy files between ASM diskgroups. Using this procedure, the following transfer scenarios are possible:

- Copy files from one ASM diskgroup to another ASM diskgroup.

- Copy files from an ASM diskgroup to external storage media such as a filesystem at the OS level.

- Copy files from a filesystem at the OS level to an ASM-configured diskgroup.

- Copy files from a filesystem at the OS level to another location or raw device at the OS level.

Follow these steps to move datafiles from one location to another using the `DBMS_FILE_TRANSFER` procedure:

1. Identify the datafile to be moved/copied from one location to another

```
SQL> SELECT FILE_NAME FROM DBA_DATA_FILES;
FILE_NAME
-----------------------------------------------------------
+ASMGRP1/sskydb/datafile/users.259.571954319
+ASMGRP1/sskydb/datafile/sysaux.257.571954317
+ASMGRP1/sskydb/datafile/undotbs1.258.571954317
+ASMGRP1/sskydb/datafile/system.256.571954317
+ASMGRP1/sskydb/datafile/example.264.571954419
+ASMGRP1/sskydb/datafile/undotbs2.265.571954545
+ASMGRP1/sskydb/datafile/undotbs3.266.571954547
+ASMGRP1/sskydb/datafile/sorac_data.272.572018797
+ASMGRP1/sskydb/datafile/bmf_data.273.572018897
```

2. Identify the destination (ASM or non-ASM) to which to copy the file. In this example, the datafile is copied to an external OCFS-based filesystem location.

3. Take the datafile offline:

```
SQL> ALTER DATABASE DATAFILE
'+ASMGRP1/SSKYDB/DATAFILE/BMF_DATA.273.572018897' OFFLINE;
```

4. Copy the file to the new location by first creating DIRECTORY_NAME for the source and target locations and using the following procedure:

```
SQL> CREATE DIRECTORY ASMSRC AS '+ASMGRP1/SSKYDB/DATAFILE';
Directory created.
SQL> CREATE DIRECTORY OSDEST AS '/ocfs9/oradata';
Directory created.
SQL> BEGIN
    DBMS_FILE_TRANSFER.COPY_FILE('ASMRC',
                                 'BMF_DATA.273.572018897',
                                 'OSDEST',
                                 'BMF.dbf');
END;
/
```

5. Bring the datafile online:

```
ALTER DATABASE DATAFILE '+ASMGRP1/SSKYDB/DATAFILE/BMF_
DATA.273.572018897' ONLINE;
```

6. Verify the copied file:

```
[oracle@irvadbl01 oradata]$ ls -ltr /ocfs9/oradata
```

Transferring Non-ASM Datafiles to ASM Using FTP

Adding to the other methods of file transfer to and from ASM diskgroups, using the virtual folder feature in Extensible Markup Language (XML) Database (DB), you can manipulate ASM files and folders via XML DB protocols such as File Transfer Protocol (FTP), Hypertext Transfer Protocol (HTTP)/ Web-based Distributed Authoring and Versioning (WebDAV), and programmatic application program interfaces (APIs).

Under this method, the ASM virtual folder is mounted as /sys/asm within the XML DB hierarchy. The folder is virtual—that is, the ASM folders and files are not physically stored within the XML DB. However, the underlying ASM component handles any operation on the ASM virtual folder transparently.

To use this method of file transfer, it is important that the DBA install and configure the XML DB.

NOTE
*If they are not already installed, you can create the
XML DB base objects using the* `scatqm.sql` *script
located in $ORACLE_HOME/rdbms/admin directory
on all supported platforms.*

The ASM virtual folder is created by default during the installation of XML DB.
If the database is not configured to use ASM, then this folder will be empty and no
operations will be permitted on it. If ASM is configured, the ASM virtual folder, /sys/asm,
is mounted within the XML DB hierarchy. Any operation on the ASM virtual folder is
transparently handled by the underlying ASM component. The ASM folder contains one
subfolder for every mounted diskgroup. Each diskgroup folder contains one subfolder
corresponding to every database name. In addition, it may contain additional files and
folders corresponding to the aliases that the administrators have created.

Accessing an ASM Virtual Folder via FTP

FTP is also available for copying datafiles in and out of the ASM diskgroup, offering
additional flexibility for managing your files. Determine the appropriate FTP port
defined for your environment. The example in this section describes how to extract,
copy, and delete DataPump dumpsets from an ASM directory, +Flash/dumpsets,
which equates to the XML DB folder /sys/asm/flash/dumpsets.

To set up and configure XML DB FTP and also to see how files move into and
out of ASM, follow these steps (follow Note 243554.1 found at metalink.oracle.com
"How to Deinstall and Reinstall XML Database [XDB]" to install XDB):

1. As root, check whether the FTP service is running:

```
# netstat -a | grep ftp
tcp        0        0 *:ftp  *:*   LISTEN
```

If no output is returned, start FTP and configure it to start automatically.

2. Configure the FTP and HTTP ports of XML DB as follows:

```
connect / as sysdba
SQLPLUS> EXECUTE DBMS_XDB.SETHTTPPORT(8080);
SQLPLUS> EXECUTE DBMS_XDB.SETFTPPORT(2100);
SQLPLUS> COMMIT;
```

Verify the steps above using the following:

```
SQLPLUS> SELECT DBMS_XDB.GETFTPPORT() FROM DUAL;
SQLPLUS> SELECT DBMS_XDB.GETHTTPPORT() FROM DUAL;
```

3. Check the dispatchers configuration for XML DB; if it is not set, set it up for a single instance:

```
SQLPLUS> ALTER SYSTEM SET DISPATCHERS  = (PROTOCOL=TCP) (SERVICE
=<sid>XDB)" SCOPE=BOTH
```

To set up the configuration for RAC instances, use the following:

```
ALTER SYSTEM SET dbprod1.dispatchers = "(PROTOCOL=TCP) (SERVICE=
<sid1>XDB)" SCOPE=BOTH
ALTER SYSTEM SET dbprod2.dispatchers = "(PROTOCOL=TCP) (SERVICE=
<sid2>XDB)" SCOPE=BOTH
```

4. Set the init.ora parameter LOCAL_LISTENER if the default settings for listener will not be used; for example, you might set it to port number 1521. Restart the listener if necessary.

5. Validate that the listener has the FTP and HTTP registered. The listener output should include the following lines:

```
(DESCRIPTION =(ADDRESS = (PROTOCOL = tcp)(HOST = <host>)(PORT =
2100))(Presentation = FTP)(Session = RAW))

(DESCRIPTION = (ADDRESS = (PROTOCOL = tcp)(HOST = <host>)(PORT =
8080))(Presentation = HTTP)(Session = RAW))
```

6. Verify that there are no invalid XML DB-related packages in the database:

```
SQL> SELECT COUNT(*)FROM DBA_OBJECTS WHERE OWNER='XDB' AND
STATUS='INVALID';
```

7. Verify the XML DB status in the DBA_REGISTRY:

```
SQL>SELECT COMP_NAME, STATUS, VERSION FROM DBA_REGISTRY WHERE
COMP_NAME = 'Oracle XML Database';
Connect to ASM via XMLDB FTP
[oracle@edrsr14p1 oracle]$ ftp edrsr14p1 2100
Connected to edrsr14p1 (139.185.35.114).
220- edrsr14p1
220 edrsr14p1 FTP Server (Oracle XML DB/Oracle Database) ready.
Name (edrsr14p1:oracle): system
331 pass required for SYSTEM
Password:
230 SYSTEM logged in
Remote system type is Unix.
```

The following are examples that illustrate the use of XMLDB FTP. Note that these commands are exactly the same as standard FTP commands.

```
ftp> cd /sys/asm/flash/orcl/dumpsets
250 CWD Command successful
ftp> get expdp_5_5.dat
```

```
local: expdp_5_5.dat remote: expdp_5_5.dat
227 Entering Passive Mode (139,185,35,114,100,234)
150 ASCII Data Connection
278530 bytes received in 0.153 secs (1.8e+03 Kbytes/sec)
ftp> put expdp_03_26.dat
ftp> del expdp_03_20.dat
ftp> rename expdp_03_26.dat latest_dumpset.dmp
```

NOTE
*Currently, only files created by Oracle Database
and its clients can be stored in an ASM diskgroup.
These must be file types such as datafiles, redo logs,
RMAN backups, and DataPump dumpsets. When
the FTP server receives a request to write a file in an
ASM diskgroup, it examines the first 64K of the file
to determine what kind of file it is and what block
size it has. If the file is not recognized as one of the
file types created by Oracle, then the write will fail.
The same is true when creating files with DBMS_
FILE_TRANSFER. You cannot store arbitrary data
in an ASM diskgroup. It is a common misconception
that ASM somehow stores file contents differently
than other filesystems. The contents of a datafile
stored in ASM and the contents of a datafile stored
in an OS file are exactly the same. The same is true
of all other file types that ASM supports. The only
difference is that ASM keeps some extra metadata ,
such as file type and block size.*

Using EM to Simplify ASM Migration

The EM Migration utility is a feature available starting in Oracle Database 10g Release
2 that provides simplified database migration to ASM-based storage. This utility
migrates 10.2 and later databases residing on filesystem or raw devices to ASM on the
same host. The EM Migration utility can be accessed from the Maintenance tab of the
Database Instance page of EM.

The purpose of the EM Migration utility is to automate and simplify the database
migration process to ASM. The EM Migration utility provides the following benefits:

- Supports migrating all database files, recovery related files, and Spfiles

- Provides a wizard walkthrough to create migration requests, process and
  schedule migration requests, and report statuses of migration requests

■ Migrates databases using the same database name, database identifier (DBID), and system identifier (SID)

■ Provides a fully recoverable fallback database in case the user decides to return to non-ASM based storage (assuming that ASM storage and the existing storage exist at the same time)

■ Monitors the migration process

■ Supports online and offline database migration

The EM Migration utility uses RMAN commands to migrate control files, datafiles, and recovery-related files from the filesystem to ASM. (The utility migrates files such as online logs and temp files by dropping them, using PL/SQL procedures, and then recreating them in ASM.) The migration task is created and submitted as a job via the EM job system. The task specification process includes walking through the wizard, which involves real-time validation of user requests. The submitted job includes the following major substeps:

1. Construct the init parameters.

2. Migrate the database files using RMAN.

3. Migrate the temp files and online logs using PL/SQL procedures.

4. Clean up.

TIP
The following site describes how to perform migration to ASM: http://www.oracle.com/ technology/deploy/availability/pdf/MAA_WP_ 10gASMMigration.pdf.

ASM Performance Monitoring Using EM

Because ASM diskgroups present raw devices to the database, databases inherently benefit from raw device performance (as well as the filesystem interface). ASYNC_IO must be enabled on the database side, but you need not set any other parameters to take advantage of the raw device performance.

However, there are always users who are testing the I/O performance of ASM in juxtaposition to the filesystem. Often users reach incorrect conclusions regarding ASM performance drawn from invalid benchmark comparisons. Here's why:

■ ASM uses a character or "unbuffered" I/O interface. No I/O caching occurs at the OS level.

■ Filesystems use a block or buffered I/O interface. OS virtual memory is used extensively for I/O caching.

As a result of the different I/O code paths, and in particular the use of additional memory, a direct comparison is invalid. Large amounts of available memory on the server always benefit filesystems, because the filesystem driver caches recently used blocks in virtual memory. Performance is directly affected, because database physical I/Os can be serviced from the filesystem buffer cache, thus providing a faster I/O response time. Note that this debate is not necessarily one of ASM versus raw, but rather of raw versus cooked.

Therefore, to level the playing field, you should determine the amount of memory used by the filesystem for the application being benchmarked (the working set size) and add that to the database buffer cache or the `SGA_TARGET` of the database using ASM storage. This is the same technique that has been applied to cooked versus raw comparisons of database performance for many years to make an "apples-to-apples" comparison of raw and filesystems. For example, a filesystem that houses the datafiles for a database consumes an average of 200MB of memory. This working set size of 200MB should rolled into the database buffer cache or added to the pool of `SGA_TARGET`.

Alternatively, if the filesystem can support `o_direct` or DIRECTIO, than that option should be enabled when benchmarking against ASM-based databases. This technique is used to eliminate the cache from the filesystem I/O path.

The comparison of cooked and raw has been going on for over a dozen years. The conclusion has always been that raw devices usually provide better performance than filesystems; however, the lack of manageability of raw devices makes it a cumbersome choice. ASM provides the best of both worlds: the performance of raw with manageability of filesystems, with the additional benefit of being optimized specifically for database I/O patterns.

Given equivalent operating conditions, ASM will always perform at least as well as, if not better than, filesystems.

To improve performance of the database, consider the following best practices:

■ Ensure that the database can leverage asynchronous I/O. Starting with Oracle Database 10g, asynchronous I/O is enabled and is the default setting.

■ Make sure that the lower I/O stack components, such as host bus adapters (HBAs), Fabric switches, and storage array adapters are configured correct and the ratio between the HBA and controllers are proportional for optimal I/O performance. Additionally, ensure that the firmware on these components is up-to-date and certified by the storage vendor.

■ Maximize the I/O read and write size through all the I/O stack layers, such as the OS, multipathing drivers, hardware device drivers, and the storage array. Configure an OS I/O size that is at least 1MB and make certain that multipathing drivers and device drivers do not excessively break up I/O requests into smaller units.

ASM–Database Multiversion Support

Starting in Oracle Database 10g Release 2, ASM transparently supports both older and newer software versions of the database. Both forward and backward compatibility are also maintained between Oracle Database 10g Releases 1 and 2. Therefore, any combination of 10.1.*0.x* and 10.2.*0.y* and 11.1.0.*z* for either ASM or RDBMS instances interoperate seamlessly without administrative intervention. The only requirement is that an RDBMS instance connecting to a 10.2 or 11.1 ASM instance must be at version 10.1.0.3 or later. Additionally, CSS must be at the highest level.

Allowing mixed versions of the ASM and RDBMS instances makes for relaxed migration strategies and higher availability possible. For example, a database upgrade will not force an upgrade of the ASM instance.

When mixing software versions, ASM functionality reverts to the functionality of the earliest version in use. For example, an Oracle 10.1.0.5 RDBMS instance working with a 10.2.0.3 ASM instance does not exploit new features in ASM 10.2. Conversely, a 10.2 RDBMS instance working with a 10.1.0.5 ASM instance cannot exploit any of the 10.2 features of ASM, such as XML DB folders. V$ASM_CLIENT has two columns that give you information about the software version number and corresponding database compatibility level. Note that V$ASM_CLIENT exists on both ASM and RDBMS instances, so the content of the view will reflect the instance from which it is queried.

Oracle Database 11g Release 1 introduced the COMPATBILE.ASM and COMPATIBLE.RDBMS diskgroup attributes. Setting these attributes to 11.1 enables additional ASM functionality, but restricts the RDBMS clients to those with their compatible init.ora parameter set to 11.0 or higher. The compatible diskgroup attributes are discussed in further detail in Chapter 4.

Transportable Tablespaces and ASM

This section describes the method for creating transportable tablespaces (TTSs) where the source and destination databases are ASM-based. This method uses standard utilities such as DataPump and the database package DBMS_FILE_TRANSFER. This package is used to transfer the DataPump metadata and datafiles to the remote database server. For completeness, the 10.2 command CONVERT DATABASE is covered in the last subsection.

We will examine a working example of creating and plugging in transportable tablespaces. In the example two servers, host1 and host2, are in disparate locations, with each one on an independent Hitachi storage array. Server host1 is the source database and will house database named db1. The server host2, which is deemed the target server and will subscribe to the transportable tables, will house the database SSKYDB.

Performing the Preliminary Steps to Set Up TTS

Before setting up the TTSs, you need to take the following steps:

1. Create or use two existing tablespaces on the source database:

```
SQL> SHOW PARAMETER DB_CREATE_FILE_DEST
NAME TYPE VALUE
-------------------- ----------- ------------------------------
db_create_file_dest string +DATA
SQL> CREATE TABLESPACE TTS_1;
SQL> CREATE TABLESPACE TTS_2;
```

Although having two tablespaces is not necessary in all cases, we will need them for this example to demonstrate object dependency.

NOTE
OMF is being employed in this example, so set the init.ora parameter DB_CREATE_FILE_DEST to the appropriate diskgroup name.

2. Create a table in TTS_1 and an index in TTS_2 to ensure that the tablespaces have object dependencies:

```
SQL> CONNECT scott/tiger
Connected.
SQL> CREATE TABLE EMP_COPY TABLESPACE TTS_1 AS SELECT * FROM EMP;
SQL> SELECT COUNT(*) FROM EMP_COPY;
10 rows returned
SQL> CREATE INDEX EMP_COPY_I ON EMP_COPY (EMPNO);
2 TABLESPACE TTS_2;
```

3. Check to make sure that you have a self-contained transportable set. Oracle provides a PL/SQL package that aids in this check:

```
SQL> EXECUTE DBMS_TTS.TRANSPORT_SET_CHECK ('TTS_1, TTS_2' TRUE);
```

4. Then query the TRANSPORT_SET_VIOLATIONS view, to see whether any dependency violations exist:

```
SQL> SELECT * FROM TRANSPORT_SET_VIOLATIONS;
No rows returned
```

5. Create a new service names entry, which will point to the destination database to which the tablespaces will be transported. For example, add the following lines to tnsnames.ora:

```
SSKYDB =
DESCRIPTION =
ADDRESS_LIST =
ADDRESS = (PROTOCOL = TCP)(HOST = host2)(PORT = 1521))
)
CONNECT_DATA =
SERVICE_NAME = host2.us.oracle.com)
INSTANCE_NAME = SSKYDB)
)
)
```

6. As SYSTEM, create a database link between the two databases. This is needed because you will be using the DBMS_FILE_TRANSFER package to move metadata between the two databases.

```
SQL> CREATE DATABASE LINK SSKYDB CONNECT TO SYSTEM IDENTIFIED BY
MANAGER1 USING 'SSKYDB';
```

7. Create a directory object in the source database db1 to hold the dumpfile. Because you we are using ASM, this needs to be an ASM object; make sure that the directory path ends with a slash (/):

```
SQL> CREATE DIRECORY TTS_DUMP AS '+DATA/';
```

8. Create another directory object in the source database that points to an operating system path for the log file:

```
SQL> CREATE DIRECTORY TTS_DUMP_LOG AS '/export/home/tts_log/';
```

9. Create a directory object in the source database that points to the datafiles:

```
SQL> CREATE DIRECTORY TTS_DATAFILE AS '+DATA/db1/datafile/';
```

10. Grant read/write access to the user as whom you will perform the export (you need only perform this step if you are using a nonprivileged user):

```
SQL> GRANT READ, WRITE ON DIRECTORY TTS_DUMP TO SYSTEM;
SQL> GRANT READ, WRITE ON DIRECTORY TTS_DUMP_LOG TO SYSTEM;
SQL> GRANT READ, WRITE ON DIRECTORY TTS_DUMP_DATAFILE TO SYSTEM;
```

11. Repeat steps 7 through 10 for the target database SSKYDB as well.

12. Make all tablespaces in the transportable set to read-only:

```
SQL> ALTER TABLESPACE tts_1 READ ONLY;
SQL> ALTER TABLESPACE tts_2 READ ONLY;
```

13. Check the status of the tablespaces on the source database:

```
SQL> SELECT TABLESPACE_NAME, STATUS FROM DBA_TABLESPACES;
```

```
TABLESPACE_NAME                STATUS
------------------------------ ---------
SYSTEM                         ONLINE
UNDOTBS1                       ONLINE
SYSAUX                         ONLINE
TEMP                           ONLINE
USERS                          ONLINE
UNDOTBS2                       ONLINE
TTS_1                          READ ONLY
TTS_2                          READ ONLY
Export metadata
```

14. Export the metadata for the two tablespaces:

```
[ora10g@host1]$ expdp system/manager1 directory=tts_dump
dumpfile=tts1_db1.dmp
logfile=tts_dump_log:tts.log
transport_tablespaces=tts_1,tts_2 transport_full_check=y
Starting "SYSTEM"."SYS_EXPORT_TRANSPORTABLE_02": system/********
directory=tts_datafile dumpfile=tts1.dmp
logfile=tts_dump_log:tts.log transport
_tablespaces=tts_1,tts_2 transport_full_check=y
Processing object type TRANSPORTABLE_EXPORT/PLUGTS_BLK
Processing object type TRANSPORTABLE_EXPORT/TABLE
Processing object type TRANSPORTABLE_EXPORT/INDEX
Processing object type TRANSPORTABLE_EXPORT/INDEX_STATISTICS
Processing object type TRANSPORTABLE_EXPORT/TABLE_STATISTICS
Processing object type TRANSPORTABLE_EXPORT/POST_INSTANCE/PLUGTS_BLK
Master table "SYSTEM"."SYS_EXPORT_TRANSPORTABLE_02" successfully
loaded/unloaded
************************************************************************
**Dump file set for SYSTEM.SYS_EXPORT_TRANSPORTABLE_02 is:
+DATA/tts1.dmp
Job "SYSTEM"."SYS_EXPORT_TRANSPORTABLE_02" successfully completed at
14:00:34
```

15. Use DBMS_FILE_TRANSFER to send the dump file across to the target:

```
[ora10g@host1]$ sqlplus system/manager
SQL> BEGIN
2 DBMS_FILE_TRANSFER.PUT_FILE
3 (SOURCE_DIRECTORY_OBJECT => 'TTS_DUMP',
4 SOURCE_FILE_NAME => 'tts1.db1.dmp',
5 DESTINATION_DIRECTORY_OBJECT => 'TTS_DUMP',
6 DESTINATION_FILE_NAME => 'tts1.db1.dmp',
7 DESTINATION_DATABASE => 'SSKYDB');
8 END;
9 /
```

16. Check the filenames on the source database for the two tablespaces being transported:

```
SQL> SELECT FILE_NAME FROM DBA_DATA_FILES
2 WHERE TABLESPACE_NAME LIKE 'TTS%';
FILE_NAME
-------------------------------------------------
+DATA/sskydb/datafile/tts_1.294.590721319
+DATA/sskydb/datafile/tts_2.295.586721335
```

17. Transfer the two datafiles to the target database using DBMS_FILE_TRANSFER:

```
TTS1 datafile
SQL> BEGIN
2 DBMS_FILE_TRANSFER.PUT_FILE
3 (SOURCE_DIRECTORY_OBJECT => 'TTS_DATAFILE',
4 SOURCE_FILE_NAME => 'tts_1.294.570721319',
5 DESTINATION_DIRECTORY_OBJECT => 'TTS_DATAFILE',
6 DESTINATION_FILE_NAME => 'tts1.db1.dbf',
7 DESTINATION_DATABASE => 'SSKYDB');
8 END;
9 /
TTS2 datafile
SQL> BEGIN
2 DBMS_FILE_TRANSFER.PUT_FILE
3 (SOURCE_DIRECTORY_OBJECT => 'TTS_DATAFILE',
4 SOURCE_FILE_NAME => 'tts_2.295.586721335',
5 DESTINATION_DIRECTORY_OBJECT => 'TTS_DATAFILE',
6 DESTINATION_FILE_NAME => 'tts2.db1.dbf',
7 DESTINATION_DATABASE => 'SSKYDB');
8 END;
9 /
```

18. On host2 (the target server), import the datafile metadata using DataPump:

```
imp.par has the following contents:
DIRECTORY=TTS_DUMP
DUMPFILE=TTS1_DB1.DMP
LOGFILE=TTS_DUMP_LOG:TTS1.LOG
TRANSPORT_DATAFILES='+DATA1/tts1_db1.dbf','+DATA1/tts2_db1.dbf'
KEEP_MASTER=y

[ora10g@host2]$ impdp system/oracle parfile=imp.par
Master table "SYSTEM"."SYS_IMPORT_TRANSPORTABLE_03" successfully
loaded/unloaded
Starting "SYSTEM"."SYS_IMPORT_TRANSPORTABLE_03": system/********
parfile=impdp.par
Processing object type TRANSPORTABLE_EXPORT/PLUGTS_BLK
```

```
Processing object type TRANSPORTABLE_EXPORT/TABLE
Processing object type TRANSPORTABLE_EXPORT/INDEX
Processing object type TRANSPORTABLE_EXPORT/INDEX_STATISTICS
Processing object type TRANSPORTABLE_EXPORT/TABLE_STATISTICS
Processing object type TRANSPORTABLE_EXPORT/POST_INSTANCE/
PLUGTS_BLK
Job "SYSTEM"."SYS_IMPORT_TRANSPORTABLE_03" successfully
completed at 15:05:00
```

NOTE
*For the TRANSPORT_DATAFILES parameter,
you can either use the alias names (filenames in
the DBMS_FILE_TRANSFER) or use the names
generated by DBMS_FILE_TRANSFER (these start
with the name File_Transfer.xxxx.xxxxxx). To
determine the latter system-generated names, use the
asmcmd line tool by simply entering cd +DATA/
sskydb/datafile followed by the ls -l
command.*

19. Switch the tablespaces back to read/write mode:

```
SQL> ALTER TABLESPACE tts_1 READ WRITE;
SQL> ALTER TABLESPACE tts_2 READ WRITE;
```

20. Verify that the datafiles are successfully plugged in:

```
SQL> SELECT NAME FROM V$DATAFILE;
NAME
--------------------------------------------------
+DATA/sskydb/datafile/system.271.599658207
+DATA/sskydb/datafile/undotbs1.268.599658207
+DATA/sskydb/datafile/sysaux.270.599658207
+DATA/sskydb/datafile/users.267.599658209
+DATA/sskydb/datafile/example.262.599658459
+DATA/sskydb/datafile/tts2_db1.dbf
+DATA/sskydb/datafile/tts1_db1.dbf
```

21. To validate that the data were imported, select the required tables:

```
SQL> CREATE TABLE EMP_COPY TABLESPACE TTS_1 AS SELECT * FROM EMP;
SQL> SELECT COUNT(*) FROM EMP_COPY;
10 rows returned
```

Converting the Database

The RMAN CONVERT DATABASE command was introduced in Oracle Database
10*g* Release 2. The feature provides the capability to convert a database between
platforms that use the same endianness—for example, between AIX and Solaris, or

between SPARC Solaris and HP-UX (PA-RISC). It does not support conversion across endianness, such as between Linux (Intel) and SPARC Solaris.

In the following example, we will convert a database that resides on SPARC Solaris (on filesystem) to an AIX server. Additionally, this conversion will also convert directly into an ASM diskgroup.

```
RMAN> CONVERT DATABASE ON TARGET PLATFORM
CONVERT SCRIPT '/tmp/convert_newdb.rman'
TRANSPORT SCRIPT '/tmp/transport_newdb.sql'
NEW DATABASE 'newdb'
FORMAT '/tmp/newdb'
DB_FILE_NAME_CONVERT '/u01/oradata/db1/datafile','+DATA' ;
```

The convert script will generate CONVERT DATAFILE commands in the following form:

```
CONVERT DATAFILE '/u01/oradata/db1/datafile/o1_mf_system_21g3905p_.dbf'
FROM PLATFORM '<your src platform here>'

FORMAT '+DATA';
```

To reduce downtime for this process, give some thought to how to make the source files available to the target system prior to running the convert script. The usual method is to copy the files over the network (or restore a backup), but there may be other options available, depending on the storage infrastructure you have available. For example, NFS may be a viable option. Suppose that the NFS mount on the AIX system is /net/solaris/oradata (from Solaris filesystem). You would then need to edit the convert script to reference the NFS-mounted directory as the location of the source datafiles to convert, changing the preceding command as follows:

```
CONVERT DATAFILE '/net/solaris/oradata/DBUA/datafile/o1_mf_system_21g3905p_.dbf'
FROM PLATFORM '<your src platform here>'
FORMAT '+DATA';
```

Taking this approach, rather than transferring all files over the network and writing them to a temporary location, may save time. Then, while running the convert script, read the files from that temporary location and write them to the final destination—in this case, ASM.

Summary

ASM is a storage management solution from Oracle Corporation that has made the storage management layer more suitable and flexible. In this chapter, we discussed this technology and through these discussions we have learned how the ASM storage management solution differs from other solutions available on the market and how ASM complements RAC.

   This chapter covered using ASM with an RDBMS instance, starting with the basic installation and configuration through maintenance administration and performance monitoring. While configuring the RDBMS instance using DBCA, we followed the best practice of using two diskgroups, one for data and the other for FRA. Irrespective of whether the database is clustered solution or a single-instance configuration and deployment of ASM is no different. We covered the various methods in which data can be migrated from a non-ASM based Oracle Database into ASM and finally looked into the monitoring options.

CHAPTER
10

ASM Persistent Data Structures

ike traditional filesystems and volume managers, ASM stores metadata to describe and track diskgroup contents. All of the metadata that describe the composition and contents of an ASM diskgroup are stored within the diskgroup itself, which makes each diskgroup self-describing. ASM has two main classes of metadata: physical metadata and virtual metadata. Physical metadata are located at a fixed location on disk. Virtual metadata are stored in ASM files, and thus such metadata are spread evenly across the disks in the diskgroup like any other ASM file. Relational database management system (RDBMS) instances cannot open ASM metadata directories and they cannot perform input/output (I/O) to ASM physical metadata locations.

Myth: ASM uses a database to store metadata.

Although ASM does run an Oracle instance, ASM does not mount a database within the instance. The ASM metadata are stored within the diskgroup using the data structures described in this chapter. All ASM metadata are stored in 4K metadata blocks that include a header and checksum.

Physical Metadata

Physical metadata are located at fixed locations on disk. This fixed location is necessary for ASM bootstrapping. As such, physical metadata cannot be stored in ASM files. The following structures comprise the physical metadata:

- Disk Header

- Allocation Table (AT)

- Free Space Table (FST)

- Partnership Status Table (PST)

Disk Header

Each ASM disk has a disk header. The disk header, which identifies the disk to ASM, occupies the first block (block 0) of the first allocation unit (AU 0) of each disk.

The disk header entries include:

- disk name

- disk number

- diskgroup name

- failure group name

- disk size

- allocation unit (AU) size

- creation time

- mount time

- ASM compatibility

- RDBMS compatibility

- file directory pointer

- ASMLIB reserved block

The purpose of most of the fields is obvious from their names. The mount time and creation time are used to help determine the correct disk to use at mount time if two disks claim to have the same disk name and number in a given diskgroup. Such a condition could occur in the case of a transient disk failure with another disk added to the diskgroup.

ASM compatibility indicates the minimum software version for the ASM instance to mount the diskgroup. Oracle Database 10g software always uses 10.1 for this field. When the COMPATIBLE.ASM attribute is advanced to 11.1, ASM stores this version number in the PST, but also updates the disk headers in the disk group to ensure that Oracle Database 10g software does not access incompatible diskgroups.

RDBMS compatibility indicates the minimum setting for the compatible initialization parameter for an RDBMS instance to access the diskgroup. This field in the disk header will always be 10.1. Oracle Database 10g software never updates this field, and Oracle Database 11g software consults the attribute directory for RDBMS compatibility if COMPATIBLE.ASM is 11.1 or higher.

The file directory pointer describes the location of the first extent of the File Directory if the disk contains it. This pointer is necessary to bootstrap the virtual ASM metadata. The File Directory is described later in this chapter.

ASMLIB vendors can store up to 32 bytes of information in the ASMLIB reserved block of the disk header. Oracle's ASMLIB stores the ASMLIB name for the disk in this field. For more information on ASMLIB see Chapter 6.

Because the disk header is disk-specific, it does not make sense to mirror it on another disk. As described later in this chapter, the Disk Directory contains some of the same information as the disk header. The ALTER DISKGROUP ... CHECK command verifies that the Disk Directory and disk headers are consistent.

Allocation Table (AT)

Each ASM disk has an Allocation Table to track free and allocated space within the disk. The Allocation Table begins immediately after the disk header. The table contains an Allocation Table Entry (ATE) for every allocation unit in the disk. ATEs are grouped into Allocation Table Blocks (ATBs). ATBs always contain a multiple of 64 ATEs to ensure that multi-AU extents never span ATBs. Typically, the entire Allocation Table fits in one allocation unit; however, for large disks, the Allocation Table can span multiple AUs. In this case, the second AU for the Allocation Table is located after the last AU addressed by the first AU of the Allocation Table. The space between allocation units for Allocation Tables is called the *stride*. Strides allow the allocation units for Allocation Tables to be in fixed locations and to address 2^{32} allocation units, while not wasting AUs unnecessarily for small disks.

ATEs describe how a particular allocation unit is used. They contain the file number and extent number if the AU is allocated to an ASM file. For extents that span multiple allocation units, multiple ATEs will point to the same file extent.

Unallocated AUs are marked as free in the Allocation Table. The free extents are kept in a linked list to facilitate quickly finding a free AU for allocation.

If an RDBMS or ASM instance is unable to read part of an AU but is able to access other parts of the disk, the ATE indicates that the AU is unusable (starting with Oracle Database 11g Release 1). ASM will mark AUs as unusable only in normal- and high-redundancy diskgroups. Handling of unusable AUs is discussed in greater detail in the "Read Errors" section of Chapter 11, "ASM Operations."

The Allocation Table and the File Directory (described later in this chapter) are complementary data structures. The ALTER DISKGROUP ... CHECK command validates that the Allocation Table and File Directory agree on the diskgroup contents.

Free Space Table (FST)

The FST indicates which ATBs might contain free allocation units. ASM consults a disk's FST when that disk is selected for allocation. This allows ASM to skip over ATBs that are fully allocated. The FST contains an entry for each ATB. Each entry indicates the estimated number of total and free extents for each extent size. The FST is an optimization for allocation. The truth about what is allocated resides in the Allocation Table. The Free Space Table occupies the second block (block 1) of each AT.

Partnership Status Table (PST)

The PST tracks diskgroup membership and the disk partnerships. ASM consults the PST to determine whether a sufficient set of disks is online to mount the diskgroup. Each disk in a diskgroup reserves the second allocation unit (AU 1) for the PST. At any given time, however, a diskgroup has only a limited number of active PSTs. The number of PSTs is determined by the diskgroup redundancy and the number of failure groups. External redundancy diskgroups have a single PST. Normal-redundancy diskgroups contain three PSTs if at least three failure groups exist. Otherwise, normal-redundancy diskgroups have one PST per failure group. High-redundancy diskgroups have five PSTs if sufficient failure groups exist. Otherwise, high-redundancy diskgroups have one PST per failure group.

The PST is shadow paged to ensure that the active version of the PST on any disk is always consistent, even though the PST spans multiple blocks. AU1 has sufficient space to write two complete PSTs. One copy is the active copy, and the other copy is written when the PST is updated. Once the write to update the PST is complete, the former shadow becomes the active PST, and the other copy becomes the shadow for the next update. The RDBMS uses a similar technique for control files.

The first part of the PST contains information about the PST itself:

- version number

- timestamp

- PST size (number of disks)

- number of PST copies

- list of disks containing the PST

- value of compatible.asm (if COMPATIBLE.ASM >= 11.1)

ASM stores COMPATIBLE.ASM in the PST to reduce the number of locations it needs to update to commit changes to the parameter. As described previously in the disk header section of this chapter, ASM also updates the value of COMPATIBLE.ASM in all the disk headers to prevent Oracle Database 10g software from mounting incompatible diskgroups, but Oracle Database 11g software uses the value in the PST.

The PST then contains an array of entries for each disk in the diskgroup. For each disk, the PST tracks the following:

- disk status (for example, whether it is online or offline)

- number of partners

- list of partners

The last block of the PST is reserved for the diskgroup heartbeat. ASM uses this block to prevent diskgroups from being simultaneously mounted in different clusters. Just like RAC, ASM relies on Cluster Synchronization Services (CSS) to prevent split brain within the same cluster. The PST heartbeat is an additional mechanism to prevent cross-cluster split brain. This is similar to the heartbeat that the RDBMS writes to the controlfile to prevent two instances that are not members of the same cluster from mounting the same database.

Usually, a diskgroup must be able to access a quorum of the PSTs to mount the diskgroup. Normal-redundancy diskgroups with two failure groups and high-redundancy diskgroups with fewer than five failure groups are degenerate cases where a smaller number of PSTs is sufficient to mount a diskgroup.

Virtual Metadata

ASM virtual metadata are stored in ASM files. Directories are the metadata files that are accessed exclusively by the ASM instance. File numbers for directories begin at 1. Registries are reserved ASM files that may be accessed by RDBMS instances as well as ASM instances. Registry numbers count down from 255. File numbers that are not mentioned in this section are reserved for future use. V$ASM_FILE does not display metadata directories or registries.

Like other ASM files, virtual metadata files are mirrored according to the diskgroup redundancy type. ASM does not provide mirroring for external redundancy diskgroups. Virtual metadata are triple-mirrored in both normal- and high-redundancy diskgroups. The following structures comprise the virtual metadata:

- File Directory

- Disk Directory

- Active Change Directory (ACD)

- Continuing Operations Directory (COD)

- Template Directory

- Alias Directory

- Attribute Directory

- Staleness Directory

- Staleness Registry

File Directory

The File Directory contains all of the metadata relevant to ASM files. The directory contains an entry for every ASM file and is indexed by file number. The File Directory is file number one (F1) in every diskgroup.

Fields in the File Directory include the following:

- Incarnation number

- File size

- File block size

- File type

- Redundancy (none, normal, or high)

- Striping (coarse or fine-grained)

- File creation time

- File modification time (the time that the file was last opened for writing)

- File layout

If a file is deleted and ASM reuses its file number for a newly created file, then the files will have unique, distinct incarnation numbers. The incarnation number is derived from the time when the file is created, which guarantees that the incarnation numbers are unique for the same file number.

The block size for ASM files is independent of the ASM metadata block size. All of the ASM metadata directories have a 4K block size. RDBMS data files can be 2K, 4K, 8K, 16K, or 32K as specified at tablespace creation time. RDBMS redo log files typically have 512 byte blocks. ASM tracks both the logical file size, as seen by the database, and the physical space occupied in the diskgroup, taking into account file redundancy. The RDBMS also provides the file type at file creation time. For files that are not created explicitly by an RDBMS instance (such as files created by the XML DB ftp command or the ASMCMD cp command), ASM inspects the file header at creation time to determine the file type.

The file creation time has the obvious semantics. The file modification time, however, is not updated every time that the file is written. Instead, the file modification time is updated when the file is opened for write. This means that the modification time can change even if the file is not written and that the stored modification time may be earlier than the time of the last change to the file's contents. Also, to reduce the contention for the File Directory blocks in the buffer cache of clustered ASM instances, the modification time is truncated to the precision of an hour. Thus, if several instances in a cluster open the file within a short period of time, only the first instance to access to file needs to update the file modification time.

The file layout information consists of a series of extent pointers. Extent pointers specify the disk number and allocation unit number where the extent resides. The File Directory entry contains the first 60 extent pointers for a file, sometimes called *direct extents*. The rest of the File Directory contains pointers to indirect extents. Indirect extents are other virtual metadata extents that contain extent pointers for ASM files. Each indirect extent is one allocation unit. Each File Directory entry can have up to 300 indirect extents. The concept of indirect pointers exists in most traditional filesystems, such as Unix BSD filesystems. The interpretation of the file layout, also known as the extent map, and how the file layout is affected by the striping and redundancy are discussed in detail in Chapter 11, "ASM Operations."

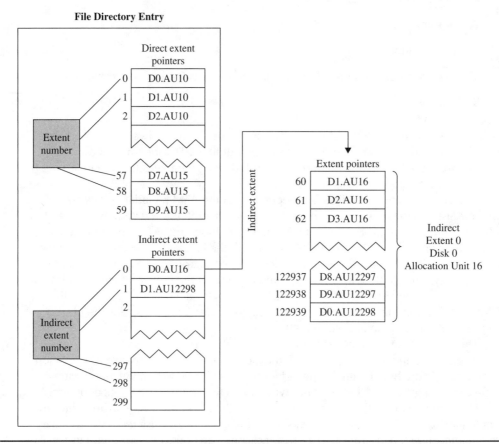

FIGURE 10-1. *File Directory and an indirect extent*

Figure 10-1 shows an example of a file large enough to have indirect extents. Note that the indirect extent is a metadata extent outside of the File Directory. The file in the example is in a diskgroup with 10 ASM disks (D0 through D9).

Figure 10-2 shows the relationship between extent pointers and Allocation Tables. In this example, file 256 has five extents (0 through 4) and file 257 has four extents (0 through 3). The diskgroup has three disks (0 through 2). The figure shows only small sections of the Allocation Table that are relevant to the files in the example.

Disk Directory

The Disk Directory contains information about all of the disks in the diskgroup. Disk Directory information is more detailed than that of the PST. Each disk in the diskgroup has an entry in the Disk Directory indexed by disk number. The Disk Directory is file number two (F2) in every diskgroup.

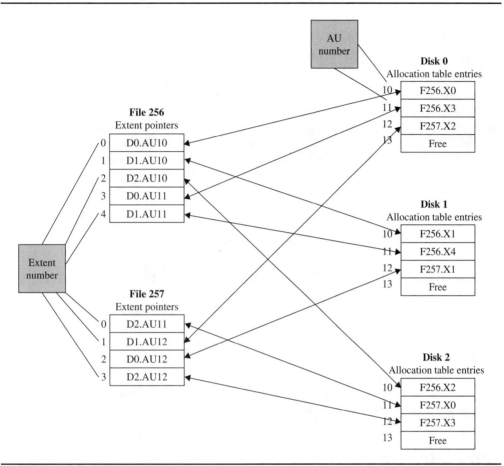

FIGURE 10-2. *File Directory and an Allocation Table*

Fields in a Disk Directory entry include the following:

■ Disk name

■ Failure group name

■ Disk size

■ Disk free space

■ Disk creation time

Much of the information in the Disk Directory is also available in the disk headers. `ALTER DISKGROUP … CHECK` verifies that these structures agree about disk details.

The Disk Directory is always available when a diskgroup is mounted, so it can provide information about disks that are offline in normal- or high-redundancy diskgroups.

Active Change Directory (ACD)

The ACD is a log that allows ASM to make atomic changes to multiple data structures. It is similar to the redo logs used by the Oracle RDBMS. Each instance gets a 42MB chunk of the ACD. (As Douglas Adams explained in *Hitchhiker's Guide to the Galaxy*, "42" is the answer to the ultimate question of Life, the Universe and Everything.) The first block of each chunk contains the open/close status and checkpoint. The checkpoint is updated every 3 sec. The remaining blocks are used as a circular buffer of ACD change records. (Yes, "Active Change Directory Change record" is redundant, but without the second "change," we could not call it an ACDC record.) The ACD grows dynamically as needed to accommodate new ASM instances. ASM uses the ACD to perform crash recovery and instance recovery to ensure that the ASM metadata is consistent. The ACD is file number three (F3) in every diskgroup.

Continuing Operations Directory (COD)

The COD tracks long-running diskgroup operations, such as file creation and rebalance. The scope of the long-running operations is not suitable for the Active Change Directory. COD entries allow ASM to recover from failures during long-running operations. For instance, ASM can roll back the allocations for a file creation that did not complete. RDBMS failures or user actions could lead to such a scenario. For diskgroup rebalance, if the instance performing rebalance fails, ASM can restart the rebalance on a surviving node in the cluster or restart the rebalance when the diskgroup is mounted again in the case of single-instance ASM. The COD is file number four (F4) in every diskgroup.

Template Directory

The Template Directory contains information about all of the file templates for the diskgroup. Diskgroup creation populates the diskgroup with default system templates for each supported file type. New entries are added if users create their own templates. The Template Directory is indexed by template number.

Each template entry contains the following information:

- Template name
- File redundancy
- File striping policy
- System flag

The Template Directory is file number five (F5) in every diskgroup. The template names for the default templates correspond to the file types. The file redundancy defaults to the diskgroup redundancy. The file striping default is file-type–specific. The system flag is set for the default (or system) templates. User-created templates do not set the system flag.

Alias Directory

The Alias Directory contains all alias metadata as well as entries for each system alias, system directory, user directory, and user alias. It is indexed by alias number.
Alias Directory entries include the following fields:

- Alias name (or directory name)
- Alias incarnation number
- File number
- File incarnation number
- Parent directory
- System flag

The Alias Directory is file number six (F6) in every diskgroup. The alias incarnation number, much like the file incarnation number, is provided to distinguish aliases or directories that might reuse the same alias number. The system flag is set for system-created aliases and directories, but is not set for user-created aliases or directories.

Attributes Directory

The Attributes Directory contains metadata about diskgroup attributes. The directory exists only in diskgroups where COMPATIBLE.ASM is 11.1 or higher. In such diskgroups, the Attribute Directory is file number nine (F9). (File numbers seven and eight are reserved for future features.) The AU_SIZE attribute is actually stored in the disk header for bootstrapping reasons. COMPATIBLE.ASM is stored in the PST if the value is 11.1 or higher; otherwise it is stored in the disk header. In Oracle Database 11g Release 1, COMPATIBLE.RDBMS and DISK_REPAIR_TIME and their values are stored in the Attribute Directory. Future releases will support additional attributes.

Staleness Directory

The Staleness Directory contains metadata to map slots in the Staleness Registry to particular disks and ASM clients. The Staleness Directory is file 12 (F12). It is allocated along with the Staleness Registry when it is needed.

Staleness Registry (SR)

The Staleness Registry is used to track allocation units that become stale when disks are offline. This registry is file 254 (file 255 is reserved for a future feature) in normal- and high-redundancy diskgroups with the attribute COMPATIBLE.RDBMS set to 11.1 or higher. The Staleness Registry is created when needed, and can grow dynamically as necessary to accommodate additional offline disks or new ASM or RDBMS instances.

When a disk goes offline, each RDBMS instance gets a slot in the Staleness Registry for that disk. This slot has a bit for each allocation unit in the offline disk. When the RDBMS instance write is targeted for an offline disk, the RDBMS instance sets the corresponding bit in the Staleness Registry slot for that disk if it is not already set.

When a disk is brought online, ASM performs a bitwise OR operation on the slices used by the RDBMS instances for the disk being brought online. Any allocation unit that has its bit set must be copied from its mirror extent. Any allocation unit whose bit is clear need not be updated as part of bringing the disk online. Because only allocation units that should have changed while the disk was offline are updated, bringing a disk online is more efficient than replacing the disk with a newly added one.

Summary

An ASM diskgroup is a self-describing entity that stores all of its metadata within the diskgroup. Each disk has a small amount of physical metadata. The rest of the metadata—the virtually addressed metadata—are stored in ASM files, which enables the metadata to leverage the same data distribution and redundancy features enjoyed by the database files stored in diskgroups.

CHAPTER
11

ASM Operations

his chapter describes the flow of the critical operations for ASM diskgroups and files. It also describes the key interactions between the ASM and relational database management system (RDBMS) instances. This chapter refers to the persistent data structures described in Chapter 10, "ASM Persistent Data Structures."

ASM Instance Discovery

The first time that an RDBMS instance tries to access an ASM file, it needs to establish its connection to the local ASM instance. Rather than requiring a static configuration file to locate the ASM instance, the RDBMS contacts the Cluster Synchronization Services (CSS) daemon where the ASM instance has registered. CSS provides the necessary connect string for the RDBMS to spawn a bequeath connection to the ASM instance. The RDBMS authenticates itself to the ASM instance via operating system (OS) authentication by connecting as SYSDBA. This initial connection between the ASM instance and the RDBMS instance is known as the *umbilicus,* and remains active as long as the RDBMS instance has any ASM files open. The RDBMS side of this connection is the ASMB process. (See the "File Open" section for an explanation of why ASMB can appear in an ASM instance). The ASM side of the connection is a foreground process called the umbilicus foreground (UFG). RDBMS and ASM instances exchange critical messages over the umbilicus. Failure of the umbilicus is fatal to the RDBMS instance because the connection is critical to maintaining the integrity of the diskgroup. Some of the umbilicus messages are described later in the "Relocation" section. The ASMB process exits within a few minutes of the last ASM file being closed by the instance where ASMB is running.

RDBMS Operations on ASM Files

This section describes the interaction between the RDBMS and ASM instances for the following operations on ASM files:

- File create
- File open
- File input/output (I/O)
- File close
- File delete

File Create

ASM filenames in the RDBMS are distinguished by the fact that they start with a plus sign (+). ASM file creation consists of three phases:

- File allocation in the ASM instance
- File initialization in the RDBMS instance
- File creation commit in the RDBMS and ASM instance

When an RDBMS instance wants to create an ASM file, it sends a request to create the ASM file. In Oracle Database 10g, the RDBMS spawns a foreground process that connects to a network foreground process (NFG) in the ASM instance. In Oracle Database 11g, the RDBMS has a pool of processes (the o0nn processes) that have connections to NFGs in the ASM instance. The file-creation request sent over the appropriate connection includes the following information:

- Diskgroup name
- File type
- File block size
- File size
- File tag

The request may optionally include the following additional information:

- Template name
- Alias name

ASM uses this information to allocate the file. (File allocation is described in greater detail in the "ASM File Allocation" section). ASM determines the appropriate striping and redundancy for the file based on the template. If the template was not explicitly specified in the request, the default template is used based on the file type. ASM uses the file type and tag information to create the system-generated filename. The system-generated filename is formed as follows:

```
+diskgroup name/db unique name/file type/file tag.file #.incarnation#
```

After allocating the file, ASM sends extent map information to the RDBMS instance. ASM creates a Continuing Operations Directory (COD) entry to track the pending file creation. The RDBMS instance subsequently issues the appropriate I/O to initialize the file. When initialization is complete, the RDBMS instance messages ASM to commit the creation of the file.

When ASM receives the commit message, ASM's LGWR flushes the Active Change Directory (ACD) change record with the file-creation information. DBWR subsequently asynchronously writes the appropriate allocation table, File Directory, and Alias Directory entries to disk.

If the RDBMS instance explicitly or implicitly aborts the file creation without committing the creation, then ASM uses the COD to roll back the file creation. Rollback marks the allocation table entries as free, releases the file directory entry, and removes the appropriate alias directory entries.

File Open

When an RDBMS instance needs to open an ASM file, it sends to the ASM instance a file-open request, with the filename, via one of the o0nn processes. ASM consults the File Directory to get the extent map for the file. ASM sends the extent map to the RDBMS instance. In Oracle Database 10g, for datafiles, ASM sends the entire extent map to the RDBMS instance at file-open time. In Oracle Database 11g, for datafiles, ASM initially sends the 60 direct extents to the RDBMS instance. For the remaining extents, which are located in indirect extents, the RDBMS requests subsequent extent map sections on demand. ASM delivers all the extent map pointers in the same indirect extent as the requested file extent.

Opening the Spfile at RDBMS instance startup is a special code path. This open cannot follow the typical open path, because the RDBMS instance System Global Area (SGA) does not yet exist to hold the extent map; the SGA sizing information is contained in the Spfile. In this specific case, the RDBMS does proxy I/O through the ASM instance. When the ASM instance reads user data, it does a loop-back connection to itself. This results in ASM having an ASMB process during RDBMS instance startup. After the RDBMS has gotten the initial contents of the Spfile, it allocates the SGA, closes the proxy open of the Spfile, and opens the Spfile again using the normal method used for all other files.

ASM tracks all of the files that an RDBMS instance has open. This allows ASM to prevent deletion of open files. ASM also needs to know what files an RDBMS instance has open so that it can coordinate extent relocation, as described later in this chapter.

File I/O

Myth: RDBMS instances proxy all I/O to ASM files through an ASM instance.

RDBMS instances perform ASM file I/O directly to the ASM disks. Each RDBMS instance uses the extent maps that it obtains during file open to determine where on the ASM disks to direct its reads and writes.

File Close

When an RDBMS instance closes a file, it sends a message to the ASM instance. ASM cleans up its internal state when the file is closed. Closed files do not require messaging to RDBMS instances when their extents are relocated.

ASM administrators can issue `ALTER DISKGROUP ... DROP FILE...` to delete closed files manually. The `DROP FILE` command fails for open files (generating an ORA-15028 error message: "ASM file *filename*' not dropped; currently being accessed"). Generally, manual deletion of files is not required if the ASM files are Oracle-managed files (OMF). OMF files are automatically deleted when they are no longer needed. For instance, when the RDBMS drops a tablespace, it will also delete the underlying datafiles if they are OMF files.

File Delete

When an RDBMS instance deletes a file, it sends a request to the ASM instance. The ASM instance creates a COD entry to record the intent to delete the file. ASM then marks the appropriate allocation table entries as free, releases the file directory entry, and removes the appropriate alias directory entries. If the instance fails during file deletion, COD recovery completes the deletion.

ASM File Allocation

This section describes how ASM allocates files within an external redundancy diskgroup. For simplicity, this section explains ASM striping and variable-sized extents for ASM files in the absence of ASM redundancy. The concepts in striping and variable-sized extents also apply to files with ASM redundancy. A later section explains allocation of file with ASM redundancy.

External Redundancy Diskgroups

ASM allocates files so that they are evenly spread across all disks in a diskgroup. ASM uses the same algorithm for choosing disks for file allocation and for file rebalance. In the case of rebalance, if multiple disks are equally desirable for extent placement, ASM chooses the disk where the extent is already allocated if that is one of the choices.

Myth: ASM chooses disks for allocation based on I/O statistics.

Myth: ASM places the same number of megabytes from a file on each disk regardless of disk size.

ASM chooses the disk for the first extent of a file to optimize for space usage in the diskgroup. It strives to fill each disk evenly (proportional to disk size if disks are not the same size). Subsequently, ASM tries to spread the extents of the file evenly across all disks. As described in the file directory persistent structure, ASM extent placement is not bound by strict modulo arithmetic; however, extent placement tends to follow an approximately round-robin pattern across the disks in a diskgroup. ASM allocation on a disk begins at the lower-numbered AUs (typically the outer tracks of disks). Keeping allocations concentrated in the lower-numbered AUs tends to reduce seek time and takes advantage of the highest-performing tracks of the disk. Note that the assumption about the mapping of lower numbered AUs to higher performing tracks is generally true for physical disks, but may not hold true for LUNs presented by storage arrays. ASM is not aware of the underlying physical layout of the ASM disks.

A potentially nonintuitive side-effect of ASM's allocation algorithm is that ASM may report out-of-space errors even when it shows adequate free space for the diskgroup. This side effect can occur if the diskgroup is out of balance. For external redundancy diskgroups, the primary reason for diskgroup imbalance is an incomplete rebalance operation. This can occur if a user stops a rebalance operation by specifying rebalance power 0. Also, if a diskgroup is almost full when new disks are added, allocation may fail on the existing disks until rebalance has freed sufficient space.

Variable-Sized Extents

In diskgroups with COMPATIBLE.RDBMS lower than 11.1, all extents are a fixed size of one allocation unit (AU). If COMPATIBLE.RDBMS is 11.1 or higher, extent sizes increase for datafiles as the file size grows. A multi-AU extent consists of multiple contiguous allocation units on the same disk. The first 20,000 extents in a file are 1 AU. The next 20,000 extents are 8 AUs. All extents beyond 40,000 are 64 AUs. This allows ASM to address larger files more efficiently. For the first 20,000 extents, allocation occurs exactly as with fixed–extent-size files. For multi-AU extents, ASM must find contiguous extents on a disk. ASM's allocation pattern tends to concentrate allocations in the lower-numbered AUs and leave free space in the higher-numbered AUs. File shrinking or deletion can lead to free space fragmentation. ASM attempts to maintain defragmented disks during diskgroup rebalance. If during file allocation ASM is unable to find sufficient contiguous space on a disk for a multi-AU extent, it consolidates the free space until enough contiguous space is available for the allocation. Defragmentation uses the relocation locking mechanism described later in this chapter.

ASM Striping

ASM offers two types of striping for files. Coarse striping is done at the AU level. Fine-grained striping is done at 128K granularity. Coarse striping provides better throughput, whereas fine-grained striping provides better latency. The file template indicates which type of striping is performed for the file. If a template is not specified during file creation, ASM uses the default template for the file type.

ASM striping is performed logically at the client level. In other words, RDBMS instances interpret extent maps differently based on the type of striping for the file. Striping is opaque to ASM operations such as extent relocation; however, ASM takes striping into account during file allocation.

Coarse Striping

With single AU extents, each extent contains a contiguous logical chunk of the file. Because ASM distributes files evenly across all disks at the extent level, such files are effectively striped at AU-sized boundaries.

With multi-AU extents, the ASM file is logically striped at the AU level across a stripe set of eight disks. For instance, with 1MB AUs, the first MB of the file is written to the first disk, the second MB is written to the second disk, the third MB is written to the third disk, and so on. The file allocation dictates the set of eight disks involved in the stripe set and the order in which they appear in the stripe set. If fewer than eight disks exist in the diskgroup, then disks may be repeated within a stripe set.

Figure 11-1 shows a file with coarse striping and 1MB fixed extents. The logical database file is 6.5MB. In the figure, each letter represents 128K, so uppercase *A* through *Z* followed by lowercase *a* through *z* cover 6.5MB. Each extent is 1MB (represented by eight letters, or 8 × 128K) and holds the contiguous logical content of the database file. ASM must allocate seven extents to hold a 6.5MB file with coarse striping.

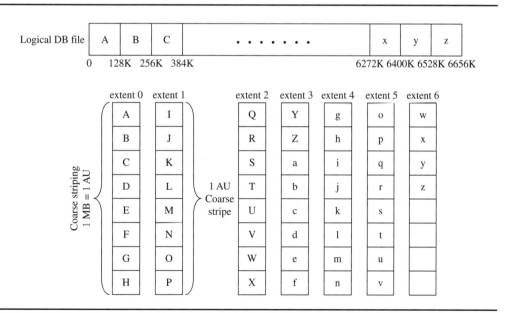

FIGURE 11-1. *Coarse striping*

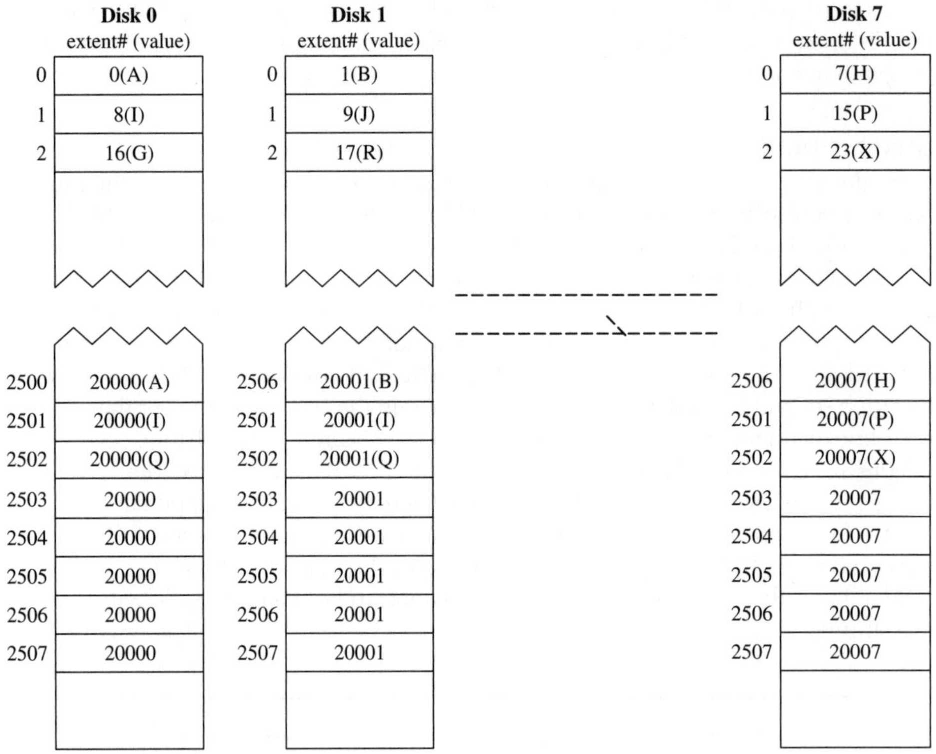

Disk 0 extent# (value)		**Disk 1** extent# (value)		**Disk 7** extent# (value)	
0	0(A)	0	1(B)	0	7(H)
1	8(I)	1	9(J)	1	15(P)
2	16(G)	2	17(R)	2	23(X)

Disk 0		**Disk 1**		**Disk 7**	
2500	20000(A)	2506	20001(B)	2506	20007(H)
2501	20000(I)	2501	20001(I)	2501	20007(P)
2502	20000(Q)	2502	20001(Q)	2502	20007(X)
2503	20000	2503	20001	2503	20007
2504	20000	2504	20001	2504	20007
2505	20000	2505	20001	2505	20007
2506	20000	2506	20001	2506	20007
2507	20000	2507	20001	2507	20007

FIGURE 11-2. *Coarse striping variable-sized extents*

Figure 11-2 represents a file with variable-sized extents and coarse striping. To make the figure fit on one page, the figure represents a diskgroup with eight disks. The file represented is 20024MB. In the figure, each capital letter represents 1MB in the database file. The file has 20,008 extents. The first 20,000 are one AU, whereas the next eight are 8 AU extents. Notice that the eight AU extents are allocated in sets of eight so that ASM can continue to stripe at the AU level. This file uses 20,064MB of space in the diskgroup.

Fine-Grained Striping

Fine-grained striped ASM files are logically striped at 128K.

Myth: Fine-grained striped ASM files have smaller extent sizes than files with coarse striping.

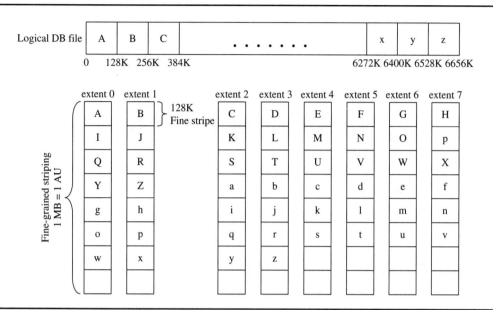

FIGURE 11-3. *Fine-grained striping*

For each set of eight extents, the file data are logically striped in a round-robin fashion: bytes 0K through 127K go on the first disk, 128K through 255K on the second disk, 256K through 383K on the third disk, and so on. The file allocation determines the set of eight disks involved in the stripe set and the order in which they appear in the stripe set. If fewer than eight disks exist in the diskgroup, then disks may be repeated within a stripe set.

Figure 11-3 shows a file with fine-grained striping and 1MB fixed extents. The logical database file is 6.5MB (and is the same as in the file shown in Figure 11-1). In the figure, each letter represents 128K, so uppercase *A* through *Z* followed by lowercase *a* through *z* cover 6.5MB. Each extent is 1MB (representing eight letters or 8 × 128K). ASM must allocate eight extents to hold a 6.5MB file with fine-grained striping. As described previously, the logical contents of the database file are striped across the eight extents in 128K stripes.

ASM Redundancy

Unlike traditional volume managers, ASM mirrors extents rather than mirroring disks. ASM's extent-based mirroring provides load balancing and hardware utilization advantages over traditional redundancy methods.

In traditional RAID 1 mirroring, the disk that mirrors a failed disk suddenly must serve all of the reads that were intended for the failed drive, and it also serves all of the reads needed to populate the hot spare disk that replaces the failed drive. When an ASM disk fails, the load of the I/Os that would have gone to that disk are distributed among the disks that contain the mirror copies of extents on the failed disk.

Myth: ASM mirroring makes two disks look identical.

RAID 5 and RAID 1 redundancy schemes have a rigid formula that dictates the placement of the data relative to the mirror or parity copies. As a result, these schemes require hot spare disks to replace drives when they fail. "Hot spare" is a euphemism for usually idle. During normal activity, applications cannot take advantage of the I/O capacity of a hot spare disk. ASM, on the other hand, does not require any hot spare disks; it requires only spare capacity. During normal operation, all disks are actively serving I/O for the diskgroup. When a disk fails, ASM's flexible extent pointers allow extents from a failed disk to be reconstructed from the mirror copies distributed across the disk partners of the failed disk. The reconstructed extents can be placed on the remaining disks in the diskgroup.

Failure Groups

Because of the physical realities of disk connectivity, disks do not necessarily fail independently. Certain disks share common single points of failure, such as a power supply, a host bus adapter (HBA), or a controller. Different users have different ideas about which component failures they want to be able to tolerate. Users can specify the shared components whose failures they want to tolerate by specifying failure groups. By default, each disk is in its own failure group.

ASM allocates mirror extents such that they are always in a different failure group than the primary extent. In the case of high-redundancy files, each extent copy in an extent set is in a different failure group. By placing mirror copies in different failure groups, ASM guarantees that even with the loss of all disks in a failure group, a diskgroup will still have at least one copy of every extent available.

Disk Partners

ASM disks store the mirror copies of their extents on their disk partners. A disk partnership is a symmetric relationship between two disks in the same diskgroup but different failure groups. ASM selects partners for a disk from failure groups other than the failure group to which the disk belongs, but an ASM disk may have multiple partners that are in the same failure group. Limiting the number of partners for each disk minimizes the number of disks whose overlapping failures could lead to loss of data in a diskgroup. Consider a diskgroup with 100 disks. If an extent could be mirrored between any two disks, the failure of any two of the 100 disks could lead to data loss. If a disk mirrors its extents on only up to 10 disks, then when one disk fails, its 10 partners must remain online until the lost disk's contents are reconstructed by rebalance, but a failure of any of the other 89 disks could be tolerated without loss of data.

ASM stores the partnership information in the Partnership Status Table (PST). Users do not specify disk partners; ASM chooses disk partners automatically based on the diskgroup's failure group definitions. A disk never has any partners in its own failure group. Disk partnerships may change when the diskgroup configuration changes. Disks have a maximum of 10 active partnerships. When diskgroup reconfigurations cause disks to drop existing partnerships and form new partnerships, the PST tracks the former partnerships until rebalance completes to ensure that former partners no longer mirror any extent between them. PST space restrictions limit each disk to a total of 20 total and former partners. For this reason, it is more efficient to perform disk reconfiguration (that is, to add or drop a disk) in batches. Too many nested diskgroup reconfigurations can exhaust the PST space, and result in an ORA-15074 error message: "diskgroup requires rebalance completion."

Allocation with ASM Redundancy

File allocation in normal- and high-redundancy diskgroups is similar to allocation in external redundancy diskgroups. ASM uses the same algorithm for allocating the primary extent for each extent set. ASM then balances mirror extent allocation among the partners of the disk that contains the primary extent.

Because mirror extent placement is dictated by disk partnerships, which are influenced by failure group definitions, it is important that failure groups in a diskgroup be of similar sizes. If some failure groups are smaller than others, ASM may return out-of-space errors during file allocation if the smaller failure group fills up sooner than the other failure groups.

I/O to ASM Mirrored Files

When all disks in an ASM diskgroup are online, ASM writes in parallel to all copies of an extent and reads from the primary extent. Writes to all extent copies are necessary for correctness. Reads from the primary extent provide the best balance of I/O across disks in a diskgroup.

Myth: ASM needs to read from all mirror sides to balance I/O across disks.

Most traditional volume managers distribute reads evenly among the mirror sides in order to balance I/O load among the disks that mirror each other. Because each ASM disk contains a combination of primary and mirror extents, I/O to primary extents of ASM files spreads the load evenly across all disks. Although the placement of mirror extents is constrained by failure group definitions, ASM can allocate primary extents on any disk to optimize for even distribution of primary extents.

Read Errors

When an RDBMS instance encounters an I/O error trying to read a primary extent, it will try to read the mirror extent. If the read from the mirror extent is successful, the

RDBMS can satisfy the read request, and upper-layer processing continues as usual. For a high-redundancy file, the RDBMS tries to read the second mirror extent if the first mirror extent returns an I/O error. If reads fail to all extent copies, the I/O error propagates to the upper layers, which take the appropriate action (such as taking a tablespace offline). A read error in an RDBMS instance never causes a disk to go offline.

The ASM instance handles read errors in a similar fashion. If ASM is unable to read any copy of a virtual metadata extent, it forces the dismounting of the diskgroup. If ASM is unable to read physical metadata for a disk, it takes the disk offline, because physical metadata are not mirrored.

Read errors can be due to the loss of access to the entire disk or due to bad sectors on an otherwise healthy disk. With Oracle Database 10g software, ASM does not distinguish between these two cases. With Oracle Database 11g software, ASM tries to recover from bad sectors on a disk. Read errors in the RDBMS or ASM instance trigger the ASM instance to attempt bad block remapping. ASM reads a good copy of the extent and copies it to the disk that had the read error. If the write to the same location succeeds, then the underlying allocation unit is deemed healthy (because the underlying disk likely did its own bad block relocation). If the write fails, ASM attempts to write the extent to a new allocation unit of the same disk. If that write succeeds, the original allocation unit is marked as unusable. If the write to the new allocation unit fails, the disk is taken offline. The process of relocating a bad allocation unit uses the same locking logic discussed later in this chapter for rebalance.

One unique benefit on ASM-based mirroring is that the RDBMS instance is aware of the mirroring. For many types of logical file corruptions, if the RDBMS instance reads unexpected data (such as a bad checksum or incorrect System Change Number (SCN)) from the primary extent, the RDBMS proceeds through the mirror sides looking for valid content. If the RDBMS can find valid data on an alternate mirror, it can proceed without errors (although it will log the problem in the alert log). If the process in the RDBMS that encountered the read is in a position to obtain the appropriate locks to ensure data consistency, it writes the correct data to all mirror sides.

Write Errors

When an RDBMS instance encounters a write error, it sends to the ASM instance a "disk offline" message indicating which disk had the write error. If the RDBMS can successfully complete a write to at least one extent copy and receive acknowledgment of the offline disk from the ASM instance, the write is considered successful for the purposes of the upper layers of the RDBMS. If writes to all mirror sides fail, the RDBMS takes the appropriate actions in response to a write error (such as taking a tablespace offline).

When the ASM instance receives a write error message from an RDBMS instance (or when an ASM instance encounters a write error itself), ASM attempts to take the disk offline. ASM consults the PST to see whether any of the disk's partners are offline. If too many partners are already offline, ASM forces the dismounting of the diskgroup. Otherwise, ASM takes the disk offline. In Oracle Database 11*g* and some versions of Oracle Database 10*g*, ASM also tries to read the disk header for all of the other disks in the same failure group as the disk that had the write error. If the disk header read fails for any of those disks, they are also taken offline. This optimization allows ASM to handle potential diskgroup reconfigurations more efficiently.

Disk offline is a global operation. The ASM instance that initiates the offline sends a message to all other ASM instances in the cluster. The ASM instances all relay the offline status to their client RDBMS instances. With Oracle Database 10*g* software (or if COMPATIBLE.RDBMS is less than 11.1), ASM immediately force-drops disks that have gone offline. If COMPATIBLE.RDBMS is 11.1 or higher, disks stay offline until the administrator issues an online command or until the timer specified by the DISK_REPAIR_TIME attribute expires. If the timer expires, ASM force-drops the disk. The "Resync" section later in this chapter describes how ASM handles I/O to offline disks.

Mirror Resilvering

Because the RDBMS writes in parallel to multiple copies of extents, in the case of a process or node failure, it is possible that a write completed to one extent copy but not another. Mirror resilvering ensures that two mirror sides (that may be read) are consistent.

Myth: ASM needs a Dirty Region Log to keep mirrors in sync after process or node failure.

Most traditional volume managers handle mirror resilvering by maintaining a Dirty Region Log (DRL). The DRL is a bitmap with 1 bit per chunk (typically 512K) of the volume. Before a mirrored write can be issued, the DRL bit for the chunk must be set on disk. This results in a performance penalty if an additional write to the DRL is required before the mirrored write can be initiated. A write is unnecessary if the DRL bit is already set because of a prior write. The volume manager lazily clears DRL bits as part of other DRL accesses. Following a node failure, for each region marked in the DRL, the volume manager copies one mirror side to the other as part of recovery before the volume is made available to the application. The lazy clearing of bits in the DRL and coarse granularity inevitably result in more data than necessary being copied during traditional volume manager resilvering.

Because the RDBMS must recover from process and node failure anyway, RDBMS recovery also addresses potential ASM mirror inconsistencies if necessary. Some files, such as archived logs, are simply recreated if there was a failure while it was being written, so no resilvering is required. This is possible because an archive log's creation is not committed until all of its contents are written. For some operations, such as writing intermediate sort data, the failure means that the data will never be read, so the mirror sides need not be consistent and no recovery is required. If the redo log indicates that a datafile needs a change applied, the RDBMS reads the appropriate blocks from the datafile and checks the SCN. If the SCN in the block indicates that the change must be applied, the RDBMS writes the change to both mirror sides (just as with all other writes). If the SCN in the block indicates that the change is already present, the RDBMS writes the block back to the datafile in case an unread mirror side does not contain the change.

The ASM resilvering algorithm also provides better data integrity guarantees. For example, a crash could damage a block that was in the midst of being written. Traditional volume manager resilvering has a 50 percent chance of copying the damaged block over the good block as part of applying the DRL. When RDBMS recovery reads a block, it verifies that the block is not corrupt. If the block is corrupt and mirrored by ASM, then each mirrored copy is examined to find a valid version. Thus a valid version is always used for ASM resilvering.

ASM's mirror resilvering is more efficient and more effective than traditional volume managers both during normal I/O operation and during recovery.

Preferred Read

Some customers deploy extended clusters for high availability. Extended clusters consist of servers and storage that reside in separate data centers at sites that are usually several kilometers apart. In these configurations, ASM normal-redundancy diskgroups have two failure groups: one for each site. From a given server in an extended cluster, the I/O latency is greater for the disks at the remote site than for the disks in the local site. When COMPATIBLE.RDBMS is set to 11.1 or higher, users can set the PREFERRED_READ_FAILURE_GROUPS initialization parameter for each ASM instance to specify the local failure group in each diskgroup for that instance. When this parameter is set, reads are preferentially directed to the disk in the specified failure group rather than always going to the primary extent first. In the case of I/O errors, reads can still be satisfied from the nonpreferred failure group. To ensure that all mirrors have the correct data, writes must still go to all copies of an extent.

Rebalance

Whenever the diskgroup configuration changes—whenever a disk is added or dropped—ASM rebalances the diskgroup to ensure that all of the files are evenly spread across the disks in the diskgroup. ASM creates a COD entry to indicate that a rebalance is in progress. If the instance terminates abnormally, a surviving instance restarts the rebalance. If no other ASM instances are running, when the instance restarts, it restarts the rebalance.

Myth: An ASM rebalance places data on disks based on I/O statistics.

Myth: ASM rebalances dynamically in response to hot spots on disks.

ASM spreads every file evenly across all of the disks in the diskgroup. Because of the access patterns of the database, including the caching that occurs in the database's buffer cache, ASM's even distribution of files across the disks in a diskgroup usually leads to an even I/O load on each of the disks as long as the disks share similar size and performance characteristics.

Because ASM maintains pointers to each extent of a file, rebalance can minimize the number of extents that it moves during configuration changes. For instance, adding a fifth disk to an ASM diskgroup with four disks results in moving 20 percent of the extents. If modulo arithmetic were used—changing placement to every fifth extent of a file on each disk from every fourth extent of a file on each disk—then almost 100 percent of the extents would have needed to move. Figures 11-4 and 11-5 show the differences in data movement required when adding a one disk to a four-disk diskgroup using ASM rebalance and traditional modulo arithmetic.

The RBAL process on the ASM instance that initiates the rebalance coordinates rebalance activity. For each file in the diskgroup—starting with the metadata files and continuing in ascending file number order—RBAL creates a plan for even placement

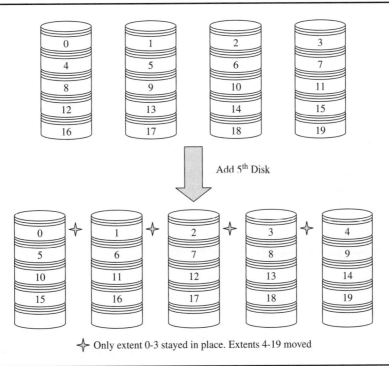

Add 5th Disk

Only extent 0-3 stayed in place. Extents 4-19 moved

FIGURE 11-4. *Data movement using traditional module arithmetic.*

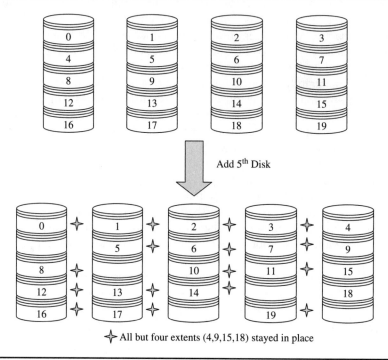

FIGURE 11-5. *Data movement using ASM rebalance*

of the file across the disks in the diskgroup. RBAL dispatches the rebalance plans to the ARBn processes in the instance. The number of ARBs is dictated by the power of the rebalance. Each ARBn relocates the appropriate extents according to its plan. Coordination of extent relocation among the ASM instances and RDBMS instances is described in the next section.

ASM displays the progress of the rebalance in V$ASM_OPERATION. ASM estimates the number of extents that need to be moved and the time required to complete the task. As rebalance progresses, ASM reports the number of extents moved and updates the estimates.

Resync

Resync is the operation that restores the updated contents of disks that are brought online from an offline state. Bringing online a disk that has had a transient failure is more efficient than adding the disk back to the diskgroup. When you add a disk, all of the contents of the disk must be restored via a rebalance. Resync restores only the extents that would have been written while the disk was offline.

When a disk goes offline, ASM distributes an initialized slot of the Staleness Registry (SR) to each RDBMS and ASM instance that has mounted the diskgroup with the offline disk. Each SR slot has a bit per allocation unit in the offline disk. Any instance that needs to perform a write to an extent on the offline disk persistently sets the corresponding bit in its SR slot and performs the writes to the extent set members on other disks.

When a disk is being brought online, the disk is enabled for writes, so the RDBMS and ASM instances stop setting bits in their SR slots for that disk. Then ASM reconstructs the allocation table (AT) and free space table for the disk. Initially, all of the AUs (except for the physical metadata and AUs marked as unreadable by block remapping) are marked as free. At this point de-allocation is allowed on the disk. ASM then examines all of the file extent maps and updates the AT to reflect the extents that are allocated to the disk being brought online. The disk is enabled for new allocations. To determine which AUs are stale, ASM performs a bitwise OR of all of the SR slots for the disk. Those AUs with set bits are restored using the relocation logic described in the following section. After all of the necessary AUs have been restored, ASM enables the disk for reads. When the online is complete, ASM cleats the SR slots.

Relocation

Relocation is the act of moving an extent from one place to another in an ASM diskgroup. Relocation takes place most commonly during rebalance. It also occurs during resync and during bad block remapping. The relocation logic guarantees that the active RDBMS clients always read the correct data and that no writes are lost during the relocation process.

Relocation operates on a per-extent basis. For a given extent, ASM first checks whether the file is open by any instance. If the file is closed, ASM can relocate the file without messaging any other instances. Recovery Manager (RMAN) backup pieces and archive logs often account for a large volume of the space used in ASM diskgroups, especially if the diskgroup is used for the flashback recovery area (FRA), but these files are usually not open. For closed files, ASM reads the extent contents from the source disk and writes them to the specified location on the target disk.

If the file being relocated is open, the instance performing the relocation sends to all other ASM instances in the cluster a message stating its intent to relocate an extent. All ASM instances send a message, which indicates the intent to relocate the extent over the umbilicus to any RDBMS clients that have the file open. At this point, the RDBMS instances delay any new writes until the new extent location is available. Because only one extent (per ARB) is relocated at a time, the chances are very small of an RDBMS instance writing to the extent being relocated at its time of relocation. Each RDBMS instance acknowledges receipt of this message to its ASM instance. The ASM instances in turn acknowledge receipt to the coordinating ASM instance. After all acknowledgments arrive, the coordinating ASM instance reads the extent contents from the source disk and writes them to the target disk. After this is complete, the same messaging sequence occurs, this time to indicate the new location of the extent set. At this time, in-flight reads from the old location are still valid. Subsequent reads are issued to the new location. Writes that were in-flight must be reissued to the new location. Writes that were delayed based on the first relocation message can now be issued to the new location. After all in-flight writes issued before the first relocation message are complete, the RDBMS instances use the same message-return sequence to notify the coordinating ASM instance that they are no longer referencing the old extent location. At this point, ASM can return the allocation unit(s) from the old extent to the free pool. Note that the normal RDBMS synchronization mechanisms remain in effect in addition to the relocation logic.

ASM Instance Recovery and Crash Recovery

When ASM instances exit unexpectedly due to a shutdown abort or an instance crash, ASM performs recovery. As with the RDBMS, ASM can perform crash recovery or instance recovery. ASM performs instance recovery when an ASM instance mounts a diskgroup following abnormal instance termination. In a clustered configuration, surviving ASM instances perform crash recovery following the abnormal termination of another ASM instance in the cluster. ASM recovery is similar to the recovery performed by the RDBMS. For ASM recovery the ACD is analogous to the redo logs in the RDBMS instance. The ASM COD is similar to the undo tablespaces in the RDBMS. With ASM, recovery is performed on a diskgroup basis. In a cluster, different ASM instances can perform recovery on different diskgroups.

CSS plays a critical role in RAC database recovery. With RAC databases, CSS ensures that all I/O-capable processes from a crashed RDBMS instance have exited before a surviving RDBMS instance performs recovery. The OS guarantees that terminated processes do not have any pending I/O requests. This effectively fences off the crashed RDBMS instance. The surviving RDBMS instances can then proceed with recovery with the assurance that the crashed RDBMS instances cannot corrupt the database.

CSS plays a similar role in ASM recovery. Even a single-node ASM deployment involves multiple Oracle instances. When an ASM instance mounts a diskgroup, it registers with CSS. Each RDBMS instance that accesses ASM storage registers with CSS, which associates the RDBMS instance with the diskgroup that it accesses and with its local ASM instance. Each RDBMS instance has an umbilicus connection between its ASMB process and the UFG in the local ASM instance. Because ASMB is a fatal background process in the RDBMS, and the failure of a UFG kills ASMB, the failure of an ASM instance promptly terminates all of its client RDBMS instances.

CSS tracks the health of all of the I/O-capable processes in RDBMS and ASM instances. If an RDBMS client terminates, CSS notifies the local ASM instance when all of the I/O-capable processes have exited. At this point, ASM can clean up any resource held on behalf of the terminated RDBMS instances. When an ASM instance exits abnormally, its client RDBMS instances terminate shortly thereafter because of the severed umbilicus connection. CSS notifies the surviving ASM instances after all of the I/O-capable processes from the terminated ASM instance and its associated RDBMS instances have exited. At this point, the surviving ASM instances can perform recovery knowing that the terminated instance can no longer perform any I/Os.

During ASM diskgroup recovery, an ASM instance first applies the ACD thread associated with the terminated ASM instance. Applying the ACD records ensures that the ASM cache is in a consistent state. The surviving ASM instance will eventually flush its cache to ensure that the changes are recorded in the other persistent diskgroup data structures. After ACD recovery is complete, ASM performs COD recovery. COD recovery performs the appropriate actions to handle long-running operations that were in progress on the terminated ASM instance. For example, COD recovery restarts a rebalance operation that was in progress on a terminated instance. It rolls back file creations that were in progress on terminated instances. File creations are rolled back because the RDBMS instance could not have committed a file creation that was not yet complete. The "Mirror Resilvering" section earlier in this chapter describes how ASM ensures mirror consistency during recovery.

ASM recovery is based on the same technology that the Oracle Database has used successfully for years.

Disk Discovery

Disk discovery is the process of examining disks that are available to an ASM instance. ASM performs disk discovery in several scenarios, including the following:

- Mount diskgroup

- Create diskgroup

- Add disk

- Online disk

- Select from V$ASM_DISKGROUP or V$ASM_DISK

The set of disks that ASM examines is called the *discovery set* and is constrained by the ASM_DISKSTRING initialization parameter and the disks to which ASM has read/write permission. The default value for ASM_DISKSTRING varies by platform, but usually matches the most common location for raw devices on the platform. For instance, on Linux, the default is /dev/raw/*. On Solaris, the default is /dev/rdsk/*. The ASM_DISKSTRING value should be broad enough to match all of the disks that will be used by ASM. Making ASM_DISKSTRING more restrictive than the default can make disk discovery more efficient.

Myth: ASM persistently stores the path to each disk in a diskgroup.

The basic role of disk discovery is to allow ASM to operate on disks based on their content rather than the path to them. This allows the paths to disks to vary between reboots of a node and across nodes of a cluster. It also means that ASM diskgroups are self-describing: All of the information required to mount a diskgroup is found on the disk headers. Users need not enumerate the paths to each disk in a diskgroup to mount it. This makes ASM diskgroups easily transportable from one node to another.

Mount Diskgroup

When mounting a diskgroup, ASM scans all of the disks in the discovery set to find each disk whose header indicates that it is a member of the specified diskgroup. ASM also inspects the PSTs to ensure that the diskgroup has a quorum of PSTs and that it has a sufficient number of disks to mount the diskgroup. If discovery finds each of the disks listed in the PST (and does not find any duplicate disks), the mount completes and the mount timestamp is updated in each disk header.

If some disks are missing, the behavior depends on the version of ASM and the redundancy of the diskgroup. For external redundancy diskgroups, the mount fails if any disk is missing. For normal-redundancy diskgroups, the mount can succeed as long as none of the missing disks are partners of each other. In Oracle Database 10*g* Release 1, the mount succeeds in the preceding circumstances and the missing disks are taken offline. In Oracle Database 10*g* Release 2, the mount succeeds if the instance is the first in the cluster to mount the diskgroup. If the diskgroup is already mounted by other instances, the mount will fail. The rationale for this behavior is that if the missing disk had truly failed, the instances with the diskgroup mounted would have already taken the disk offline. As a result, the missing disk on the node trying to mount is likely to be the result of local problems, such as incorrect permissions, an incorrect discovery string, or a local connection problem. Rather than continuing the schizophrenic mount behavior in Oracle Database 11*g*, ASM introduced a FORCE option to mount. If you do not specify FORCE (which is equivalent to specifying NOFORCE), the mount fails if any disks are missing. If you specify FORCE to the mount command, ASM takes the missing disks offline (if it finds a sufficient number of disks) and completes the mount. A mount with the FORCE option fails if no disks need to be taken offline as part of the mount. This is to prevent the gratuitous use of FORCE during a mount.

If multiple disks have the same name in the disk header, ASM does its best to pick the right one for the mount. If another ASM instance already has the diskgroup mounted, the mounting ASM instance chooses the disk with the mount timestamp that matches the mount timestamp cached in the instance that already has the diskgroup mounted. If no other instance has the diskgroup mounted or if multiple disks have the same ASM disk name and mount timestamp, the mount fails. With multipathing the ASM_DISKSTRING or disk permissions should be set such that the discovery set contains only the path to the multipathing pseudo-device. The discovery set should not contain each individual path to each disk.

Create Diskgroup

When creating a diskgroup, ASM writes a disk header to each of the disks specified in the CREATE DISKGROUP SQL statement. ASM recognizes disks that are formatted as ASM disks. Such disks have a MEMBER in the HEADER_STATUS field of V$ASM_DISK. Other patterns, such as those of database files, the Oracle Clusterware voting disk, or the Oracle Cluster Registry (OCR) appear as FOREIGN in the HEADER_STATUS of V$ASM_DISK. By default, ASM disallows the use of disks that have a header status of FOREIGN or MEMBER. Specifying the FORCE option to a disk specification allows the use of disks with these header statuses. ASM does not allow reuse of any disk that is a member of a mounted diskgroup. ASM then verifies that it is able to find exactly one copy of each specified disk by reading the headers in the discovery set. If any disk is not found during this discovery, the diskgroup creation fails. If any disk is found more than once, then the diskgroup creation also fails.

Add Disk

When adding a disk to a diskgroup, ASM writes a disk header to each of the disks specified in the ADD DISK SQL statement. ASM verifies that it can discover exactly one copy of the specified disk in the discovery set. In clusters, the ASM instance adding the disk sends a message to all peers that have the diskgroup mounted to verify that they can also discover the new disk. If any peer ASM instance with the diskgroup mounted fails to discover the new disk, the ADD DISK operation fails. In this case, ASM marks the header as FORMER. ADD DISK follows the same rules for FORCE option usage as CREATE DISKGROUP.

Online Disk

The online operation specifies an ASM disk name, not a path. The ASM instance searches for the disk with the specified name in its discovery set. In a cluster, ASM sends a message to all peer instances that have the diskgroup mounted to verify that they can discover the specified disk. If any instance fails to discover the specified disk, ASM returns the disk to the OFFLINE state.

Select from V$ASM_DISK and V$ASM_DISKGROUP

Select from V$ASM_DISK or V$ASM_DISKGROUP reads all the disk headers in the discovery set to populate the tables. V$ASM_DISK_STAT and V$ASM_DISKGROUP_STAT return the same information as the V$ASM_DISK and V$ASM_DISKGROUP, but the _STAT views do not perform discovery. If any disks were added since the last discovery, they will not be displayed in the _STAT views.

Summary

ASM is a sophisticated storage product that performs complex internal operations to provide simplified storage management to the user. Most of the operations described in this chapter are transparent to the user, but understanding what happens behind the curtains can be useful for planning and monitoring an ASM deployment.

CHAPTER
12

From Discussion
to Deployment

New technology such as ASM is bound to draw various types of reactions from those who are affected by it. Database administrators (DBAs) love it, but system administrators and vendors of storage and volume managers might freak out over it. DBAs love the manageability of ASM. System administrators worry about losing control. Vendors of storage and volume managers lose sleep because Oracle Corporation is giving away a "volume manager" at no extra cost. One can only imagine the politics that surround ASM, and, not surprisingly, ASM finds itself in an uphill battle against many assailants.

The ASM technology is simple and good, but the politics are a major stumbling block. This chapter prepares DBAs for the critical first step: convincing the system or storage administrator. Until these administrators are on board, widespread use of ASM will only be wishful thinking.

Why System Administrators Freak Out over ASM

System administrators freak out over ASM mainly because of the way that Oracle Corporation defines ASM, and also because of the FUD (fear, uncertainty, and doubt) that are sown by ASM's competitors. ASM, according to Oracle Corporation, is the database file system and volume manager. The two words "volume manager" raise red flags in system administrators' minds. It is fun to watch their reactions in ASM presentations: The moment the words "volume manager" roll off the presenter's tongue, they immediately perk up with their eyes wide open and fixed on the presenter and their jaws drop. "Whoa, wait a minute," they say. This reaction is usually followed by a series of questions such as, "Does ASM handle multipath I/O?" "Does ASM handle nondatabase files?" "Do we have to swap Veritas out for ASM?" "Will the DBAs have control over storage provisioning?" At the heart of such questions are concerns over job security and control. These are all important questions, and unprepared DBAs who fail to provide clear and convincing answers may fail to win support for ASM.

Traditionally, volume managers belong to the system administration group. The thought of transferring that ownership, control, and initiative to the DBA group is unimaginable to system administrators. You would probably feel the same way if you were to transfer database control to end users. Also, why would any system administrator want to exchange a familiar volume manager for a new technology such as ASM that he or she has to learn? (People would rather deal with the devil they know than the devil they don't know.) From the system administrator's perspective, there simply is no incentive to make the change. ASM is free and other volume managers are costly, you say. So what? Such savings do not impact the system administrators' salaries and bonuses.

Why Vendors of Storage and Volume Managers Dislike ASM

Storage vendors dislike ASM because it is included with the relational database management system (RDBMS) license. ASM can manage a bunch of raw disks and bypass their proprietary volume managers. Essentially, Oracle is giving away their core product for free. Can you blame the vendors for not being excited about ASM? Big storage vendors are not interested in selling just raw disks because there is no money in it. They are not in the disk-manufacturing business like Seagate Technology or Western Digital Corporation. The money is in proprietary volume managers, storage configuration software, and maintenance contracts. So when Oracle introduced ASM in Oracle Database 10g Release 1, the vendors danced around the issue of ASM support. Their standard answer was that they would support ASM, but they quickly diverted their customers' attention to their proprietary volume managers, which they claimed were much more sophisticated. (Although this is undoubtedly true, Oracle did not design ASM to replace general-purpose volume managers for non-database files.) As time went by and the dust settled, the vendors realized that ASM was compatible with their volume managers, so the tension eased somewhat.

ASM—What's in It for the Business

ASM may be useful to DBAs, but it would be valueless if it did not solve any business problems. ASM implementation should not be a technology exercise; rather, it should be a value exercise. Having an understanding of the business problems that ASM solves helps you articulate the benefits to the business or the application owner. Such owners can be your strong allies when you propose ASM to the system administrators. You should also be proud of yourself for using a disruptive technology to solve real business problems.

ASM offers four distinct business value propositions:

- Improves storage utilization through consolidation

- Lowers storage administration cost through automated and simplified management

- Improves application availability through online and dynamic storage provisioning

- Lowers deployment cost when used as a volume manager

Improves Storage Utilization

In most large corporations, storage requirements puzzle capacity planners and storage administrators. How can it be that requirements for new storage grow by 30 percent year after year when the actual usage remains at less than 50 percent? Although the 30 and 50 are arbitrary numbers, they serve to illustrate the conflicting scenarios that exist in many businesses today. On one hand, there is low utilization, and on the other hand, there is an insatiable demand for new storage. This is a big and costly problem. The root cause could be business uncertainties, which make capacity forecasting very challenging. Seasoned DBAs are well aware that the initial data volume metrics from applications are no good, so they normally fudge the numbers. Seasoned storage administrators know the initial storage capacity requirements from DBAs are no good, so they too fudge the numbers. Slow provisioning also drives administrators and capacity planners to err on the excess side. The silo-computing paradigm in most organizations only helps to magnify the problem. Each application has its own storage resources and they are not shared with other applications. So there you have it—acres of tier-1 storage waiting to be used. Now, what if there was a way to improve storage utilization and reduce capital expenditures through sharing? ASM allows multiple databases to share the same diskgroups. Additional capacity can be added online and on demand so that businesses do not have to overprovision as they do with traditional capacity planning.

Lowers Storage Administration Cost

Those who understand storage will agree that the total cost of ownership is not just *x* dollars per gigabyte. Unfortunately, many corporate buyers still evaluate storage on that basis. One should always take into consideration the administration cost, which includes provisioning, tuning, backup, restoring, and information lifecycle management (ILM). Storage solutions with simpler and user-friendlier procedures reduce operation costs.

In the DBA world, manual database hot spots tuning in dynamic business environments is not only time consuming and costly, it is almost a lost cause. DBAs spend a lot of time monitoring for and identifying hot spots. By the time they find the hot spots, reorganize schema objects, or shuffle data files around in the database (which may require application downtime), the business's behavior often changes, which may be in the form of processing extra months of data or loading more data than usual. As a result, new hot spots may develop and the tuning process must restart all over again. Businesses are also notorious for keeping data online for too long, which calls for additional storage capacity and an updated storage configuration. To achieve a balanced capacity, DBAs would have to move and rebalance data across the new infrastructure manually. Wouldn't it be nice if data were automatically distributed across all available disks for optimal performance and automatically rebalanced whenever the diskgroup configuration changed? ASM reduces administrative cost by relieving the DBAs from the manual tasks of balancing data and data file placements for different workloads, allowing them to be more proactive and productive in other areas. (The white paper *Take the Guesswork out of DB Tuning* available on the Oracle Technology Network website—http://www.oracle.com/technology/products/database/

asm/pdf/take%20the%20guesswork%20out%20of%20db%20tuning%2001-06.pdf, is a good read.) ASM also reduces the work that system administrators have to do and speeds up storage provisioning because traditional cooked volumes need not be created.

Improves Application Availability

Depending on the storage vendor and the volume manager, logical unit numbers (LUNs), once created, are normally rigid. LUN modifications to accommodate dynamic growth can severely impact business availability. A LUN rebuild may take hours depending on the LUN's size. Needless to say, this is a costly proposition for the business. What if LUNs could be added or removed without a database outage? With ASM, DBAs can dynamically add or remove ASM disks (which is an abstraction layer of LUNs) from a diskgroup and have ASM automatically rebalance the data. While the rebalance operation is ongoing, query, insert, update, and delete statements can continue to access the data. There is no impact on application availability. The performance impact of the rebalancing can be controlled with the ASM_POWER_ LIMIT initialization parameter.

ILM is another area where ASM improves business availability. With proper partitioning schemes, ASM can move cold data to cheaper tier-2 or tier-3 storage without business interruption.

Lowers Deployment Cost

In most information technology (IT) organizations, applications and databases are by default deployed on some type of file system for manageability, but at the expense of performance. This includes local file systems, logical volume managers (LVM), network attached storage (NAS) systems, network file systems (NFS), cluster file systems (CFS), and storage array network file systems (SAN FS). A handful of databases are deployed on raw devices for performance, but at the expense of manageability. The following table shows the common storage management systems and their general attributes:

Storage Management System	General Attributes
Local file systems, LVM	Manageable, slow
Raw device	Fast, complex
NAS, NFS	Manageable, slow
CFS	Expensive, slow
SAN FS	Expensive, slow, complex, cross-platform
ASM	Low cost, fast, more manageable than a raw device

It is amazing how much money IT organizations spend on storage management systems each year for database projects without considering a cheaper alternative. Most IT organizations would cut costs by reducing headcount, outsourcing, consolidating systems and databases, or replacing enterprise-class hardware with commodity hardware, but few would attempt to replace their storage management system. Perhaps until ASM, there simply was not a storage management system that struck a good balance among price, performance, and manageability. When used as a volume manager, ASM offers the best price and manageability. There is no additional cost to use ASM, and it is much more manageable than raw devices. It also delivers raw device-like performance. Furthermore, ASM is also cluster-aware, so it supports both single-instance and Real Application Clusters (RAC) databases. Starting with Oracle10g Release 2, multiple single-instance databases running on multiple nodes can share ASM diskgroups without the need for an RAC license.

NOTE
As of Oracle Database 11g Release 2, ASM handles only database files (data files, online and archived redo logs, control files, and Recovery Manager [RMAN] backups). Oracle binaries, SQL and PL/SQL scripts, alert logs, and other nondatabase files are not supported and usually remain on the local or clustered file system.

What DBAs Need to Know before Talking to System Administrators about ASM

You can save yourself a lot of trouble by doing a little homework before talking to your system administrators about ASM. If you simply call a meeting to propose ASM, chances are your proposal will be rejected. Do not ever approach your system administrators with a question such as the following: "We would like to use ASM, will you support it?" Also, understand this is not your regular "we need more storage" meeting. You are dealing with a new technology that changes normal business operations; you are messing with your system administrators' holy grail; you are leading an initiative that traditionally is theirs. Equipping yourself with the following before the first meeting is highly advisable:

- **A good ASM concept**   This is the foundation and it is covered in Chapters 2-4.

- **ASM storage configuration best practices**   This knowledge is mandatory and it is covered in Chapters 4 and 5.

■ **A good understanding of the Oracle Clusterware** Such an understanding is necessary if the ASM diskgroups will be shared by Oracle instances running on multiple nodes. This may be for an RAC database or single-instance databases. The Oracle Clusterware is beyond the scope of this chapter, but you can read about it in the *Oracle Clusterware and Oracle Real Application Clusters Administration and Deployment Guide.*

■ **An insight into the storage system that you want ASM to manage** DBAs understand mount points and most do not care about or have little understanding of what lies beneath. A typical request for storage is along the line of "give me *x* mount points of *y* size and make sure they do not contend with each other." To configure ASM storage effectively, you have to go below the mount points. You need to understand how raw physical disks in the drive trays are configured for redundancy and sliced or partitioned into LUNs. Take a typical EMC storage system, for example. Physical disks are sliced into Hyper volumes of a certain size and then grouped into Meta volumes. Meta volumes are presented to the operating system as LUNs. Each LUN is an ASM disk. You also need to be able to map out or relate the LUNs with the I/O channels on the hosts. For example, a LUN is associated with controller-A, switch-1 port 3, and HBA port 2 (if you are using fibre channel). This can be rather intimidating if your experience with storage is only at the mount-point level. To make things worse, each brand of storage can be configured in multiple ways. The best way to learn about your storage setup is to talk to your system or storage administrators and the storage vendor.

■ **Preparation to address common objections and differentiate real objections from FUD** Most objections arise from the FUD that are sown by ASM competitors. You can safely bet that they have beaten you to your system administrators and have done a good job of influencing them. It is not an easy task to change a predetermined mind. Common FUD or myths include the following: ASM constantly rebalances data and increases CPU utilization; ASM is a chokepoint because it takes over database I/Os; ASM works only with RAC; the creation and management of ASM instances require the effort of savvy Oracle DBAs; ASM is a single point of failure; ASM has no I/O fencing capability and data may be corrupted when the instance fails; and one has to choose between ASM and an LVM. There are valid considerations, however. Among them are multipath I/O, LUN ownership and control, future use of the existing LVM, visibility into ASM-managed storage, ASM disks overwrite prevention, and new backup and recovery strategies for ASM files. Multipath I/O is the most common objection. This is because many people have mistaken ASM for a volume manager and expect it to offer the same functionality. It is important to understand that LVM and multipath I/O are two different things. Storage and volume manager vendors bundle them for licensing and competition reasons. ASM supports many multipath I/O software packages to provide failover and redundancy for host bus adapters (HBAs). Many of the FUD are addressed as myths in the earlier chapters.

■ **Readiness to share how ASM benefits system administrators** They do less work with ASM than with the conventional file system without giving up any control. When provisioning storage for ASM, their work is complete at the LUN level, but they have to continue to build logical volumes and mount points with the conventional file system.

■ **A strong cadre of allies** You will need them, especially if your storage group is set on a certain LVM technology and not willing to budge despite the clear and indisputable value and return on investment (ROI) offered by ASM. In this situation, escalations to the vice-presidential level are necessary. Business units and application owners are your best allies, so start building relationships if you haven't already done so.

Peer Politics

Your DBA coworkers may be nervous about ASM because it is a change agent. Those who resist change, who are inexperienced with storage configurations, and who haven't considered the importance of having a real-life ASM experience on their resumes may impede your ASM initiative. You should proactively help them to envision life with ASM and transition them into the new paradigm. Job-posting websites are a good place to start. Encourage such coworkers to browse the DBA job openings and see how many require the ASM skill set.

ASM changes the way Oracle databases are being cloned, backed up, and recovered. Because of this, your existing file system–based database cloning scripts will not work with ASM and must be changed and an additional standard must be maintained. If RMAN is not currently used for backup and recovery, you must also change your existing backup and recovery scripts. (RMAN is the only way of accessing ASM files in Oracle10g Release 1. In Oracle10g Release 2, ASM files can be accessed through RMAN, the DBMS_FILE_TRANSFER package, or the File Transfer Protocol [FTP] tool that is part of the XML DB.) You may also have to change your transportable tablespace scripts. The additional scripts and operation standards needed to support ASM may be a stumbling block for junior DBAs. Perhaps the biggest fear is that the DBA group will now own the "volume manager." If ASM crashes, DBAs will get more pages and blame—just what they don't need. They already get more than their fair share daily.

Those are the common objections from operation DBAs. DBAs in the architect role who are mindful of the business will support ASM once they understand the value that ASM brings to the business and to DBAs. The challenge is to help operation DBAs see that they are solving real business problems with ASM and not just focus on the changes that they will have to make.

Summary

Prior to ASM, DBAs could take for granted that system administrators would provision storage for databases—cooked file systems or raw devices did not matter. But some system administrators will deny storage if DBAs decide to use ASM for database storage management. All of a sudden, the system administrators become the chokepoint. Until the issues are resolved (whatever makes the system administrators uneasy, whether FUD, myths, or real concerns), the hope of using ASM is only wishful thinking. Important tips can be found in the section "What DBAs Need to Know before Talking to System Administrators about ASM."

ASM offers the best price/manageability, is valuable to the business, and is useful to both system administrators and DBAs. ASM is free; its unique automation features reduce database storage management costs. ASM simplifies storage configuration and reconfiguration. It improves storage utilization and reduces storage management–related downtime. It also opens up an alternative for businesses to use low-cost commodity storage (if appropriate) where the functionality of redundant array of independent drives (RAID) is not available, by providing normal (two-way) or high-redundancy (three-way) mirroring. For DBAs, ASM means manageability and performance—no more manual balancing of data or chasing after hot spots like Wile E. Coyote chasing after the Road Runner. For system administrators, ASM means less work without giving up any control.

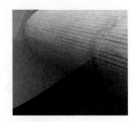

APPENDIX
A

ASM and Storage
Array Configurations

Best Practices for EMC Clariion and ASM

This section describes how to design and configure an EMC Clariion storage array that is to be used in an ASM environment.

To review, an ASM diskgroup consists of ASM disks, and an ASM disk maps to a Clariion logical unit number (LUN), which is properly formatted as a usable disk device under the server operating system (OS). As a best practice, format the host disk device (for example, using `fdisk`) and create only one disk device partition that consumes all the usable space on that disk device. So, an ASM disk is essentially one disk device partition that consumes all the available free space on that disk device, or alternatively, the Clariion LUN. A Clariion LUN is carved out of the usable free space from a Clariion redundant array of independent drives (RAID) group (RG).

To clarify, in the Clariion storage array, a set of physical disk spindles is selected and grouped together as an RG. The RG may be of type RAID 5, RAID 3, RAID 0, or RAID 1/0. (There is also a degenerate RAID type called *Singly Bound Disk*, which is essentially a single-disk RG with no striping or redundancy—that is, Just a Bunch of Disks [JBOD].) Inside the Clariion array, an RG is identified by an RG number. The Clariion array also has two service processors (SPs) that are responsible for processing the input/output (I/O) requests that arrive from the Clariion front-end adapters. As LUNs are carved out of a single RG, each LUN is assigned to one of the two SPs in the Clariion array. Because the SPs have a peer relationship, it is possible for a LUN to trespass (fail over) to the peer SP if it is manually redirected or if the SP that owns it fails.

In general, you should carve no more than two LUNs out of the usable space from one RG. Slicing more LUNs out of the same RG does not increase the IOPS or MB/sec from the back end. This is due to the fact that the net amount of usable capacity, the maximum random IOPS, and maximum MB/sec sustainable remain invariant and governed by the physics and geometry of the actual physical disk spindles making up that Clariion RG.

These Clariion LUNs can then be presented to ASM as two separate ASM disks, with each of these LUNs owned by a different SP. This enables ASM to drive parallelism of I/O requests to the Clariion and keep the Clariion SPs close to their maximum I/O operations per second (IOPS) and MB/sec rate.

For example, if the host is already driving ASM concurrent I/O against 16 distinct LUNs, each consuming a full RG from one or more Clariions, trying to subdivide each of those 16 RGs and create 32 ASM disks is inadvisable. This is because the application is unlikely to be able to sustain enough real parallelism, either from the host outbound to the Clariion or from within the Clariion.

The following are some best-practice considerations when configuring the EMC Clariion:

- Create external redundancy diskgroups for Clariion storage arrays

- For each ASM disk required, create Clariion RAID 10 or RAID 5 groups. Typical RAID 5 groups can be 4+P or 8+P. For RAID 5 RGs, 4+P provides a good balance among performance, cost of redundant data protection, and rebuild time for failed spindle data. Use RAID 10 groups if the write I/O rate is high (70/30 read/write ratio).

- Make sure LUNs are evenly distributed across both the SPs (SPa and SPb).

- Disable Clariion read-ahead caching for ASM-associated LUNs, particularly if the ASM group is primarily holding datafiles.

- Create multiple ASM diskgroups if LUNs are from different storage types— such as from Fibre Channel (FC) and Advanced Technology Attachment (ATA) drives, or from FC drives at 10 and 15k rpm—and group LUNs from different drive technologies into distinct and separate ASM groups.

- Ensure that the Flare code, host bus adapter (HBA) firmware, and OS patches are up to date.

Best Practices for HP StorageWorks EVA 8000 and ASM

This section describes how to design and configure a Hewlett-Packard (HP) Enterprise Virtual Arrays (EVA) 8000 storage array to be used in an ASM environment.

Similar to ASM, the EVA storage array consists of diskgroups, which are essentially containers for physical disks. An EVA diskgroup can contain different RAID sets (VRAIDs), such as VRAID 5 or VRAID 10. When database files are allocated from a given RAID set, the datafile extents are distributed across all the disks contained with that EVA diskgroup, leveraging all the disks in the EVA diskgroup.

As an example, for a 2TB database, the following would be a practical configuration of EVA 8000 for ASM that consists of three EVA diskgroups:

- EVA diskgroup A contains 88 146GB, 15k rpm disks. Allocate eight 500GB VRAID 10 LUNs and present them to the ASM DATA diskgroup. This ASM DATA (external) diskgroup houses all datafiles, a set of online redo log files, and a set of controlfiles.

- EVA diskgroup B contains 88 146GB, 15k rpm disks. Allocate eight 700GB VRAID 10 LUNs to the ASM FLASH diskgroup. This ASM (external) FLASH diskgroup contains archive log files, Recovery Manager (RMAN) backups, flashback logs, a set of online redo log files, and a set of controlfiles. Note that the FLASH diskgroup is larger than the DATA diskgroup to accommodate a complete level 0 backup of the database, several incremental backups, and archive log files. The size of the FLASH area depends entirely on how many backups are needed to meet the recovery service level agreement (SLA).

■ (Optional) EVA diskgroup C contains 24 300GB, 10k rpm disks. Allocate six 500GB VRAID 5 LUNs to the ASM (external) BACKUP diskgroup. This optional ASM diskgroup can hold RMAN backups if it is not feasible to maintain them in the FLASH diskgroup. This diskgroup can also be used to house the TEMPORARY tablespaces.

Configuring ASM with EMC DMX-3

This section describes how to deploy ASM on an EMC DMX-3 storage array system. EMC DMX-3 is EMC's latest flagship array which builds on EMC's Symmetrix Direct Matrix Architecture Symmetrix DMX-3 provides the ability to scale back-end performance incrementally by adding disk directors and storage bays. Each disk director pair supports 32–480 physical disk drives via eight FC loops.

The following are considerations when building an ASM-based database environment. Note that these are high-level generic guidelines; consult your EMC representative to analyze the requirements that will best fit your environment.

■ Applications characterized by high I/O rates (a high percentage of disk read and write activity) can achieve best performance with 15-drive loops and smaller drive sizes with faster speeds (for example, 73GB or 146GB drives running at 15k rpm).

■ Applications that do not have mixed workloads or high I/O rates or are considered DSS systems usually have an I/O profile that does not impose a huge impact on the back-end performance. For these applications, longer drive loops (30 drives or higher) with large drive capacities (146 GB and 300 GB) are appropriate. Typically, loops of up to 30 drives will easily meet the performance requirements of the vast majority of applications.

■ Ensure that enough host central processing unit (CPU) cycles and HBAs are available to drive and sustain the I/O rate of the application.

■ Use EMC PowerPath for failover and load balancing.

■ If you are deploying RAID 5, you should configure it with either four members (3+1) or eight members (7+1) in each RG. Having more members in an RG will produce longer rebuild times (due to the large physical drive capacity) and may increase the chances of a second drive failure within an RG during rebuild.

- Create 4:1 splits of the physical spindles.

- Standardize on the use of metavolumes. Metavolumes can be of type RAID 10 or RAID 5 and should have equal number of hypervolumes, such as 8 or 16.

- Standardize on a metavolume LUN size.

- Each of these metavolumes' LUNs should span all the back-end disk directors.

- Consult with EMC System Engineer (SE) to determine whether EMC's Dynamic Cache Partitioning or Symmetrix Priority Controls are appropriate for your application.

Consider, for example, a 10TB mixed-workload Oracle 11*g* Database built on the DMX-3 system. The DMX array is dedicated for the use of this application. This system is standardized on the following:

- 146GB 15k rpm disks.

- Four-to-one disk splits, providing approximately 36GB hypervolumes.

- Eight-way metavolumes producing 288GB LUNs. If you need to minimize the number of LUNs presented, then you can use 16-way metavolumes instead.

- Ninety 288GB LUNs: 40 LUNs for the ASM DATA diskgroup, and 50 LUNs to support the Flash Recovery Area (archive logs, flashback logs, and RMAN backups).

- PowerPath deployed for path management to the disks.

Configuring the Initial ASM Diskgroup with CVM/VxVM

The following example illustrates how to create a cluster volume manager (CVM)/ Veritas Virtual Machine (VxVM) diskgroup using four disks. Note that if this were an RAC environment, you would need to do this only on one node in the cluster.

```
racnode1@root# vxdiskunsetup -C c2t1d13

racnode1@root# vxdisksetup -i c2t1d13
racnode1@root# vxdiskunsetup -C c2t1d14
racnode1root# vxdisksetup -i c2t1d14
racnode1@root# vxdiskunsetup -C c2t1d15
```

```
racnode1root# vxdisksetup -i c2t1d15
racnode1@root# vxdiskunsetup -C c2t1d16
racnode1@root# vxdisksetup -i c2t1d16
racnode1@root# vxdg -s init ora_asm_dg c2t1d13 c2t1d14 c2t1d15 c2t1d16
racnode1@root# vxassist -g ora_asm_dg make ora_asm_vol 2000M
racnode1@root# vxedit -g ora_asm_dg \
set group=dba user=oracle mode=660 ora_asm_vol
```

The following are considerations when creating ASM over CVM/VxVM devices:

■ This configuration does not support Veritas Storage Foundation commands vxresize or vxassist.

■ Do not attempt VxVM/CVM virtualization operations, such as volume resizing or concatenation with LUNs that are under ASM control.

■ Coordinator disks for I/O fencing cannot be configured under ASM. The coordinator disks can be configured only under the Veritas SFRAC stack.

■ Do not combine ASM and CVM or cluster filesystem (CFS) volumes within the same CVM diskgroup. You must create separate diskgroups for ASM and CFS/CVM volumes.

■ Do not attempt to have ASM directly address the DMP meta nodes. All access to DMP meta nodes should be through the appropriate Veritas Volume Manager (clustered or unclustered).

■ Do not change ownership or permissions on the DMP meta nodes, as this could prevent access to storage devices under DMP (for example, /dev/vx/dmp/[devicename] and /dev/vx/rdmp/[devicename]).

■ Do not stripe or mirror using Veritas Volume Manager. ASM implements an additional layer of striping above the hardware RAID configuration.

■ A CVM/VxVM volume should consist of a single disk or LUN as presented to the operating system. Do not stripe, mirror, or concatenate the volumes.

ASM and NetApp NAS

Customers who are currently using NetApp network attached storage (NAS) for their database storage typically ask whether there are any advantages to using ASM on NAS. Although customers who deploy ASM and NetApp storage typically use FC or Internet small computer interface (iSCSI) devices, ASM can also leverage NetApp NFS-based files as ASM disks. However, this is not considered to be the most optimal architecture because of the several filesystem layers involved—for example, ASM (which is a filesystem) over NFS over the Write Anywhere File Layout (WAFL) (NetApp's filer internal filesystem). Additionally, because NFS-based storage from NetApp and ASM provides some overlapping functionality, it is difficult to deploy ASM over NetApp NFS without reducing the benefit of either component's core features.

Nevertheless, there are circumstances where ASM on NFS is applicable, such as when you need to provide uniformity of operating procedures or to satisfy product, host OS, and/or other environmental constraints. In these cases, ASM can achieve the following:

- Load balancing across filers.

- Mirroring between filers.

- Abstracting of the underlying storage. ASM enables you to migrate seamlessly from NAS to a storage area network (SAN) or between vendors while the database and applications remain online.

When implementing ASM on NFS, it is advisable to combine the guidelines for deploying Oracle directly on NFS with those for implementing ASM on SAN storage, including the following:

- Use NFS mount options as recommended for non-ASM Oracle files on NAS.

- Create NFS-based files according to the guidelines for LUNs discussed in the ASM diskgroup in Chapter 4. You can follow either the shared diskgroups or separate diskgroups model as appropriate. Multiple files and/ or mount points from a single WAFL volume can be used to overcome I/O concurrency limits.

- Use the Unix mkfile or dd commands to create the files to be incorporated into the ASM diskgroups (as if they were LUNs). The files must be a multiple of 512 bytes.

- Set the permissions on the files to allow oracle:dba read/write access.

- Use an ASM diskstring that allows the ASM instance to find the file, such as /oradata/<db_name>/*. You can use symbolic links to make such a diskstring work for files spread across multiple NFS mount points.

There are two deployment models based on the proposed use of the NetApp filer management features as well as ASM best practices:

- Separate diskgroups.
- Common diskgroups.

For the separate diskgroup model, ASM deployment leverages filer-based features such as full database backup and restore, cloning, mirroring, and migration. In this scenario, separate ASM diskgroups should be established for each database deployed, and each diskgroup should be stored within a single WAFL volume.

If filer-based data management will not be used, then multiple databases can be grouped into a common shared pool. This deployment model is referred to as the common diskgroup model. In this model, all data management methods are based exclusively on Oracle tools such as ASM and RMAN.

The following additional recommendations are specific to this common diskgroup model:

Use two or more Oracle ASM diskgroups to store the databases. The database datafile diskgroup should be stored in separate disk groups from their respective flashback recovery areas (FRAs).

Some database applications may impose stringent SLA requirements and thus necessitate greater control over the underlying storage resources; for example, such control might be necessary to ensure quality of service or independent data migration capabilities. In these cases, it is prudent to assign databases into distinct ASM diskgroups.

Each ASM diskgroup may include storage from one or more WAFL volumes or filers. Spreading a diskgroup across multiple WAFL volumes improves performance by distributing the diskgroup storage and throughput demands across volumes based on the aggregate size of the LUNs that each volume contributes to the diskgroup.

When adding storage (disk drives) to existing volumes to increase storage capacity or throughput, expand all the WAFL volumes and the diskgroup LUNs within them to maintain uniform throughput-per-capacity ratios and to minimize unneeded data movement due to load balancing.

If you are adding storage from a new filer within a diskgroup, configure the new filer's LUNs with similar throughput-per-capacity properties to those already in the diskgroup. If the new filer contains multiple LUNs for host I/O concurrency, then all LUNs should be added to the diskgroup at once to limit ASM's load-balancing movement to only what is required.

General Recommendations

The following recommendations apply to both the common diskgroup and separate diskgroup deployment models:

- Use host filesystems or NFS to store Oracle binaries and other non–ASM-enabled files. In Oracle10g RAC environments, NFS can simplify deployment using a shared Oracle Home.

- For high-throughput applications, use either FC or iSCSI SAN protocols to access the storage.

■ Combine each filer's disk drives into fewer larger WAFL volumes to minimize administrative overhead.

■ Make sure that the LUNs within each diskgroup are balanced in terms of throughput per capacity so that the I/O throughput available to a diskgroup from each LUN is proportional to the LUN's size; in other words, ensure that all LUNs within the diskgroup deliver equivalent I/O operations per second per gigabyte. Usually this is accomplished using disk drives with very similar capacity and performance properties throughout the underlying WAFL volume(s).

■ Configure a minimum of four LUNs per ASM diskgroup per WAFL volume.

■ Configuring multiple LUNs can maximize I/O concurrency to the diskgroup, overcoming any per-LUN limits of the host driver stack (the operating system, host bus adapter driver, and/or multipath driver).

■ Use NetApp cluster failover to ensure that there is no single point of failure.

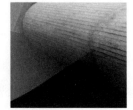

APPENDIX

B

Troubleshooting ASM

he ASM instance is typically a passive instance that does not need much tending. However, there may be cases where ASM does not start up or diskgroups fail to mount because of external issues, such as an incorrect setup or configuration. The following appendix describes the troubleshooting steps that you should take to ensure that the ASM environment runs properly.

ASM Startup Issues

If ASM has problems starting, check the following:

■ If ASM cannot start and the message "Cannot contact Cluster Manager" displays, Make sure that CSS is started and is running in the correct mode. CSS should be started from the ASM home in single-instance setups and from the Oracle Clusterware home in a Real Application Clusters (RAC) environment. For RAC environments, ensure that the Oracle Clusterware is running properly before ASM is started.

■ Make sure that enough memory is available on the host and that ASM System Global Areas (SGA) init.ora parameters are set correctly. See Chapter 2 for guidance on setting ASM SGA parameters.

■ Review and check the ASM alert log for errors and messages. Additionally, check the CRS/CSS log files for ASM issues. Contact Oracle support if necessary.

■ For Oracle Database 10g, each ASM instance has bdump, cdump, and udump directory structures. If error messages exist in the ASM alert log, then check the any relevant files in the udump, cdump, and bdump directories for trace files or core dumps.

■ For Oracle Database 11g, check the trace dump direct of the DIAG_DEST directory.

Diskgroup Cannot be Mounted

Diskgroups that have not been mounted result in relational database management system (RDBMS) instances not being able to start up. When diskgroups do not get mounted, this typically is a result of discovering an insufficient number of disks make up the diskgroup.

To troubleshoot unmounted diskgroup problems, check the following:

1. Check on all nodes of an RAC cluster whether the `ASM_DISKSTRING` parameter matches the disk path.

2. Perform a query against the `V$ASM_DISK` view (on the ASM instance) to determine which disks were discovered and their respective states.

3. Make sure that the operating system (OS) permissions on the underlying device are both readable and writable by ASM on all nodes of an RAC cluster.

4. Make sure that there are not duplicate paths or names that point to the same physical disk. Such duplication results in the following error message:

   ```
   ORA-15020: discovered duplicate ASM disk "DATA_0000"
   ```

   If there are duplicate paths, ASM reports them in the alert log but otherwise ignores them.

5. Make sure that the disk device is on a valid OS partition that does not include the volume table of contents (VTOC).

6. If you are using ASMLIB, make sure that the ASMLIB `listdisks` commands list all required disks. Also make sure that that ASMLIB `scandisk` returns OK, and that the correct library-specific discovery string is used—that is, the string should be left at its default value or set to `ORCL:*`. See Chapter 6 for more details on ASMLIB.

7. For Windows systems, ensure that ASM disk devices are visible by the Windows OS. It's a best practice to enable automount using the `diskpart` utility so that Windows can see the disks upon reboot.

8. Make sure to stamp the Windows disks with the `asmtool`.

   If an ORA-15063 error is incurred, users will be unable to get the diskgroup mounted or dropped, as in the following example:

```
SQL> ALTER DISKGROUP DATA mount;
ALTER DISKGROUP DATA   mount
*
ERROR at line 1:
ORA-15032: not all alterations performed
ORA-15063: diskgroup "DATA" lacks quorum of 1 PST disks; 0 found
```

The main issue here is that users need to get this diskgroup dropped so that they can use the disks in another diskgroup or repurpose them. In Oracle Database 10*g*, a diskgroup must be mounted before it is dropped. If you are certain that the disk will not be needed again, then there are several ways to reclaim this disk:

1. You can use dd to write a block of zeroes on the disk header in block 0.

2. A safer option is creating a new diskgroup using all the disks in the old diskgroup with the FORCE option. The following steps would be one way to accomplish this.

```
SQL > CREATE DISKGROUP DATA EXTERNAL REDUNDANCY
DISK 'ORCL:VOLUME1' FORCE
DISK 'ORCL:VOLUME2' FORCE;
```

For Oracle Database 11g, the diskgroup can be forcibly dropped using the DROP DISKGROUP FORCE command. For force drop to succeed, the diskgroup cannot be mounted anywhere in the cluster.

An ORA-15072 error message may be displayed for an external diskgroup, as in the following example:

```
SQL > CREATE DISKGROUP DATA EXTERNAL REDUNDANCY DISK 'ORCL:VOLUME1' SIZE 34816M;

CREATE DISKGROUP DATA EXTERNAL REDUNDANCY DISK 'ORCL:VOLUME1' SIZE 34816M
*

ERROR at line 1:

ORA-15018: diskgroup cannot be created

ORA-15072: command requires at least 1 failure groups, discovered only 0

SQL> SELECT STATE, HEADER_STATUS, SUBSTR (NAME,1,12) NAME, FREE_MB, SUBSTR(PATH,1,16)
PATH FROM V$ASM_DISK;

STATE    HEADER_STATU NAME         FREE_MB PATH
-------- ------------ ------------ ---------- ----------------
NORMAL   PROVISIONED                      0 ORCL:VOLUME2
NORMAL   MEMBER       VOLUME1        34766 ORCL:VOLUME1

NODE2_SQL> SELECT STATE, HEADER_STATUS, SUBSTR(NAME,1,12) NAME, FREE_MB,
SUBSTR (PATH,1,16) PATH FROM V$ASM_DISK;

STATE    HEADER_STATU NAME         FREE_MB PATH
-------- ------------ ------------ ---------- ----------------
NORMAL   UNKNOWN                          0 ORCL:VOLUME2
NORMAL   UNKNOWN                          0 ORCL:VOLUME1
```

If you see UNKNOWN in the HEADER_STATUS, then you have not discovered correctly. This is commonly because the scan order is not set up correctly for ASMLIB and multipathing.

Although initially the error message may seem misleading for an external redundancy diskgroup, the error message is accurate because you are creating a diskgroup with an unknown disk type—a null device—and you need at least one device to create a diskgroup.

Disk Space–Related Issues

The following message indicates that ASM could not allocate the extent for the requested file because no space is left in the diskgroup:

```
WARNING: allocation failure on disk DATA_0012 for file
1582 xnum 90033
```

There are a couple of reasons that this failure might occur:

- The diskgroup is out of balance. If this is the case, then a manual rebalance will resolve it.

- The diskgroup is truly running out of space. This would require that you add more disk space to the diskgroup or back up unnecessary files and remove them from the diskgroup. This is seen most often in the flashback recovery area (FRA):

```
SQL> ALTER DATABASE DATAFILE
'+DATA/orcl/datafile/users01.272.594387433' RESIZE 4000M;
ALTER DATABASE DATAFILE
'+DATA/orcl/datafile/users01.272.594387433' RESIZE 4000M
*
ERROR at line 1:
ORA-01237: cannot extend datafile 15
ORA-01110: data file 15:
'+DATA/orcl/datafile/users01.272.594387433'
ORA-17505: ksfdrsz:1 Failed to resize file to size 512000 blocks
ORA-15041: diskgroup space exhausted

SQL> SELECT NAME, TOTAL_MB, USABLE_FILE_MB
FROM V$ASM_DISKGROUP;
NAME                                 TOTAL_MB FREE_MB
------------------------------- ---------- --------------
DATA                                    43155           3603
```

A negative USABLE_FILE_MB implies that this is a normal redundancy diskgroup. Therefore, to allocate a file of 4,000MB requires 8,000MB of free space. According to the output, there is only 8,055MB free space. Note that if there were a disk failure, there would no longer be enough space to hold the files that have already been allocated. That is why USABLE_FILE_MB is negative. This diskgroup needs at least one more disk.

A Walkthrough of an ASM Alert Log

The rest of this appendix walks you through an example ASM alert log, explaining what is happening in each part of the log:

```
Starting ORACLE instance (normal)    ← ASM starts here for the first time.

LICENSE_MAX_SESSION = 0
LICENSE_SESSIONS_WARNING = 0          ← ASM interconnect and public interface usage follows.
Interface type 1 eth1 192.168.0.0 configured from OCR for use as a cluster
interconnect
Interface type 1 eth0 130.35.164.0 configured from OCR for use as a public interface
Shared memory segment for instance monitoring created
Picked latch-free SCN scheme 2
Using LOG_ARCHIVE_DEST_1 parameter default value as   ← This is disabled in ASM.
/u01/app/oracle/product/11.1.0/070521/db/dbs/arch
Autotune of undo retention is turned off.             ← This is disabled in ASM.
LICENSE_MAX_USERS = 0
Starting up ORACLE RDBMS Version: 11.1.0.6.0.
Using parameter settings in server-side pfile
/u01/app/oracle/product/11.1.0/070521/db/dbs/init+ASM1.ora
System parameters with non-default values:    ← Nondefault init.ora settings.
  large_pool_size        = 12M
  spfile                 = "/dev/raw/raw3"    ← Raw device Spfile location.
  instance_type          = "asm"
  cluster_database       = TRUE               ← Set to TRUE for RAC.
  instance_number        = 1
  diagnostic_dest        = "/u01/app/oracle"
Cluster communication is configured to use the following interface(s) for this
instance
  192.168.0.5                                 ← Cluster interconnect IP address.
cluster interconnect IPC version:Oracle UDP/IP (generic)
IPC Vendor 1 proto 2
Wed May 23 14:17:34 2007                       ← All background (nonslave) processes start here.
PMON started with pid=2, OS id=16679
Wed May 23 14:17:34 2007
VKTM started with pid=3, OS id=16681 at elevated priority
VKTM running at (20)ms precision
Wed May 23 14:17:34 2007
DIAG started with pid=4, OS id=16685
Wed May 23 14:17:34 2007
PING started with pid=5, OS id=16687
Wed May 23 14:17:34 2007
PSP0 started with pid=6, OS id=16689
Wed May 23 14:17:34 2007
DSKM started with pid=7, OS id=16696
Wed May 23 14:17:34 2007
DIA0 started with pid=8, OS id=16698
Wed May 23 14:17:34 2007
LMON started with pid=7, OS id=16700
Wed May 23 14:17:35 2007
LMD0 started with pid=9, OS id=16702
Wed May 23 14:17:35 2007
LMS0 started with pid=10, OS id=16704 at elevated priority   ← LMS is running in Real Time class.
```

```
Wed May 23 14:17:35 2007
MMAN started with pid=11, OS id=16708
Wed May 23 14:17:35 2007
DBW0 started with pid=12, OS id=16710
Wed May 23 14:17:35 2007
LGWR started with pid=13, OS id=16712
Wed May 23 14:17:35 2007
CKPT started with pid=14, OS id=16714
Wed May 23 14:17:35 2007
SMON started with pid=15, OS id=16716
Wed May 23 14:17:35 2007
RBAL started with pid=16, OS id=16718
Wed May 23 14:17:35 2007
GMON started with pid=17, OS id=16720
lmon registered with NM - instance id 1 (internal mem no 0)
Reconfiguration started (old inc 0, new inc 2)
ASM instance
List of nodes:            ← When creating an initial diskgroup, only one ASM instance is active.
 Global Resource Directory frozen        ← Global Resource Directory (GRD) and RAC recovery are part of
the standard startup.
The next couple of messages are standard RAC-DLM messages
* allocate domain 0, invalid = TRUE
 Communication channels reestablished
 Master broadcasted resource hash value bitmaps
 Non-local Process blocks cleaned out
 LMS 0: 0 GCS shadows cancelled, 0 closed, 0 Xw survived
 Set master node info
 Submitted all remote-enqueue requests
 Dwn-cvts replayed, VALBLKs dubious
 All grantable enqueues granted
 Post SMON to start 1st pass IR
 LMS 0: 0 GCS shadows traversed, 0 replayed
 Submitted all GCS remote-cache requests
 Fix write in gcs resources
Reconfiguration complete           ← GRD reconfiguration is completed here.
Wed May 23 14:17:35 2007
LCK0 started with pid=18, OS id=16730  ← ASM LCK process starts here.

ORACLE_BASE from environment = /u01/app/oracle
Spfile /dev/raw/raw3 is in old pre-11 format and compatible >= 11.0.0;
converting to new H.A.R.D. compliant format.  ← The Spfile is converted to 11g format.
Wed May 23 14:17:36 2007
SQL> ALTER DISKGROUP ALL MOUNT          ← This is the standard diskgroup ALL MOUNT command;
however, no diskgroups have been created yet.
ALTER SYSTEM SET asm_diskgroups='' SCOPE=BOTH;
Wed May 23 14:17:40 2007
SQL> alter diskgroup all mount

Wed May 23 14:17:48 2007
Reconfiguration started (old inc 2, new inc 4)
List of nodes:
 0 1                                        ← Second ASM instance starts.
 Global Resource Directory frozen       ← The GRD and RAC recovery phase for membership change
begins here.
 Communication channels reestablished
 Master broadcasted resource hash value bitmaps
```

```
 Non-local Process blocks cleaned out
Wed May 23 14:17:48 2007
 LMS 0: 0 GCS shadows cancelled, 0 closed, 0 Xw survived
 Set master node info
 Submitted all remote-enqueue requests
 Dwn-cvts replayed, VALBLKs dubious
 All grantable enqueues granted
 LMS 0: 0 GCS shadows traversed, 0 replayed
 Submitted all GCS remote-cache requests
 Post SMON to start 1st pass IR
 Fix write in gcs resources
Reconfiguration complete
Wed May 23 14:17:51 2007
NOTE:Loaded lib: /opt/oracle/extapi/32/asm/orcl/1/libasm.so   ← ASMLIB is detected and loaded.
Wed May 23 14:26:50 2007
SQL> CREATE DISKGROUP DATA                    ← ASM diskgroup DATA is created here.
FAILGROUP DATA1_lower DISK
'ORCL:DATA1L*'
FAILGROUP DATA1_upper DISK
'ORCL:DATA1U*'
FAILGROUP DATA2_lower DISK
'ORCL:DATA2L*'
FAILGROUP DATA_upper DISK
'ORCL:DATA2U*'
WARNING: Deprecated privilege SYSDBA for command 'CREATE DISKGROUP'   ← SYSDBA was used
                                                                       instead of SYSASM.
NOTE: Assigning number (1,0) to disk (ORCL:DATA1LCD1)   ← ASM disk numbers are assigned to the
                                                          disks in the diskgroup.
NOTE: Assigning number (1,1) to disk (ORCL:DATA1LCD2)
NOTE: Assigning number (1,2) to disk (ORCL:DATA1LCD3)
NOTE: Assigning number (1,3) to disk (ORCL:DATA1LCD4)
NOTE: Assigning number (1,4) to disk (ORCL:DATA1LCD5)
..............................................  .             ← The remaining 23 disks are omitted here for brevity.

NOTE: initializing header on grp 1 disk DATA1LCD1   ← The assigned disks are initialized.
NOTE: initializing header on grp 1 disk DATA1LCD2
NOTE: initializing header on grp 1 disk DATA1LCD3
NOTE: initializing header on grp 1 disk DATA1LCD4
.................................................................  . .        ← The remaining 23 disks are omitted here for brevity.

NOTE: initiating PST update: grp = 1   ← This begins updating the Partnership Status Table (PST) for the
                                         DATA diskgroup.
Wed May 23 14:26:52 2007
NOTE: group DATA: initial PST location: disk 0000 (PST copy 0)   ← Each PST (3 total for normal
                                                                   redundancy) is in a separate failgroup.
NOTE: group DATA: initial PST location: disk 0007 (PST copy 1)
NOTE: group DATA: initial PST location: disk 0014 (PST copy 2)
NOTE: PST update grp = 1 completed successfully
NOTE: cache registered group DATA number=1 incarn=0x40f3fad2
NOTE: cache opening disk 0 of grp 1: DATA1LCD1 label:DATA1LCD1   ← Open the enabled disks.
NOTE: cache opening disk 1 of grp 1: DATA1LCD2 label:DATA1LCD2
NOTE: cache opening disk 2 of grp 1: DATA1LCD3 label:DATA1LCD3
NOTE: cache opening disk 3 of grp 1: DATA1LCD4 label:DATA1LCD4
..................................................................  . .            ← The remaining 23 disks are omitted here for brevity.
```

```
Wed May 23 14:26:52 2007
* allocate domain 1, invalid = TRUE
kjbdomatt send to node 1
Wed May 23 14:26:52 2007
NOTE: attached to recovery domain 1
NOTE: cache creating group 1/0x40F3FAD2 (DATA)
NOTE: cache mounting group 1/0x40F3FAD2 (DATA) succeeded
NOTE: allocating F1X0 on grp 1 disk DATA1LCD1
NOTE: allocating F1X0 on grp 1 disk DATA1UCD1
NOTE: allocating F1X0 on grp 1 disk DATA2LCD3
NOTE: diskgroup must now be re-mounted prior to first use   ← The diskgroup will be dismounted
```
and remounted.
```
NOTE: cache dismounting group 1/0x40F3FAD2 (DATA)
NOTE: lgwr not being msg'd to dismount
kjbdomdet send to node 1
detach from dom 1, sending detach message to node 1
freeing rdom 1
NOTE: detached from domain 1
NOTE: cache dismounted group 1/0x40F3FAD2 (DATA)
NOTE: De-assigning number (1,0) from disk (ORCL:DATA1LCD1)   ← Deassign disks with dismount.
NOTE: De-assigning number (1,1) from disk (ORCL:DATA1LCD2)
NOTE: De-assigning number (1,2) from disk (ORCL:DATA1LCD3)
NOTE: De-assigning number (1,3) from disk (ORCL:DATA1LCD4)
NOTE: De-assigning number (1,4) from disk (ORCL:DATA1LCD5)
.................................................... . .          ← The remaining 23 disks are omitted here for brevity.


SUCCESS: diskgroup DATA was created   ← The diskgroup DATA has been successfully created.
NOTE: cache registered group DATA number=1 incarn=0x6503fada

NOTE: start heartbeating (grp 1)
Wed May 23 14:27:01 2007
NOTE: cache opening disk 0 of grp 1: DATA1LCD1 label:DATA1LCD1
.................................................... . .
NOTE: F1X0 found on disk 7 fcn 0.0
.................................................... . .
.................................................... . .
* allocate domain 1, invalid = TRUE   ← The next couple of lines communicate the diskgroup and disk
```
states to other ASM instances.
```
kjbdomatt send to node 1
NOTE: attached to recovery domain 1
NOTE: cache recovered group 1 to fcn 0.0
Wed May 23 14:27:01 2007
NOTE: opening chunk 1 at fcn 0.0 ABA
NOTE: seq=2 blk=0
NOTE: cache mounting group 1/0x6503FADA (DATA) succeeded
Wed May 23 14:27:01 2007
NOTE: Instance updated compatible.asm to 10.1.0.0.0 for grp 1   ← This line indicates
```
ASM attributes.
```
SQL> drop diskgroup DATA                        ← This is the command to drop the diskgroup DATA.
NOTE: cache dismounting group 1/0xF803FB05 (DATA)   ← Begin messaging DATA dismount to other
```
ASM instances.

```
kjbdomdet send to node 1
detach from dom 1, sending detach message to node 1
freeing rdom 1
Wed May 23 14:33:19 2007
NOTE: detached from domain 1
NOTE: cache dismounted group 1/0xF803FB05 (DATA)
NOTE: erasing header on grp 1 disk DATA1LCD1    ← Begin expelling and cleaning up DATA disks.
NOTE: erasing header on grp 1 disk DATA1LCD2
NOTE: erasing header on grp 1 disk DATA1LCD3
NOTE: erasing header on grp 1 disk DATA1LCD4
.........................................  . .        ← The remaining disks erased are omitted here for brevity.

NOTE: De-assigning number (1,0) from disk (ORCL:DATA1LCD1)
NOTE: De-assigning number (1,1) from disk (ORCL:DATA1LCD2)
NOTE: De-assigning number (1,2) from disk (ORCL:DATA1LCD3)
NOTE: De-assigning number (1,3) from disk (ORCL:DATA1LCD4)
NOTE: De-assigning number (1,4) from disk (ORCL:DATA1LCD5)
.........................................  . .        ← The remaining disks deassigned are omitted here for brevity.

SUCCESS: diskgroup DATA was dropped
SUCCESS: drop diskgroup DATA      ← The DATA diskgroup was dropped successfully.
Wed May 23 14:33:39 2007
```

.... For the remainder of the example, it is assumed that the DATA diskgroup has been re-created.
....

```
SQL> alter diskgroup DATA SET ATTRIBUTE 'compatible.asm' = '11.1'    ← Advance the
```
ASM attribute.

```
NOTE: Advancing ASM compatibility to 11.1.0.0.0 for grp 1
NOTE: initiating PST update: grp = 1
Thu May 24 06:45:37 2007
NOTE: Advancing compatible.asm on grp 1 disk DATA1LCD1    ← Each disk in the DATA diskgroup will
```
have the attribute updated in the header.
```
NOTE: Advancing compatible.asm on grp 1 disk DATA1LCD2
NOTE: Advancing compatible.asm on grp 1 disk DATA1LCD3
NOTE: Advancing compatible.asm on grp 1 disk DATA1LCD4
NOTE: Advancing compatible.asm on grp 1 disk DATA1LCD5

NOTE: group DATA: updated PST location: disk 0000 (PST copy 0)
NOTE: group DATA: updated PST location: disk 0007 (PST copy 1)
NOTE: group DATA: updated PST location: disk 0014 (PST copy 2)
NOTE: PST update grp = 1 completed successfully
SUCCESS: Advanced compatible.asm to 11.1.0.0.0 for grp 1   ← The attribute has been successfully
```
advanced.
```
Thu May 24 06:45:37 2007
NOTE: Instance updated compatible.asm to 11.1.0.0.0 for grp 1
```

The next set of outputs illustrates process flow of diskgroup mount.

```
SUCCESS: ALTER DISKGROUP ALL MOUNT      ← Mount all the diskgroups—in this case, DATA only.
Fri May 25 12:54:50 2007
Starting background process ASMB
Fri May 25 12:54:50 2007
```

```
ASMB started with pid=20, OS id=833
Fri May 25 12:59:49 2007
Reconfiguration started (old inc 12, new inc 14)
List of nodes:
 0
 Global Resource Directory frozen
* dead instance detected - domain 1 invalid = TRUE
 Communication channels reestablished
 Master broadcasted resource hash value bitmaps
 Non-local Process blocks cleaned out
Fri May 25 12:59:49 2007
 LMS 0: 0 GCS shadows cancelled, 0 closed, 0 Xw survived
 Set master node info
 Submitted all remote-enqueue requests
 Dwn-cvts replayed, VALBLKs dubious
 All grantable enqueues granted
 Post SMON to start 1st pass IR
 LMS 0: 49 GCS shadows traversed, 0 replayed
 Submitted all GCS remote-cache requests
 Fix write in gcs resources
Reconfiguration complete
Fri May 25 12:59:49 2007
NOTE: PST enabling heartbeating (grp 1)
Fri May 25 12:59:49 2007
NOTE: SMON starting instance recovery for group 1 (mounted)
NOTE: F1X0 found on disk 0 fcn 0.0
NOTE: F1X0 found on disk 7 fcn 0.0
NOTE: F1X0 found on disk 14 fcn 0.0
NOTE: starting recovery of thread=2 ckpt=2.6543 group=1
NOTE: advancing ckpt for thread=2 ckpt=2.6543
NOTE: smon did instance recovery for domain 1
.........
.........
.........
```

The following output illustrates process flow of a diskgroup disk add.

SQL> alter diskgroup DATA add disk 'ORCL:DATA1LCD1' rebalance wait   ← **This SQL command adds the disk and begins a rebalance.**
NOTE: Assigning number (2,0) to disk (ORCL:DATA1LCD1)   ← **ASM assigns a disk number to the new disk.**
NOTE: requesting all-instance membership refresh for group=2 ← **This cross-instance communication refreshes the cluster buffer cache with new membership.**
NOTE: initializing header on grp 2 disk DATA1LCD1   ← **Initialize the new disk.**
NOTE: cache opening disk 0 of grp 2: DATA1LCD1 label:DATA1LCD1
NOTE: requesting all-instance disk validation for group=2 ← **This cross-instance communication validates that the new disk is discovered by all instances in the cluster.**
Tue Jun 12 17:59:33 2007
NOTE: disk validation pending for group 2/0x24156d5c (DATA)
SUCCESS: validated disks for 2/0x24156d5c (DATA)
NOTE: initiating PST update: grp = 2   ← **After successful disk validation, the PSTs will be updated with the new partnership info.**
Tue Jun 12 17:59:36 2007
NOTE: group DATA: updated PST location: disk 0007 (PST copy 0)
NOTE: group DATA: updated PST location: disk 0014 (PST copy 1)
NOTE: group DATA: updated PST location: disk 0001 (PST copy 2)

```
NOTE: group DATA: updated PST location: disk 0000 (PST copy 3)
NOTE: PST update grp = 2 completed successfully
NOTE: membership refresh pending for group 2/0x24156d5c (DATA)
SUCCESS: refreshed membership for 2/0x24156d5c (DATA)
```
← **This message marks the successful completion of the logistics of the disk addition; now the rebalance begins.**
```
NOTE: starting rebalance of group 2/0x24156d5c (DATA) at power 8
```
← **Rebalance started with power 8. This starts ARB processes 0–7.**
```
Starting background process ARB0
Starting background process ARB1
Tue Jun 12 17:59:39 2007
ARB0 started with pid=26, OS id=16597
Starting background process ARB2
Tue Jun 12 17:59:40 2007
ARB1 started with pid=27, OS id=16599
Starting background process ARB3
Tue Jun 12 17:59:40 2007
ARB2 started with pid=28, OS id=16601
Starting background process ARB4
Tue Jun 12 17:59:40 2007
ARB3 started with pid=29, OS id=16603
Starting background process ARB5
Tue Jun 12 17:59:40 2007
ARB4 started with pid=30, OS id=16610
Starting background process ARB6
Tue Jun 12 17:59:40 2007
ARB5 started with pid=31, OS id=16613
Starting background process ARB7
Tue Jun 12 17:59:41 2007
ARB6 started with pid=32, OS id=16615
NOTE: assigning ARB0 to group 2/0x24156d5c (DATA)
Tue Jun 12 17:59:41 2007
ARB7 started with pid=33, OS id=16617
NOTE: assigning ARB1 to group 2/0x24156d5c (DATA)
```
← **ARBs are assigned to the correct diskgroup.**
```
NOTE: assigning ARB2 to group 2/0x24156d5c (DATA)
NOTE: assigning ARB3 to group 2/0x24156d5c (DATA)
NOTE: assigning ARB4 to group 2/0x24156d5c (DATA)
NOTE: assigning ARB5 to group 2/0x24156d5c (DATA)
NOTE: assigning ARB6 to group 2/0x24156d5c (DATA)
NOTE: assigning ARB7 to group 2/0x24156d5c (DATA)
NOTE: F1B3 extent pointer being modified, kfpxn=14
```
← **F1B3 is the file directory entry for the Active Change Directory (ACD) Extent 14 of the ACD is being relocated.**
```
NOTE: disk=5 au=12141 changing to disk=0 au=2
Tue Jun 12 17:59:43 2007
NOTE: ACD relocation: group=2 msgCount=2 msgId=0 locator=1.3
```
← **Relocation of the ACD cannot be recorded in the ACD; it is recorded in the disk header and also written to the alert log.**
```
NOTE: ACD relocation: group=2 msgCount=2 msgId=1
NOTE: F1B3 extent pointer being modified, kfpxn=39
NOTE: disk=20 au=11916 changing to disk=0 au=16
NOTE: F1B3 extent pointer being modified, kfpxn=41
NOTE: disk=4 au=12144 changing to disk=17 au=12153
NOTE: ACD relocation: group=2 msgCount=3 msgId=0 locator=1.3
NOTE: ACD relocation: group=2 msgCount=3 msgId=1
NOTE: ACD relocation: group=2 msgCount=3 msgId=2
NOTE: F1B3 extent pointer being modified, kfpxn=43
Tue Jun 12 18:27:39 2007
```

```
NOTE: stopping process ARB0              ← ARBs stopped as a result of the end of the rebalance.
NOTE: stopping process ARB7
Tue Jun 12 18:41:19 2007
NOTE: stopping process ARB5
Tue Jun 12 18:41:34 2007
NOTE: stopping process ARB6
Tue Jun 12 18:42:28 2007
NOTE: stopping process ARB3
Tue Jun 12 18:42:58 2007
NOTE: stopping process ARB4
Tue Jun 12 18:44:49 2007
NOTE: stopping process ARB1
Tue Jun 12 18:45:31 2007
NOTE: stopping process ARB2
SUCCESS: rebalance completed for group 2/0x24156d5c (DATA)  ← The rebalance completed
```
successfully.
```
Tue Jun 12 18:45:34 2007
NOTE: requesting all-instance membership refresh for group=2  ← This request refreshes the
```
diskgroup info for all instances.
```
Tue Jun 12 18:45:52 2007
NOTE: initiating PST update: grp = 2   ← After the refresh is complete, update the PSTs with new disk
```
partnership info.
```
NOTE: PST update grp = 2 completed successfully
NOTE: initiating PST update: grp = 2
NOTE: PST update grp = 2 completed successfully
Tue Jun 12 18:45:52 2007
NOTE: membership refresh pending for group 2/0x24156d5c (DATA)
SUCCESS: refreshed membership for 2/0x24156d5c (DATA)  ← Declare the complete cluster refresh of
```
the diskgroup a success.

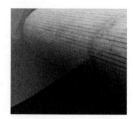

APPENDIX
C

Scripts and Tips

Leveraging Unix Files as ASM

There may be cases where you need to use standard Linux files as an ASM disk. For example, you might be performing basic functional testing on a system that does not have any external storage devices. Such testing will not work for Real Application Cluster (RAC) environments.

NOTE
This practice is not recommended in a production environment; it is shown here simply for illustration.

1. Generate the files that will be used as disk devices for ASM. The Oracle user can be used to execute the dd command to generate these disk files.

   ```
   $ dd if=/dev/zero of=asm_file_disk1 bs=1k count=1000000
   $ dd if=/dev/zero of=asm_file_disk2 bs=1k count=1000000
   ```

   These commands will create to disk files of 1GB each.

2. Enter the following command to list the file attributes of the newly created files:

   ```
   $ ls -l
   -rw-r--r--    1 oracle    dba        1024000000 Mar 19 23:58 asm_file_disk1
   -rw-r--r--    1 oracle    dba        1024000000 Mar 19 23:58 asm_file_disk2
   ```

3. Associate with raw devices and change the ownership of the raw devices:

   ```
   # chown oracle:dba /dev/raw/raw1
   # chown oracle:dba /dev/raw/raw2


   # chmod 660 /dev/raw/raw1
   # chmod 660 /dev/raw/raw2
   ```

   ASM should now be able to discover these disks.

4. Incorporate these disks into an ASM diskgroup. You can do so using SQLPlus or Database Configuration Assistant (DBCA).

   ```
   % export ORACLE_SID=+ASM
   ```

5. Make sure that the appropriate ASM init.ora (init+ASM.ora) settings are defined, including the following parameter, which allows standard files to be used as ASM disks:

   ```
   _ASM_ALLOW_ONLY_RAW_DISKS=FALSE
   ```

6. Using SQLPlus, create a diskgroup called DATA_FL:

```
sqlplus "/ as sysdba"
SQL> STARTUP NOMOUNT
SQL> CREATE DISKGROUP DATA_FL external REDUNDANCY DISK
'/dev/raw/raw1', '/dev/raw/raw2';
```

7. When you are done, validate that the DATA_FL diskgroup is using the new disks:

```
SQL> SELECT NAME, STATE, TOTAL_MB, FREE_MB FROM V$ASM_DISK;
```

```
NAME            STATE      TOTAL_MB    FREE_MB PATH
-------------   --------   ----------  ---------- ----------
DATA_FL_0000    EXTERNAL   1076             996 /dev/raw/raw1
DATA_FL_0001    EXTERNAL   1076             996 /dev/raw/raw2
```

Automatically Starting Up and Shutting Down ASM Instances in Non-RAC Environments

The following scripts can be used to start up and shut down ASM instance in non-RAC environments, using a customized version of the standard dbora, dbstart, and dbshut scripts:

```
#!/bin/sh
export ORA_DB_HOME=/apps/oracle/product/10.2.0/DB
export SH=/apps/oracle/general/sh
ORA_OWNER=oracle


case "$1" in
    'start')
        # Start the Oracle databases:
        # The following command assumes that the oracle login
        # will not prompt the user for any values
        su - $ORA_OWNER -c "$SH/start_shutdown_asm.ksh start" >
/tmp/start_asm.log
        su - $ORA_OWNER -c "$ORA_DB_HOME/bin/dbstart $ORA_DB_HOME" >
/tmp/dbstart.log
        ;;
    'stop')
```

```
        # Stop the Oracle databases:
        # The following command assumes that the oracle login
        # will not prompt the user for any values
        su - $ORA_OWNER -c $ORA_DB_HOME/bin/dbshut >/tmp/dbshut.log
        su - $ORA_OWNER -c "$SH/start_shutdown_asm.ksh stop" >
/tmp/shutdown_asm.log
        ;;

esac
```

dbstart and dbshut are Oracle's standard scripts and reside in $ORACLE_HOME/bin. The ASM startup and shutdown script looks like this:

```
#!/bin/ksh
export START_SHUTDOWN_FLAG=$1


#-------------------------------------------------------------------
# Setup the Oracle Environment and pass the ORACLE_SID
#-------------------------------------------------------------------
export PATH=$PATH:/usr/local/bin
export ORAENV_ASK=NO
export ORACLE_SID=+ASM1
. oraenv


[ "$START_SHUTDOWN_FLAG" = "" ] &&
{
  echo "No startup or shutdown flag specified!"
  echo "Aborting!"
  exit 1;
}

[ "$START_SHUTDOWN_FLAG" = "start" ] &&
{
sleep 60;  # Adjust the sleep time as necessary
export MODE="startup"
echo "$MODE"  |sqlplus / as sysdba
}


[ "$START_SHUTDOWN_FLAG" = "stop" ] &&
{
export MODE="shutdown immediate"
echo "$MODE"  |sqlplus / as sysdba

}
```

Migrating Individual Non-ASM Datafiles to ASM

This section describes how to migrate individual tablespaces to ASM while the database is online. This illustration assumes that there is a tablespace named `ISHAN` located on a mounted filesystem. Additionally, this same procedure can also be used to move a datafile from one diskgroup to another diskgroup.

1. Connect to Recovery Manager (RMAN):

   ```
   RMAN> CONNECT TARGET
   ```

2. Make the target tablespace offline or read-only:

   ```
   RMAN> SQL "ALTER TABLESACE ISHAN OFFLINE";
   ```

3. Copy the `ISHAN` tablespace to the DATA diskgroup:

   ```
   RMAN> BACKUP AS COPY TABLESPACE ISHAN FORMAT '+DATA';
   ```

4. After successfully copying the tablespace, switch all the datafiles in the `ISHAN` tablespace to ASM. Determine the file number of the files to be switched (use V$DATAFILE). In this example, it is assumed that ISHAN tablespace has one datafile and its datafile number is 6:

   ```
   RMAN> SWITCH DATAFILE 6 TO COPY;
   ```

   When you receive the following message, the tablespace has migrated successfully:

   ```
   datafile 6 switched to datafile copy "+DATA/orcl/datafile/
   ishan.314.1"
   ```

NOTE
The original filesystem copy still exists and can be deleted.

You can use the `SET NEWNAME` command to move the restored database to one or more ASM diskgroups. The datafile number or the datafile name of a database filename can be used to migrate the database from non-ASM to ASM.

Here's a simple script to generate `SET NEWNAME` syntax for all the datafiles for a database:

```
SELECT 'SET NEWNAME FOR DATAFILE '|| CHAR(39)||D.FILE_NAME || CHR(39)||
' TO '||CHR(39)||'+DATA'||CHR(39)||';' FROM DBA_DATA_FILES D
/
```

The output generated from this script can be incorporated in the RMAN restore command.

```
RMAN> run
{ allocate channel d1 type disk;
  allocate channel d2 type disk;
 SET NEWNAME FOR DATAFILE 1 to '+DG_OF_PD101';
 SET NEWNAME FOR DATAFILE 2to '+DG_OF_PD101';
 SET NEWNAME FOR DATAFILE 3 to '+DG_OF_PD101';
 SET NEWNAME FOR DATAFILE 5 to '+DG_OF_PD101';
 SET NEWNAME FOR DATAFILE '/u02/oradata/DBATOOLS/tools_01.dbf' to
'+DG_OF_PD101';
 SET NEWNAME FOR DATAFILE '/u02/oradata/DBATOOLS/users_01.dbf' to
'+DG_OF_PD101';
 SET NEWNAME FOR DATAFILE '/u02/oradata/DBATOOLS/undo_rsa_01.dbf' to
'+DG_OF_PD101';
restore database;
switch datafile all;
release channel d1;
release channel d2;
}
```

Alternatively, you can take advantage of the DB_FILE_NAME_CONVERT and the LOG_FILE_NAME_CONVERT initialization parameters. With these correct settings, you can also restore a non-ASM database into an ASM instance.

Creating DataPump Filesets and ASM

This section describes how to create DataPump export dumpsets within ASM diskgroups:

1. Create a directory from ASM. This step is necessary only if you plan on storing the dumpset in a specific directory.

   ```
   ALTER DISKGROUP FLASH ADD DIRECTORY '+flash/dumpsets';
   ```

2. Create a directory in the database:

   ```
   CREATE DIRECTORY DUMPSETS AS '+flash/dumpsets';
   ```

3. Create a logfile directory, since logfiles cannot be stored in ASM:

   ```
   CREATE DIRECTORY LOGFILE_DEST AS '/u01/admin/dumpsets';
   ```

4. Perform a DataPump export and write the output file to expdp_6_26.dat, which will be in an ASM diskgroup.

   expdp parfile=expdp_parfile where expdp_parfile contents are:

   ```
   userid=system/manager1 directory='DUMPSETS' dumpfile=expdp_6_26.dat
   job_name=full_export logfile=logfile_dest:exp6_26.log
   ```

```
Hint:  The dumpfile and logfile can be specified at dumpfile=DIRECTORY:
DUMPFILE such as dumpfile=DUMPSETS.expdp_6_26.dat.
```

5. Validate that the file is created within ASM:

```
SQL> SELECT FILE_NUMBER, BYTES, CREATION_DATE FROM V$ASM_FILE
WHERE TYPE ='DUMPSET';
 FILE_NUMBER  BYTES      CREATION_
 -----------  ---------- ---------
  581         2785280    07-JUN-26
```

Creating Extra Controlfiles in ASM

The following procedure can be used to create additional controlfiles in the ASM diskgroup:

1. Create a new directory in your diskgroup using commands similar to the following (this step is optional):

```
alter diskgroup <DG_name> add directory '+<DG_name>/<DB_name>';
alter diskgroup <DG_name> add directory '+<DG_name>/<DB_name>/
controlfile';
```

2. Edit the controlfile entry in your spfile/init.ora to point to the new controlfile, where the new controlfile is

`'+DATA2/ora10g/controlfile/control03.ctl'`

```
*.control_files='+DATA/Ora10g/controlfile/current.260.3,
'+FLASH/Ora10G/controlfile/o1_mf_0fh3t83f_.ctl,'DATA2/ora10g/
controlfile/control03.ctl'
```

3. Cleanly shut down your database (including all instances if you are using RAC):

```
SHUTDOWN IMMEDIATE;
```

4. Start up the database in NOMOUNT mode:

```
STARTUP NOMOUNT;
```

5. Using RMAN, restore the controlfile from one of the existing locations to the new one:

```
RESTORE CONTROFILE TO  'DATA2/Ora10g/controlfile/control03.ctl'
FROM '+FLASH/Ora10g/conrolfile/current.260.3';
```

6. Mount the database and recover it if necessary:

```
SQL> ALTER DATABASE MOUNT;
```

7. Open the database:

```
SQL> ALTER DATABASE OPEN;
```

NOTE
If you are using an Spfile for your database, your
CONTROL_FILES parameter will be automatically
updated to reflect the fully qualified filename if you
create the controlfiles with incomplete filenames
(such as +DATA). If you are using a Pfile, then you
need to update the value of the CONTROL_FILES
parameter manually for your database if you created
the controlfiles with incomplete filenames. You
can find the fully qualified filename by querying
V$CONTROLFILE.NAME. If you specify aliases (such
as +DATA/mycontrolfile), the alias name can be
used to open the file as well as create it, so there is
no need to update the CONTROL_FILES parameter.

Using ASM SQL Scripts

The following scripts are outlined to assist you in managing ASM files, specifically
listing or deleting them.

NOTE
Oracle recommends using 10g Enterprise Manager
Grid Control or Database Control when performing
these functions.

The following SQL statement generates a script to list the ASM files for a given
database. This script is ordered by listing first the directory structure and then the
files. The script assumes that the files were created using the ASM filename
conventions; in particular, it assumes that the given database name is present in the
alias name (the FULL_PATH column). The query prompts for the database name.
The FULL_PATH variable in the query refers to the alias name. The DIR column
indicates whether it is a directory or not, and SYS column indicates whether the
alias was created by the system or not.

```
COL FULL_PATH FORMAT a120
COL dir FORMAT a3
COL sys FORMAT a3
SET ECHO OFF
SET VERIFY OFF
SET FEEDBACK OFF
SET PAGESIZE 39
SET LINESIZE 130
--get database name
ACCEPT database PROMPT 'Enter the database name: '
--spool file
```

```
spool lis_&database..lst
--generates  list
SELECT FULL_PATH, DIR, SYS FROM
(SELECT CONCAT ('+'|| GNAME, SYS_CONNECT_BY_PATH (ANAME,'/'))
FULL_PATH, DIR, SYS FROM (SELECT G.NAME GNAME, A.PARENT_INDEX PINDEX,
A.NAME ANAME, A.REFERENCE_INDEX RINDEX, A.ALIAS_DIRECTORY DIR,
A.SYSTEM_CRETED SYS FROM V$ASM_ALIAS A, V$ASM_DISKGROUP G WHERE
A.GROUP_NUMBER = G.GROUP_NUBER)
START WITH (MOD(pindex, POWER(2, 24))) = 0
CONNECT BY PRIOR rindex = pindex
ORDER BY dir desc, full_path asc)
WHERE FULL_PATH LIKE UPPER('%/&database%');

--end spool
spool off
-- resetting format
COL full_path CLEAR
COL dir CLEAR
COL sys CLEAR
SET VERIFY ON
SET HEADING ON
SET FEEDBACK ON
```

This SQL statement generates a script that deletes files in ASM for a given database. The script assumes that the files were created using the ASM naming conventions. Specifically, it assumes that the given database name is present in the alias name (the FULL_PATH column), in the form of */db_name/*. The scripts prompt for the database name.

```
COL gsql FORMAT a300
SET ECHO OFF
SET VERIFY OFF
SET HEADING OFF
SET FEEDBACK OFF
SET PAGESIZE 0
SET LINESIZE 600
SET TRIMSPOOL ON
--get database name
ACCEPT database PROMPT 'Enter the database name: '
--spool file
spool del_&database..sql
--generates file list
SELECT 'ALTER DISKGROUP '||GNAME||' DROP FILE '''||FULL_PATH||''';'
QSQL FROM

(SELECT CONCAT ('+'|| GNAME, SYS_CONNECT_BY_PATH(ANAME,'/')) FULL_PATH,
QNAME FROM
(SELECT Q.NAME QNAME, A.PARENT_INDEX PINDEX, A.NAME ANAME,
A.REFERENCE_INDEX RINDEX, A.ALIAS_DIRECTORY ADIR FROM V$ASM_ALIAS A,
```

```
V$ASM_DISKGROUP G WHERE A.GROUP_NUMBER = G.GROUP_NUMBER) AND A.DIR ='N'
START WITH (MOD (PINDEX, POWER (2,24))) = 0 CONNECT BY PRIOR RINDEX =
PINDEX) WHERE FULL_PATH LIKE UPPER('%/&database/%');
```

This SQL statement generates a script to drop ASM directories:

```
SELECT 'ALTER DISKGROUP '||gname||' DROP DIRECTORY '''||full_
path||''';' QSQL FROM
(SELECT CONCAT ('+'|| GNAME, SYS_CONNECT_BY_PATH(ANAME,'/')) FULL_PATH,
QNAME FROM
(SELECT Q.NAME QNAME, A.PARENT_INDEX PINDEX, A.NAME ANAME,
A.REFERENCE_INDEX RINDEX, A.ALIAS_DIRECTORY ADIR
FROM V$ASM_ALIAS A, V$ASM_DISKGROUP G
WHERE A.GROUP_NUMBER = G.GROUP_NUMBER)
WHERE ADIR='Y'
START WITH ( MOD( PINDEX, POWER(2, 24))) = 0
CONNECT BY PRIOR RINDEX = PINDEX
ORDER BY FULL_PATH DESC)
WHERE FULL_PATH LIKE UPPER('%/&&database%');
--end spool
spool off
-- resetting format
COL gsql CLEAR
SET VERIFY ON
SET HEADING ON
SET FEEDBACK ON
SET PAGESIZE 30
SET LINESIZE 600
SET TRIMSPOOL OFF
```

Reporting Disk Imbalances

The following SQLPlus script reports the percentage of imbalance in all mounted diskgroups. Additionally, it displays the symmetry of failure groups for any normal- or high-redundancy diskgroups. This script requires privileges to connect as SYSDBA in order to be run when connected to an ASM instance. If the imbalance is too high, then it is wise to do a manual rebalance. It can also be used to track the progress of a long-running rebalance. It runs as is on Oracle Database 10g Release 2 and Oracle Database 11g. For Oracle Database 10g Release 1, you must uncomment two lines near the top of the listing. This will make it run slower as there will be unnecessary disk header reads. Ensure that the following environment variables are set for the ASM instance:

```
ORACLE_SID=+ASM
export ORACLE_SID
sqlplus "/ as sysdba"
```

The Script

The script for the imbalance reporting program follows:

```
/*
 * RUN THIS SQL*PLUS SCRIPT WHILE CONNECTED TO AN ASM INSTANCE WITH
 * DISKGROUPS MOUNTED. "no rows selected" IF NO DISKGROUPS ARE MOUNTED
 */
set verify off
clear columns
/* THE FOLLOWING ERROR WILL BE REPORTED IF THIS SCRIPT IS RUN ON 10gR1
ORA-01219: database not open: queries allowed on fixed tables/views only
 * This script is intended to work with 10gR2 and later. To make it work with
 * 10gR1 you must remove the "_stat" in the following two defines by
 * uncommenting the redefines that follow. The _stat tables eliminate disk
 * header reads, but they were not available in 10.1
 */
define asm_disk = v$asm_disk_stat
define asm_diskgroup = v$asm_diskgroup_stat
/* for 10.1 uncomment the following redefines
define asm_disk = v$asm_disk
define asm_diskgroup = v$asm_diskgroup
*/
/*
 * Query to see if any diskgroups are out of balance
 */
column "Diskgroup" format A30
column "Diskgroup" Heading " Columns Described in Script||Diskgroup Name"
/*
 * The imbalance measures the difference in space allocated to the fullest and
 * emptiest disks in the diskgroup. Comparison is in percent full since ASM
 * tries to keep all disks equally full as a percent of their size. The
 * imbalance is relative to the space allocated, not the space available. An
 * imbalance of a couple percent is reasonable.
 */
column   "Imbalance" format 99.9 Heading "Percent|Imbalance"

/*
 * Percent disk size variance gives the percentage difference in size between
 * the largest and smallest disks in the diskgroup. This will be zero if
 * best practices have been followed and all disks are the same size. Small
 * differences in size are acceptable. Large differences can result in some
 * disks getting much more I/O than others. With normal- or high-redundancy
 * diskgroups, a large size variance can make it impossible to reduce the
 * percent imbalance to a small value.
 */
column   "Variance" format 99.9 Heading "Percent|Disk Size|Variance"
/*
 * Minimum percent free gives the amount of free disk space on the fullest
 * disk as a percent of the disk size. If the imbalance is zero, then this
```

```
 * represents the total freespace. Since all allocations are done evenly
 * across all disks, the minimum free space limits how much space can be
 * used. If one disk has only 1 percent free, then only 1 percent of the
 * space in the diskgroup is really available for allocation, even if the
 * rest of the disks are only half full.
 */
column  "MinFree" format 99.9 Heading "Minimum|Percent|Free"
/*
 * The number of disks in the diskgroup gives a sense of how widely the
 * files can be spread.
 */
column "DiskCnt" format 9999 Heading "Disk|Count"
/*
 * External redundancy diskgroups can always be rebalanced to have a small
 * percent imbalance. However the failure group configuration of a normal- or
 * high-redundancy diskgroup may make it impossible to make the diskgroup well
 * balanced.
 */
column  "Type"  format A10 Heading "Diskgroup|Redundancy"
select
/*
    Name of the diskgroup */
    g.name
    "Diskgroup",
/*
    Percent diskgroup allocation is imbalanced  */
    100*(max((d.total_mb-d.free_mb)/d.total_mb)-min((d.total_mb-d.free_mb)/
d.total_mb))/max((d.total_mb-d.free_mb)/d.total_mb)
    "Imbalance",
/*
     Percent difference between largest and smallest disk */
    100*(max(d.total_mb)-min(d.total_mb))/max(d.total_mb)
    "Variance",
/*
    The disk with the least free space as a percent of total space */
    100*(min(d.free_mb/d.total_mb))
    "MinFree",
/*
    Number of disks in the diskgroup */
    count(*)
    "DiskCnt",
/*
    Diskgroup redundancy */
    g.type
    "Type"
from
    &asm_disk d ,
    &asm_diskgroup g
```

```
where
    d.group_number = g.group_number and
    d.group_number <> 0 and
    d.state = 'NORMAL' and
    d.mount_status = 'CACHED'
group by
    g.name ,
    g.type
;
/*
 * Query to see if there are partner imbalances.
 *
 * This query only returns rows for normal- or high-redundancy diskgroups.
 * You will not get any rows if all your diskgroups are external.
 */
/*
 * This query checks how even the partnerships are laid out for the diskgroup.
 * If the disks are different sizes or the failure groups are different sizes,
 * then the partnerships may not be balanced. Uneven numbers of disks in
 * failure groups can result in some disks having fewer partners. Uneven
 * disk sizes result in some disks having more partner space than others.
 * Primary extents are allocated to a disk based on its size. The secondary
 * extents for those primaries are allocated on its partner disks. A disk with
 * less partner space will fill up those partners more than a disk with more
 * partner space. At the beginning of a rebalance, partnerships may be
 * rearranged. The partnerships being dropped are marked as inactive. This
 * query only examines active partnerships since it is attempting to
 * evaluate problems based on the structure of the diskgroup, not the
 * transient state that may exist at the moment. At the completion of a
 * successful rebalance, the inactive partnerships will be deleted.
 */
/*
 * Partner count imbalance gives the difference in the number of partners for
 * the disk with the most partners and the disk with the fewest partners. It
 * may not be possible for every disk to have the same number of partners
 * even when all the failure groups are the same size. However, an imbalance
 * of more than one indicates that the failure groups are different sizes.
 * In any case, it maybe impossible to get a percent imbalance of zero when
 * some disks have more partners than others.
 */
column  "PImbalance" format 99 Heading "Partner|Count|Imbalance"
/*
 * Partner space imbalance indicates if some disks have more space in their
 * partners than others. The partner space is calculated as a ratio between
 * the size of a disk and the sum of the sizes of its active partners. This
 * ratio is compared for all the disks. The difference in the highest and
 * lowest partner space is reported as a percentage. It is impossible to
 * achieve a percent imbalance of zero unless this is zero. An imbalance of
 * 10 percent is acceptable.
```

```
       * Inactive partners are not considered in this calculation since the
       * allocations across an inactive partnership will be relocated by rebalance.
       */
column  "SImbalance" format 99.9 Heading "Partner|Space %|Imbalance"
/*
       * Failgroup Count reports the number of failure groups. This gives a sense
       * of how widely the partners of a disk can be spread across different
       * failure groups.
       */
column  "FailGrpCnt" format 9999 Heading "Failgroup|Count"
/*
       * Inactive Partnership Count reports the number of partnerships that are
       * no longer used for allocation. A successful rebalance will eliminate these
       * partnerships. If this is not zero, then a rebalance is needed or is in
       * progress.
       */
column "Inactive" format 9999 Heading "Inactive|Partnership|Count"
select
/*
       Name of the diskgroup */
       g.name
       "Diskgroup",
 /*
       partner imbalance */
       max(p.cnt)-min(p.cnt)
       "PImbalance",
/*
       total partner space imbalance */
       100*(max(p.pspace)-min(p.pspace))/max(p.pspace)
       "SImbalance",
/*
       Number of failure groups in the diskgroup */
       count(distinct p.fgrp)
       "FailGrpCnt",
/*
       Number of inactive partnerships in the diskgroup */
       sum(p.inactive)/2
       "Inactive"
from
       &asm_diskgroup g ,
       ( /* One row per disk with count of partners and total space of partners
         * as a multiple of the space in this disk. It is possible that all
         * partnerships are inactive, giving a pspace of 0. To avoid this,
         * divide by zero. When this happens for all disks, we return a number
         * very small for total partner space. This happens in a diskgroup
         * with only two failure groups when one failure group fails. */
         select
              x.grp grp,
              x.disk disk,
              sum(x.active) cnt,
              greatest(sum(x.total_mb/d.total_mb),0.0001) pspace,
```

```
            d.failgroup fgrp,
            count(*)-sum(x.active) inactive
    from
        &asm_disk d ,
        ( /* One row per partner of a disk with partner size. We return
          * size of zero for inactive partnerships since they will
          * be eliminated by rebalance. */
          select
              y.grp grp,
              y.disk disk,
              z.total_mb*y.active_kfdpartner total_mb,
              y.active_kfdpartner active
          from
              x$kfdpartner y,
              &asm_disk z
          where
              y.number_kfdpartner = z.disk_number and
              y.grp = z.group_number
        ) x
    where
        d.group_number = x.grp and
        d.disk_number = x.disk and
        d.group_number <> 0 and
        d.state = 'NORMAL' and
        d.mount_status = 'CACHED'
    group by
        x.grp, x.disk, d.failgroup
    ) p
where
    g.group_number = p.grp
group by
    g.name
;
```

The Sample Script Output

The output of the imbalance reporting program follows:

Columns Described in Script	Percent	Percent Minimum Disk Size	Percent	Disk	Diskgroup
Diskgroup Name	Imbalance	Variance	Free	Count	Redundancy
---	---	---	---	---	---
XRAID	.2	.0	96.0	28	HIGH

Columns Described in Script	Partner Count	Partner Space %	Failgroup	Inactive Partnership
Diskgroup Name	Imbalance	Imbalance	Count	Count
---	---	---	---	---
XRAID	0	.0	4	0

Reporting ASM `iostat` Information—asmiostat.sh

This script is used to provide Unix `iostat`-like information on ASM disks. The user must be connected to an ASM instance. The script itself has information on setting environment variables and scripts options.

The Sample Script

The script for the asmiostat.sh utility follows:

```ksh
#!/bin/ksh
#
# NAME
#   asmiostat.sh
#
# DESCRIPTION
#   iostat-like output for ASM
#   $ asmiostat.sh [-s ASM ORACLE_SID] [-h ASM ORACLE_HOME] [-g Diskgroup]
#                  [-f disk path filter] [<interval>] [<count>]
#
# NOTES
#   Creates persistent SQL*Plus connection to the +ASM instance implemented
#   as a ksh co-process
#
#
#
#ORACLE_SID=+ASM

NLS_LANG=AMERICAN_AMERICA.WE8ISO8859P1
NLS_DATE_FORMAT='DD-MON-YYYY HH24:MI:SS'


endOfOutput="_EOP$$"


typeset -u diskgroup
typeset diskgroup_string="Disk Group: All diskgroups"
typeset usage="
$0 [-s ASM ORACLE_SID] [-h ASM ORACLE_HOME] [-g diskgroup] [<interval>] [<count>]

Output:
  DiskPath - Path to ASM disk
  DiskName - ASM disk name
  Gr       - ASM diskgroup number
  Dsk      - ASM disk number
  Reads    - Reads
  Writes   - Writes
  AvRdTm   - Average read time (in msec)
  AvWrTm   - Average write time (in msec)
  KBRd     - Kilobytes read
  KBWr     - Kilobytes written
  AvRdSz   - Average read size (in bytes)
```

```
   AvWrSz   - Average write size (in bytes)
   RdEr     - Read errors
   WrEr     - Write errors
"

while getopts ":s:h:g:f" option; do
  case $option in
    s)  ORACLE_SID="$OPTARG" ;;
    h)  ORACLE_HOME="$OPTARG"
        PATH=$ORACLE_HOME/bin:$PATH
        LD_LIBRARY_PATH=$ORACLE_HOME/lib:$LD_LIBRARY_PATH ;;
    g)  diskgroup="$OPTARG"
        diskgroup_string="Disk Group: $diskgroup" ;;
    f)  print '-f option not implemented' ;;
    :)  print "Option $OPTARG needs a value"
        print "$usage"
        exit 1 ;;
    \?) print "Invalid option $OPTARG"
        print "$usage"
        exit 1 ;;
  esac
done
shift OPTIND-1

# Must be exported for asmcmd to work
export ORACLE_SID ORACLE_HOME LD_LIBRARY_PATH PATH

typeset -i interval=${1:-10} count=${2:-0} index=0

#
# Verify interval and count arguments are valid
#
(( interval <=0 || count<0 )) && {
  print 'Invalid parameter: <interval> must be > 0; <count> must be >= 0'
  print "$usage"
  exit 1
}

#
# Query to run against v$asm_disk_stat
#
if [[ -z $diskgroup ]]; then
  query="select group_number, disk_number, name, path, reads, writes, read_errs,
write_errs, read_time, write_time, bytes_read, bytes_written from v\$asm_disk_stat
where group_number>0 order by group_number, disk_number;"
else
  query="select group_number, disk_number, name, path, reads, writes, read_errs,
write_errs, read_time, write_time, bytes_read, bytes_written from v\$asm_disk_stat
where group_number=(select group_number from v\$asm_diskgroup_stat where name=regexp_
replace('$diskgroup','^\+','')) order by group_number, disk_number;"
fi
#
# Check for version 10.2 or later
```

```
#
typeset version minversion=10.2
version=$($ORACLE_HOME/bin/exp </dev/null 2>&1 | grep "Export: " | sed -e 's/^Export:
Release \([0-9][0-9]*\.[0-9][0-9]*\).*/\1/')
if ! (print "$version<$minversion" | bc >/dev/null 2>&1); then
  print "$0 requires Oracle Database Release $minversion or later"
  exit 1
fi

###############################################################################
#
# Fatal error
#-----------------------------------------------------------------------------
function fatalError {
  print -u2 -- "Error: $1"
  exit 1
}

###############################################################################
#
# Drain all of the sqlplus output - stop when we see our well-known string
#-----------------------------------------------------------------------------
function drainOutput {
  typeset dispose=${1:-'dispose'} output
  while :; do
    read -p output || fatalError 'Read from co-process failed [$0]'
    if [[ $QUERYDEBUG == ON ]]; then print $output; fi
    if [[ $output == $endOfOutput* ]]; then break; fi
    [[ $dispose != 'dispose' ]] && print -- $output
  done
}

###############################################################################
#
# Ensure the instance is running and it is of type ASM
#-----------------------------------------------------------------------------
function verifyASMinstance {
  typeset asmcmdPath=$ORACLE_HOME/bin/asmcmd
  [[ ! -x $asmcmdPath ]] && fatalError "Invalid ORACLE_HOME $ORACLE_HOME: $asmcmdPath
does not exist"
  $asmcmdPath pwd 2>/dev/null | /bin/grep -q '^\+$' || fatalError "$ORACLE_SID is not
an ASM instance"

}

###############################################################################
#
# Start the sqlplus coprocess
#-----------------------------------------------------------------------------
function startSqlplus {
  # start sqlplus, set up the env
  $ORACLE_HOME/bin/sqlplus -s '/ as sysdba' |&
```

```
   print -p 'whenever sqlerror exit failure' \
   && print -p "set pagesize 9999 linesize 9999 feedback off heading off" \
   && print -p "prompt $endOfOutput" \
   || fatalError 'Write to co-process failed (startSqlplus)'
   drainOutput dispose
}

###########################################################################
###########################################################################
# MAIN
#-------------------------------------------------------------------------
verifyASMinstance
startSqlplus

#
# Loop as many times as requested or forever
#
while :; do
  print -p "$query" \
  && print -p "prompt $endOfOutput" \
  || fatalError 'Write to co-process failed (collectData)'
  stats=$(drainOutput keep)

  print -- "$stats\nEOL"

  index=index+1
  (( count<index && count>0 )) && break

  sleep $interval
done  | \
awk '
BEGIN { firstSample=1
}
/^EOL$/ {
  firstSample=0; firstLine=1
  next
}
{
  path=$4
  if (path ~ /^ *$/) next
  group[path]=$1; disk[path]=$2; name[path]=$3

  reads[path]=$5;      writes[path]=$6
  readErrors[path]=$7; writeErrors[path]=$8
  readTime[path]=$9;   writeTime[path]=$10
  readBytes[path]=$11; writeBytes[path]=$12

  # reads and writes
  readsDiff[path]=(reads[path]-readsPrev[path])
  writesDiff[path]=(writes[path]-writesPrev[path])
  rps=(reads[path]-readsPrev[path])/'"$interval"'
  wps=(writes[path]-writesPrev[path])/'"$interval"'

  # read errors and write errors
```

```
    readErrorsDiff[path]=readErrors[path]-readErrorsPrev[path]
    writeErrorsDiff[path]=writeErrors[path]-writeErrorsPrev[path]

    # read time and write time
    readTimeDiff[path]=readTime[path]-readTimePrev[path]
    writeTimeDiff[path]=writeTime[path]-writeTimePrev[path]

    # average read time and average write time in msec (data provided in csec)
    avgReadTime[path]=0; avgWriteTime[path]=0
    if ( readsDiff[path] ) avgReadTime[path]=(readTimeDiff[path]/readsDiff[path])*1000
    if ( writesDiff[path]) avgWriteTime[path]=(writeTimeDiff[path]/writesDiff[path])*1000

    # bytes and KB read and bytes and KB written
    readBytesDiff[path]=readBytes[path]-readBytesPrev[path]
    writeBytesDiff[path]=writeBytes[path]-writeBytesPrev[path]
    readKb[path]=readBytesDiff[path]/1024
    writeKb[path]=writeBytesDiff[path]/1024
    rkbps=readBytesDiff[path]/1024/'"$interval"'
    wkbps=writeBytesDiff[path]/1024/'"$interval"'

    # average read size and average write size
    avgReadSize[path]=0; avgWriteSize[path]=0
    if ( readsDiff[path] ) avgReadSize[path]=readBytesDiff[path]/readsDiff[path]
    if ( writesDiff[path] ) avgWriteSize[path]=writeBytesDiff[path]/writesDiff[path]

    if (!firstSample) {
      if (firstLine) {
        "date" | getline now; close("date")
        printf "\n"
        printf "Date: %s    Interval: %d secs    %s\n\n", now, '"$interval"',
"'"$diskgroup_string"'"
        printf "%-40s %2s %3s %8s %8s %6s %6s %8s %8s %7s %7s %4s %4s\n", \
          "DiskPath - DiskName","Gr","Dsk","Reads","Writes","AvRdTm",\
          "AvWrTm","KBRd","KBWr","AvRdSz","AvWrSz", "RdEr", "WrEr"
        firstLine=0
      }
      printf "%-40s %2s %3s %8d %8d %6.1f %6.1f %8d %8d %7d %7d %4d %4d\n", \
        path " - " name[path], group[path], disk[path], \
        rps, wps, \
        avgReadTime[path], avgWriteTime[path], \
        rkbps, wkbps, \
        avgReadSize[path], avgWriteSize[path], \
        readErrorsDiff[path], writeErrorsDiff[path]
    }

    readsPrev[path]=reads[path];           writesPrev[path]=writes[path]
    readErrorsPrev[path]=readErrors[path]; writeErrorsPrev[path]=writeErrors[path]
    readTimePrev[path]=readTime[path];     writeTimePrev[path]=writeTime[path]
    readBytesPrev[path]=readBytes[path];   writeBytesPrev[path]=writeBytes[path]
  }
END {
  }
'

exit 0
```

The Sample Script Output

The output for the asmiostat.sh script follows:

```
[oracle@racnode1]$ asmiostat 2 10

Date: Sat Aug 11 20:33:34 PDT 2007     Interval: 2 secs     Disk Group: All diskgroups
```

DiskPath - DiskName	Gr	Dsk	Reads	Writes	AvRdTm	AvWrTm	KBRd	KBWr	AvRdSz
AvWrSz RdEr WrEr									
ORCL:FLGRP1_D1 - FLGRP1_D1	1	0	0	0	4.0	0.0	2	0	4096
0 0 0									
ORCL:FLGRP1_D2 - FLGRP1_D2	1	1	0	0	4.0	0.0	2	0	4096
0 0 0									
ORCL:FLGRP1_D3 - FLGRP1_D3	1	2	0	0	4.0	0.0	2	0	4096
0 0 0									
ORCL:FLGRP1_D4 - FLGRP1_D4	1	3	0	0	3.0	0.0	2	0	4096
0 0 0									
ORCL:FLGRP1_D5 - FLGRP1_D5	1	4	0	0	3.0	0.0	2	0	4096
0 0 0									
ORCL:FLGRP1_D6 - FLGRP1_D6	1	5	0	0	3.0	0.0	2	0	4096
0 0 0									

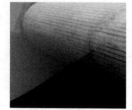

APPENDIX
D

Typical ASM
Diskgroup Commands

his appendix discusses commands that are typically used to manage an ASM diskgroup.

The following are some examples of commands that alter a diskgroup.

Mount a Diskgroup

The command for mounting a diskgroup is as follows:

```
SQL> ALTER DISKGROUP DATA MOUNT;
```

The commands that follow are new in Oracle Database 11*g*.
The MOUNT RESTRICTED keywords are used as part of the new Fast Rebalance feature:

```
SQL> ALTER DISKGROUP DATA MOUNT RESTRICTED;
```

or

```
SQL> ALTER DISKGROUP DATA MOUNT FORCE;
```

With the MOUNT FORCE option, ASM attempts to mount the diskgroup forcibly even if all disks in the diskgroup were not found. Disks that were missing are forcibly taken offline. ASM successfully mounts the diskgroup only if enough disks are found to make all data available. This option can be used with ASM redundancy diskgroups.

Dismount a Diskgroup

The command for dismounting a diskgroup is as follows:

```
SQL> ALTER DISKGROUP DATA DISMOUNT
```

- Add diskgroup templates:

```
SQL> ALTER DISKGROUP DATA ADD TEMPLATE FINE_NOPROT (FINE unprotected);
```

Add ASM Disks to the Diskgroup

The command for adding ASM disks to the diskgroup is as follows:

```
SQL> ALTER DISKGROUP DATA ADD DISK '/dev/rdsk/c3t19d5s4';
```

or

```
SQL> ALTER DISKGROUP DATA ADD DISK '/dev/rdsk/c3t19d5s4' WAIT;
```

Typically, when a disk is added to a diskgroup, its space is not immediately available for allocation, and because every file is evenly allocated, extents must be rebalanced off other disks to the new disk to make space evenly available. Because rebalance takes a while, users may not be able to allocate files even though plenty freespace is available. The WAIT option is useful when the database administrator (DBA) wants the rebalance to finish completely before taking advantage of the new disk.

Drop ASM Disks from the Diskgroup

The command for dropping ASM disks from the diskgroup is as follows:

```
SQL> ALTER DISKGROUP DATA DROP DISK DATA_0009;
```

NOTE
Do not inadvertently remove the disk unit physically from the storage array before it is completely dropped from the diskgroup. When a disk is dropped, it is not immediately expelled from the diskgroup. Verify that the HEADER_STATUS from the V$ASM_DISK view shows FORMER status, not DROPPING. Additionally, check to make sure that the rebalance operation from the DROP DISK is completed.

Check Diskgroup Consistency

The command for checking diskgroup consistency is as follows:

```
SQL> ALTER DISKGROUP DATA CHECK;
```

Occasionally there will be inconsistencies in the diskgroup metadata, similar to standard filesystems. The ALTER DISKGROUP CHECK REPAIR is used to check and repair these metadata inconsistencies. Note that it does not validate any stored database content such as tablespace headers or table data; rather, it checks that the metadata is consistent. Alias and template checks are new in Oracle Database 11*g*.

Modify the Rebalance Power Level

The command for modifying the rebalance power level is as follows:

```
SQL> ALTER DISKGROUP DATA REBALANCE POWER 11;
```

This also restarts the rebalance if it is running and starts a new rebalance if none is running. To change the default power of all new rebalances, change the ASM_POWER_LIMIT parameter value using ALTER SYSTEM or edit the init.ora file.

Drop a Diskgroup

The command for dropping a diskgroup is as follows:

```
SQL> DROP DISKGROUP DATA INCLUDING CONTENTS;
```

The following command works only on an empty diskgroup:

```
SQL> DROP DISKGROUP DATA;
```

In Oracle Database 10*g*, before a diskgroup could be dropped, it had to be mounted on exactly one node. If the diskgroup could not be mounted and the disks were to be repurposed for non-ASM uses, the user typically cleared the disks using the Unix dd command to copy zeroes into the header. If the disks were to be repurposed as an ASM disk for a new diskgroup, then users could use the FORCE option in the CREATE DISKGROUP command. This behavior changes in Oracle Database 11*g*; now if diskgroup is not mounted, the user can drop it using the FORCE option. Note that it is a best practice to mount the diskgroup, if possible, and then drop the diskgroup. That way, you are guaranteed that all of the disks are updated. DROP DISKGROUP FORCE simply clears the header (actually it just changes the HEADER_STATUS from MEMBER to FORMER) for whatever disks are found at the time with the specified diskgroup name. If the mount is not possible, then use the FORCE option, as follows:

```
SQL> DROP DISKGROUP DATA FORCE INCLUDING CONTENTS;
```

The following output shows the entries in the ASM alert log for the DROP DISKGROUP command:

```
SQL> DROP DISKGROUP DATA
NOTE: cache dismounting group 1/0x6268E569 (DATA)
kjbdomdet send to node 1
detach from dom 1, sending detach message to node 1
freeing rdom 1
Wed Mar 07 17:08:10 2007
NOTE: detached from domain 1
NOTE: cache dismounted group 1/0x6268E569 (DATA)
NOTE: erasing header on grp 1 disk DATA_0000
NOTE: erasing header on grp 1 disk DATA_0001
NOTE: erasing header on grp 1 disk DATA_0002
NOTE: erasing header on grp 1 disk DATA_0003
NOTE: De-assigning number (1,0) from disk (/dev/rdsk/c3t19d5s4)
NOTE: De-assigning number (1,1) from disk (/dev/rdsk/c3t19d16s4)
NOTE: De-assigning number (1,2) from disk (/dev/rdsk/c3t19d17s4)
NOTE: De-assigning number (1,3) from disk (/dev/rdsk/c3t19d18s4)
SUCCESS: diskgroup DATA was dropped
```

APPENDIX
E

References

1. Loaiza, Juan. "Optimal Storage Configuration Made Easy," White Paper, Oracle Corporation. Available at http://www.oracle.com.

2. NetApp. "NetApp Architectural Overview." Available online at www.netapp.com/tech_library/3001.html.

3. NetApp and ASM. "NetApp & 10*g* RAC/ASM Performance Report with FCP, NFS and iSCSI," White Paper.

4. Vaidyanatha, Gaja Krishna. "Implementing RAID on Oracle Systems," "Proceedings of Oracle Open World 2000." Available online at www.oracle.com.

5. Adams, Steve. "IXORA." Available online at www.ixora.com.au.

6. Morle, James. *Scaling Oracle 8i*. New York: Addison Wesley, 2000. Available online at www.aw.com/cseng.

7. Zafar, Mahmood; Fernandez, Anthony; Scalzo, Bert; and Vallath, Murali. "Testing Oracle 10*g* RAC Sacalability," DELL PowerSolutions, March 2005.

8. Vengurlekar, Nitin. "ASM Technical Best Practices," Metalink Note 265633.1 Available online at http://metalink.oracle.com

9. Vallath, Murali. *Oracle 10g RAC Grid, Services and Clustering*, Elsevier, August 2007. Available online at www.elsevier.com.

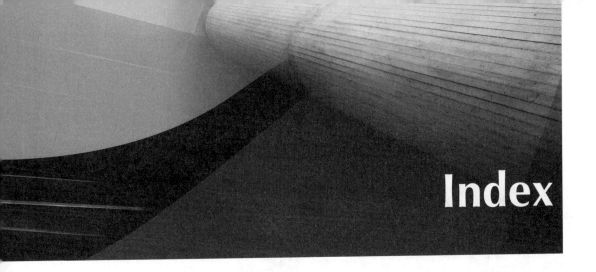

Index

G

S

The RAC SIG organizes at least one live web seminar every month. Admission is free, all you need is some time to join the webcast and learn from the experts!

The RAC SIG also hosts a discussion forum on OTN. Have a question? Post it and you will find an answer from another RAC SIG member or directly from Oracle ...

Share your knowledge and learn from your peers, that's what the RAC SIG is all about!

Join the
Oracle RAC SIG...

at

www.oracleracsig.org